Comprehensive Criminal Procedure

Second Edition

2010 Supplement

ASPEN PUBLISHERS

2010 Supplement

Comprehensive Criminal Procedure

Second Edition

Ronald Jay Allen

John Henry Wigmore Professor of Law
Northwestern University

Joseph L. Hoffmann

Harry Pratter Professor of Law
Indiana University Maurer School of Law–Bloomington

Debra A. Livingston

Vice Dean and Paul J. Kellner Professor of Law
Columbia University

William J. Stuntz

Henry J. Friendly Professor of Law
Harvard University

Wolters Kluwer
Law & Business

AUSTIN BOSTON CHICAGO NEW YORK THE NETHERLANDS

Aspen Publishers
Attn: Permissions Department
76 Ninth Avenue, 7th Floor
New York, NY 10011-5201

To contact Customer Care, e-mail customer.service@aspenpublishers.com,
call 1-800-234-1660, fax 1-800-901-9075, or mail correspondence to:

Aspen Publishers
Attn: Order Department
PO Box 990
Frederick, MD 21705

Printed in the United States of America.

1 2 3 4 5 6 7 8 9 0

ISBN 978-0-7355-9035-9

Library of Congress Cataloging-in Publication Data

Comprehensive criminal procedure/Ronald Jay Allen . . . . [et al.].—2nd ed.
p. cm.
Includes index.
ISBN 0-7355-4622-3 (text)
ISBN 978-0-7355-9035-9 (supplement)
I. Criminal procedure—United States. I. Allen, Ronald J. (Ronald Jay), 1948-
KF9618.C66 2001
345.73'05—dc21

00-053608

About Wolters Kluwer Law & Business

Wolters Kluwer Law & Business is a leading provider of research information and workflow solutions in key specialty areas. The strengths of the individual brands of Aspen Publishers, CCH, Kluwer Law International and Loislaw are aligned within Wolters Kluwer Law & Business to provide comprehensive, in-depth solutions and expert-authored content for the legal, professional and education markets.

CCH was founded in 1913 and has served more than four generations of business professionals and their clients. The CCH products in the Wolters Kluwer Law & Business group are highly regarded electronic and print resources for legal, securities, antitrust and trade regulation, government contracting, banking, pension, payroll, employment and labor, and healthcare reimbursement and compliance professionals.

Aspen Publishers is a leading information provider for attorneys, business professionals and law students. Written by preeminent authorities, Aspen products offer analytical and practical information in a range of specialty practice areas from securities law and intellectual property to mergers and acquisitions and pension/benefits. Aspen's trusted legal education resources provide professors and students with high-quality, up-to-date and effective resources for successful instruction and study in all areas of the law.

Kluwer Law International supplies the global business community with comprehensive English-language international legal information. Legal practitioners, corporate counsel and business executives around the world rely on the Kluwer Law International journals, loose-leafs, books and electronic products for authoritative information in many areas of international legal practice.

Loislaw is a premier provider of digitized legal content to small law firm practitioners of various specializations. Loislaw provides attorneys with the ability to quickly and efficiently find the necessary legal information they need, when and where they need it, by facilitating access to primary law as well as state-specific law, records, forms and treatises.

Wolters Kluwer Law & Business, a unit of Wolters Kluwer, is headquartered in New York and Riverwoods, Illinois. Wolters Kluwer is a leading multinational publisher and information services company.

Contents

Table of Cases *xiii*

PART ONE THE CRIMINAL PROCESS

Chapter 2 The Idea of Due Process 3

C. The Residual Due Process Clause 3
Hamdi v. Rumsfeld *3*
Notes and Questions 21

PART TWO THE RIGHT TO COUNSEL—THE LINCHPIN OF CONSTITUTIONAL PROTECTION

Chapter 3 The Right to Counsel and Other Assistance 27

A. The Constitutional Requirements 27
2. Further Emanations of the Right to Counsel — Counsel on Appeal and Other Forms of Assistance 27
3. Critical Stages of the Proceedings 28
B. Effective Assistance of Counsel 29
1. The Meaning of Effective Assistance 29
Rompilla v. Beard *30*
Notes and Questions 42
Note on Ineffective Assistance, Habeas Corpus, and the Death Penalty 44
C. Some Implications of the Right to Counsel 46
1. The Right to Proceed Pro Se 46
3. The Right to Counsel of One's Choice 50
United States v. Gonzalez-Lopez *51*
Notes and Questions 60

PART THREE THE RIGHT TO BE LET ALONE—AN EXAMINATION OF THE FOURTH AND FIFTH AMENDMENTS AND RELATED AREAS

Chapter 5 The Fourth Amendment 65

B. The Scope of the Fourth Amendment 65
1. The Meaning of "Searches" 65
a. The Relationship Between Privacy and Property 65
Illinois v. Caballes *65*
Notes and Questions 73
c. Privacy and Technology 74
3. To Whom Does the Fourth Amendment Apply? 76
C. Probable Cause and Warrants 77
1. The Probable Cause Standard 77
2. The Warrant "Requirement" 80
United States v. Grubbs *80*
Notes and Questions 86
Muehler v. Mena *88*
Notes and Questions 97
3. "Exceptions" to the Warrant "Requirement" 100
a. Exigent Circumstances 100
Brigham City v. Stuart *100*
Notes on Punitive and Protective Policing 105
e. Searches Incident to Arrest 108
Arizona v. Gant *108*
Notes and Questions 119
Virginia v. Moore *120*
Notes and Questions 127
D. Reasonableness 128
1. Stops and Frisks 128
3. "Special Needs" 129
b. Non-Police Searches 129
4. Reasonableness and Police Use of Force 133
Scott v. Harris *134*
Notes and Questions 144
E. Consent Searches 146
Georgia v. Randolph *146*
Notes and Questions 162
F. Remedies 163
1. Limits on the Exclusionary Remedy 163
a. The "Good Faith" Exception 163
Herring v. United States *164*
Notes and Questions 170

c. "Fruit of the Poisonous Tree" Doctrine 171
Hudson v. Michigan *171*
Notes and Questions 185
189

Chapter 6 The Fifth Amendment

B. The Contours of the Privilege Against Self-Incrimination 189
1. "No Person . . . Shall Be Compelled": The Meaning of Compulsion 189
D. Police Interrogation 190
1. Police Interrogation and the *Miranda* Revolution 190
2. The Scope of *Miranda* 192
c. What Constitutes a Valid *Miranda* Waiver? 192
4. The Right to Counsel Reconsidered 202

Chapter 7 Investigating Complex Crimes 207

A. Electronic Surveillance and the Search of Electronic Data 207
1. Wiretapping and Related Electronic Surveillance 207
2. Grand Jury Secrecy 207
D. Law Enforcement and Counterterrorism 211

PART FOUR THE ADJUDICATION PROCESS

Chapter 8 The Charging Decision 217

A. Prosecutorial Discretion 217
2. Enforcement Discretion for Low-Level Crimes 217

Chapter 9 Bail, Detention, and the Right to a Speedy Trial 219

B. The Right to a Speedy Trial 219

Chapter 10 Guilty Pleas and Plea Bargaining 223

A. Guilty Pleas as a Substitute for Trials 223
1. The Plea Process 223

Chapter 11 Discovery and Disclosure 225

A. Disclosure by the Government 225
2. The Prosecutor's Constitutional Disclosure Obligations 225
United States v. Ruiz *226*
Notes and Questions 231

Chapter 12 The Jury and the Criminal Trial 235

B. Jury Composition 235
Miller-El v. Dretke *238*

C. Influences upon the Jury 263
1. Publicity 263
Skilling v. United States *263*
Notes and Questions 287

D. The Defendant's Rights to Be Present, to Testify, to Obtain Evidence, to Confront His Accusers, and to Present a Defense at Trial 289
Davis v. Washington *290*
Notes and Questions 306

F. Criminal Trials and Factual Accuracy 312

G. Alternatives to the Traditional Criminal Trial—The Proposed Special Military Tribunal 315

PART FIVE POSTTRIAL PROCEEDINGS

Chapter 13 Sentencing 319

A. Introduction to Sentencing 319
3. Substantive Limits on Sentencing—Eighth Amendment Proportionality 319
Roper v. Simmons *320*
Notes and Questions 342

C. Do the Rules of Constitutional Criminal Procedure Apply to Sentencing? 344
Gall v. United States *344*
Notes and Questions 359

Chapter 14 Double Jeopardy 363

A. "Twice Put in Jeopardy" 363
1. Acquittals 363
Smith v. Massachusetts *363*
Notes and Questions 372

Chapter 15 Appellate and Collateral Review 375

A. Appellate Review 375
5. Prejudice and Harmless Error 375

B. Collateral Review 375
2. The Nature and Purposes of Federal Habeas 375

Selected Statutes and Rules 377

Federal Rules of Criminal Procedure 377
Rule 6. The Grand Jury 377
Rule 8. Joinder of Offenses or Defendants 382
Rule 11. Pleas 382
Rule 14. Relief from Prejudicial Joinder 386
Rule 16. Discovery and Inspection 386
Rule 26.2. Producing a Witness's Statement 390
Rule 41. Search and Seizure 391
Rule 44. Right to and Appointment of Counsel 395
Rule 52. Harmless and Plain Error 396

Bail Reform Act of 1984 (as amended) 396
18 U.S.C. §§ 3141-3150 396

Speedy Trial Act of 1974 (as amended) 409
18 U.S.C. §§ 3161, 3162, 3164, 3173 409

Criminal Appeals Act of 1970 (as amended) 417
18 U.S.C. § 3731 417

Habeas Corpus Act of 1867 (as amended by Antiterrorism and Effective Death Penalty Act of 1996) 418
28 U.S.C. §§ 2241-2244, 2253-2254 418

Collateral Review for Federal Prisoners 425
28 U.S.C. § 2255 425

Table of Cases

Italics indicate principal cases.

$242,484.00; United States v., 69
Abdul-Saboor; United States v., 117
Adams v. St. Lucie County Sheriff's Dep't, 48, 49, 139
Addington v. Texas, 9
Agurs; United States v., 228
Ake v. Oklahoma, 229
Allen v. Florida, 255
Antelope; United States v., 189
Apprendi v. New Jersey, 319, 360, 361, 362
Arizona v. Evans, 164, 165, 167
Arizona v. Gant, 108, 119, 120
Arizona v. Hicks, 184
Arizona v. Johnson, 128, 129
Arkansas v. Sullivan, 79
Atkins v. Virginia, 320, 322, 323, 324, 325, 326, 328, 332, 335, 336, 338
Atwater v. Lago Vista, 111, 120, 123, 125
Avellino; United States v., 232

Banks; United States v., 171, 173, 181
Batson v. Kentucky, 235, 236, 237, 238, 239, 240, 241, 242, 245, 246, 247, 250, 251, 252, 253, 254, 255, 256, 257, 258, 259, 260, 261, 262, 263
Beck v. Washington, 277
Bell v. Cone, 29, 43
Bellotti v. Baird, 338
Berghuis v. Thompkins, 197
Bivens v. Six Unknown Fed. Narcotics Agents, 339
Blakely v. Washington, 344, 358, 359, 360, 361, 362, 375
Bond v. United States, 72, 103
Booker; United States v., 344, 348, 349, 356, 357, 358, 359, 360, 375
Boumediene v. Bush, 212, 282, 375, 376
Bousley v. United States, 223, 224
Boyd v. United States, 133
Bradshaw v. Stumpf, 223, 224
Brady v. Maryland, 228, 231, 279, 281
Brady v. United States, 225, 226, 228, 229, 231, 232, 233, 279, 281
Brendlin v. California, 75, 76
Brigham City v. Stuart, 100, 105, 106, 107, 108, 161
Broce; United States v., 229

Brower v. County of Inyo, 75, 76, 138, 140n10, 144
Burger v. Kemp, 33
Burks v. United States, 369
Burnet v. Coronado Oil & Gas Co., 115
Butler case, 197

Calandra; United States v., 164, 167, 168, 171, 191
Calderon; United States v., 368
California v. Greenwood, 123, 161
Caplin & Drysdale, Chartered v. United States, 51
Carey v. Musladin, 289
Carr; United States v., 69
Ceccolini; United States v., 172
Chadwick; United States v., 84, 85
Chagra; United States v., 271
Chambers v. State, 250
Chapman v. United States, 149
Chavez v. Martinez, 189
Chimel v. California, 108, 109, 110, 111, 114, 116, 117, 118, 119, 120
Claiborne v. United States, 345
Claiborne; United States v., 348
Collins; State v., 367
Coolidge v. New Hampshire, 156
Cosme; People v., 158
Cote; Commonwealth v., 367
Cox; People v., 66
Coy v. Iowa, 270
Crawford v. Washington, 52, 60, 289, 293, 294, 295, 296, 297, 298, 299, 300, 301, 302, 303, 304, 308, 309, 311, 312
Crawford; United States v., 131
Cunningham v. California, 360, 362

Davis v. Washington, 290, 273, 274, 275, 276, 280
Davis; United States v., 159
Defore; People v., 166
Devenpeck v. Alford, 77
Di Re; United States v., 122
Dickerson v. United States, 115, 270
Diebold, Inc.; United States v., 136
District Attorney's Office for the Third Judicial District v. Osborne, 280
Drayton case, 75
Dutton v. Evans, 269

Eddings v. Oklahoma, 45, 355
Edmonson v. Leesville Concrete Co., 240
Edwards; Commonwealth v., 203, 204, 301
Elkins v. United States, 125, 167
Esparza-Mendoza; United States v., 76
Estes v. Texas, 270, 271n14, 272

Faretta case, 46, 47, 48
Ferguson v. Charleston, 131, 133
Flippo v. West Virginia, 102
Florida v. Bostick, 75, 92
Florida v. Nixon, 29
Florida v. Powell, 192
Florida v. Wells, 103
Fong Foo v. United States, 365, 369, 374
Frazier v. Cupp, 156

Gall v. United States, 344, 359, 360
Garcetti v. Ceballos, 225, 226
Garcia; United States v., 82
Georgia v. McColum, 240
Georgia v. Randolph, 107, *146*, 160, 161

Giglio v. United States, 228, 229
Giles v. California, 274, 275
Godinez v. Moran, 46
Gonzalez-Lopez; United States v., 51, 60, 61
Graham v. Connor, 88, 91, 92, 93, 95, 96, 103, 138, 143
Graham v. Florida, 343
Gregg v. Georgia, 342
Griffin v. Wisconsin, 131, 133
Groh v. Ramirez, 84, 85, 102
Grubbs; United States v., 80, 86, 87

Halbert v. Michigan, 27
Hamdan v. Rumsfeld, 281, 282
Hamdi v. Rumsfeld, *3*, 21, 22, 23, 24, 213, 214
Hammon v. Indiana, 292, 298, 301, 303n1, 305, 305n4, 306, 306n6
Harden v. State, 367
Harlow v. Fitzgerald, 168
Harmelin v. Michigan, 319, 326, 339, 342
Harris v. Coweta County, 135, 138n9
Harris v. United States, 117, 361
Hartman v. Moore, 217, 218
Haskell; Commonwealth v., 370
Hatter; United States v., 341
Henderson v. Morgan, 223
Hendrix; United States v., 158
Hernandez v. New York, 236, 237, 261, 262
Herring v. United States, 164, 168, 169
Hiibel v. Sixth Judicial Dist. Court of Nev., 296, 300
Hill v. Lockhart, 233
Hodari D case, 75
Holloway v. Horn, 237
Holmes v. South Carolina, 289, 279
Horton v. California, 79
Hotal; United States v., 81
House v. Bell, 275, 279, 280
Hudson v. Michigan, 164, 165, 170, *171*, 184, 185, 186

Idaho v. Horiuchi, 134
Illinois v. Allen, 47
Illinois v. Caballes, 65, 73, 74
Illinois v. Gates, 77, 82, 83, 166
Illinois v. McArthur, 154
Illinois v. Rodriguez, 146, 148, 152, 155, 158, 161
Inadi; United States v., 297
Indiana v. Edwards, 46, 47, 191, 203, 193
Indianapolis v. Edmond, 103, 104, 107, 133
INS v. Delgado, 92
Irwin v. Dowd, 270, 275, 276, 284, 287

J. E. B. v. Alabama ex rel. T. B., 240, 253, 254, 259
Jacobsen; United States v., 66, 67, 70
Johnson v. California, 236, 237
Johnson v. New Jersey, 202
Johnson v. Texas, 325, 326, 355
Johnson; United States v., 348
Jones v. United States, 49, 83, 148

Kansas v. Hendricks, 23
Kansas v. Ventris, 202
Katz v. United States, 82, 87, 102, 148
Kennedy v. Louisiana, 343
Kennedy; United States v., 68
Ker v. California, 102
Kimbrough v. United States, 356, 357, 359, 360

King v. Brasier, 297, 275
King v. Dingler, 297
King v. Parkin, 369
Knowles v. Iowa, 111, 112, 120, 126, 127
Knowles v. Mirzayance, 49
Koon v. United States, 352
Kyles v. Whitley, 226, 228, 231
Kyllo v. United States, 299n5, 300

Laime v. State, 68
Lawrence v. Texas, 113
Leon; United States v., 164, 165, 166, 169, 171, 173, 186, 191
Lilly v. Virginia, 296
Limares; United States v., 68
Lindh; United States v., 15
Lockett v. Ohio, 45
LoRusso; United States v., 370
Los Angeles County v. Rettele, 98, 99, 100
Lowe; United States v., 82
Ludwig; United States v., 72

Mapp v. Ohio, 171, 174, 175, 178, 339
Martin Linen Supply Co.; United States v., 366, 369
Martinez-Fuerte; United States v., 130n4
Maryland v. Craig, 52
Maryland v. Pringle, 77, 78
Maryland v. Shatzer, 194
Maryland v. Wilson, 91, 92, 129
Massiah case, 202, 191
Mathews v. Eldridge, 9, 10, 11, 18, 20, 23
Matlock; United States v., 146, 148, 149, 152, 155, 158, 161, 162
Matsushita Elec. Industrial Co. v. Zenith Radio Corp., 137
Mattox v. United States, 269
McDonald v. United States, 172
McGautha v. California, 368
McKaskle v. Wiggins, 47
McMann v. Richardson, 53, 229
McNabb v. United States, 191
Melendez-Diaz v. Massachusetts, 276, 278
Mena v. Simi Valley, 90
Merryman, Ex parte, 16
Michigan v. Chesternut, 75
Michigan v. Jackson, 203, 204, 205
Michigan v. Summers, 89, 90, 91, 92, 93, 94n4, 95, 99
Michigan v. Tyler, 102
Mickens v. Taylor, 52
Miller-El v. Cockrell, 237, 238, 239, 241, 242, 245, 247, 248, 249, 250, 251, 258, 260, 261
Miller-El v. Dretke, 238
Miller-El v. Johnson, 239
Miller-El v. State, 239
Mincey v. Arizona, 102
Minnesota v. Olson, 150
Minnick case, 195, 196, 203, 204
Miranda v. Arizona, 173, 190, 191, 190, 191, 192, 193, 194, 195, 196, 197, 198, 199, 200, 201, 202, 203, 204, 270n13, 294, 298
Monell v. New York, 168
Monroe v. Pape, 174
Montejo v. Louisiana, 203, 204
Moran case, 193
Moran v. Burbine, 198
Mosley case, 198
Moyer v. Peabody, 20
Mu'Min v. Virginia, 271, 284
Muehler v. Mena, 88, 97, 98, 99, 100
Murphy v. Florida, 270, 284, 285

Nardone v. United States, 172
Nebraska Press Assn. v. Stuart, 272, 274n21
Neder v. United States, 58, 360, 375
New York v. Belton, 108, 109, 110, 111, 112, 113, 114, 115, 116, 118, 119, 120, 184
New York v. Class, 112
New York v. Harris, 175, 176, 177, 182
New York v. Quarles, 298, 271
Nix v. Whiteside, 43
Norris v. Alabama, 240

Ohio v. Roberts, 52
Ohio v. Robinette, 152
Ontario v. Quon, 129
Oregon v. Guzek, 280
Oregon v. Ice, 360, 362

Padilla v. Hanft, 213
Padilla v. Kentucky, 29
Patterson v. McLean Credit Union, 115
Patterson v. New York, 361
Patton v. Yount, 270, 270n13, 278
Paulino v. Castro, 237
Payne case, 115
Payton v. New York, 102, 176, 182
Pennsylvania Board of Probation and Parole v. Scott, 171, 173
Pennsylvania v. Goldhammer, 367
Pennsylvania v. Rompilla, 36
Penry v. Lynaugh, 322, 323, 324, 336
Place; United States v., 65, 67, 68, 69, 72, 74, 139
Planned Parenthood of Central Mo. v. Danforth, 338
Powers v. Ohio, 240
Price v. Georgia, 366n3
Purkett v. Elem, 236, 237, 241, 261, 262

Quinn; United States v., 72
Quirin, Ex parte, 7

Rabinowitz; United States v., 117
Rakas v. Illinois, 155
Ramirez v. Butte-Silver Bow County, 84
Ramirez; United States v., 175, 176, 182, 183
Randall v. Sorrell, 115
Recognition Equipment, Inc.; United States v., 218
Reed; State v., 296
Reyes; People v., 132
Reyes; United States v., 131
Rice v. Collins, 262
Richards v. Wisconsin, 171, 172, 173, 181
Rideau v. Louisiana, 269, 272, 282, 283, 287
Rita v. United States, 344, 349, 350, 352, 356, 357, 358
Rivera v. Illinois, 235
Riverside, County of v. McLaughlin, 19
Robinson; United States v., 126
Rochin v. California, 144
Rodriguez de Quijas v. Shearson/American Express, Inc., 341
Roe v. Wade, 339
Rompilla v. Beard, 30, 42, 43, 44, 45, 46
Rompilla v. Horn, 31
Roper v. Simmons, 320, 342, 343
Rothgery v. Gillespie County, Texas, 28
Ruiz; United States v., 226, 231, 232, 280

Sacramento, County of v. Lewis, 136n4, 144, 145
Salerno; United States v., 19, 22, 23
Samson v. California, 131, 133, 163
Sanabria v. United States, 368, 369n7
Sanchez-Llamas v. Oregon, 190, 191, 190
Santana; United States v., 102
Saucier v. Katz, 135, 136, 136n4, 141, 142, 144
Scarborough; United States v., 68
Schneckloth v. Bustamonte, 202
Schriro v. Landrigan, 46
Scott v. Harris, 134, 144, 145, 146
Scott v. United States, 79, 103
Scott; United States v., 301, 371, 374
Segura v. United States, 172, 175, 176, 177, 182
Sheehy v. Plymouth, 79
Sheppard v. Maxwell, 270, 271n14, 272, 285, 287
Silverthorne Lumber Co. v. United States, 179
Skilling v. United States, 263
Smalis v. Pennsylvania, 365, 366, 368, 371, 372, 373
Smith v. Massachusetts, 363, 372, 373, 374
Snyder v. Louisiana, 263
Spector Motor Service, Inc. v. McLaughlin, 142
Sperrazza; Commonwealth v., 371
Stanford v. Kentucky, 320, 321, 322, 323, 324, 325, 328, 329, 331, 334, 335, 336, 337, 341
State Oil Co. v. Khan, 341
Stefonek; United States v., 84
Stewart; United States v., 296
Strauder v. West Virginia, 239, 240
Strickland v. Washington, 30, 31, 33, 37, 38, 39, 40, 42, 43, 44, 45, 46, 50, 52, 53, 58, 232, 233
Swain v. Alabama, 238, 239, 240, 241, 259, 260

Tennessee v. Garner, 135, 138, 138n9, 139, 143, 145, 146
Thompson v. Oklahoma, 321, 324, 325, 326, 328
Thornton v. United States, 108, 109, 111, 112, 113, 114, 115, 116, 118, 119, 120
Tollett v. Henderson, 229
Trammel v. United States, 156
Treasury Employees; United States v., 136
Trejo v. Perez, 79
Trop v. Dulles, 320, 329

United States ex rel. Darcy v. Handy, 274n21
Uttecht v. Brown, 235

Ventresca; United States v., 151
Vermont v. Brillon, 220
Vieth v. Jubelirer, 115
Virginia v. Moore, 120, 127

Washington v. Recuenco, 360, 375
Watson v. State, 367
Wayne v. United States, 102
Weeks v. United States, 164, 178, 183
Weems v. United States, 320
Welsh v. Wisconsin, 104

Wheat v. United States, 47, 53n3
White v. Illinois, 295, 302, 269, 271
White; United States v., 155, 161
Whitely v. Warden, 165
Whorton v. Bockting, 289
Whren v. United States, 79, 103, 123, 125, 158
Wiggins v. Smith, 31, 33, 36, 38, 43, 44, 45, 48
Williams v. Taylor, 36, 43, 44, 45
Williams; United States v., 71
Wilson v. Arkansas, 170, 171, 178
Wilson; United States v., 365
Withrow v. Williams, 201
Wolf v. Colorado, 178
Wong Sun v. United States, 84, 126
Wood; United States v., 273
Wyoming v. Houghton, 122, 123

Youngblood v. West Virginia., 279
Youngstown Sheet & Tube Co. v. Sawyer, 16

Zadvydas v. Davis, 9
Zedner v. United States, 219
Zerbst case, 201

PART ONE

THE CRIMINAL PROCESS

Chapter 2

The Idea of Due Process

C. *The Residual Due Process Clause*

Replace Note 5, pages 109-111, with the following main case and notes:

HAMDI v. RUMSFELD

Certiorari to the United States Court of Appeals for the Fourth Circuit
542 U.S. 507 (2004)

JUSTICE O'CONNOR announced the judgment of the Court and delivered an opinion, in which CHIEF JUSTICE REHNQUIST, JUSTICE KENNEDY, and JUSTICE BREYER join.

At this difficult time in our Nation's history, we are called upon to consider the legality of the Government's detention of a United States citizen on United States soil as an "enemy combatant" and to address the process that is constitutionally owed to one who seeks to challenge his classification as such. . . .

I

On September 11, 2001, the al Qaeda terrorist network used hijacked commercial airliners to attack prominent targets in the United States. Approximately 3,000 people were killed in those attacks. One week later, in response to these "acts of treacherous violence," Congress passed a resolution authorizing the President to "use all necessary and appropriate force against those nations, organizations, or persons he determines planned, authorized, committed, or aided the terrorist attacks" or "harbored such organizations or persons, in order to prevent any future acts of international terrorism against the United States by such nations, organizations or persons." Authorization for Use of Military Force ("the AUMF"), 115 Stat 224. Soon thereafter, the President ordered United States Armed Forces to Afghanistan, with a mission to subdue al Qaeda and quell the Taliban regime that was known to support it.

This case arises out of the detention of a man whom the Government alleges took up arms with the Taliban during this conflict. His name is Yaser Esam Hamdi. Born an American citizen in Louisiana in 1980, Hamdi moved with his family to Saudi Arabia as a child. By 2001, the parties agree, he resided in Afghanistan. At some point that year, he was seized by members of the Northern Alliance, a coalition of military groups opposed to the Taliban government, and eventually was turned over to the United States military. The Government asserts that it initially detained and interrogated Hamdi in Afghanistan before transferring him to the United States Naval Base in Guantanamo Bay in January 2002. In April 2002, upon learning that Hamdi is an American citizen, authorities transferred him to a naval brig in Norfolk, Virginia, where he remained until a recent transfer to a brig in Charleston, South Carolina. The Government contends that Hamdi is an "enemy combatant," and that this status justifies holding him in the United States indefinitely—without formal charges or proceedings—unless and until it makes the determination that access to counsel or further process is warranted.

In June 2002, Hamdi's father, Esam Fouad Hamdi, filed the present petition for a writ of habeas corpus under 28 U.S.C. § 2241 in the Eastern District of Virginia, naming as petitioners his son and himself as next friend. The elder Hamdi alleges in the petition that he has had no contact with his son since the Government took custody of him in 2001, and that the Government has held his son "without access to legal counsel or notice of any charges pending against him." . . . The habeas petition asks that the court, among other things, (1) appoint counsel for Hamdi; (2) order respondents to cease interrogating him; (3) declare that he is being held in violation of the Fifth and Fourteenth Amendments; (4) "[t]o the extent Respondents contest any material factual allegations in this Petition, schedule an evidentiary hearing, at which Petitioners may adduce proof in support of their allegations"; and (5) order that Hamdi be released from his "unlawful custody." Although his habeas petition provides no details with regard to the factual circumstances surrounding his son's capture and detention, Hamdi's father has asserted in documents found elsewhere in the record that his son went to Afghanistan to do "relief work," and that he had been in that country less than two months before September 11, 2001, and could not have received military training. The 20-year-old was traveling on his own for the first time, his father says, and "[b]ecause of his lack of experience, he was trapped in Afghanistan once that military campaign began."

The District Court . . . appointed the federal public defender as counsel for the petitioners, and ordered that counsel be given access to Hamdi. The United States Court of Appeals for the Fourth Circuit reversed that order, holding that the District Court had failed to extend appropriate deference to the Government's security and intelligence interests. 296 F.3d 278, 279, 283 (2002). It directed the District Court to consider "the most cautious procedures first," id., at 284, and to conduct a deferential inquiry into Hamdi's status, id., at 283. It opined that "if Hamdi is indeed an 'enemy combatant' who was captured during hostilities in Afghanistan, the government's present detention of him is a lawful one." Ibid.

On remand, the Government filed a response and a motion to dismiss the petition. It attached to its response a declaration from one Michael Mobbs (hereinafter "Mobbs Declaration"), who identified himself as Special Advisor to the Under Secretary of Defense for Policy. Mobbs indicated that in this position, he has been "substantially involved with matters related to the detention of enemy combatants in the current war against the al Qaeda terrorists and those who support and harbor them (including the Taliban)." . . . Mobbs . . . set forth what remains the sole evidentiary support that the Government has provided to the courts for Hamdi's detention. The declaration states that Hamdi "traveled to Afghanistan" in July or August 2001, and that he thereafter "affiliated with a Taliban military unit and received weapons training." It asserts that Hamdi "remained with his Taliban unit following the attacks of September 11" and that, during the time when Northern Alliance forces were "engaged in battle with the Taliban," "Hamdi's Taliban unit surrendered" to those forces, after which he "surrender[ed] his Kalishnikov assault rifle" to them. The Mobbs Declaration also states that, because al Qaeda and the Taliban "were and are hostile forces engaged in armed conflict with the armed forces of the United States," "individuals associated with" those groups "were and continue to be enemy combatants." Mobbs states that Hamdi was labeled an enemy combatant "[b]ased upon his interviews and in light of his association with the Taliban." According to the declaration, a series of "U.S. military screening team[s]" determined that Hamdi met "the criteria for enemy combatants," and "a subsequent interview of Hamdi has confirmed that he surrendered and gave his firearm to Northern Alliance forces, which supports his classification as an enemy combatant."

After the Government submitted this declaration, the Fourth Circuit directed the District Court to proceed in accordance with its earlier ruling and, specifically, to "'consider the sufficiency of the Mobbs Declaration as an independent matter before proceeding further.'" 316 F.3d 450, 462 (2003). The District Court found that the Mobbs Declaration fell "far short" of supporting Hamdi's detention. . . . It ordered the Government to turn over numerous materials for *in camera* review, including copies of all of Hamdi's statements and the notes taken from interviews with him that related to his reasons for going to Afghanistan and his activities therein; a list of all interrogators who had questioned Hamdi and their names and addresses; statements by members of the Northern Alliance regarding Hamdi's surrender and capture; a list of the dates and locations of his capture and subsequent detentions; and the names and titles of the United States Government officials who made the determinations that Hamdi was an enemy combatant and that he should be moved to a naval brig. . . .

The Government sought to appeal the production order, and the District Court certified the question of whether the Mobbs Declaration, "'standing alone, is sufficient as a matter of law to allow meaningful judicial review of [Hamdi's] classification as an enemy combatant.'" 316 F.3d at 462. The Fourth Circuit reversed, but did not squarely answer the certified question. It instead stressed that, because it was "undisputed that Hamdi was captured in a zone of active combat in a foreign theater of conflict," no factual inquiry or evidentiary hearing allowing Hamdi to be heard or to rebut the Government's assertions was necessary or proper. *Id.*, at 459. Concluding that the factual averments in the Mobbs Declaration, "if accurate," provided a sufficient basis upon which to conclude that the President had constitutionally detained Hamdi pursuant to the President's war powers, it ordered the habeas petition dismissed. *Id.*, at 473. . . .

II

The threshold question before us is whether the Executive has the authority to detain citizens who qualify as "enemy combatants." There is some debate as to the proper scope of this term, and the Government has never provided any court with the full criteria that it uses in classifying individuals as such. It has made clear, however, that, for purposes of this case, the "enemy combatant" that it is seeking to detain is an individual who, it alleges, was "'part of or supporting forces hostile to the United States or coalition partners'" in Afghanistan and who "'engaged in an armed conflict against the United States'" there. Brief for Respondents 3. We therefore answer only the narrow question before us: whether the detention of citizens falling within that definition is authorized. . . .

The Government . . . maintains that [18 U.S.C.] § 4001(a)[1] is satisfied, because Hamdi is being detained "pursuant to an Act of Congress" — the

1. "No citizen shall be imprisoned or otherwise detained by the United States except pursuant to an Act of Congress." — Eds.

AUMF. Id., at 21-22. . . . [W]e conclude that the AUMF is explicit congressional authorization for the detention of individuals in the narrow category we describe (assuming, without deciding, that such authorization is required), and that the AUMF satisfied § 4001(a)'s requirement that a detention be "pursuant to an Act of Congress" (assuming, without deciding, that § 4001(a) applies to military detentions). . . .

There is no bar to this Nation's holding one of its own citizens as an enemy combatant. In [Ex parte Quirin, 317 U.S. 1 (1942)], one of the detainees, Haupt, alleged that he was a naturalized United States citizen. 317 U.S., at 20. We held that "[c]itizens who associate themselves with the military arm of the enemy government, and with its aid, guidance and direction enter this country bent on hostile acts, are enemy belligerents within the meaning of . . . the law of war." *Id.*, at 37-38. While Haupt was tried for violations of the law of war, nothing in *Quirin* suggests that his citizenship would have precluded his mere detention for the duration of the relevant hostilities. See id., at 30-31. . . . A citizen, no less than an alien, can be "part of or supporting forces hostile to the United States or coalition partners" and "engaged in an armed conflict against the United States," Brief for Respondents 3; such a citizen, if released, would pose the same threat of returning to the front during the ongoing conflict. . . .

Hamdi objects, nevertheless, that Congress has not authorized the *indefinite* detention to which he is now subject. . . . We take Hamdi's objection to be not to the lack of certainty regarding the date on which the conflict will end, but to the substantial prospect of perpetual detention. We recognize that the national security underpinnings of the "war on terror," although crucially important, are broad and malleable. As the Government concedes, given its unconventional nature, the current conflict is unlikely to end with a formal cease-fire agreement. The prospect Hamdi raises is therefore not far-fetched. If the Government does not consider this unconventional war won for two generations, and if it maintains during that time that Hamdi might, if released, rejoin forces fighting against the United States, then the position it has taken throughout the litigation of this case suggests that Hamdi's detention could last for the rest of his life. . . .

. . . Certainly, we agree that indefinite detention for the purpose of interrogation is not authorized. Further, we understand Congress' grant of authority for the use of "necessary and appropriate force" to include the authority to detain for the duration of the relevant conflict, and our understanding is based on longstanding law-of-war principles. If the practical circumstances of a given conflict are entirely unlike those of the conflicts that informed the development of the law of war, that understanding may unravel. But that is not the situation we face as of this date. Active combat operations against Taliban fighters apparently are ongoing in Afghanistan. . . . The United States may detain, for the duration of these hostilities, individuals legitimately determined to be Taliban combatants who "engaged in an armed conflict against the United States." If the record establishes that United States troops are still involved in active combat in Afghanistan, those detentions are part of the exercise of "necessary and appropriate force," and therefore are authorized by the AUMF. . . .

III

Even in cases in which the detention of enemy combatants is legally authorized, there remains the question of what process is constitutionally due to a citizen who disputes his enemy-combatant status. Hamdi argues that he is owed a meaningful and timely hearing and that "extra-judicial detention [that] begins and ends with the submission of an affidavit based on third-hand hearsay" does not comport with the Fifth and Fourteenth Amendments. Brief for Petitioners 16. The Government counters that any more process than was provided below would be both unworkable and "constitutionally intolerable." Brief for Respondents 46. Our resolution of this dispute requires a careful examination both of the writ of habeas corpus, which Hamdi now seeks to employ as a mechanism of judicial review, and of the Due Process Clause, which informs the procedural contours of that mechanism in this instance. . . .

The Government [argues] that further factual exploration is unwarranted and inappropriate in light of the extraordinary constitutional interests at stake. Under the Government's most extreme rendition of this argument, "[r]espect for separation of powers and the limited institutional capabilities of courts in matters of military decision-making in connection with an ongoing conflict" ought to eliminate entirely any individual process, restricting the courts to investigating only whether legal authorization exists for the broader detention scheme. Brief for Respondents 26. At most, the Government argues, courts should review its determination that a citizen is an enemy combatant under a very deferential "some evidence" standard. *Id.*, at 34. Under this review, a court would assume the accuracy of the Government's articulated basis for Hamdi's detention, as set forth in the Mobbs Declaration, and assess only whether that articulated basis was a legitimate one. Brief for Respondents 36. . . .

In response, Hamdi emphasizes that this Court consistently has recognized that an individual challenging his detention may not be held at the will of the Executive without recourse to some proceeding before a neutral tribunal to determine whether the Executive's asserted justifications for that detention have basis in fact and warrant in law. See, e.g., Zadvydas v. Davis, 533 U.S. 678, 690 (2001); Addington v. Texas, 441 U.S. 418, 425- 427 (1979). He argues that the Fourth Circuit inappropriately "ceded power to the Executive during wartime to define the conduct for which a citizen may be detained, judge whether that citizen has engaged in the proscribed conduct, and imprison that citizen indefinitely," Brief for Petitioners 21, and that due process demands that he receive a hearing in which he may challenge the Mobbs Declaration and adduce his own counter evidence. The District Court, agreeing with Hamdi, apparently believed that the appropriate process would approach the process that accompanies a criminal trial. It therefore disapproved of the hearsay nature of the Mobbs Declaration and anticipated quite extensive discovery of various military affairs. Anything less, it concluded, would not be "meaningful judicial review."

Both of these positions highlight legitimate concerns. And both emphasize the tension that often exists between the autonomy that the Government asserts is necessary in order to pursue effectively a particular goal and the process that a citizen contends he is due before he is deprived of a constitutional right. The ordinary mechanism that we use for balancing such serious competing interests, and for determining the procedures that are necessary to ensure that a citizen is not "deprived of life, liberty, or property, without due process of law," U.S. Const., Amdt. 5, is the test that we articulated in Mathews v. Eldridge, 424 U.S. 319 (1976). *Mathews* dictates that the process due in any given instance is determined by weighing "the private interest that will be affected by the official action" against the Government's asserted interest, "including the function involved" and the burdens the Government would face in providing greater process. 424 U.S., at 335. The *Mathews* calculus then contemplates a judicious balancing of these concerns, through an analysis of "the risk of an erroneous deprivation" of the private interest if the process were reduced and the "probable value, if any, of additional or substitute safeguards." *Ibid.* . . .

It is beyond question that substantial interests lie on both sides of the scale in this case. Hamdi's "private interest . . . affected by the official action," *ibid.*, is the most elemental of liberty interests—the interest in being free from physical detention by one's own government. . . .

On the other side of the scale are the weighty and sensitive governmental interests in ensuring that those who have in fact fought with the enemy during a war do not return to battle against the United States. . . .

The Government also argues at some length that its interests in reducing the process available to alleged enemy combatants are heightened by the practical difficulties that would accompany a system of trial-like process. In its view, military officers who are engaged in the serious work of waging battle would be unnecessarily and dangerously distracted by litigation half a world away, and discovery into military operations would both intrude on the sensitive secrets of national defense and result in a futile search for evidence buried under the rubble of war. Brief for Respondents 46-49. To the extent that these burdens are triggered by heightened procedures, they are properly taken into account in our due process analysis.

Striking the proper constitutional balance here is of great importance to the Nation during this period of ongoing combat. But it is equally vital that our calculus not give short shrift to the values that this country holds dear or to the privilege that is American citizenship. It is during our most challenging and uncertain moments that our Nation's commitment to due process is most severely tested; and it is in those times that we must preserve our commitment at home to the principles for which we fight abroad. . . .

With due recognition of these competing concerns, we believe that neither the process proposed by the Government nor the process apparently envisioned by the District Court below strikes the proper constitutional balance when a United States citizen is detained in the United States as an enemy combatant. That is, "the risk of erroneous deprivation" of a detainee's liberty interest is unacceptably high under the Government's proposed rule, while some of the "additional or substitute procedural safeguards" suggested by the District Court are unwarranted in light of their limited "probable value" and the burdens they may impose on the military in such cases. *Mathews,* 424 U.S., at 335.

We therefore hold that a citizen-detainee seeking to challenge his classification as an enemy combatant must receive notice of the factual basis for his classification, and a fair opportunity to rebut the Government's factual assertions before a neutral decisionmaker. . . . These essential constitutional promises may not be eroded.

At the same time, the exigencies of the circumstances may demand that, aside from these core elements, enemy combatant proceedings may be tailored to alleviate their uncommon potential to burden the Executive at a time of ongoing military conflict. Hearsay, for example, may need to be accepted as the most reliable available evidence from the Government in such a proceeding. Likewise, the Constitution would not be offended by a presumption in favor of the Government's evidence, so long as that presumption remained a rebuttable one and fair opportunity for rebuttal were provided. Thus, once the Government puts forth credible evidence that the habeas petitioner meets the enemy-combatant criteria, the onus could shift to the petitioner to rebut that evidence with more persuasive evidence that he falls outside the criteria. A burden-shifting scheme of this sort would meet the goal of ensuring that the errant tourist, embedded journalist, or local aid worker has a chance to prove military error while giving due regard to the Executive once it has put forth meaningful support for its conclusion that the detainee is in fact an enemy combatant. In the words of *Mathews,* process of this sort would sufficiently address the "risk of erroneous deprivation" of a detainee's liberty interest while eliminating certain procedures that have questionable additional value in light of the burden on the Government. 424 U.S., at 335. . . .

In sum, while the full protections that accompany challenges to detentions in other settings may prove unworkable and inappropriate in the enemy-combatant setting, the threats to military operations posed by a basic system of independent review are not so weighty as to trump a citizen's core rights to challenge meaningfully the Government's case and to be heard by an impartial adjudicator.

In so holding, we necessarily reject the Government's assertion that separation of powers principles mandate a heavily circumscribed role for the courts in such circumstances. Indeed, the position that the courts must forgo any examination of the individual case and focus exclusively on the legality of the broader detention scheme cannot be mandated by any reasonable view of separation of powers, as this approach serves only to *condense* power into a single branch of government. . . . Thus, while we do not question that our due process assessment must pay keen attention to the particular burdens faced by the Executive in the context of military action, it would turn our system of checks and balances on its head to suggest that a citizen could not make his way to court with a challenge to the factual basis for his detention by his government, simply because the Executive opposes making available such a challenge. Absent suspension of the writ [of habeas corpus] by Congress, a citizen detained as an enemy combatant is entitled to this process. . . .

There remains the possibility that the standards we have articulated could be met by an appropriately authorized and properly constituted military tribunal. . . . In the absence of such process, however, a court that receives a petition for a writ of habeas corpus from an alleged enemy combatant must itself ensure that the minimum requirements of due process are achieved. . . . We have no reason to doubt that courts faced with these sensitive matters will pay proper heed both to the matters of national security that might arise in an individual case and to the constitutional limitations safeguarding essential liberties that remain vibrant even in times of security concerns.

IV

Hamdi asks us to hold that the Fourth Circuit also erred by denying him immediate access to counsel upon his detention and by disposing of the case without permitting him to meet with an attorney. Brief for Petitioners 19. Since our grant of certiorari in this case, Hamdi has been appointed counsel, with whom he has met for consultation purposes on several occasions, and with whom he is now being granted unmonitored meetings. He unquestionably has the right to access to counsel in connection with the proceedings on remand. No further consideration of this issue is necessary at this stage of the case.

The judgment of the United States Court of Appeals for the Fourth Circuit is vacated, and the case is remanded for further proceedings. . . .

JUSTICE SOUTER, with whom JUSTICE GINSBURG joins, concurring in part, dissenting in part, and concurring in the judgment.

. . . The Government [argues] that Hamdi's incommunicado imprisonment as an enemy combatant seized on the field of battle falls within the President's power as Commander in Chief under the laws and usages of war, and is in any event authorized by two statutes. Accordingly, the Government contends that Hamdi has no basis for any challenge by petition for habeas except to his own status as an enemy combatant; and even that challenge may go no further than to enquire whether "some evidence" supports Hamdi's designation, see Brief for Respondents 34-36; if there is "some evidence," Hamdi should remain locked up at the discretion of the Executive. . . .

The plurality rejects any such limit on the exercise of habeas jurisdiction and so far I agree with its opinion. The plurality does, however, accept the Government's position that if Hamdi's designation as an enemy combatant is correct, his detention (at least as to some period) is authorized by an Act of Congress as required by § 4001(a). . . . Here, I disagree and respectfully dissent. The Government has failed to demonstrate that the Force Resolution authorizes the detention complained of here even on the facts the Government claims. If the Government raises nothing further than the record now shows, . . . Hamdi [should] be released. . . .

Because I find Hamdi's detention forbidden by § 4001(a) and unauthorized by the Force Resolution, I would not reach any questions of what process he may be due in litigating disputed issues in a proceeding under the habeas statute or prior to the habeas enquiry itself. For me, it suffices that the Government has failed to justify holding him in the absence of a further Act of Congress, criminal charges, a showing that the detention conforms to the laws of war, or a demonstration that § 4001(a) is unconstitutional. I would therefore vacate the judgment of the Court of Appeals and remand for proceedings consistent with this view.

Since this disposition does not command a majority of the Court, however, the need to give practical effect to the conclusions of eight members of the Court rejecting the Government's position calls for me to join with the plurality in ordering remand on terms closest to those I would impose. Although I think litigation of Hamdi's status as an enemy combatant is unnecessary, the terms of the plurality's remand will allow Hamdi to offer evidence that he is not an enemy combatant, and he should at the least have the benefit of that opportunity.

It should go without saying that in joining with the plurality to produce a judgment, I do not adopt the plurality's resolution of constitutional issues that I would not reach. It is not that I could disagree with the plurality's determinations (given the plurality's view of the Force Resolution) that someone in Hamdi's position is entitled at a minimum to notice of the Government's claimed factual basis for holding him, and to a fair chance to rebut it before a neutral decision maker; nor, of course, could I disagree with the plurality's affirmation of Hamdi's right to counsel. On the other hand, I do not mean to imply agreement that the Government could claim an evidentiary presumption casting the burden of rebuttal on Hamdi, or that an opportunity to litigate before a military tribunal might obviate or truncate enquiry by a court on habeas.

Subject to these qualifications, I join with the plurality in a judgment of the Court vacating the Fourth Circuit's judgment and remanding the case.

JUSTICE SCALIA, with whom JUSTICE STEVENS joins, dissenting.

. . . Where the Government accuses a citizen of waging war against it, our constitutional tradition has been to prosecute him in federal court for treason or some other crime. Where the exigencies of war prevent that, the Constitution's Suspension Clause, Art. I, § 9, cl. 2, allows Congress to relax the usual protections temporarily. Absent suspension, however, the Executive's assertion of military exigency has not been thought sufficient to permit detention without charge. No one contends that the congressional Authorization for Use of Military Force, on which the Government relies to justify its actions here, is an implementation of the Suspension Clause. Accordingly, I would reverse the decision below.

I

. . . The gist of the Due Process Clause, as understood at the founding and since, was to force the Government to follow those common-law procedures traditionally deemed necessary before depriving a person of life, liberty, or property. When a citizen was deprived of liberty because of alleged criminal conduct, those procedures typically required committal by a magistrate followed by indictment and trial. 3 J. Story, Commentaries on the Constitution of the United States § 1783, p. 661 (1833) (hereinafter Story) (equating "due process of law" with "due presentment or indictment, and being brought in to answer thereto by due process of the common law"). The Due Process Clause "in effect affirms the right of trial according to the process and proceedings of the common law." *Ibid.* See also T. Cooley, General Principles of Constitutional Law 224 (1880) ("When life and liberty are in question, there must in every instance be judicial proceedings; and that requirement implies an accusation, a hearing before an impartial tribunal, with proper jurisdiction, and a conviction and judgment before the punishment can be inflicted" (internal quotation marks omitted)). . . .

These due process rights have historically been vindicated by the writ of habeas corpus. . . . The writ of habeas corpus was preserved in the Constitution—the only common-law writ to be explicitly mentioned. See Art. I, § 9, cl. 2. Hamilton lauded "the establishment of the writ of habeas corpus" in his Federalist defense as a means to protect against "the practice of arbitrary imprisonments . . . in all ages, [one of] the favourite and most formidable instruments of tyranny." The Federalist No. 84. . . .

II

The allegations here, of course, are no ordinary accusations of criminal activity. Yaser Esam Hamdi has been imprisoned because the Government believes he participated in the waging of war against the United States. The relevant question, then, is whether there is a different, special procedure for imprisonment of a citizen accused of wrongdoing *by aiding the enemy in wartime*.

JUSTICE O'CONNOR, writing for a plurality of this Court, asserts that captured enemy combatants (other than those suspected of war crimes) have traditionally been detained until the cessation of hostilities and then released. That is probably an accurate description of wartime practice with respect to enemy *aliens*. The tradition with respect to American citizens, however, has been quite different. Citizens aiding the enemy have been treated as traitors subject to the criminal process. . . .

The modern treason statute is 18 U.S.C. § 2381; it basically tracks the language of the constitutional provision. Other provisions of Title 18 criminalize various acts of warmaking and adherence to the enemy. See, e.g., § 32 (destruction of aircraft or aircraft facilities), § 2332a (use of weapons of mass destruction), § 2332b (acts of terrorism transcending national boundaries), § 2339A (providing material support to terrorists), § 2339B (providing material support to certain terrorist organizations), § 2382 (misprision of treason), § 2383 (rebellion or insurrection), § 2384 (seditious conspiracy), § 2390 (enlistment to serve in armed hostility against the United States). See also 31 CFR § 595.204 (2003) (prohibiting the "making or receiving of any contribution of funds, goods, or services" to terrorists); 50 U.S.C. § 1705(b) (criminalizing violations of 31 CFR § 595.204). The only citizen other than Hamdi known to be imprisoned in connection with military hostilities in Afghanistan against the United States *was* subjected to criminal process and convicted upon a guilty plea. See United States v. Lindh, 212 F. Supp. 2d 541 (ED Va. 2002) (denying motions for dismissal); Seelye, N. Y. Times, Oct. 5, 2002, p. A1, col. 5.

There are times when military exigency renders resort to the traditional criminal process impracticable. English law accommodated such exigencies by allowing legislative suspension of the writ of habeas corpus for brief periods. Blackstone explained:

> "And yet sometimes, when the state is in real danger, even this [i.e., executive detention] may be a necessary measure. But the happiness of our constitution is, that it is not left to the executive power to determine when the danger of the state is so great, as to render this measure expedient. For the parliament only, or legislative power, whenever it sees proper, can authorize the crown, by suspending the habeas corpus act for a short and limited time, to imprison suspected persons without giving any reason for so doing. . . . In like manner this experiment ought only to be tried in case of extreme emergency; and in these the nation parts with it[s] liberty for a while, in order to preserve it for ever." 1 Blackstone 132.

Where the Executive has not pursued the usual course of charge, committal, and conviction, it has historically secured the Legislature's explicit approval of a suspension. In England, Parliament on numerous occasions passed temporary suspensions in times of threatened invasion or rebellion. . . .

Our Federal Constitution contains a provision explicitly permitting suspension, but limiting the situations in which it may be invoked: "The privilege of the Writ of Habeas Corpus shall not be suspended, unless when in Cases of Rebellion or Invasion the public Safety may require it." Art. I, § 9, cl. 2. Although this provision does not state that suspension must be effected by, or authorized by, a legislative act, it has been so understood, consistent with English practice and the Clause's placement in Article I. See Ex parte Merryman, 17 F. Cas. 144, 151-152 (CD Md. 1861) (Taney, C. J., rejecting Lincoln's unauthorized suspension); 3 Story § 1336, at 208-209.

The Suspension Clause was by design a safety valve, the Constitution's only "express provision for exercise of extraordinary authority because of a crisis," Youngstown Sheet & Tube Co. v. Sawyer, 343 U.S. 579, 650 (1952) (Jackson, J., concurring). . . .

III

. . . President Lincoln, when he purported to suspend habeas corpus without congressional authorization during the Civil War, apparently did not doubt that suspension was required if the prisoner was to be held without criminal trial. In his famous message to Congress on July 4, 1861, he argued only that he could suspend the writ, not that even without suspension, his imprisonment of citizens without criminal trial was permitted. . . .

The proposition that the Executive lacks indefinite wartime detention authority over citizens is consistent with the Founders' general mistrust of military power permanently at the Executive's disposal. In the Founders' view, the "blessings of liberty" were threatened by "those military establishments which must gradually poison its very fountain." The Federalist No. 45, p. 238 (J. Madison). No fewer than 10 issues of the Federalist were devoted in whole or part to allaying fears of oppression from the proposed Constitution's authorization of standing armies in peacetime. Many safeguards in the Constitution reflect these concerns. Congress's authority "[t]o raise and support Armies" was hedged with the proviso that "no Appropriation of Money to that Use shall be for a longer Term than two Years." U.S. Const., Art. 1, § 8, cl. 12. Except for the actual command of military forces, all authorization for their maintenance and all explicit authorization for their use is placed in the control of Congress under Article I, rather than the President under Article II. . . . A view of the Constitution that gives the Executive authority to use military force rather than the force of law against citizens on American soil flies in the face of the mistrust that engendered these provisions. . . .

V

It follows from what I have said that Hamdi is entitled to a habeas decree requiring his release unless (1) criminal proceedings are promptly brought, or (2) Congress has suspended the writ of habeas corpus. A suspension of the writ could, of course, lay down conditions for continued detention, similar to those that today's opinion prescribes under the Due Process Clause. Cf. Act of Mar. 3, 1863, 12 Stat. 755. But there is a world of difference between the people's representatives' determining the need for that suspension (and prescribing the conditions for it) and this Court's doing so.

The plurality finds justification for Hamdi's imprisonment in the Authorization for Use of Military Force, 115 Stat. 224, which provides:

> "That the President is authorized to use all necessary and appropriate force against those nations, organizations, or persons he determines planned, authorized, committed, or aided the terrorist attacks that occurred on September 11, 2001, or harbored such organizations or persons, in order to prevent any future acts of international terrorism against the United States by such nations, organizations or persons." § 2(a).

This is not remotely a congressional suspension of the writ, and no one claims that it is. Contrary to the plurality's view, I do not think this statute even authorizes detention of a citizen with the clarity necessary to satisfy the interpretive canon that statutes should be construed so as to avoid grave constitutional concerns,

. . . or with the clarity necessary to overcome the statutory prescription that "[n]o citizen shall be imprisoned or otherwise detained by the United States except pursuant to an Act of Congress." 18 U.S.C. § 4001(a). But even if it did, I would not permit it to overcome Hamdi's entitlement to habeas corpus relief. The Suspension Clause of the Constitution, which carefully circumscribes the conditions under which the writ can be withheld, would be a sham if it could be evaded by congressional prescription of requirements *other than the common-law requirement of committal for criminal prosecution* that render the writ, though available, unavailing. If the Suspension Clause does not guarantee the citizen that he will either be tried or released, unless the conditions for suspending the writ exist and the grave action of suspending the writ has been taken; if it merely guarantees the citizen that he will not be detained unless Congress by ordinary legislation says he can be detained; it guarantees him very little indeed.

It should not be thought, however, that the plurality's evisceration of the Suspension Clause augments, principally, the power of Congress. As usual, the major effect of its constitutional improvisation is to increase the power of the Court. Having found a congressional authorization for detention of citizens where none clearly exists; and having discarded the categorical procedural protection of the Suspension Clause; the plurality then proceeds, under the guise of the Due Process Clause, to prescribe what procedural protections it thinks appropriate. It "weigh[s] the private interest . . . against the Government's asserted interest," and—just as though writing a new Constitution—comes up with an unheard-of system in which the citizen rather than the Government bears the burden of proof, testimony is by hearsay rather than live witnesses, and the presiding officer may well be a "neutral" military officer rather than judge and jury. It claims authority to engage in this sort of "judicious balancing" from Mathews v. Eldridge, 424 U.S. 319 (1976), a case involving . . . *the withdrawal of disability benefits!* Whatever the merits of this technique when newly recognized property rights are at issue (and even there they are questionable), it has no place where the Constitution and the common law already supply an answer. . . .

There is a certain harmony of approach in the plurality's making up for Congress's failure to invoke the Suspension Clause and its making up for the Executive's failure to apply what it says are needed procedures—an approach that reflects what might be called a Mr. Fix-it Mentality. The plurality seems to view it as its mission to Make Everything Come Out Right, rather than merely to decree the consequences, as far as individual rights are concerned, of the other two branches' actions and omissions. Has the Legislature failed to suspend the writ in the current dire emergency? Well, we will remedy that failure by prescribing the reasonable conditions that a suspension should have included. And has the Executive failed to live up to those reasonable conditions? Well, we will ourselves make that failure good, so that this dangerous fellow (if he is dangerous) need not be set free. The problem with this approach is not only that it steps out of the courts' modest and limited role in a democratic society; but that by repeatedly doing what it thinks the political branches ought to do it encourages their lassitude and saps the vitality of government by the people. . . .

VI

Several limitations give my views in this matter a relatively narrow compass. They apply only to citizens, accused of being enemy combatants, who are detained within the territorial jurisdiction of a federal court. This is not likely to be a numerous group; currently we know of only two, Hamdi and Jose Padilla. Where the citizen is captured outside and held outside the United States, the constitutional requirements may be different. Moreover, even within the United States, the accused citizen-enemy combatant may lawfully be detained once prosecution is in progress or in contemplation. See, e.g., County of Riverside v. McLaughlin, 500 U.S. 44 (1991) (brief detention pending judicial determination after warrantless arrest); United States v. Salerno, 481 U.S. 739 (1987) (pretrial detention under the Bail Reform Act). The Government has been notably successful in securing conviction, and hence long-term custody or execution, of those who have waged war against the state.

I frankly do not know whether these tools are sufficient to meet the Government's security needs, including the need to obtain intelligence through interrogation. It is far beyond my competence, or the Court's competence, to determine that. But it is not beyond Congress's. If the situation demands it, the Executive can ask Congress to authorize suspension of the writ—which can be made subject to whatever conditions Congress deems appropriate, including even the procedural novelties invented by the plurality today. To be sure, suspension is limited by the Constitution to cases of rebellion or invasion. But whether the attacks of September 11, 2001, constitute an "invasion," and whether those attacks still justify suspension several years later, are questions for Congress rather than this Court. If civil rights are to be curtailed during wartime, it must be done openly and democratically, as the Constitution requires, rather than by silent erosion through an opinion of this Court. . . .

JUSTICE THOMAS, dissenting.

The Executive Branch, acting pursuant to the powers vested in the President by the Constitution and with explicit congressional approval, has determined that Yaser Hamdi is an enemy combatant and should be detained. This detention falls squarely within the Federal Government's war powers, and we lack the expertise and capacity to second-guess that decision. As such, petitioners' habeas challenge should fail, and there is no reason to remand the case. . . .

Although the President very well may have inherent authority to detain those arrayed against our troops, I agree with the plurality that we need not decide that question because Congress has authorized the President to do so. The Authorization for Use of Military Force (AUMF), 115 Stat. 224, authorizes the President to "use all necessary and appropriate force against those nations, organizations, or persons he determines planned, authorized, committed, or aided the terrorist attacks" of September 11, 2001. Indeed, the Court has previously concluded that language materially identical to the AUMF authorizes the Executive to "make the ordinary use of the soldiers . . . ; that he may kill persons who resist and, of course, that he may use the milder measure of seizing [and detaining] the bodies of those whom he considers to stand in the way of restoring peace." Moyer v. Peabody, 212 U.S. 78, 84 (1909). . . .

I agree with the plurality that the Federal Government has power to detain those that the Executive Branch determines to be enemy combatants. But I do not think that the plurality has adequately explained the breadth of the President's authority to detain enemy combatants, an authority that includes making virtually conclusive factual findings. . . . In my view, . . . we lack the capacity and responsibility to second-guess this determination. . . .

The Government's asserted authority to detain an individual that the President has determined to be an enemy combatant, at least while hostilities continue, comports with the Due Process Clause. . . . [T]he Executive's decision that a detention is necessary to protect the public need not and should not be subjected to judicial second-guessing. Indeed, at least in the context of enemy-combatant determinations, this would defeat the unity, secrecy, and dispatch that the Founders believed to be so important to the warmaking function. . . .

Accordingly, I conclude that the Government's detention of Hamdi as an enemy combatant does not violate the Constitution. By detaining Hamdi, the President, in the prosecution of a war and authorized by Congress, has acted well within his authority. Hamdi thereby received all the process to which he was due under the circumstances. I therefore believe that this is no occasion to balance the competing interests, as the plurality unconvincingly attempts to do. . . .

Although I do not agree with the plurality that the balancing approach of Mathews v. Eldridge, 424 U.S. 319 (1976), is the appropriate analytical tool with which to analyze this case,[2] I cannot help but explain that the plurality misapplies its chosen framework, one that if applied correctly would probably lead to the result I have reached. . . . In *Moyer,* the Court

2. Evidently, neither do the parties, who do not cite *Mathews* even once.

recognized the paramount importance of the Governor's interest in the tranquility of a Colorado town. At issue here is the far more significant interest of the security of the Nation. The Government seeks to further that interest by detaining an enemy soldier not only to prevent him from rejoining the ongoing fight. Rather, as the Government explains, detention can serve to gather critical intelligence regarding the intentions and capabilities of our adversaries, a function that the Government avers has become all the more important in the war on terrorism.

Additional process, the Government explains, will destroy the intelligence gathering function. Brief for Respondents 43-45. It also does seem quite likely that, under the process envisioned by the plurality, various military officials will have to take time to litigate this matter. And though the plurality does not say so, a meaningful ability to challenge the Government's factual allegations will probably require the Government to divulge highly classified information to the purported enemy combatant, who might then upon release return to the fight armed with our most closely held secrets. . . .

Undeniably, Hamdi has been deprived of a serious interest, one actually protected by the Due Process Clause. Against this, however, is the Government's overriding interest in protecting the Nation. If a deprivation of liberty can be justified by the need to protect a town, the protection of the Nation, *a fortiori,* justifies it. . . .

NOTES AND QUESTIONS

1. As Justice Scalia's opinion emphasizes, *Hamdi* isn't a criminal case. But the various opinions in *Hamdi* sound a number of themes that run through much of the law of criminal procedure: the role of the Founders' understandings in interpreting the Constitution, the role of open-ended interest balancing in deciding on the scope of proper procedures, the boundaries (if any) of enforcement discretion by the executive branch, the relevance of public safety needs to a sound interpretation of constitutional restrictions on government power, the relevance of the government's need to gather information — and its need to avoid *disclosing* information — to a sound interpretation of those restrictions, and the list could go on. Though not itself a part of the law of criminal procedure, *Hamdi* is a window on that law, a way of looking at the most fundamental debates in the field in a different context than the ones that dominate this book.

One of those debates, one that is central to the decision in *Hamdi,* concerns the nature and meaning of due process. Notice the different approaches Justices O'Connor, Scalia, and Thomas take to that basic question. Justice O'Connor seems to see due process as a question for the courts, to be decided by a common-law process, with interest balancing as the appropriate method of decision. Justice Scalia uses a different interpretive method—a mix of textualism and originalism—to reach a very different conclusion: In his preferred world, the key player in defining the process for prisoners like Hamdi is the legislative branch, not the judiciary. Justice Thomas deploys the same interpretive method as Justice Scalia, but comes to yet another conclusion: It is the executive branch that should decide what process Hamdi should receive. Which branch is best suited to defining due process? The executive? The legislature? The courts? How much should courts defer to the definitions the political branches use?

2. The *Hamdi* plurality approves a set of procedures that is significantly less protective than those used in criminal trials. It follows that it is a good deal easier for the government to detain suspected terrorists—even when they are American citizens—than it is to detain other suspected criminals. One might reasonably wonder about the incentives that procedural gap creates. If the government finds it more procedurally convenient to fight the war on terrorism with military and intelligence agencies than with criminal law enforcement agencies, what effect will that have on civil liberties? What effect will it have on the progress of the fight against terrorism?

Perhaps the answer is "not much." After all, Hamdi belongs to a very small class of people: American citizens (allegedly) fighting American armed forces in a foreign country. On the other hand, the logic of the Court's position—is it even possible to say what that is, given the fractured decision in *Hamdi*?—might apply to suspected terrorists found *within* the United States. Does it?

3. *Hamdi* is part of a substantial legal tradition, one you will encounter a number of times in this book. The essence of the tradition is this: Often, the government wishes to justify detention that looks a lot like criminal punishment without using the procedures that generally attend criminal punishment. In general, the Supreme Court has been quite receptive to government claims of this sort. The usual legal justification is that, for one or another reason, the relevant detention is something other than "punishment." Thus pretrial detention of criminal defendants is authorized based on much less protective procedures than those used in criminal trials because the detention is "regulatory" rather than punitive. See United States v. Salerno, 481 U.S. 739 (1987). (*Salerno* is excerpted in Chapter 9, at page 1119.) The long-term incarceration of sex offenders

can be authorized with less than the usual processes in criminal cases, as long as the incarceration can be seen as a response to the offenders' mental abnormality rather than punishment for their wrongful conduct. See Kansas v. Hendricks, 521 U.S. 346 (1997). (*Hendricks* is noted in Chapter 14, at page 1556.) There are other examples.

Cases like *Salerno, Hendricks,* and *Hamdi* raise the following question: What does, and doesn't, count as criminal punishment for purposes of defining appropriate procedures? How is the question to be answered? One approach would be to look at the nature of the harm to the claimant. Under that approach, whenever a prisoner is detained in circumstances that seem similar to the detention of prison or jail inmates, criminal procedure protections would be triggered. Another approach would be to allow legislatures to classify detention as punitive or not, and defer to their classification. Under that approach, legislative labels would decide such cases. Yet another approach would be to decide whether a given detention is or isn't "punishment" based on the strength of the government's interest in more flexible procedures than those used in criminal litigation. (Arguably, the last is the approach taken by the *Hamdi* plurality.) Each of these approaches has support in the case law. Which is best?

4. The government claims that its interest in detaining Hamdi justifies special—and, from the government's point of view, specially favorable—procedures. Assume for the moment that the government's claim has substantial merit. (A majority of the Justices so assumed.) Should the government get specially favorable procedures when it prosecutes serial killers? After all, there is a very strong social interest in catching and punishing murderers, especially those who keep killing until they are caught. Should that interest be weighed in the balance when deciding what murder defendants' procedural rights should include? If not, why not?

Speaking of interest balancing, Justice O'Connor's plurality opinion relied on Mathews v. Eldridge, 424 U.S. 319 (1976), to determine how much process to grant Hamdi; *Mathews* requires weighing both sides' interests as the means by which courts decide what process is due in particular cases. It would seem to follow that whatever process the Court deems necessary represents, at least in the Justices' view, the optimal accommodation of the competing interests. That is not the usual method by which criminal procedure rights are defined. Should it be? Presumably everyone wants optimal procedures. Why not perform a *Mathews*-style balance throughout the criminal process? Do the opinions in *Hamdi* suggest an answer?

5. Much of the debate in *Hamdi* concerns the proper balance between legislative and executive power. In the criminal justice system, those two sources of government power are usually allies, not competitors. Legislatures draft broad criminal statutes and allow police and prosecutors nearly total discretion in deciding when, how, and against whom to enforce those statutes. As a general matter, legislative power has not been a check on executive-branch agencies. More like a blank check, authorizing the executive to do pretty much what it pleases. Courts, not legislatures, are the source of most restrictions on executive power to enforce the criminal law. How does that affect your view of the arguments in Justice Scalia's dissent? How do you suppose he would respond?

PART TWO

THE RIGHT TO COUNSEL—THE LINCHPIN OF CONSTITUTIONAL PROTECTION

Chapter 3

The Right to Counsel and Other Assistance

A. The Constitutional Requirements

2. Further Emanations of the Right to Counsel—Counsel on Appeal and Other Forms of Assistance

Insert the following note after Note 3 on page 161:

4. In an odd opinion, the Court dealt with another question derived from the relationship between *Douglas* and *Ross* in Halbert v. Michigan, 545 U.S. 605 (2005). In order to relieve court congestion, the State of Michigan provided by statute that appeals from convictions based on plea agreements were discretionary and that counsel need not be appointed to assist an indigent defendant in filing applications for leave to appeal. The Court noted that, in reviewing applications for leaves to appeal, the Michigan Court of Appeals looks to the merits of the defendant's claim and that indigent defendants are generally ill equipped to represent themselves. In light of these considerations, the Court announced that it was *Douglas* rather than *Ross* that was the controlling precedent, and found the statute to be unconstitutional. However, as the dissent pointed out, the majority, among other failings, "fails . . . to ground its analysis in any particular provision of the Constitution or in this Court's precedents." The dissent further pointed out that the Michigan statute does not appear to make invidious discriminations on the basis of wealth, and certainly does not deprive anyone of access on that basis. More curious still, according to the dissent, the effect of the ruling will be to divert scarce state funds from cases which more likely have problems (cases involving convictions following trials) to those that more likely do not (convictions based on pleas of guilty).

3. Critical Stages of the Proceedings

Insert the following material before the first full paragraph on page 168:

As the preceding text suggests, the conventional view for close to 50 years has been that "critical stages" define the scope of the right to counsel. The belief was that one had a right to counsel at and only at critical stages of the proceedings. In Rothgery v. Gillespie County, Texas, ___ U.S. ___, 2008 U.S. LEXIS 5057 (June 23, 2008), the Court rejected that conventional understanding, although with precisely what implications is quite unclear. Rothgery had been wrongfully arrested and taken by the police before a magistrate for a probable cause hearing. No lawyer for the State of Texas was aware of this. At the hearing, the magistrate erroneously found probable cause but did not appoint a lawyer to represent Rothgery. According to Rothgery, if a lawyer had been appointed immediately, the lawyer would have demonstrated (as eventually occurred) that there was no probable cause to believe Rothgery had committed an offense. Thus, the magistrate's failure to appoint counsel resulted in Rothgery's needless incarceration for three weeks, for which he sued under 42 U.S.C. § 1983 alleging the deprivation of constitutional rights. The Court sided with Rothgery, concluding that "a criminal defendant's initial appearance before a judicial officer, where he learns the charge against him and his liberty is subject to restriction, marks the start of adversary judicial proceedings that trigger attachment of the Sixth Amendment right to counsel." And this was so even though the prosecutorial forces of the state were blithely ignorant of the event, and thus had had no chance to decide whether to prosecute or not, and even though no rights affecting a fair trial were at stake. But, according to the Court at n.15, "We do not purport to set out the scope of an individual's postattachment right to the presence of counsel. It is enough for present purposes to highlight that the enquiry into that right is a different one from the attachment analysis." In short, although Rothgery had the right to counsel, it is not at all clear that he had the right to the presence of counsel at that particular hearing. One might think this is angels dancing on the heads of pins, but it is not. As you will see in Section D, *infra*, a defendant has a right to counsel postindictment because that is a "critical stage" of a criminal proceeding, but not at a preindictment lineup. Does *Rothgery* affect that line? Stay tuned.

B. Effective Assistance of Counsel

1. The Meaning of Effective Assistance

Renumber Notes 5, 6, and 7, at pages 186-187, as Notes 3a, 3b, and 3c, respectively, and move them to follow Note 3 at page 184. Add the following new paragraph to the end of renumbered Note 3b:

In Padilla v. Kentucky, 130 S.Ct. 1473 (2010), the Court concluded the failure to fully advise the defendant concerning the consequences of pleading guilty was ineffective. Counsel did not inform Padilla, a non-citizen who had resided lawfully in the United States for 40 years and had served with honor in Vietnam, that his plea of guilty to a drug charge would render him automatically removable and further told him that he need not worry about the immigration consequences of the plea. The prior law had been reasonably clear that, at most, the right to effective assistance extended to advice concerning the direct consequences of a plea, and not to collateral consequences. The effect of a conviction on immigration status had largely been viewed as collateral. However, the Court concluded that the effect on Padilla was so dramatic—automatic deportation after having spent 40 years in the United States—that the direct/collateral distinction was blurred, and that in any event a reasonably competent lawyer would have advised of such a clear and dramatic consequence. Justice Scalia dissented on the ground that the Court's opinion impermissibly breached the direct/collateral divide, leaving a highly ambiguous admonition in its place that would lead to further instability in pleas and to substantial litigation.

Insert the following note after Note 4 on page 186:

4a. When a defense lawyer in a capital case decides to concede the defendant's guilt at trial, and to focus his efforts entirely on arguing for leniency at sentencing, should he always be required to secure the defendant's prior consent? And, if he concedes guilt without obtaining such consent, does this result in a "fail[ure] to subject the prosecution's case to meaningful adversarial testing," thus triggering the *Cronic*/Bell v. Cone presumption of prejudice? In Florida v. Nixon, 543 U.S. 175 (2004), the Supreme Court unanimously answered "no" to both of these questions (Chief Justice Rehnquist was ill and did not participate). According to the Court, the decision to concede guilt in a capital case is not the same as entering a guilty plea or waiving basic trial rights (either of which would have to be done with the defendant's express consent). Here, Nixon's defense lawyer discussed his choice of strategy with Nixon on several occasions, explaining the pros and cons thereof, but Nixon repeatedly refused to respond: "Given Nixon's constant resistance to answering inquiries put to him by counsel and court, . . . [his lawyer] was not additionally required to gain express consent before conceding Nixon's guilt." Moreover, the Court held, any review of the lawyer's decision to concede guilt should be conducted pursuant to the traditional Strickland v. Washington standards of "performance" and "prejudice," and not under the *Cronic* approach.

ROMPILLA v. BEARD

Certiorari to the United States Court of Appeals for the Third Circuit
545 U.S. 374 (2005)

JUSTICE SOUTER delivered the opinion of the Court.

This case calls for specific application of the standard of reasonable competence required on the part of defense counsel by the Sixth Amendment. We hold that even when a capital defendant's family members and the defendant himself have suggested that no mitigating evidence is available, his lawyer is bound to make reasonable efforts to obtain and review material that counsel knows the prosecution will probably rely on as evidence of aggravation at the sentencing phase of trial.

I

On the morning of January 14, 1988, James Scanlon was discovered dead in a bar he ran in Allentown, Pennsylvania, his body having been stabbed repeatedly and set on fire. Rompilla was indicted for the murder and related offenses, and the Commonwealth gave notice of intent to ask for the death penalty. Two public defenders were assigned to the case.

The jury at the guilt phase of trial found Rompilla guilty on all counts, and during the ensuing penalty phase, the prosecutor sought to prove three aggravating factors to justify a death sentence: that the murder was committed in the course of another felony; that the murder was committed by torture; and that Rompilla had a significant history of felony convictions indicating the use or threat of violence. See 42 Pa. Cons. Stat. §§ 9711(d)(6), (8), (9) (2002). The Commonwealth presented evidence on all three aggravators, and the jury found all proven. Rompilla's evidence in mitigation consisted of relatively brief testimony: five of his family members argued in effect for residual doubt, and beseeched the jury for mercy, saying that they believed Rompilla was innocent and a good man. Rompilla's 14-year-old son testified that he loved his father and would visit him in prison. The jury acknowledged this evidence to the point of finding, as two factors in mitigation, that Rompilla's son had testified on his behalf and that rehabilitation was possible. But the jurors assigned the greater weight to the aggravating factors, and sentenced Rompilla to death. The Supreme Court of Pennsylvania affirmed both conviction and sentence.

In December 1995, with new lawyers, Rompilla filed claims . . . including ineffective assistance by trial counsel in failing to present significant mitigating evidence about Rompilla's childhood, mental capacity and health, and alcoholism. The [state habeas] court found that trial counsel had done enough to investigate the possibilities of a mitigation case, and the Supreme Court of Pennsylvania affirmed the denial of relief.

Rompilla then petitioned for a writ of habeas corpus under 28 U.S.C. § 2254 in Federal District Court. . . . The District Court found that the State Supreme Court had unreasonably applied Strickland v. Washington, 466 U.S. 668 (1984), as to the penalty phase of the trial, and granted relief for ineffective assistance of counsel. . . .

A divided Third Circuit panel reversed. Rompilla v. Horn, 355 F.3d 233 (2004). The majority found nothing unreasonable in the state court's application of *Strickland*, given defense counsel's efforts to uncover mitigation material, which included interviewing Rompilla and certain family members, as well as consultation with three mental health experts. Although the majority noted that the lawyers did not unearth the "useful information" to be found in Rompilla's "school, medical, police, and prison records," it thought the lawyers were justified in failing to hunt through these records when their other efforts gave no reason to believe the search would yield anything helpful. 355 F.3d at 252. The panel thus distinguished Rompilla's case from Wiggins v. Smith, 539 U.S. 510 (2003). Whereas Wiggins's counsel failed to investigate adequately, to the point even of ignoring the leads their limited enquiry yielded, the Court of Appeals saw the Rompilla investigation as going far enough to leave counsel with reason for thinking further efforts would not be a wise use of the limited resources they had. But Judge Sloviter's dissent stressed that trial counsel's failure to obtain relevant records on Rompilla's background was owing to the lawyers' unreasonable reliance on family members and medical experts to tell them what records might be useful. . . .

II

. . . Ineffective assistance under *Strickland* is deficient performance by counsel resulting in prejudice, 466 U.S., at 687, with performance being measured against an "objective standard of reasonableness," id., at 688, "under prevailing professional norms." Ibid. This case, like some others recently, looks to norms of adequate investigation in preparing for the sentencing phase of a capital trial, when defense counsel's job is to counter the State's evidence of aggravated culpability with evidence in mitigation. . . .

A

A standard of reasonableness applied as if one stood in counsel's shoes spawns few hard-edged rules, and the merits of a number of counsel's choices in this case are subject to fair debate. This is not a case in which defense counsel simply ignored their obligation to find mitigating evidence, and their workload as busy public defenders did not keep them from making a number of efforts, including interviews with Rompilla and some members of his family, and examinations of reports by three mental health experts who gave opinions at the guilt phase. None of the sources proved particularly helpful.

Rompilla's own contributions to any mitigation case were minimal. Counsel found him uninterested in helping, as on their visit to his prison to go over a proposed mitigation strategy, when Rompilla told them he was "bored being here listening" and returned to his cell. App. 668. To questions about childhood and schooling, his answers indicated they had been normal, ibid., save for quitting school in the ninth grade, *id.*, at 677. There were times when Rompilla was even actively obstructive by sending counsel off on false leads. *Id.*, at 663-664.

The lawyers also spoke with five members of Rompilla's family (his former wife, two brothers, a sister-in-law, and his son), id., at 494, and counsel testified that they developed a good relationship with the family in the course of their representation. *Id.*, at 669. The state postconviction court found that counsel spoke to the relatives in a "detailed manner," attempting to unearth mitigating information, *id.*, at 264, although the weight of this finding is qualified by the lawyers' concession that "the overwhelming response from the family was that they didn't really feel as though they knew him all that well since he had spent the majority of his adult years and some of his childhood years in custody," *id.*, at 495; see also *id.*, at 669. Defense counsel also said that because the family was "coming from the position that [Rompilla] was innocent . . . they weren't looking for reasons for why he might have done this." *Id.*, at 494.

The third and final source tapped for mitigating material was the cadre of three mental health witnesses who were asked to look into

Rompilla's mental state as of the time of the offense and his competency to stand trial, *id.*, at 473-474, 476, but their reports revealed "nothing useful" to Rompilla's case, *id.*, at 1358, and the lawyers consequently did not go to any other historical source that might have cast light on Rompilla's mental condition.

When new counsel entered the case to raise Rompilla's postconviction claims, however, they identified a number of likely avenues the trial lawyers could fruitfully have followed in building a mitigation case [, including school records and] records of Rompilla's juvenile and adult incarcerations. . . . And while counsel knew from police reports provided in pretrial discovery that Rompilla had been drinking heavily at the time of his offense, Lodging to App. 111-120 (hereinafter Lodging), and although one of the mental health experts reported that Rompilla's troubles with alcohol merited further investigation, App. 723-724, counsel did not look for evidence of a history of dependence on alcohol that might have extenuating significance.

Before us, trial counsel and the Commonwealth respond to these unexplored possibilities by emphasizing this Court's recognition that the duty to investigate does not force defense lawyers to scour the globe on the off-chance something will turn up; reasonably diligent counsel may draw a line when they have good reason to think further investigation would be a waste. See Wiggins v. Smith, 539 U.S., at 525 (further investigation excusable where counsel has evidence suggesting it would be fruitless); Strickland v. Washington, *supra*, at 699 (counsel could "reasonably surmise . . . that character and psychological evidence would be of little help"); Burger v. Kemp, 483 U.S. 776, 794 (1987) (limited investigation reasonable because all witnesses brought to counsel's attention provided predominantly harmful information). The Commonwealth argues that the information trial counsel gathered from Rompilla and the other sources gave them sound reason to think it would have been pointless to spend time and money on . . . additional investigation . . . , and we can say that there is room for debate about trial counsel's obligation to follow at least some of those potential lines of enquiry. There is no need to say more, however, for a further point is clear and dispositive: the lawyers were deficient in failing to examine the court file on Rompilla's prior conviction.

B

There is an obvious reason that the failure to examine Rompilla's prior conviction file fell below the level of reasonable performance. Counsel knew that the Commonwealth intended to seek the death penalty by proving Rompilla had a significant history of felony convictions indicating the use or threat of violence, an aggravator under state law. Counsel further knew that the Commonwealth would attempt to establish this history by proving Rompilla's prior conviction for rape and assault, and would emphasize his violent character by introducing a transcript of the rape victim's testimony given in that earlier trial. App. 665-666. . . . It is also undisputed that the prior conviction file was a public document, readily available for the asking at the very courthouse where Rompilla was to be tried.

It is clear, however, that defense counsel did not look at any part of that file, including the transcript, until warned by the prosecution [twice]. . . . [C]rucially, even after obtaining the transcript of the victim's testimony on the eve of the sentencing hearing, counsel apparently examined none of the other material in the file.

. . . [I]t is difficult to see how counsel could have failed to realize that without examining the readily available file they were seriously compromising their opportunity to respond to a case for aggravation. The prosecution was going to use the dramatic facts of a similar prior offense, and Rompilla's counsel had a duty to make all reasonable efforts to learn what they could about the offense. Reasonable efforts certainly included obtaining the Commonwealth's own readily available file on the prior conviction to learn what the Commonwealth knew about the crime, to discover any mitigating evidence the Commonwealth would downplay and to anticipate the details of the aggravating evidence the Commonwealth would emphasize.[1] . . . The obligation to get the file was particularly pressing here owing to the similarity of the violent prior offense to the crime charged and Rompilla's sentencing strategy stressing residual doubt. Without making efforts to learn the details and rebut the relevance of the earlier crime, a convincing argument for residual doubt was certainly beyond any hope. . . .

At argument the most that Pennsylvania (and the United States as *amicus*) could say was that defense counsel's efforts to find mitigating evidence by other means excused them from looking at the prior conviction file. Tr. of Oral Arg. 37-39, 45-46. . . .

We think this [is] . . . an objectively unreasonable conclusion. It flouts prudence to deny that a defense lawyer should try to look at a file he knows the prosecution will cull for aggravating evidence, let alone when the file is sitting in the trial courthouse, open for the asking. No reasonable

1. The ease with which counsel could examine the entire file makes application of this standard correspondingly easy. Suffice it to say that when the State has warehouses of records available in a particular case, review of counsel's performance will call for greater subtlety.

lawyer would forgo examination of the file thinking he could do as well by asking the defendant or family relations whether they recalled anything helpful or damaging in the prior victim's testimony. . . . Questioning a few more family members and searching for old records can promise less than looking for a needle in a haystack, when a lawyer truly has reason to doubt there is any needle there. But looking at a file the prosecution says it will use is a sure bet: whatever may be in that file is going to tell defense counsel something about what the prosecution can produce.

The dissent thinks this analysis creates a "rigid, *per se*" rule that requires defense counsel to do a complete review of the file on any prior conviction introduced, but that is a mistake. Counsel fell short here because they failed to make reasonable efforts to review the prior conviction file, despite knowing that the prosecution intended to introduce Rompilla's prior conviction not merely by entering a notice of conviction into evidence but by quoting damaging testimony of the rape victim in that case. The unreasonableness of attempting no more than they did was heightened by the easy availability of the file at the trial courthouse, and the great risk that testimony about a similar violent crime would hamstring counsel's chosen defense of residual doubt. . . . Other situations, where a defense lawyer is not charged with knowledge that the prosecutor intends to use a prior conviction in this way, might well warrant a different assessment.

C

Since counsel's failure to look at the file fell below the line of reasonable practice, there is a further question about prejudice, that is, whether "there is a reasonable probability that, but for counsel's unprofessional errors, the result of the proceeding would have been different." 466 U.S., at 694. . . . We think Rompilla has shown beyond any doubt that counsel's lapse was prejudicial. . . .

If the defense lawyers had looked in the file on Rompilla's prior conviction, it is uncontested they would have found a range of mitigation leads that no other source had opened up. In the same file with the transcript of the prior trial were the records of Rompilla's imprisonment on the earlier conviction, which defense counsel testified she had never seen. The prison files pictured Rompilla's childhood and mental health very differently from anything defense counsel had seen or heard. An evaluation by a corrections counselor states that Rompilla was "reared in the slum environment of Allentown, Pa. vicinity. He early came to the attention of juvenile authorities, quit school at 16, [and] started a series of incarcerations in and out Penna. often of assaultive nature and commonly related to over-indulgence in alcoholic beverages." Lodging 40. The same file discloses test results that the defense's mental health experts would have viewed as pointing to schizophrenia and other disorders, and test scores showing a third grade level of cognition after nine years of schooling. Id., at 32-35.

. . . The accumulated entries would have destroyed the benign conception of Rompilla's upbringing and mental capacity defense counsel had formed from talking with Rompilla himself and some of his family members, and from the reports of the mental health experts. With this information, counsel . . . would unquestionably have gone further to build a mitigation case. Further effort would presumably have unearthed much of the material postconviction counsel found, including testimony from several members of Rompilla's family whom trial counsel did not interview. Judge Sloviter summarized this evidence:

> "Rompilla's parents were both severe alcoholics who drank constantly. His mother drank during her pregnancy with Rompilla, and he and his brothers eventually developed serious drinking problems. His father, who had a vicious temper, frequently beat Rompilla's mother, leaving her bruised and black-eyed, and bragged about his cheating on her. His parents fought violently, and on at least one occasion his mother stabbed his father. He was abused by his father who beat him when he was young with his hands, fists, leather straps, belts and sticks. All of the children lived in terror. There were no expressions of parental love, affection or approval. Instead, he was subjected to yelling and verbal abuse. His father locked Rompilla and his brother Richard in a small wire mesh dog pen that was filthy and excrement filled. He had an isolated background, and was not allowed to visit other children or to speak to anyone on the phone. They had no indoor plumbing in the house, he slept in the attic with no heat, and the children were not given clothes and attended school in rags." 355 F.3d at 279 (citations omitted) (dissenting opinion).

The jury never heard any of this and neither did the mental health experts who examined Rompilla before trial. While they found "nothing helpful to [Rompilla's] case," *Rompilla,* 554 Pa., at 385, 721 A.2d, at 790, their postconviction counterparts, alerted by information from school, medical, and prison records that trial counsel never saw, found plenty of "red flags" pointing up a need to test further. 355 F.3d at 279 (Sloviter, J., dissenting). When they tested, they found that Rompilla "suffers from organic brain damage, an extreme mental disturbance significantly impairing several of his cognitive functions." Ibid. They also said that

"Rompilla's problems relate back to his childhood, and were likely caused by fetal alcohol syndrome [and that] Rompilla's capacity to appreciate the criminality of his conduct or to conform his conduct to the law was substantially impaired at the time of the offense." *Id.*, at 280 (Sloviter, J., dissenting). . . .

. . . [A]lthough we suppose it is possible that a jury could have heard [all this evidence] and still have decided on the death penalty, that is not the test. It goes without saying that the undiscovered "mitigating evidence, taken as a whole, 'might well have influenced the jury's appraisal' of [Rompilla's] culpability," *Wiggins*, 539 U.S., at 538 (quoting Williams v. Taylor, 529 U.S., at 398), and the likelihood of a different result if the evidence had gone in is "sufficient to undermine confidence in the outcome" actually reached at sentencing, *Strickland*, 466 U.S., at 694.

The judgment of the Third Circuit is reversed, and Pennsylvania must either retry the case on penalty or stipulate to a life sentence.

JUSTICE O'CONNOR, concurring.

I write separately to put to rest one concern. The dissent worries that the Court's opinion "imposes on defense counsel a rigid requirement to review all documents in what it calls the 'case file' of any prior conviction that the prosecution might rely on at trial." But the Court's opinion imposes no such rule. Rather, today's decision simply applies our longstanding case-by-case approach to determining whether an attorney's performance was unconstitutionally deficient under Strickland v. Washington, 466 U.S. 668 (1984). Trial counsel's performance in Rompilla's case falls short under that standard, because the attorneys' behavior was not "reason-able considering all the circumstances." *Id.*, at 688. In particular, there were three circumstances which made the attorneys' failure to examine Rompilla's prior conviction file unreasonable.

First, Rompilla's attorneys knew that their client's prior conviction would be at the very heart of the *prosecution's* case. The prior conviction went not to a collateral matter, but rather to one of the aggravating circumstances making Rompilla eligible for the death penalty. The prosecutors intended not merely to mention the fact of prior conviction, but to read testimony about the details of the crime. That crime, besides being quite violent in its own right, was very similar to the murder for which Rompilla was on trial, and Rompilla had committed the murder at issue a mere three months after his release from prison on the earlier conviction. In other words, the prosecutor clearly planned to use details of the prior crime as powerful evidence that Rompilla was a dangerous man for whom the death penalty would be both appropriate punishment and a necessary means of incapacitation. This was evidence the defense should have been prepared to meet . . . .

Second, the prosecutor's planned use of the prior conviction threatened to eviscerate one of the *defense's* primary mitigation arguments. Rompilla was convicted on the basis of strong circumstantial evidence. His lawyers structured the entire mitigation argument around the hope of convincing the jury that residual doubt about Rompilla's guilt made it inappropriate to impose the death penalty. In announcing an intention to introduce testimony about Rompilla's similar prior offense, the prosecutor put Rompilla's attorneys on notice that the prospective defense on mitigation likely would be ineffective and counterproductive. . . . Such a scenario called for further investigation, to determine whether circumstances of the prior case gave any hope of saving the residual doubt argument, or whether the best strategy instead would be to jettison that argument so as to focus on other, more promising issues.

Third, the attorneys' decision not to obtain Rompilla's prior conviction file was not the result of an informed tactical decision about how the lawyers' time would best be spent. . . . Rompilla's attorneys did not ignore the prior case file in order to spend their time on other crucial leads. They did not determine that the file was so inaccessible or so large that examining it would necessarily divert them from other trial-preparation tasks they thought more promising. They did not learn at the 11th hour about the prosecution's intent to use the prior conviction, when it was too late for them to change plans. Rather, their failure to obtain the crucial file "was the result of inattention, not reasoned strategic judgment." Wiggins v. Smith, 539 U.S. 510, 534 (2003). As a result, their conduct fell below constitutionally required standards. See *id.*, at 533 ("'Strategic choices made after less than complete investigation are reasonable' only to the extent that 'reasonable professional judgments support the limitations on investigation'" (quoting *Strickland*, 466 U.S., at 690-691)). . . .

JUSTICE KENNEDY, with whom CHIEF JUSTICE REHNQUIST, JUSTICE SCALIA, and JUSTICE THOMAS join, dissenting.

Today the Court brands two committed criminal defense attorneys as ineffective — "outside the wide range of professionally competent counsel," Strickland v. Washington, 466 U.S. 668, 690 (1984) — because they did not look in an old case file and stumble upon something they had not set out to find. . . .

Rompilla was represented at trial by Fredrick Charles, the chief public defender for Lehigh County at the time, and Maria Dantos, an assistant public defender. Charles and Dantos were assisted by John Whispell, an investigator in the public defender's office. Rompilla's defense team sought to develop mitigating evidence from various sources. First, they questioned Rompilla extensively about his upbringing and background. App. 668-669. . . . Second, Charles and Dantos arranged for Rompilla to be examined by three experienced mental health professionals. . . . Finally, Rompilla's attorneys questioned his family extensively in search of any information that might help spare Rompilla the death penalty. . . .

The Court acknowledges the steps taken by Rompilla's attorneys in preparation for sentencing but finds fault nonetheless. "The lawyers were deficient," the Court says, "in failing to examine the court file on Rompilla's prior conviction." . . .

The majority . . . disregards the sound strategic calculation supporting the decisions made by Rompilla's attorneys. Charles and Dantos were "aware of [Rompilla's] priors" and "aware of the circumstances" surrounding these convictions. *Id.*, at 507. At the postconviction hearing, Dantos also indicated that she had reviewed documents relating to the prior conviction. Ibid. Based on this information, as well as their numerous conversations with Rompilla and his family, Charles and Dantos reasonably could conclude that reviewing the full prior conviction case file was not the best allocation of resources.

The majority concludes otherwise only by ignoring *Strickland*'s command that "judicial scrutiny of counsel's performance must be highly deferential." 466 U.S., at 689. According to the Court, the Constitution required nothing less than a full review of the prior conviction case file by Rompilla's attorneys. Even with the benefit of hindsight the Court struggles to explain how the file would have proved helpful, offering only the vague speculation that Rompilla's attorneys might have discovered "circumstances that extenuated the behavior described by the [rape] victim." What the Court means by "circumstances" is a mystery. If the Court is referring to details on Rompilla's mental fitness or upbringing, surely Rompilla's attorneys were more likely to discover such information through the sources they consulted: Rompilla, his family, and the three mental health experts that examined him.

Perhaps the circumstances to which the majority refers are the details of Rompilla's 1974 crimes. Charles and Dantos, however, had enough information about the prior convictions to determine that reviewing the case file was not the most effective use of their time. Rompilla had been convicted of breaking into the residence of Josephine Macrenna, who lived in an apartment above the bar she owned. App. 56-89. After Macrenna gave him the bar's receipts for the night, Rompilla demanded that she disrobe. When she initially resisted, Rompilla slashed her left breast with a knife. Rompilla then held Macrenna at knifepoint while he raped her for over an hour. Charles and Dantos were aware of these circumstances of the prior conviction and the brutality of the crime. *Id.*, at 507. It did not take a review of the case file to know that quibbling with the Commonwealth's version of events was a dubious trial strategy. At sentencing Dantos fought vigorously to prevent the Commonwealth from introducing the details of the 1974 crimes, *id.*, at 16-40, but once the transcript was admitted there was nothing that could be done. Rompilla was unlikely to endear himself to the jury by arguing that his prior conviction for burglary, theft, and rape really was not as bad as the Commonwealth was making it out to be. Recognizing this, Rompilla's attorneys instead devoted their limited time and resources to developing a mitigation case. That those efforts turned up little useful evidence does not make the ex ante strategic calculation of Rompilla's attorneys constitutionally deficient.

One of the primary reasons this Court has rejected a checklist approach to effective assistance of counsel is that each new requirement risks distracting attorneys from the real objective of providing vigorous advocacy as dictated by the facts and circumstances in the particular case. The Court's rigid requirement that counsel always review the case files of convictions the prosecution seeks to use at trial will be just such a distraction. Capital defendants often have a history of crime. . . . If the prosecution relies on these convictions as aggravators, the Court has now obligated defense attorneys to review the boxes of documents that come with them.

In imposing this new rule, the Court states that counsel in this case could review the "entire file" with "ease." There is simply no support in the record for this assumption. Case files often comprise numerous boxes. The file may contain, among other things, witness statements, forensic evidence, arrest reports, grand jury transcripts, testimony and exhibits relating to any pretrial suppression hearings, trial transcripts, trial exhibits, post-trial motions and presentence reports. Full review of even a single prior conviction case file could be time consuming, and many of the documents in a file are duplicative or irrelevant. The Court, recognizing the flaw in its analysis, suggests that cases involving "warehouses of records" "will call for greater subtlety." Yet for all we know, this is such a case. . . .

Even accepting the Court's misguided analysis of the adequacy of representation by Rompilla's trial counsel, Rompilla is still not entitled to habeas relief. *Strickland* assigns the defendant the burden of demonstrating prejudice, 466 U.S., at 692. Rompilla cannot satisfy this standard. . . .

The Court's theory of prejudice rests on serendipity. Nothing in the old case file diminishes the aggravating nature of the prior conviction. The only way Rompilla's attorneys could have minimized the aggravating force of the earlier rape conviction was through Dantos' forceful, but ultimately unsuccessful, fight to exclude the transcript at sentencing. The Court, recognizing this problem, instead finds prejudice through chance. If Rompilla's attorneys had reviewed the case file of his prior rape and burglary conviction, the Court says, they would have stumbled across "a range of mitigation leads."

The range of leads to which the Court refers is in fact a handful of notations within a single 10-page document. The document, an "Initial Transfer Petition," appears to have been prepared by the Pennsylvania Department of Corrections after Rompilla's conviction to facilitate his initial assignment to one of the Commonwealth's maximum-security prisons. Lodging 31-40.

Rompilla cannot demonstrate prejudice because nothing in the record indicates that Rompilla's trial attorneys would have discovered the transfer petition, or the clues contained in it, if they had reviewed the old file. The majority faults Rompilla's attorneys for failing to "learn what the Commonwealth knew about the crime," "discover any mitigating evidence the Commonwealth would downplay," and "anticipate the details of the aggravating evidence the Commonwealth would emphasize." Yet if Rompilla's attorneys had reviewed the case file with these purposes in mind, they almost surely would have attributed no significance to the transfer petition following only a cursory review. The petition, after all, was prepared by the Bureau of Correction after Rompilla's conviction for the purpose of determining Rompilla's initial prison assignment. It contained no details regarding the circumstances of the conviction. Reviewing the prior conviction file for information to counter the Commonwealth, counsel would have looked first at the transcript of the trial testimony, and perhaps then to probative exhibits or forensic evidence. There would have been no reason for counsel to read, or even to skim, this obscure document. . . .

The majority thus finds itself in a bind. If counsel's alleged deficiency lies in the failure to review the file for the purposes the majority has identified, then there is no prejudice: for there is no reasonable probability that review of the file for those purposes would have led counsel to accord the transfer petition enough attention to discover the leads the majority cites. Prejudice could only be demonstrated if the deficiency in counsel's performance were to be described not as the failure to perform a purposive review of the file, but instead as the failure to accord intense scrutiny to every single page of every single document in that file, regardless of the purpose motivating the review. . . . Surely, however, the Court would not require defense counsel to look at every document, no matter how tangential, included in the prior conviction file on the off chance that some notation therein might provide a lead, which in turn might result in the discovery of useful information. The Constitution does not mandate that defense attorneys perform busy work. . . .

Strickland anticipated the temptation "to second-guess counsel's assistance after conviction or adverse sentence" and cautioned that "[a] fair assessment of attorney performance requires that every effort be made to eliminate the distorting effects of hindsight, to reconstruct the circumstances of counsel's challenged conduct, and to evaluate the conduct from counsel's perspective at the time." 466 U.S., at 689. Today, the Court succumbs to the very temptation that *Strickland* warned against. In the process, the majority imposes on defense attorneys a rigid requirement that finds no support in our cases or common sense.

I would affirm the judgment of the Court of Appeals.

NOTES AND QUESTIONS

1. What, exactly, did Rompilla's lawyers do wrong? Whatever it was, did it look wrong at the time or only in hindsight?

2. Compare *Rompilla* to *Strickland*. Both are capital cases; in both, the government had strong evidence of aggravating factors that would make the defendant eligible for the death penalty. And both defendants claimed that defense counsel failed to do enough to uncover mitigating evidence. There are differences, of course—but some of the differences make Washington's claim look stronger than Rompilla's. For example: Washington's lawyer basically did nothing to come up with an argument in mitigation. Rompilla's lawyers did quite a lot. It is hard to explain why Washington's lawyer passed *Strickland*'s performance standard while Rompilla's lawyers flunked that same standard.

Was the standard really the same? Is Justice Souter's opinion consistent with Justice O'Connor's opinion for the Court in *Strickland*? Judging from her *Rompilla* concurrence, Justice O'Connor seems to think so. Is she right?

3. If Rompilla seems to have a weaker argument than Washington on attorney performance, he appears to have a much stronger argument on prejudice. Even the most comprehensive investigation would have turned up little in *Strickland*, because there wasn't much of a mitigating case to be

made. Washington had killed three people (a fourth later died)—a college student, a minister, and an elderly woman—because he was upset that he had lost his job. (In the words of one psychiatric report, he was "chronically frustrated and depressed because of his economic dilemma." *Strickland*, 466 U.S. at 676.) Even in the hands of the most skillful defense lawyer, that is not a winning argument. Rompilla's lawyers, by contrast, had a much stronger case on sentencing to begin with: Rompilla was charged with one murder rather than three, and his key prior conviction was decades old. If they managed to find it, they also had a mother lode of mitigating evidence. Where Washington was "chronically frustrated and depressed," Rompilla may have been schizophrenic. Add to that the hellish childhood described by Judge Sloviter in the passage quoted by the majority opinion, and you have a substantial case for mitigation. One can easily imagine that a jury confronted with that evidence and argument would decide that Rompilla should be incarcerated, not executed.

In short, *Rompilla* looks like *Strickland*'s mirror image. Washington had a fairly strong case on performance but a weak case on prejudice. Rompilla seems to have a strong case on prejudice but a weak performance argument. Perhaps the two decisions suggest that *Strickland*'s prejudice prong is more important than its performance prong—that a strong case on prejudice will compensate for a weak one on performance, but that such compensation only runs in one direction.

4. What, if anything, does *Rompilla* mean for non-capital cases? In general, defendants have not had much success when making *Strickland* claims based on their lawyers' inaction. Not coincidentally, inaction is the norm in criminal cases. One study of appointed counsel in New York City in the mid-1980s found that counsel filed written motions in 26% of homicide cases and 11% of other felony cases, interviewed witnesses in 21% of homicides and 4% of other felonies, employed experts in 17% of homicides and 2% of other felonies, and visited the crime scene in 12% of homicides and 4% of other felonies. See Michael McConville & Chester L. Mirsky, Criminal Defense of the Poor in New York City, 15 N.Y.U. Rev. L. & Soc. Change 581, 762-67 (1986-87).

What is the proper judicial response to data like these? Should courts ratchet up Sixth Amendment standards in order to force states and localities to provide more resources for indigent defense? Would that work? For an argument that courts should instead regulate the funding of defense counsel directly, see Note, Effectively Ineffective: The Failure of Courts to Address Underfunded Indigent Defense Systems, 118 Harv. L. Rev. 1731 (2005).

NOTE ON INEFFECTIVE ASSISTANCE, HABEAS CORPUS, AND THE DEATH PENALTY

Like most of the Supreme Court's key ineffective assistance cases—Strickland v. Washington, 466 U.S. 668 (1984), Nix v. Whiteside, 475 U.S. 157 (1986), Williams v. Taylor, 529 U.S. 362 (2000), Bell v. Cone, 535 U.S. 685 (2002), and Wiggins v. Smith, 539 U.S. 510 (2003), are all examples—*Rompilla* is a federal habeas corpus decision. That is no accident. Ineffective assistance claims are usually raised after the defendant has lost at trial and on direct appeal. Technically, defendant's trial counsel could claim that his own representation was ineffective, but that rarely happens. Instead, defendants usually raise such claims *pro se* in a state trial court after losing their direct appeals. That process, which all state court systems have (with some variation as to procedural details), is usually referred to as "state habeas corpus." In all the cases cited at the beginning of this paragraph, including *Rompilla,* the defendant's ineffective assistance claim ultimately was rejected in state habeas, whereupon the defendant filed the claim in federal district court under the *federal* habeas statute.

In the Anti-terrorism and Effective Death Penalty Act of 1996 (AEDPA), Congress established a deferential standard of review for federal habeas decisions. Federal courts are to grant relief and thereby overturn state-court decisions only when those decisions are "contrary to, or involved an unreasonable application of, clearly established Federal law, as determined by the Supreme Court of the United States." 28 U.S.C. § 2254(d)(1). In Williams v. Taylor, 529 U.S. 362 (2000), the Court construed this language as follows:

> [T]he most important point is that an *unreasonable* application of federal law is different from an *incorrect* application of federal law. . . . Under § 2254(d)(1)'s "unreasonable application" clause, then, a federal habeas court may not issue the writ simply because that court concludes in its independent judgment that the relevant state-court decision applied clearly established federal law erroneously or incorrectly. Rather, that application must also be unreasonable.

529 U.S. at 410-411 (emphasis in original).

Recall that in *Strickland,* the Supreme Court emphasized that, when judging ineffective assistance claims, courts should defer to the decision making of defense counsel. AEDPA and Williams v. Taylor command similar deference to state court judges who deny ineffective assistance claims. The result, when deference is piled on deference, is a tall mountain defendants must climb. In order to prevail in federal court, the defendant (now called a habeas petitioner) must show that trial counsel behaved so unreasonably that it was unreasonable—not merely incorrect—for the state habeas court to deny relief. (Got that?) If AEDPA and Williams v. Taylor mean what they say, federal habeas is an exceedingly unfriendly environment for ineffective assistance claims.

That is probably the reality for most ineffective assistance litigation. But the story is different in capital cases like *Rompilla*. Consider: In Williams v. Taylor itself, the defendant claimed that counsel was ineffective for failing to raise mitigating arguments. On state habeas, the Virginia Supreme Court rejected Williams' claim; notwithstanding the language quoted above, the Justices granted that claim. Wiggins v. Smith, 539 U.S. 510 (2003), was similar: Again, the defendant in a capital case claimed that counsel had failed to raise appropriate mitigating arguments; again state habeas courts denied the claim; again the Supreme Court granted the claim, notwithstanding AEDPA. *Rompilla* is the latest in this line of cases. Tellingly, Justice Souter's majority opinion had virtually nothing to say about AEDPA or Williams v. Taylor, aside from the bottom line that the Pennsylvania courts' decision was "objectively unreasonable." Justice O'Connor's concurrence is, if anything, even more cryptic:

> In the particular circumstances of this case, the attorneys' failure to obtain and review the case file from their client's prior conviction did not meet standards of "reasonable professional judgment." [*Strickland*, 466 U.S.], at 691. Because the Court's opinion is consistent with the "'case-by-case examination of the evidence'" called for under our cases, Williams v. Taylor, 529 U.S. 362, 391 (2000), I join the opinion.

That is not a ringing endorsement of deference to state courts. Evidently, AEDPA's reasonableness standard did little work in *Rompilla*.

At the least, *Williams*, *Wiggins*, and *Rompilla* stand for the proposition that the reasonableness standards in *Strickland*'s performance prong and in § 2254(d)(1) are to be applied more generously when deciding claims that challenge counsel's performance *at capital sentencing proceedings*. Why would the Court treat such cases differently? Perhaps the answer is simply that the death penalty is different from other punishments. But why is it different in a way that relates specifically to ineffective assistance claims?

One possible answer goes to an important piece of death penalty law. The Supreme Court has long held that capital defendants must be permitted to introduce any mitigating evidence or argument in capital sentencing proceedings. See Eddings v. Oklahoma, 455 U.S. 104 (1982); Lockett v. Ohio, 438 U.S. 586 (1978). States can, and to some degree must, be specific about the aggravating factors that separate capital from non-capital murder. But no exclusive list of mitigating factors can exist. That principle is justified by the view that the decision to impose death is ultimately a moral judgment, not a legal one; it cannot be reduced to a set of well-defined legal criteria. It follows that, in nearly every case — *Strickland* may be the exception that proves the rule — there is room for argument about whether this defendant and this crime merit a death sentence.

That makes capital sentencing proceedings very different from most criminal trials. Some defendants can plausibly argue that their conduct does not fit within the governing criminal statute — that the defendant lacked mens rea or acted in self defense, or fit some other legal category exempt from punishment. But most defendants can make no such arguments. That is why most criminal trials revolve around the question whether the government charged the right person or whether the defendant did what the prosecution claims he did, not whether criminal punishment is morally justified. In capital sentencing proceedings, the central question is *precisely* whether the relevant punishment — a death sentence — is morally justified. Sometimes, as in *Strickland*, the answer may be a foregone conclusion. But where (as is usually the case) there is room for argument, *Rompilla* suggests that the argument must be made. On that point, the Supreme Court seems to be saying, federal judges should defer neither to defense counsel nor to state judges.

Notwithstanding the above, there remain limits on the extent to which federal judges must go to protect capital defendants from their own decisions. In Schriro v. Landrigan, 550 U.S. 465 (2007), the defendant refused to allow his defense counsel to present mitigating evidence at capital sentencing, and indeed told the trial judge that he did not want to have such evidence introduced, preferring instead to "bring on" the death penalty. The Supreme Court, by 5-4, held that the Ninth Circuit had erroneously ordered a federal district court to hold an evidentiary hearing on the defendant's ineffective assistance claim, finding the denial of the evidentiary hearing to be within the district court's discretion in light of the defendant's own actions.

C. *Some Implications of the Right to Counsel*

1. The Right to Proceed Pro Se

On page 229, replace the last full paragraph of Note 1 with the following:

A number of states took the hint in *Godinez v. Moran* and imposed restrictions on the waiver of the right to counsel that went beyond the bare bones minimum of *Faretta*. The issue reached the Supreme Court in Indiana v. Edwards, 554 U.S. 164 (2008). In an opinion interesting for a number of reasons, the Court distinguished between a state's choice to permit as compared to forbid a marginally competent individual to proceed *pro se*. Even if due process is not violated by permitting a marginally competent individual to proceed *pro se*, the Court concluded that "the Constitution permits states to insist upon representation by counsel for those competent enough to stand trial under *Dusky* but who still suffer from severe mental illness to the point where they are not competent to conduct trial proceedings themselves." Thus, apparently, a state may permit a severely mentally ill defendant to commit judicial suicide but may also decline to do so.

As interesting as the ultimate conclusion is the manner in which the Court got to it. *Faretta* is best understood as an exegesis on the significance of autonomy—the right to control oneself and one's decisions—for understanding the Sixth Amendment. Autonomy is one of three concepts that often are intermingled under the terms of the other two—privacy and dignity. Privacy refers to the right to control information about yourself, and dignity to the manner in which others must treat you. As you will see in the next main case that closes this subsection, *McKaskle v. Wiggins*, autonomy and dignity can be at odds with each other. Indeed, to some extent, as you will see, *McKaskle* seemed to suggest that the strong focus in *Faretta* on autonomy was giving way under the pressure of pragmatism to a focus on dignitary interests. This change in focus allowed the courts ostensibly to protect *Faretta* rights in a public manner while simultaneously protecting incompetent defendants from themselves.

This same tension between autonomy and dignity is also at the heart of the dispute between the majority and the dissent in *Edwards*. According to the majority:

> [I]n our view, a right of self-representation at trial will not "affirm the dignity" of a defendant who lacks the mental capacity to conduct his defense without the assistance of counsel. *McKaskle*, 465 U.S. at 176-177 ("Dignity" and "autonomy" of individual underlie self-representation right). To the contrary, given defendant's uncertain mental state, the spectacle that could well result from his self-representation at trial is at least as likely to prove humiliating as ennobling. Moreover, insofar as a defendant's lack of capacity threatens an improper conviction or sentence, self-representation in that exceptional context undercuts the most basic of the Constitution's criminal law objectives, providing a fair trial. As Justice Brennan put it, "[t]he Constitution would protect none of us if it prevented the courts from acting to preserve the very processes that the Constitution itself prescribes." Illinois v. Allen, 397 U.S., at 350 (concurring opinion). See *Martinez*, 528 U.S., at 162,

> ("Even at the trial level . . . the government's interest in ensuring the integrity and efficiency of the trial at times outweighs the defendant's interest in acting as his own lawyer"). . . .
>
> Further, proceedings must not only be fair, they must "appear fair to all who observe them." Wheat v. United States, 486 U.S. 153, 160. . . . An amicus brief reports one psychiatrist's reaction to having observed a patient (a patient who had satisfied *Dusky*) try to conduct his own defense: "[H]ow in the world can our legal system allow an insane man to defend himself?" Brief for Ohio et al. as Amici Curiae 24 (internal quotation marks omitted). . . . The application of *Dusky's* basic mental competence standard can help in part to avoid this result. But given the different capacities needed to proceed to trial without counsel, there is little reason to believe that *Dusky* alone is sufficient. At the same time, the trial judge, particularly one such as the trial judge in this case, who presided over one of Edwards' competency hearings and his two trials, will often prove best able to make more fine-tuned mental capacity decisions, tailored to the individualized circumstances of a particular defendant.

Now compare the dissent. In addition to thinking about the distinction between dignity and autonomy, pay careful attention to Justice Scalia's point that the defendant was actually deprived of the ability to make what he believed was his best defense:

> Beyond [forbidding a defendant to disrupt the courtroom], we have never constrained the ability of a defendant to retain "actual control over the case he chooses to present to the jury"—what we have termed "the core of the *Faretta* right." *Wiggins*, supra, at 178. Thus, while *Faretta* recognized that the right of self-representation does not bar the court from appointing standby counsel, we explained in *Wiggins* that "[t]he pro se defendant must be allowed to control the organization and content of his own defense, to make motions, to argue points of law, to participate in voir dire, to question witnesses, and to address the court and the jury at appropriate points in the trial." 465 U.S., at 174. Furthermore, because "multiple voices 'for the defense'" could "confuse the message the defendant wishes to convey," *id.*, at 177, a standby attorney's participation would be barred when it would "destroy the jury's perception that the defendant is representing himself," *id.*, at 178.
>
> As I have explained, I would not adopt an approach to the right of self-representation that we have squarely rejected for other rights—allowing courts to disregard the right when doing so serves the purposes for which the right was intended. But if I were to adopt such an approach, I would remain in dissent, because I believe the Court's assessment of the purposes of the right of self-representation is inaccurate to boot. While there is little doubt that preserving individual "dignity" (to which the Court refers), is paramount among those purposes, there is equally little doubt that the loss of "dignity" the right is designed to prevent is not the defendant's making a fool of himself by presenting an amateurish or even incoherent defense. Rather, the dignity at issue is the supreme human dignity of being master of one's fate rather than a ward of the State—the dignity of individual choice.

Faretta explained that the Sixth Amendment's counsel clause should not be invoked to impair "'the exercise of [the defendant's] free choice'" to dispense with the right, 422 U.S., at 815, (quoting *Adams*, 317 U.S., at 280); for "whatever else may be said of those who wrote the Bill of Rights, surely there can be no doubt that they understood the inestimable worth of free choice," 422 U.S., at 833-834. Nine years later, when we wrote in *Wiggins* that the self-representation right served the "dignity and autonomy of the accused," 465 U.S., at 177, we explained in no uncertain terms that this meant according every defendant the right to his say in court. In particular, we said that individual dignity and autonomy barred standby counsel from participating in a manner that would "destroy the jury's perception that the defendant is representing himself," and meant that "the *pro se* defendant is entitled to preserve actual control over the case he chooses to present to the jury." *Id.*, at 178. In sum, if the Court is to honor the particular conception of "dignity" that underlies the self-representation right, it should respect the autonomy of the individual by honoring his choices knowingly and voluntarily made.

A further purpose that the Court finds is advanced by denial of the right of self-representation is the purpose of assuring that trials "appear fair to all who observe them." To my knowledge we have never denied a defendant a right simply on the ground that it would make his trial appear less "fair" to outside observers, and I would not inaugurate that principle here. But were I to do so, I would not apply it to deny a defendant the right to represent himself when he knowingly and voluntarily waives counsel. When Edwards stood to say that "I have a defense that I would like to represent or present to the Judge," it seems to me the epitome of both actual and apparent unfairness for the judge to say, I have heard "your desire to proceed by yourself and I've denied your request, so your attorney will speak for you from now on."

. . . The facts of this case illustrate this point with the utmost clarity. Edwards wished to take a self-defense case to the jury. His counsel preferred a defense that focused on lack of intent. Having been denied the right to conduct his own defense, Edwards was convicted without having had the opportunity to present to the jury the grounds he believed supported his innocence. I do not doubt that he likely would have been convicted anyway. But to hold that a defendant may be deprived of the right to make legal arguments for acquittal simply because a state-selected agent has made different arguments on his behalf is, as Justice Frankfurter wrote in *Adams*, supra, at 280, to "imprison a man in his privileges and call it the Constitution." In singling out mentally ill defendants for this treatment, the Court's opinion does not even have the questionable virtue of being politically correct. At a time when all society is trying to mainstream the mentally impaired, the Court permits them to be deprived of a basic constitutional right–for their own good.

Insert the following at the end of Note 4 on page 241:

Jones was reaffirmed in Knowles v. Mirzayance, 129 S. Ct. 1411 (2009). Mirzayance was charged with first-degree murder and pled not guilty, and then not guilty by reason of insanity. At the trial, he attempted to avoid a first-degree murder conviction on the grounds of insanity, but was convicted. The proceedings then moved to the not guilty by reason of insanity phase, in which defense counsel intended to present largely the same medical evidence, but also to bolster it with the testimony of the defendant's parents. At the first trial, the burden of proof was on the state; at this second proceeding, the burden of proof would have been on the defendant. On the eve of the trial the parents refused to testify, leaving only the evidence that had already been found, which was insufficient to raise a reasonable doubt about insanity. Defense counsel consequently advised Mirzayance to drop his not guilty by reason of insanity plea because it had already been rejected under a higher (for the state) burden of persuasion. He was convicted, and the Court of Appeals held that it was ineffective assistance to advise dropping the only possible defense, even if it was essentially hopeless. The Supreme Court reversed, concluding that neither the deficient performance nor the prejudice required by *Strickland* could be established. Counseling withdrawal of a hopeless claim did not fall below an objective standard of reasonableness. The Ninth Circuit had argued that competent counsel might have persuaded the reluctant parents to testify, but the magistrate judge who had heard the evidence had concluded to the contrary. Nor, the Court held, is there a flat rule that counsel is required to assert the only defense available when it is an almost certain loss. Moreover, Mirzayance could not demonstrate prejudice, which requires a showing of a reasonable probability of an affect on the outcome. Given that the jury concluded the evidence available did not raise a reasonable doubt about Mirzayance's sanity, it was highly unlikely that the same jury would somehow think the same evidence showed insanity by a preponderance of the evidence.

Insert the following new subsection immediately before Section D on page 255:

3. The Right to Counsel of One's Choice

Throughout this chapter, there have been intimations that the Sixth Amendment provides some protection for the right to counsel of one's choice, so long as either the defendant can afford an attorney's services or the attorney is otherwise willing to serve without reimbursement from the state for services provided. That issue came before the Court in the following case:

UNITED STATES v. GONZALEZ-LOPEZ

Certiorari to the United States Court of Appeals for the Eighth Circuit
548 U.S. 140 (2006)

JUSTICE SCALIA delivered the opinion of the Court.

We must decide whether a trial court's erroneous deprivation of a criminal defendant's choice of counsel entitles him to a reversal of his conviction.

I

Respondent Cuauhtemoc Gonzalez-Lopez was charged in the Eastern District of Missouri with conspiracy to distribute more than 100 kilograms of marijuana. His family hired attorney John Fahle to represent him. After the arraignment, respondent called a California attorney, Joseph Low, to discuss whether Low would represent him, either in addition to or instead of Fahle. Low flew from California to meet with respondent, who hired him. . . .

The following week, respondent informed Fahle that he wanted Low to be his only attorney. Low then filed an application for admission *pro hac vice*. The District Court denied his application without comment. A month later, Low filed a second application, which the District Court again denied without explanation. . . .

The case proceeded to trial, and Dickhaus represented respondent. Low again moved for admission and was again denied. The Court also denied Dickhaus's request to have Low at counsel table with him and ordered Low to sit in the audience and to have no contact with Dickhaus during the proceedings. To enforce the Court's order, a United States Marshal sat between Low and Dickhaus at trial. Respondent was unable to meet with Low throughout the trial, except for once on the last night. The jury found respondent guilty . . . .

Respondent appealed, and the Eighth Circuit vacated the conviction. The Court . . . held that the District Court erred in . . . its denials of [Low's,] . . . motions, and violated respondent's Sixth Amendment right to paid counsel of his choosing. The court then concluded that this Sixth Amendment violation was not subject to harmless-error review. We granted certiorari.

II

. . . The Government here agrees, as it has previously, that "the Sixth Amendment guarantees the defendant the right to be represented by an otherwise qualified attorney whom that defendant can afford to hire, or who is willing to represent the defendant even though he is without funds." Caplin & Drysdale, Chartered v. United States, 491 U.S. 617, 624-625 (1989). To be sure, the right to counsel of choice "is circumscribed in several important respects." But the Government does not dispute the Eighth Circuit's conclusion in this case that the District Court erroneously deprived respondent of his counsel of choice.

The Government contends, however, that the Sixth Amendment violation is not "complete" unless the defendant can show that substitute counsel was ineffective within the meaning of Strickland v. Washington—*i.e.*, that substitute counsel's performance was deficient and the defendant was prejudiced by it. In the alternative, the Government contends that the defendant must at least demonstrate that his counsel of choice would have pursued a different strategy that would have created a "reasonable probability that . . . the result of the proceedings would have been different,"—in other words, that he was prejudiced within the meaning of *Strickland* by the denial of his counsel of choice even if substitute counsel's performance was not constitutionally deficient.[1] To support these propositions, the Government points to our prior cases, which note that the right to counsel "has been accorded . . . not for its own sake, but for the effect it has on the ability of the accused to receive a fair trial." Mickens v. Taylor, 535 U.S. 162, 166 (2002). A trial is not unfair and thus the Sixth Amendment is not violated, the Government reasons, unless a defendant has been prejudiced.

Stated as broadly as this, the Government's argument in effect reads the Sixth Amendment as a more detailed version of the Due Process Clause—and then proceeds to give no effect to the details. It is true enough that the purpose of the rights set forth in that Amendment is to ensure a fair trial; but it does not follow that the rights can be disregarded so long as the trial is, on the whole, fair. What the Government urges upon us here is what was urged upon us (successfully, at one time, see Ohio v. Roberts, 448 U.S. 56 (1980)) with regard to the Sixth Amendment's right of confrontation—a line of reasoning that "abstracts from the right to its purposes, and then eliminates the

1. The dissent proposes yet a third standard—viz., that the defendant must show "'an identifiable difference in the quality of representation between the disqualified counsel and the attorney who represents the defendant at trial.'" (opinion of ALITO, J.). That proposal suffers from the same infirmities (outlined later in text) that beset the Government's positions. In addition, however, it greatly impairs the clarity of the law. How is a lower-court judge to know what an "identifiable difference" consists of? Whereas the Government at least appeals to Strickland and the case law under it, the most the dissent can claim by way of precedential support for its rule is that it is "consistent with" cases that never discussed the issue of prejudice.

right." Maryland v. Craig, 497 U.S. 836 (1990) (SCALIA, J., dissenting). Since, it was argued, the purpose of the Confrontation Clause was to ensure the reliability of evidence, so long as the testimonial hearsay bore "indicia of reliability," the Confrontation Clause was not violated. We rejected that argument (and our prior cases that had accepted it) in Crawford v. Washington, 541 U.S. 36 (2004), saying that the Confrontation Clause "commands, not that evidence be reliable, but that reliability be assessed in a particular manner: by testing in the crucible of cross-examination."

So also with the Sixth Amendment right to counsel of choice. It commands, not that a trial be fair, but that a particular guarantee of fairness be provided—to wit, that the accused be defended by the counsel he believes to be best. "The Constitution guarantees a fair trial through the Due Process Clauses, but it defines the basic elements of a fair trial largely through the several provisions of the Sixth Amendment, including the Counsel Clause." *Strickland, supra,* at 684-685. In sum, the right at stake here is the right to counsel of choice, not the right to a fair trial; and that right was violated because the deprivation of counsel was erroneous. No additional showing of prejudice is required to make the violation "complete."

The cases the Government relies on involve the right to the effective assistance of counsel, the violation of which generally requires a defendant to establish prejudice. The earliest case generally cited for the proposition that "the right to counsel is the right to the effective assistance of counsel," McMann v. Richardson, 397 U.S. 759, 771 (1970), was based on the Due Process Clause rather than on the Sixth Amendment. And even our recognition of the right to effective counsel within the Sixth Amendment was a consequence of our perception that representation by counsel "is critical to the ability of the adversarial system to produce just results." *Strickland, supra,* at 685. Having derived the right to effective representation from the purpose of ensuring a fair trial, we have, logically enough, also derived the limits of that right from that same purpose. The requirement that a defendant show prejudice in effective representation cases arises from the very nature of the specific element of the right to counsel at issue there—*effective* (not mistake-free) representation. Counsel cannot be "ineffective" unless his mistakes have harmed the defense (or, at least, unless it is reasonably likely that they have). Thus, a violation of the Sixth Amendment right to *effective* representation is not "complete" until the defendant is prejudiced.

The right to select counsel of one's choice, by contrast, has never been derived from the Sixth Amendment's purpose of ensuring a fair trial.[3] It has been regarded as the root meaning of the constitutional guarantee. Where the right to be assisted by counsel of one's choice is wrongly denied, therefore, it is unnecessary to conduct an ineffectiveness or prejudice inquiry to establish a Sixth Amendment violation. Deprivation of the right is "complete" when the defendant is erroneously prevented from being represented by the lawyer he wants, regardless of the quality of the representation he received. To argue otherwise is to confuse the right to counsel of choice—which is the right to a particular lawyer regardless of comparative effectiveness—with the right to effective counsel—which imposes a baseline requirement of competence on whatever lawyer is chosen or appointed.

III

Having concluded, in light of the Government's concession of erroneous deprivation, that the trial court violated respondent's Sixth Amendment right to counsel of choice, we must consider whether this error is subject to review for harmlessness . . . [NOTE – The general subject of harmless error is discussed *infra*, at pp. 1561-1575 – EDS.]

We have little trouble concluding that erroneous deprivation of the right to counsel of choice, "with consequences that are necessarily unquantifiable and indeterminate, unquestionably qualifies as 'structural error.'" Different attorneys will pursue different strategies with regard to investigation and discovery, development of the theory of defense, selection of the jury, presentation of the witnesses, and style of witness examination and jury argument. And the choice of attorney will affect whether and on what terms the defendant cooperates with the prosecution, plea bargains, or decides instead to go to trial. In light of these myriad aspects of representation, the erroneous denial of counsel bears directly on the "framework within which the trial proceeds,"—or indeed on whether it proceeds at all. It is impossible to know what different choices the rejected counsel would have made, and then to quantify the impact of those different choices on the outcome of the proceedings. Many counseled decisions, including those involving plea bargains and

3. In Wheat v. United States, 486 U.S. 153 (1988), where we formulated the right to counsel of choice and discussed some of the limitations upon it, we took note of the overarching purpose of fair trial in holding that the trial court has discretion to disallow a first choice of counsel that would create serious risk of conflict of interest. It is one thing to conclude that the right to counsel of choice may be limited by the need for fair trial, but quite another to say that the right does not exist unless its denial renders the trial unfair.

cooperation with the government, do not even concern the conduct of the trial at all. Harmless-error analysis in such a context would be a speculative inquiry into what might have occurred in an alternate universe.

The Government acknowledges that the deprivation of choice of counsel pervades the entire trial, but points out that counsel's ineffectiveness may also do so and yet we do not allow reversal of a conviction for that reason without a showing of prejudice. But the requirement of showing prejudice in ineffectiveness claims stems from the very definition of the right at issue; it is not a matter of showing that the violation was harmless, but of showing that a violation of the right to effective representation *occurred*. A choice-of-counsel violation occurs *whenever* the defendant's choice is wrongfully denied. Moreover, if and when counsel's ineffectiveness "pervades" a trial, it does so (to the extent we can detect it) through identifiable mistakes. We can assess how those mistakes affected the outcome. To determine the effect of wrongful denial of choice of counsel, however, we would not be looking for mistakes committed by the actual counsel, but for differences in the defense that would have been made by the rejected counsel—in matters ranging from questions asked on *voir dire* and cross-examination to such intangibles as argument style and relationship with the prosecutors. We would have to speculate upon what matters the rejected counsel would have handled differently—or indeed, would have handled the same but with the benefit of a more jury—pleasing courtroom style or a longstanding relationship of trust with the prosecutors. And then we would have to speculate upon what effect those different choices or different intangibles might have had. The difficulties of conducting the two assessments of prejudice are not remotely comparable.[5]

IV

Nothing we have said today casts any doubt or places any qualification upon our previous holdings that limit the right to counsel of choice and recognize the authority of trial courts to establish criteria for admitting lawyers to argue before them. As the dissent too discusses, the right to counsel of choice does not extend to defendants who require counsel to be appointed for them. Nor may a defendant insist on representation by

5. In its discussion of the analysis that would be required to conduct harmless-error review, the dissent focuses on which counsel was "better." This focus has the effect of making the analysis look achievable, but it is fundamentally inconsistent with the principle (which the dissent purports to accept for the sake of argument) that the Sixth Amendment can be violated without a showing of harm to the quality of representation. By framing its inquiry in these terms and expressing indignation at the thought that a defendant may receive a new trial when his actual counsel was at least as effective as the one he wanted, the dissent betrays its misunderstanding of the nature of the right to counsel of choice and its confusion of this right with the right to effective assistance of counsel.

a person who is not a member of the bar, or demand that a court honor his waiver of conflict-free representation. We have recognized a trial court's wide latitude in balancing the right to counsel of choice against the needs of fairness, and against the demands of its calendar. The court has, moreover, an "independent interest in ensuring that criminal trials are conducted within the ethical standards of the profession and that legal proceedings appear fair to all who observe them." None of these limitations on the right to choose one's counsel is relevant here. This is not a case about a court's power to enforce rules or adhere to practices that determine which attorneys may appear before it, or to make scheduling and other decisions that effectively exclude a defendant's first choice of counsel. However broad a court's discretion may be, the Government has conceded that the District Court here erred when it denied respondent his choice of counsel. Accepting that premise, we hold that the error violated respondent's Sixth Amendment right to counsel of choice and that this violation is not subject to harmless-error analysis.

* * *

The judgment of the Court of Appeals is affirmed, and the case is remanded for further proceedings consistent with this opinion.

JUSTICE ALITO, with whom THE CHIEF JUSTICE, JUSTICE KENNEDY, and JUSTICE THOMAS join, dissenting.

I disagree with the Court's conclusion that a criminal conviction must automatically be reversed whenever a trial court errs in applying its rules regarding *pro hac vice* admissions and as a result prevents a defendant from being represented at trial by the defendant's first-choice attorney. Instead, a defendant should be required to make at least *some* showing that the trial court's erroneous ruling adversely affected the quality of assistance that the defendant received. In my view, the majority's contrary holding is based on an incorrect interpretation of the Sixth Amendment and a misapplication of harmless-error principles. I respectfully dissent.

I

The majority makes a subtle but important mistake at the outset in its characterization of what the Sixth Amendment guarantees. The majority states that the Sixth Amendment protects "the right of a defendant who does not require appointed counsel to choose who will represent him." What the Sixth Amendment actually protects, however, is the right to have *the assistance* that the defendant's counsel of choice is able to provide. It follows that if the erroneous disqualification of a defendant's counsel of choice does not impair the assistance that a defendant receives at trial, there is no violation of the Sixth Amendment.

The language of the Sixth Amendment supports this interpretation. The Assistance of Counsel Clause focuses on what a defendant is entitled to receive ("Assistance"), rather than on the identity of the provider. The background of the adoption of the Sixth Amendment points in the same direction. The specific evil against which the Assistance of Counsel Clause was aimed was the English common-law rule severely limiting a felony defendant's ability to be assisted by counsel. . . .

There is no doubt, of course, that the right "to have the Assistance of Counsel" carries with it a limited right to be represented by counsel of choice. At the time of the adoption of the Bill of Rights, when the availability of appointed counsel was generally limited, that is how the right inevitably played out: A defendant's right to have the assistance of counsel necessarily meant the right to have the assistance of whatever counsel the defendant was able to secure. But from the beginning, the right to counsel of choice has been circumscribed.

For one thing, a defendant's choice of counsel has always been restricted by the rules governing admission to practice before the court in question. . . .

The right to counsel of choice is also limited by conflict-of-interest rules. Even if a defendant is aware that his or her attorney of choice has a conflict, and even if the defendant is eager to waive any objection, the defendant has no constitutional right to be represented by that attorney.

Similarly, the right to be represented by counsel of choice can be limited by mundane case-management considerations. If a trial judge schedules a trial to begin on a particular date and defendant's counsel of choice is already committed for other trials until some time thereafter, the trial judge has discretion under appropriate circumstances to refuse to postpone the trial date and thereby, in effect, to force the defendant to forgo counsel of choice.

These limitations on the right to counsel of choice are tolerable because the focus of the right is the quality of the representation that the defendant receives, not the identity of the attorney who provides the representation. Limiting a defendant to those attorneys who are willing, available, and eligible to represent the defendant still leaves a defendant with a pool of attorneys to choose from—and, in most jurisdictions today, a large and diverse pool. Thus, these restrictions generally have no adverse effect on a defendant's ability to secure the best assistance that the defendant's circumstances permit.

Because the Sixth Amendment focuses on the quality of the assistance that counsel of choice would have provided, I would hold that the erroneous disqualification of counsel does not violate the Sixth Amendment unless the ruling diminishes the quality of assistance that the defendant would have otherwise received. This would not require a defendant to show that the second-choice attorney was constitutionally ineffective within the meaning of Strickland v. Washington. Rather, the defendant would be entitled to a new trial if the defendant could show "an identifiable difference in the quality of representation between the disqualified counsel and the attorney who represents the defendant at trial."

II

But even accepting, as the majority holds, that the erroneous disqualification of counsel of choice always violates the Sixth Amendment, it still would not follow that reversal is required in all cases. The Constitution, by its terms, does not mandate any particular remedy for violations of its own provisions. Instead, we are bound in this case by Federal Rule of Criminal Procedure 52(a), which instructs federal courts to "disregar[d]" "[a]ny error . . . which does not affect substantial rights." The only exceptions we have recognized to this rule have been for "a limited class of fundamental constitutional errors that 'defy analysis by "harmless error" standards.'" Neder v. United States, 527 U.S. 1, 7 (1999) (quoting Arizona v. Fulminante).

Thus, in *Neder,* we rejected the argument that the omission of an element of a crime in a jury instruction "*necessarily* render[s] a criminal trial fundamentally unfair or an unreliable vehicle for determining guilt or innocence." In fact, in that case, "quite the opposite [was] true: Neder was tried before an impartial judge, under the correct standard of proof and with the assistance of counsel; a fairly selected, impartial jury was instructed to consider all of the evidence and argument in respect to Neder's defense. . . ."

Neder's situation—with an impartial judge, the correct standard of proof, assistance of counsel, and a fair jury—is much like respondent's. Fundamental unfairness does not inexorably follow from the denial of first-choice counsel. The "decision to retain a particular lawyer" is "often uninformed"; a defendant's second-choice lawyer may thus turn out to be better than the defendant's first-choice lawyer. More often, a defendant's first- and second-choice lawyers may be simply indistinguishable. These possibilities would not justify violating the right to choice of counsel, but they do make me hard put to characterize the violation as "*always* render

[ing] a trial unfair." Fairness may not limit the right, but it does inform the remedy.

Nor is it always or nearly always impossible to determine whether the first choice would have provided better representation than the second choice. There are undoubtedly cases in which the prosecution would have little difficulty showing that the second-choice attorney was better qualified than or at least as qualified as the defendant's initial choice, and there are other cases in which it will be evident to the trial judge that any difference in ability or strategy could not have possibly affected the outcome of the trial.

Requiring a defendant to fall back on a second-choice attorney is not comparable to denying a defendant the right to be represented by counsel at all. Refusing to permit a defendant to receive the assistance of any counsel is the epitome of fundamental unfairness, and as far as the effect on the outcome is concerned, it is much more difficult to assess the effect of a complete denial of counsel than it is to assess the effect of merely preventing representation by the defendant's first-choice attorney. To be sure, when the effect of an erroneous disqualification is hard to gauge, the prosecution will be unable to meet its burden of showing that the error was harmless beyond a reasonable doubt. But that does not justify eliminating the possibility of showing harmless error in all cases....

III

Either of the two courses outlined above—requiring at least some showing of prejudice, or engaging in harmless-error review—would avoid the anomalous and unjustifiable consequences that follow from the majority's two-part rule of error without prejudice followed by automatic reversal.

Under the majority's holding, a defendant who is erroneously required to go to trial with a second-choice attorney is automatically entitled to a new trial even if this attorney performed brilliantly. By contrast, a defendant whose attorney was ineffective in the constitutional sense . . . cannot obtain relief without showing prejudice.

Under the majority's holding, a trial court may adopt rules severely restricting *pro hac vice* admissions, but if it adopts a generous rule and then errs in interpreting or applying it, the error automatically requires reversal of any conviction, regardless of whether the erroneous ruling had any effect on the defendant.

Under the majority's holding, some defendants will be awarded new trials even though it is clear that the erroneous disqualification of their first-choice counsel did not prejudice them in the least. Suppose, for example, that a defendant is initially represented by an attorney who previously represented the defendant in civil matters and who has little criminal experience. Suppose that this attorney is erroneously disqualified and that the defendant is then able to secure the services of a nationally acclaimed and highly experienced criminal defense attorney who secures a surprisingly favorable result at trial—for instance, acquittal on most but not all counts. Under the majority's holding, the trial court's erroneous ruling automatically means that the Sixth Amendment was violated—even if the defendant makes no attempt to argue that the disqualified attorney would have done a better job. In fact, the defendant would still be entitled to a new trial on the counts of conviction even if the defendant publicly proclaimed after the verdict that the second attorney had provided better representation than any other attorney in the country could have possibly done. . . .

Because I believe that some showing of prejudice is required to establish a violation of the Sixth Amendment, I would vacate and remand to let the Court of Appeals determine whether there was prejudice. However, assuming for the sake of argument that no prejudice is required, I believe that such a violation, like most constitutional violations, is amenable to harmless-error review. Our statutes demand it, and our precedents do not bar it. I would then vacate and remand to let the Court of Appeals determine whether the error was harmless in this case.

NOTES AND QUESTIONS

1. The majority opinion purports to be a straightforward application of the literal command of the Sixth Amendment, but is it? Where in the amendment does it refer to the counsel the defendant "believes to be best"?

2. The majority opinion is another example of what might be a growing tendency among the Justices to be willing to reconsider established precedent and return to literal or original meanings of constitutional text. This is certainly an apt description of the *Crawford* case that the Court relies upon heavily in its opinion. To that extent, though, is *Gonzalez-Lopez* a case that may come back to haunt all the members of this majority opinion except its author, Justice Scalia? What if this case had arisen in a state prosecution? The Sixth Amendment does not apply against the states; the Due Process Clause does. Whatever one's views of policy, there is no serious linguistic theory that permits the conclusion that the Due Process Clause actually merely adopted various of the provisions of the

Bill of Rights. If this case had arisen from a state prosecution, what opinion might Justice Scalia and the four dissenters have written?

3. Putting aside formal matters of interpretive theory, which opinion is more persuasive? The dissent is surely right that there is a critical distinction between right and remedy that the majority elides. But what about the dissent's view of the right remedy? There is a certain intuitive appeal to the dissent's position that the focus should be on whether the disallowed counsel would have been better, but what exactly does it mean and how could it be implemented in fact? For example, how could it be shown that some other counsel might have been more effective in cross-examining a witness or making a closing argument? One cannot simply rely on reputation here presumably; one needs evidence, but where would that evidence come from? If trial counsel were so bad as to meet the ineffectiveness standard, that would be one thing, but then the holding in *Gonzalez-Lopez* would be unnecessary. Perhaps more troublesome, suppose trial counsel did botch a cross-examination. What about all the other examinations and cross-examinations counsel conducted? What if they were spectacularly effective? The measure of the level of assistance is not just how one discrete moment at trial went, but how the trial as a whole went. But if that is true, the dissent implicitly calls for a complex comparison of how this trial went with how some counter-factual trial would have gone. Is that possible? Sensible?

4. Given the curious linguistic difficulties of the majority's opinion and the practical difficulties of the dissent's, should the Court have simply focused on whether the defendant received constitutionally adequate representation and been done with it?

5. What effect will the case have on substantive decisions concerning the right to counsel? The government conceded in *Gonzalez-Lopez* that the decision to deny Low's motions to represent the defendant was erroneous. Does the case increase the pressure on courts to find to the contrary simply to avoid automatic reversal? Reconsider Note 2, p. 230, *supra*.

PART THREE

THE RIGHT TO BE LET ALONE—AN EXAMINATION OF THE FOURTH AND FIFTH AMENDMENTS AND RELATED AREAS

Chapter 5

The Fourth Amendment

B. The Scope of the Fourth Amendment

1. The Meaning of "Searches"

a. The Relationship Between Privacy and Property

Insert the following notes and main case after Note 3 on page 366:

3a. The Court returned to the subject of "sniff tests" some twenty years after *Place,* reaffirming its approach but raising some new questions at the same time:

ILLINOIS v. CABALLES

Certiorari to the Illinois Supreme Court
543 U.S. 405 (2005)

JUSTICE STEVENS delivered the opinion of the Court.

Illinois State Trooper Daniel Gillette stopped respondent for speeding on an interstate highway. When Gillette radioed the police dispatcher to report the stop, a second trooper, Craig Graham, a member of the Illinois State Police Drug Interdiction Team, overheard the transmission and immediately headed for the scene with his narcotics-detection dog. When they arrived, respondent's car was on the shoulder of the road and respondent was in Gillette's vehicle. While Gillette was in the process of writing a warning ticket, Graham walked his dog around respondent's car. The dog alerted at the trunk. Based on that alert, the officers searched the trunk, found marijuana, and arrested respondent. The entire incident lasted less than 10 minutes.

Respondent was convicted of a narcotics offense and sentenced to 12 years' imprisonment and a $256,136 fine. The trial judge denied his motion to suppress the seized evidence and to quash his arrest. . . . Although the Appellate Court affirmed, the Illinois Supreme Court reversed, concluding that because the canine sniff was performed without any "'specific and articulable facts'" to suggest drug activity, the use of the dog "unjustifiably enlarg[ed] the scope of a routine traffic stop into a drug investigation." 207 Ill.2d 504, 510 (2003).

The question on which we granted certiorari is narrow: "Whether the Fourth Amendment requires reasonable, articulable suspicion to justify using a drug-detection dog to sniff a vehicle during a legitimate traffic stop." Thus, we proceed on the assumption that the officer conducting the dog sniff had no information about respondent except that he had been stopped for speeding; accordingly, we have omitted any reference to facts about respondent that might have triggered a modicum of suspicion.

Here, the initial seizure of respondent when he was stopped on the highway was based on probable cause, and was concededly lawful. It is nevertheless clear that a seizure that is lawful at its inception can violate the Fourth Amendment if its manner of execution unreasonably infringes interests protected by the Constitution. United States v. Jacobsen, 466 U.S. 109, 124 (1984). A seizure that is justified solely by the interest in issuing a warning ticket to the driver can become unlawful if it is prolonged beyond the time reasonably required to complete that mission. In an earlier case involving a dog sniff that occurred during an unreasonably prolonged traffic stop, the Illinois Supreme Court held that use of the dog and the subsequent discovery of contraband were the product of an unconstitutional seizure. People v. Cox, 202 Ill.2d 462 (2002). We may assume that a similar result would be warranted in this case if the dog sniff had been conducted while respondent was being unlawfully detained.

In the state-court proceedings, however, the judges carefully reviewed the details of Officer Gillette's conversations with respondent and the precise timing of his radio transmissions to the dispatcher to determine whether he had improperly extended the duration of the stop to enable the dog sniff to occur. We have not recounted those details because we accept the state court's conclusion that the duration of the stop in this case was entirely justified by the traffic offense and the ordinary inquiries incident to such a stop.

Despite this conclusion, the Illinois Supreme Court held that the initially lawful traffic stop became an unlawful seizure solely as a result of the canine sniff that occurred outside respondent's stopped car. That is, the court characterized the dog sniff as the cause rather than the consequence of a constitutional violation. In its view, the use of the dog converted the citizen-police encounter from a lawful traffic stop into a drug investigation, and because the shift in purpose was not supported by any reasonable suspicion that respondent possessed narcotics, it was unlawful. In our view, conducting a dog sniff would not change the character of a traffic stop that is lawful at its inception and otherwise executed in a reasonable manner, unless the dog sniff itself infringed respondent's constitutionally protected interest in privacy. Our cases hold that it did not.

Official conduct that does not "compromise any legitimate interest in privacy" is not a search subject to the Fourth Amendment. *Jacobsen,* 466 U.S., at 123. We have held that any interest in possessing contraband cannot be deemed "legitimate," and thus, governmental conduct that *only* reveals the possession of contraband "compromises no legitimate privacy interest." Ibid. This is because the expectation "that certain facts will not come to the attention of the authorities" is not the same as an interest in "privacy that society is prepared to consider reasonable." *Id.*, at 122 (punctuation omitted). In United States v. Place, 462 U.S. 696 (1983), we treated a canine sniff by a well-trained narcotics-detection dog as "sui generis" because it "discloses only the presence or absence of narcotics, a contraband item." *Id.*, at 707. Respondent likewise concedes that "drug sniffs are designed, and if properly conducted are generally likely, to reveal only the presence of contraband." Brief for Respondent 17. Although respondent argues that the error rates, particularly the existence of false positives, call into question the premise that drug- detection dogs alert only to contraband, the record contains no evidence or findings that support his argument. Moreover, respondent does not suggest that an erroneous alert, in and of itself, reveals any legitimate private information, and, in this case, the trial judge found that the dog sniff was sufficiently reliable to establish probable cause to conduct a full- blown search of the trunk.

Accordingly, the use of a well-trained narcotics-detection dog—one that "does not expose noncontraband items that otherwise would remain hidden from public view," *Place,* 462 U.S., at 707—during a lawful traffic stop, generally does not implicate legitimate privacy interests. In this case, the dog sniff was performed on the exterior of respondent's car while he was lawfully seized for a traffic violation. Any intrusion on respondent's privacy expectations does not rise to the level of a constitutionally cognizable infringement. . . .

The judgment of the Illinois Supreme Court is vacated, and the case is remanded for further proceedings not inconsistent with this opinion. . . .

THE CHIEF JUSTICE took no part in the decision of this case.

JUSTICE SOUTER, dissenting.

I would hold that using the dog for the purposes of determining the presence of marijuana in the car's trunk was a search unauthorized as an incident of the speeding stop and unjustified on any other ground. I would accordingly affirm the judgment of the Supreme Court of Illinois, and I respectfully dissent.

In United States v. Place, 462 U.S. 696 (1983), we categorized the sniff of the narcotics-seeking dog as "sui generis" under the Fourth Amendment and held it was not a search. *Id.*, at 707. The classification rests not only upon the limited nature of the intrusion, but on a further premise that experience has shown to be untenable, the assumption that trained sniffing dogs do not err. What we have learned about the fallibility of dogs in the years since *Place* was decided would itself be reason to call for reconsidering *Place*'s decision against treating the intentional use of a trained dog as a search. . . .

At the heart both of *Place* and the Court's opinion today is the proposition that sniffs by a trained dog are sui generis because a reaction by the dog in going alert is a response to nothing but the presence of contraband. See ibid. ("[T]he sniff discloses only the presence or absence of narcotics, a contraband item"); *ante*, at 837-38 (assuming "that a canine sniff by a well- trained narcotics dog will only reveal 'the presence or absence of narcotics, a contraband item'" (quoting *Place, supra*, at 707)). Hence, the argument goes, because the sniff can only reveal the presence of items devoid of any legal use, the sniff "does not implicate legitimate privacy interests" and is not to be treated as a search. *Ante*, at 838.

The infallible dog, however, is a creature of legal fiction. Although the Supreme Court of Illinois did not get into the sniffing averages of drug dogs, their supposed infallibility is belied by judicial opinions describing well-trained animals sniffing and alerting with less than perfect accuracy, whether owing to errors by their handlers, the limitations of the dogs themselves, or even the pervasive contamination of currency by cocaine. See, e.g., United States v. Kennedy, 131 F.3d 1371, 1378 (C.A.10 1997) (describing a dog that had a 71% accuracy rate); United States v. Scarborough, 128 F.3d 1373, 1378, n. 3 (C.A.10 1997) (describing a dog that erroneously alerted 4 times out of 19 while working for the postal service and 8% of the time over its entire career); United States v. Limares, 269 F.3d 794, 797 (C.A.7 2001) (accepting as reliable a dog that gave false positives between 7 and 38% of the time); Laime v. State, 347 Ark. 142, 159 (2001) (speaking of a dog that made between 10 and 50 errors); United States v. $242,484.00, 351 F.3d 499, 511 (C.A.11 2003) (noting that because as much as 80% of all currency in circulation contains drug residue, a dog alert "is of little value"), vacated on other grounds by rehearing en banc, 357 F.3d 1225 (C.A.11 2004); United States v. Carr, 25 F.3d 1194, 1214-1217 (C.A.3 1994) (Becker, J., concurring in part and dissenting in part)("[A] substantial portion of United States currency . . . is tainted with sufficient traces of controlled substances to cause a trained canine to alert to their presence"). Indeed, a study cited by Illinois in this case for the proposition that dog sniffs are "generally reliable" shows that dogs in artificial testing situations return false positives anywhere from 12.5 to 60% of the time, depending on the length of the search. See Reply Brief for Petitioner 13; K. Garner et al., Duty Cycle of the Detector Dog: A Baseline Study 12 (Apr.2001) (prepared under Federal Aviation Administration grant by the Institute for Biological Detection Systems of Auburn University). In practical terms, the evidence is clear that the dog that alerts hundreds of times will be wrong dozens of times.

Once the dog's fallibility is recognized, however, that ends the justification claimed in *Place* for treating the sniff as sui generis under the Fourth Amendment: the sniff alert does not necessarily signal hidden contraband, and opening the container or enclosed space whose emanations the dog has sensed will not necessarily reveal contraband or any other evidence of crime. This is not, of course, to deny that a dog's reaction may provide reasonable suspicion, or probable cause, to search the container or enclosure; the Fourth Amendment does not demand certainty of success to justify a search for evidence or contraband. The point is simply that the sniff and alert cannot claim the certainty that *Place* assumed, both in treating the deliberate use of sniffing dogs as sui generis and then taking that characterization as a reason to say they are not searches subject to Fourth Amendment scrutiny. And when that aura of uniqueness disappears, there is no basis in *Place*'s reasoning, and no good reason otherwise, to ignore the actual function that dog sniffs perform. They are conducted to obtain information about the contents of private spaces beyond anything that human senses could perceive, even when conventionally enhanced. The information is not provided by independent third parties beyond the reach of constitutional limitations, but gathered by the government's own officers in order to justify searches of the traditional sort, which may or may not reveal evidence of crime but will disclose anything meant to be kept private in the area searched. Thus in practice the government's use of a trained narcotics dog functions as a limited search to reveal undisclosed facts about private enclosures, to be used to justify a further and complete search of the enclosed area. . . .

It makes sense, then, to treat a sniff as the search that it amounts to in practice, and to rely on the body of our Fourth Amendment cases . . . in deciding whether such a search is reasonable. . . .

Nothing in the case relied upon by the Court, United States v. Jacobsen, 466 U.S. 109 (1984), [changes this analysis.] In *Jacobsen,* the Court found that no Fourth Amendment search occurred when federal agents analyzed powder they had already lawfully obtained. The Court noted that because the test could only reveal whether the powder was cocaine, the owner had no legitimate privacy interest at stake. 466 U.S., at 123. As already explained, however, the use of a sniffing dog in cases like this is significantly different and properly treated as a search that does indeed implicate Fourth Amendment protection.

In *Jacobsen,* once the powder was analyzed, that was effectively the end of the matter: either the powder was cocaine, a fact the owner had no legitimate interest in concealing, or it was not cocaine, in which case the test revealed nothing about the powder or anything else that was not already legitimately obvious to the police. But in the case of the dog sniff, the dog does not smell the disclosed contraband; it smells a closed container. An affirmative reaction therefore does not identify a substance the police already legitimately possess, but informs the police instead merely of a reasonable chance of finding contraband they have yet to put their hands on. The police will then open the container and discover whatever lies within, be it marijuana or the owner's private papers. Thus, while *Jacobsen* could rely on the assumption that the enquiry in question would either show with certainty that a known substance was contraband or would reveal nothing more, both the certainty and the limit on disclosure that may follow are missing when the dog sniffs the car.

The Court today does not go so far as to say explicitly that sniff searches by dogs trained to sense contraband always get a free pass under the Fourth Amendment, since it reserves judgment on the constitutional significance of sniffs assumed to be more intrusive than a dog's walk around a stopped car, *ante,* at 838. For this reason, I do not take the Court's reliance on *Jacobsen* as actually signaling recognition of a broad authority to conduct suspicionless sniffs for drugs in any parked car . . . or on the person of any pedestrian minding his own business on a sidewalk. But the Court's stated reasoning provides no apparent stopping point short of such excesses. For the sake of providing a workable framework to analyze cases on facts like these, which are certain to come along, I would treat the dog sniff as the familiar search it is in fact, subject to scrutiny under the Fourth Amendment.[2]

JUSTICE GINSBURG, with whom JUSTICE SOUTER joins, dissenting.

Illinois State Police Trooper Daniel Gillette stopped Roy Caballes for driving 71 miles per hour in a zone with a posted speed limit of 65 miles per hour. Trooper Craig Graham of the Drug Interdiction Team heard on the radio that Trooper Gillette was making a traffic stop. Although Gillette requested no aid, Graham decided to come to the scene to conduct a dog sniff. Gillette informed Caballes that he was speeding and asked for the usual documents—driver's license, car registration, and proof of insurance. Caballes promptly provided the requested documents but refused to consent to a search of his vehicle. After calling his dispatcher to check on the validity of Caballes' license and for outstanding warrants, Gillette returned to his vehicle to write Caballes a warning ticket. Interrupted by a radio call on an unrelated matter, Gillette was still writing the ticket when Trooper Graham arrived with his drug-detection dog. Graham walked the dog around the car, the dog alerted at Caballes' trunk, and, after opening the trunk, the troopers found marijuana. . . . The Court [holds] that a dog sniff does not render a seizure that is reasonable in time unreasonable in scope. Dog sniffs that detect only the possession of contraband may be employed without offense to the Fourth Amendment, the Court reasons, because they reveal no lawful activity and hence disturb no legitimate expectation of privacy.

In my view, the Court diminishes the Fourth Amendment's force. . . . A drug-detection dog is an intimidating animal. Cf. United States v. Williams, 356 F.3d 1268, 1276 (C.A.10 2004) (McKay, J., dissenting) ("drug dogs are not lap dogs"). Injecting such an animal into a routine traffic stop changes the character of the encounter between the police and the motorist. The stop becomes broader, more adversarial, and (in at least some cases) longer. Caballes—who, as far as Troopers Gillette and Graham knew, was guilty solely of driving six miles per hour over the speed limit—was exposed to the embarrassment and intimidation of being investigated, on a public thoroughfare, for drugs. . . .

The Illinois Supreme Court, it seems to me, correctly apprehended the danger in allowing the police to search for contraband despite the

2. I should take care myself to reserve judgment about a possible case significantly unlike this one. All of us are concerned not to prejudge a claim of authority to detect explosives and dangerous chemical or biological weapons that might be carried by a terrorist who prompts no individualized suspicion. Suffice it to say that what is a reasonable search depends in part on demonstrated risk. Unreasonable sniff searches for marijuana are not necessarily unreasonable sniff searches for destructive or deadly material if suicide bombers are a societal risk.

absence of cause to suspect its presence. Today's decision, in contrast, clears the way for suspicionless, dog-accompanied drug sweeps of parked cars along sidewalks and in parking lots. Compare, e.g., United States v. Ludwig, 10 F.3d 1523, 1526-1527 (C.A.10 1993) (upholding a search based on a canine drug sniff of a parked car in a motel parking lot conducted without particular suspicion), with United States v. Quinn, 815 F.2d 153, 159 (C.A.1 1987) (officers must have reasonable suspicion that a car contains narcotics at the moment a dog sniff is performed), and *Place,* 462 U.S., at 706-707 (Fourth Amendment not violated by a dog sniff of a piece of luggage that was seized, pre-sniff, based on suspicion of drugs). Nor would motorists have constitutional grounds for complaint should police with dogs, stationed at long traffic lights, circle cars waiting for the red signal to turn green.

Today's decision also undermines this Court's situation-sensitive balancing of Fourth Amendment interests in other contexts. For example, in Bond v. United States, 529 U.S. 334, 338-339 (2000), the Court held that a bus passenger had an expectation of privacy in a bag placed in an overhead bin and that a police officer's physical manipulation of the bag constituted an illegal search. If canine drug sniffs are entirely exempt from Fourth Amendment inspection, a sniff could substitute for an officer's request to a bus passenger for permission to search his bag, with this significant difference: The passenger would not have the option to say "No."

The dog sniff in this case, it bears emphasis, was for drug detection only. A dog sniff for explosives, involving security interests not presented here, would be an entirely different matter. Detector dogs are ordinarily trained not as all-purpose sniffers, but for discrete purposes. For example, they may be trained for narcotics detection or for explosives detection or for agricultural products detection. See, e.g., U.S. Customs & Border Protection, Canine Enforcement Training Center, Training Program Course Descriptions, *http://www.cbp.gov/xp/cgov/border_security/canines/training_program.xml* (all Internet materials as visited Dec. 16, 2004, and available in the Clerk of Court's case file) (describing Customs training courses in narcotics detection); Transportation Security Administration, Canine and Explosives Program, *http://www.tsa.gov/public/display?theme=32* (describing Transportation Security Administration's explosives detection canine program); U.S. Dept. of Agriculture, Animal and Plant Health Inspection Service, USDA's Detector Dogs: Protecting American Agriculture (Oct.2001), available at *http://www.aphis.usda.gov/*

oa/pubs/detdogs.pdf (describing USDA Beagle Brigade detector dogs trained to detect prohibited fruits, plants, and meat); see also Jennings, Origins and History of Security and Detector Dogs, in Canine Sports Medicine and Surgery 16, 18-19 (M. Bloomberg, J. Dee, & R. Taylor eds. 1998) (describing narcotics detector dogs used by Border Patrol and Customs, and bomb detector dogs used by the Federal Aviation Administration and the Secret Service, but noting the possibility in some circumstances of cross training dogs for multiple tasks); S. Chapman, Police Dogs in North America 64, 70-79 (1990) (describing narcotics- and explosives- detection dogs and noting the possibility of cross training). There is no indication in this case that the dog accompanying Trooper Graham was trained for anything other than drug detection. See 207 Ill.2d, at 507 ("Trooper Graham arrived with his drug-detection dog. . . . "); Brief for Petitioner 3 ("Trooper Graham arrived with a drug-detection dog. . . . "). . . .

For the reasons stated, I would hold that the police violated Caballes' Fourth Amendment rights when, without cause to suspect wrongdoing, they conducted a dog sniff of his vehicle. I would therefore affirm the judgment of the Illinois Supreme Court.

NOTES AND QUESTIONS

1. What does the majority mean by its statement that the use of a well-trained narcotics-detection dog during a lawful traffic stop does not *generally* implicate legitimate privacy interests? Assume that a traffic stop is prolonged so that a dog can be brought to the scene. This fact might bear on whether the motorist's continued detention is lawful, but should it also bear on whether the dog sniff constitutes a search? Should it make a difference whether the dog is given access to the interior of the car? (In *Caballes,* the dog sniff was performed on the car's *exterior*.) What if the dog in *Caballes* had been cross-trained to alert to the presence of marijuana *and* tomatoes (the latter being an agricultural product that one might need to declare at the border, but that is perfectly lawful to obtain and possess in the country's interior)? Would this fact bring the dog sniff within the scope of Fourth Amendment—regulated activity? Why or why not?

2. Is Justice Souter correct that the fallibility of sniffing dogs trained to detect narcotics should weigh in the decision whether dog sniffs

constitute a search? On what theory? What about the purpose of the dog sniff? Are the dissenters suggesting that dogs trained to sniff cars parked on Capitol Hill and to alert to explosives are a different matter for Fourth Amendment purposes than dogs trained to detect narcotics? How so? Should the purpose for which a dog sniff is conducted count in the determination whether a sniff is a search or merely in the determination whether the "search" is reasonable?

3. At oral argument, Justice Souter asked the Illinois Attorney General whether adhering to the approach in *Place* would mean that "nothing prevents the police from taking the dogs through every municipal garage in the United States and . . . from taking the dogs up to any homeowner's door, ringing the bell, and seeing if the dog[s] get[ ] a sniff of something when the door is opened." After *Caballes,* are police free to use sniffing dogs wherever they wish? Why or why not?

c. *Privacy and Technology*

Insert the following note after Note 6 on page 393:

6a. Reconsider your answer to the preceding question in light of the Court's decision in Illinois v. Caballes, 543 U.S. 405 (2005), which can be found in this supplement on page 63. Doesn't the majority in *Caballes* reaffirm that governmental conduct that reveals *only* the presence of contraband compromises no legitimate privacy interest? If this is correct, presumably a scanner that detected only the presence of explosives that would be illegal to possess should not implicate the Fourth Amendment, even if used to determine whether such explosives might be found in a home. Any interest in possessing unlawful explosives cannot be deemed "legitimate."

But scanners may not be so precise. Suppose a scanner could reveal the presence of certain chemicals in the home. Possession of such chemicals is most commonly associated with the manufacture of explosive devices, but the chemicals are not unlawful to possess and have other purposes— albeit purposes not usually associated with the home. Should it make a difference for Fourth Amendment coverage purposes whether the scanner reveals, narrowly, the presence of explosives or, more generally, the presence of chemicals that might be used to produce explosives but that might also have some other limited uses?

Insert the following note after Note 8 on page 409:

9. *Bostick* and *Drayton* rest on a paradigm: One or two police officers approach one or two individuals, and start asking questions. The "reasonable person" / "free to terminate" standard the Court applies in those cases determines when the conversation becomes coercive enough to require the police to offer some justification for their actions. The other two seizure doctrines discussed in the preceding Notes—*Hodari D*'s requirement that the police achieve physical control over the suspect, and *Brower*'s requirement that such control be achieved through "means intentionally applied"—rest on a similar model: A small number of police officers are pursuing one or two individual suspects. *Hodari D* and *Brower,* like *Bostick* and *Drayton,* answer a timing question: When—at what point in the encounter between these few officers and this individual suspect—does the Fourth Amendment apply?

Sometimes, though, the police deal with suspects not singly, but in groups. (As the public demonstration cases discussed in Note 8 illustrate, the groups are sometimes quite large.) Those circumstances give rise to a different doctrinal question: not *when* the Fourth Amendment applies, but *to whom*. Suppose, for example, that the police stopped Bostick's and Drayton's buses just as they were about to leave their respective bus stations and head toward the highway; otherwise, the facts of the cases remain the same. Who, if anyone, has been "seized"?

The answer appears to be: both drivers and all the passengers on the two buses. Brendlin v. California, 551 U.S. 249 (2007), raised a variant of the hypothetical just posed. In *Brendlin,* the police stopped a car, not a bus, and the car held two people, not two dozen. The police stopped the car to check on a possibly expired registration—even though the car had a valid registration tag posted. Once the car was stopped, one of the officers recognized the passenger as a parole violator with an outstanding arrest warrant. The passenger was then placed under arrest; a subsequent search turned up various items used to manufacture methamphetamine. The California Supreme Court held that Brendlin (the passenger) was not "seized" when the car was first stopped, but only when the officer placed him under arrest. The Supreme Court unanimously disagreed:

> California defends the State Supreme Court's ruling . . . by citing our cases holding that seizure requires a purposeful, deliberate act of detention. But [Michigan v. Chesternut, 486 U.S. 567 (1988)], answers that argument. The intent that counts under the Fourth Amendment is the "intent [that] has been conveyed to the person confronted," *id.,* at 575 n. 7, and the criterion of

> willful restriction on freedom of movement is no invitation to look to subjective intent when determining who is seized. . . . Nor is [Brower v. County of Inyo, 489 U.S. 593 (1989)], to the contrary, where it was dispositive that "Brower was meant to be stopped by the physical obstacle of the roadblock— and that he was so stopped." *Id.*, at 599. California reads this language to suggest that for a specific occupant of the car to be seized he must be the motivating target of an officer's show of authority, as if the thrust of our observation were that Brower, and not someone else, was "meant to be stopped." But our point was not that Brower alone was the target but that officers detained him "through means intentionally applied"; if the car had had another occupant, it would have made sense to hold that he too had been seized when the car collided with the roadblock. . . .
>
> . . . [T]he Supreme Court of California assumed that Brendlin, "as the passenger, had no ability to submit to the deputy's show of authority" because only the driver was in control of the moving vehicle. But what may amount to submission depends on what a person was doing before the show of authority: a fleeing man is not seized until he is physically overpowered, but one sitting in a chair may submit to authority by not getting up to run away. Here, Brendlin had no effective way to signal submission while the car was still moving on the roadway, but once it came to a stop he could, and apparently did, submit by staying inside.

551 U.S. at 260-261. *Brendlin* suggests that, when the police detain a number of people in order to investigate one, *all* members of the group have been "seized."

3. To Whom Does the Fourth Amendment Apply?

Insert the following note after Note 7 on page 419:

7a. Esparza-Mendoza appealed his conviction, continuing to assert that the evidence used to support the conviction had been obtained in violation of his Fourth Amendment right and should have been suppressed. The Tenth Circuit, however, found it unnecessary to consider whether Esparza-Mendoza, as a previously deported felon, could claim the protection of the Fourth Amendment; the Court determined, instead, that Esparza-Mendoza's encounter with police was consensual and involved no search or seizure in any event. See United States v. Esparza-Mendoza, 386 F.3d 953, 955 (10th Cir. 2004). The Government on this appeal did not confess error with regard to the District Court's conclusion that the Fourth Amendment did not apply to Esparza-Mendoza but did elect not to defend this decision—urging the Tenth Circuit to affirm on other grounds (as the Circuit Court ultimately did). The Tenth

Circuit noted that this position on appeal was "somewhat surprising." *Id.* at 957. Do you agree?

Insert the following at the end of Note 8 on page 420:

The application of the Fourth Amendment in the foreign intelligence context is considered in greater detail in Chapter 7. See especially infra pp. 1017-1031.

C. *Probable Cause and Warrants*

1. The Probable Cause Standard

Insert the following note after Note 4 on page 446:

5. In Note 2 on page 434, in connection with our discussion of Illinois v. Gates, 462 U.S. 213 (1983), we said that for an arrest, there must be probable cause to believe that the suspect has committed or is committing a crime. In *Pringle,* the problem was apportioning probable cause among those present at a crime scene—or, to put it more clearly, distinguishing the suspects from the bystanders. What if the problem is, instead, figuring out what crime is being committed?

Consider Devenpeck v. Alford, 543 U.S. 146 (2004). Officer Joi Haner of the Washington State Patrol pulled over Jerome Alford's car, believing that Alford was impersonating a police officer. (As he stopped to assist some stranded motorists, Haner observed Alford, who had previously stopped and begun to help the motorists, hurry back to his car and drive away. The motorists told Haner that Alford's statements to them, as well as the flashing, wig-wag headlights on his car, had given them the impression that he was an officer.) Through the passenger-side window of Alford's car, Haner observed that Alford was listening to the Kitsap County Sheriff's Office police frequency on a special radio, and that his automobile contained handcuffs and a hand-held police scanner. Moreover, Alford appeared evasive, telling Haner that he had previously worked for the "State Patrol," but then under further questioning claiming instead to have worked in law enforcement in Texas and at a shipyard. Alford claimed that his flashing headlights were part of a recently installed car alarm system; although Alford acted as if he was unable to trigger the system, Haner noticed that Alford appeared to avoid pushing a button near his knee, which Haner suspected (correctly, as it turned out) to be the switch for the lights.

Haner was joined at the scene by his supervisor, Sergeant Gerald Devenpeck. While questioning Alford, Devenpeck discovered that Alford was taping their conversation. Devenpeck arrested Alford for violating Washington State's Privacy Act, Wash. Rev. Code § 9.73.030 (1994), not realizing that taping police at a traffic stop is not a crime in Washington. A state trial court subsequently dismissed the charge and Alford, invoking 42 U.S.C. § 1983, filed suit in federal court, claiming that his arrest violated the Fourth Amendment. The jury ruled in favor of the officers, but the Ninth Circuit reversed, concluding that the officers could not have had probable cause to arrest because they cited only the Privacy Act charge. The Ninth Circuit rejected the officers' claim that probable cause existed to arrest for the offenses of impersonating an officer, Wash. Rev. Code § 9A.60.040(3) (1994), and obstructing a law enforcement officer, § 9A.76.020, stating that these offenses were not "closely related" to the offense invoked by Sergeant Devenpeck as he took Alford into custody. The Circuit Court also held that there was no evidence to support the officers' claim of qualified immunity because no objectively reasonable officer could have concluded that arresting Alford for taping conversation at a traffic stop was permissible.

At issue before the Supreme Court was whether an arrest is lawful under the Fourth Amendment when the criminal offense for which there is probable cause to arrest (in Alford's case, arguably impersonating or obstructing an officer) is not "closely related" to the offense stated by the arresting officer at the time of arrest. In an opinion by Justice Scalia, the Supreme Court reiterated that a warrantless arrest is reasonable under the Fourth Amendment if, given the facts known to the officer, there is probable cause to believe that a crime has been or is being committed. The Court found no basis for imposing an additional limitation that the offense establishing probable cause be "closely related" to, and based on the same conduct as, the offense identified by the arresting officer at the time of arrest:

> Whether probable cause exists depends upon the reasonable conclusion to be drawn from the facts known to the arresting officer at the time of the arrest. Maryland v. Pringle, 540 U.S. 366, 371 (2003). In this case, the Court of Appeals held that the probable-cause inquiry is further confined to the known facts bearing upon the offense actually invoked at the time of arrest, and that (in addition) the offense supported by these known facts must be "closely related" to the offense that the officer invoked. We find no basis in precedent or reason for this limitation.

> Our cases make clear that an arresting officer's state of mind (except for the facts that he knows) is irrelevant to the existence of probable cause. See Whren v. United States, 517 U.S. 806, 812-813 (1996)(reviewing cases); Arkansas v. Sullivan, 532 U.S. 769 (2001)(per curiam). That is to say, his subjective reason for making the arrest need not be the criminal offense as to which the known facts provide probable cause. As we have repeatedly explained, "'the fact that the officer does not have the state of mind which is hypothecated by the reasons which provide the legal justification for the officer's action does not invalidate the action taken as long as the circumstances, viewed objectively, justify that action.'" *Whren, supra,* at 813 (quoting Scott v. United States, 436 U.S. 128, 138 (1978)). "[T]he Fourth Amendment's concern with 'reasonableness' allows certain actions to be taken in certain circumstances, whatever the subjective intent." *Whren, supra,* at 814. "[E]venhanded law enforcement is best achieved by the application of objective standards of conduct, rather than standards that depend upon the subjective state of mind of the officer." Horton v. California, 496 U.S. 128, 138 (1990).
>
> The rule that the offense establishing probable cause must be "closely related" to, and based on the same conduct as, the offense identified by the arresting officer at the time of arrest is inconsistent with this precedent. Such a rule makes the lawfulness of an arrest turn upon the motivation of the arresting officer—eliminating, as validating probable cause, facts that played no part in the officer's expressed subjective reason for making the arrest, and offenses that are "closely related" to that subjective reason. See, e.g., Sheehy v. Plymouth, 191 F.3d 15, 20 (C.A.1 1999); Trejo v. Perez, 693 F.2d 482, 485- 486 (C.A.5 1982). This means that the constitutionality of an arrest under a given set of known facts will "vary from place to place and from time to time," *Whren, supra,* at 815, depending on whether the arresting officer states the reason for the detention and, if so, whether he correctly identifies a general class of offense for which probable cause exists. An arrest made by a knowledgeable, veteran officer would be valid, whereas an arrest made by a rookie in precisely the same circumstances would not. We see no reason to ascribe to the Fourth Amendment such arbitrarily variable protection.

543 U.S. at 152-154. The Court noted that while it is good practice for officers to inform arrestees of the reason for arrest at the time they are taken into custody, the Court has never held this to be constitutionally required. A rule limiting the probable-cause inquiry to offenses closely related to those identified by the arresting officer, the Court noted, would thus have the perverse consequence of discouraging officers from providing reasons for arrest. The Court reversed and remanded the case so that the Ninth Circuit might in the first instance consider whether the evidence established probable cause to arrest for obstructing or impersonating a law enforcement officer.

2. The Warrant "Requirement"

Insert the following main case after the discussion of the particularity requirement on page 452:

Insert the following main case after the discussion of the particularity requirement on page 452:

Finally, consider how the particularity requirement might (or might not) apply to so-called "anticipatory warrants":

UNITED STATES v. GRUBBS

Certiorari to the United States Court of Appeals for the Ninth Circuit
547 U.S. 90 (2006)

JUSTICE SCALIA delivered the opinion of the Court . . . .

I

Respondent Jeffrey Grubbs purchased a videotape containing child pornography from a Web site operated by an undercover postal inspector. Officers from the Postal Inspection Service arranged a controlled delivery of a package containing the videotape to Grubbs' residence. A postal inspector submitted a search warrant application to a Magistrate Judge for the Eastern District of California, accompanied by an affidavit describing the proposed operation in detail. The affidavit stated:

> "Execution of this search warrant will not occur unless and until the parcel has been received by a person(s) and has been physically taken into the residence. . . . At that time, and not before, this search warrant will be executed by me and other United States Postal inspectors, with appropriate assistance from other law enforcement officers in accordance with this warrant's command." App. to Pet. for Cert. 72a.

In addition to describing this triggering condition, the affidavit referred to two attachments, which described Grubbs' residence and the items officers would seize. These attachments, but not the body of the affidavit, were incorporated into the requested warrant. The affidavit concluded:

> "Based upon the foregoing facts, I respectfully submit there exists probable cause to believe that the items set forth in Attachment B to this affidavit and the search warrant, will be found [at Grubbs' residence], which residence is further described at Attachment A." *Ibid.*

The Magistrate Judge issued the warrant as requested. Two days later, an undercover postal inspector delivered the package. Grubbs' wife signed for it and took the unopened package inside. The inspectors detained Grubbs as he left his home a few minutes later, then entered the house and commenced the search. Roughly 30 minutes into the search, Grubbs was provided with a copy of the warrant, which included both attachments but not the supporting affidavit that explained when the warrant would be executed. Grubbs consented to interrogation by the postal inspectors and admitted ordering the videotape. He was placed under arrest, and various items were seized, including the videotape.

A grand jury for the Eastern District of California indicted Grubbs on one count of receiving a visual depiction of a minor engaged in sexually explicit conduct. See 18 U.S.C. § 2252(a)(2). He moved to suppress the evidence seized during the search of his residence, arguing as relevant here that the warrant was invalid because it failed to list the triggering condition. After an evidentiary hearing, the District Court denied the motion. Grubbs pleaded guilty, but reserved his right to appeal the denial of his motion to suppress.

The Court of Appeals for the Ninth Circuit reversed. Relying on Circuit precedent, it held that "the particularity requirement of the Fourth Amendment applies with full force to the conditions precedent to an anticipatory search warrant." 377 F.3d [1072, 1077-1078, amended 389 F.3d 1306 (2004)](citing United States v. Hotal, 143 F.3d 1223, 1226 (C.A.9 1998)). An anticipatory warrant defective for that reason may be "cur [ed]" if the conditions precedent are set forth in an affidavit that is incorporated in the warrant and "presented to the person whose property is being searched." 377 F.3d, at 1079. Because the postal inspectors "failed to present the affidavit — the only document in which the triggering conditions were listed" — to Grubbs or his wife, the "warrant was . . . inoperative, and the search was illegal." *Ibid*. We granted certiorari.

II

Before turning to the Ninth Circuit's conclusion that the warrant at issue here ran afoul of the Fourth Amendment's particularity requirement, we address the antecedent question whether anticipatory search warrants are categorically unconstitutional. An anticipatory warrant is "a warrant based upon an affidavit showing probable cause that at some future time (but not presently) certain evidence of crime will be located at a specified place." 2 W. LaFave, Search and Seizure § 3.7(c), p. 398 (4th ed. 2004). Most anticipatory warrants subject their execution to some condition precedent other than the mere passage of time — a so-called "triggering condition." The affidavit at issue here, for instance, explained that "[e] xecution of th[e] search warrant will not occur unless and until the parcel [containing child pornography] has been received by a person(s) and has been physically taken into the residence." App. to Pet. for Cert. 72a. If the government were to execute an anticipatory warrant before the triggering condition occurred, there would be no reason to believe the item described in the warrant could be found at the searched location; by definition, the triggering condition which establishes probable cause has not yet been satisfied when the warrant is issued. Grubbs argues that for this reason anticipatory warrants contravene the Fourth Amendment's provision that "no Warrants shall issue, but upon probable cause."

We reject this view, as has every Court of Appeals to confront the issue. Probable cause exists when "there is a fair probability that contraband or evidence of a crime will be found in a particular place." Illinois v. Gates, 462 U.S. 213, 238 (1983). Because the probable-cause requirement looks to whether evidence will be found *when the search is conducted*, all warrants are, in a sense, "anticipatory." In the typical case where the police seek permission to search a house for an item they believe is already located there, the magistrate's determination that there is probable cause for the search amounts to a prediction that the item will still be there when the warrant is executed. The anticipatory nature of warrants is even clearer in the context of electronic surveillance. See, e.g., Katz v. United States, 389 U.S. 347 (1967). When police request approval to tap a telephone line, they do so based on the probability that, during the course of the surveillance, the subject will use the phone to engage in crime-related conversations. . . . Thus, when an anticipatory warrant is issued, "the fact that the contraband is not presently located at the place described in the warrant is immaterial, so long as there is probable cause to believe that it will be there when the search warrant is executed." United States v. Garcia, 882 F.2d 699, 702 (C.A.2 1989) (quoting United States v. Lowe, 575 F.2d 1193, 1194 (C.A.6 1978); internal quotation marks omitted).

Anticipatory warrants are, therefore, no different in principle from ordinary warrants. They require the magistrate to determine (1) that it is *now probable* that (2) contraband, evidence of a crime, or a fugitive *will be* on the described premises (3) when the warrant is executed. It should be noted, however, that where the anticipatory warrant places a condition (other than the mere passage of time) upon its execution, the first of these determinations goes not merely to what will probably be found *if* the condition is met. (If that were the extent of the probability determination, an anticipatory warrant could be issued for every house in the country, authorizing search and seizure *if* contraband should be delivered—though for any single location there is no likelihood that contraband will be delivered.) Rather, the probability determination for a conditioned anticipatory warrant looks also to the likelihood that the condition will occur, and thus that a proper object of seizure will be on the described premises. In other words, for a conditioned anticipatory warrant to comply with the Fourth Amendment's requirement of probable cause, two prerequisites of probability must be satisfied. It must be true not only that *if* the triggering condition occurs "there is a fair probability that contraband or evidence of a crime will be found in a particular place," *Gates, supra*, at 238, but also that there is probable cause to believe the triggering condition *will occur*. The supporting affidavit must provide the magistrate with sufficient information to evaluate both aspects of the probable-cause determination.

In this case, the occurrence of the triggering condition—successful delivery of the videotape to Grubbs' residence—would plainly establish probable cause for the search. In addition, the affidavit established probable cause to believe the triggering condition would be satisfied. Although it is possible that Grubbs could have refused delivery of the videotape he had ordered, that was unlikely. The Magistrate therefore "had a 'substantial basis for . . . conclud[ing]' that probable cause existed." *Gates*, 462 U.S., at 238-239 (quoting Jones v. United States, 362 U.S. 257, 271 (1960)).

III

The Ninth Circuit invalidated the anticipatory search warrant at issue here because the warrant failed to specify the triggering condition. The Fourth Amendment's particularity requirement, it held, "applies with full force to the conditions precedent to an anticipatory search warrant." 377 F.3d, at 1077-1078.

The Fourth Amendment, however, does not set forth some general "particularity requirement." It specifies only two matters that must be "particularly describ[ed]" in the warrant: "the place to be searched" and "the persons or things to be seized." . . .

Respondent, drawing upon the Ninth Circuit's analysis below, relies primarily on two related policy rationales. First, he argues, setting forth the triggering condition in the warrant itself is necessary "to delineate the limits of the executing officer's power." Brief for Respondent 20. This is an application, respondent asserts, of the following principle: "[I]f there is a precondition to the valid exercise of executive power, that precondition must be particularly identified on the face of the warrant." *Id.*, at 23. That principle is not to be found in the Constitution. The Fourth Amendment does not require that the warrant set forth the magistrate's basis for finding probable cause, even though probable cause is the quintessential "precondition to the valid exercise of executive power." Much less does it require description of a triggering condition.

Second, respondent argues that listing the triggering condition in the warrant is necessary to "'assur[e] the individual whose property is searched or seized of the lawful authority of the executing officer, his need to search, and the limits of his power to search.'" *Id.*, at 19 (quoting United States v. Chadwick, 433 U.S. 1, 9 (1977)). The Ninth Circuit went even further, asserting that if the property owner were not informed of the triggering condition, he "would 'stand [no] real chance of policing the officers' conduct.'" 377 F.3d, at 1079 (quoting Ramirez v. Butte-Silver Bow County, 298 F.3d 1022, 1027 (C.A.9 2002)). This argument assumes that the executing officer must present the property owner with a copy of the warrant before conducting his search. See 377 F.3d, at 1079, n. 9. In fact, however, neither the Fourth Amendment nor Rule 41 of the Federal Rules of Criminal Procedure imposes such a requirement. See Groh v. Ramirez, 540 U.S. 551, 562, n. 5 (2004). "The absence of a constitutional requirement that the warrant be exhibited at the outset of the search, or indeed until the search has ended, is . . . evidence that the requirement of particular description does not protect an interest in monitoring searches." United States v. Stefonek, 179 F.3d 1030, 1034 (C.A.7 1999) (citations omitted). The Constitution protects property owners not by giving them license to engage the police in a debate over the basis for the warrant, but by interposing, *ex ante*, the "deliberate, impartial judgment of a judicial officer . . . between the citizen and the police." Wong Sun v. United States, 371 U.S. 471, 481-482 (1963), and by providing, *ex post*, a right to suppress evidence improperly obtained and a cause of action for damages.

* * *

Because the Fourth Amendment does not require that the triggering condition for an anticipatory search warrant be set forth in the warrant itself, the Court of Appeals erred in invalidating the warrant at issue here. The judgment of the Court of Appeals is reversed, and the case is remanded for further proceedings consistent with this opinion.

It is so ordered.

JUSTICE ALITO took no part in the consideration or decision of this case.

JUSTICE SOUTER, with whom JUSTICE STEVENS and JUSTICE GINSBURG join, concurring in part and concurring in the judgment.

I agree with the Court that anticipatory warrants are constitutional for the reasons stated in Part II of the Court's opinion, and I join in the disposition of this case. But I would qualify some points made in Part III.

The Court notes that a warrant's failure to specify the place to be searched and the objects sought violates an express textual requirement of the Fourth Amendment, whereas the text says nothing about a condition placed by the issuing magistrate on the authorization to search (here, delivery of the package of contraband). That textual difference is, however, no authority for neglecting to specify the point or contingency intended by the magistrate to trigger authorization, and the government should beware of banking on the terms of a warrant without such specification. The notation of a starting date was an established feature even of the objectionable 18th-century writs of assistance, see, e.g., Massachusetts Writs of Assistance Bill, 1762, reprinted in M. Smith, The Writs of Assistance Case 567-568 (1978); Writ of Assistance (English) of George III, 1761, reprinted in *id.*, at 524-527. And it is fair to say that the very word "warrant" in the Fourth Amendment means a statement of authority that sets out the time at which (or, in the case of anticipatory warrants, the condition on which) the authorization begins. An issuing magistrate's failure to mention that condition can lead to several untoward consequences with constitutional significance. To begin with, a warrant that fails to tell the truth about what a magistrate authorized cannot inform the police officer's responsibility to respect the limits of authorization, see Groh v. Ramirez, 540 U.S. 551, 560-563, 561, and n. 4 (2004), a failing assuming real significance when the warrant is not executed by the official who applied for it and happens to know the unstated condition. . . .

Nor does an incomplete anticipatory warrant address an owner's interest in an accurate statement of the government's authority to search property. To be sure, the extent of that interest is yet to be settled; in Groh v. Ramirez, *supra*, the Court was careful to note that the right of an owner to demand to see a copy of the warrant before making way for the police had not been determined, *id.*, at 562, n. 5, and it remains undetermined today. But regardless of any right on the owner's part, showing an accurate warrant reliably "assures the individual whose property is searched or seized of the lawful authority of the executing officer, his need to search, and the limits of his power to search." United States v. Chadwick, 433 U.S. 1, 9 (1977), quoted in Groh v. Ramirez, *supra*, at 561. And if a later case holds that the homeowner has a right to inspect the warrant on request, a statement of the condition of authorization would give the owner a right to correct any misapprehension on the police's part that the condition had been met when in fact it had not been. If the police were then to enter anyway without a reasonable (albeit incorrect) justification, the search would certainly be open to serious challenge as unreasonable within the meaning of the Fourth Amendment.

NOTES AND QUESTIONS

1. The Court concludes that anticipatory warrants are "no different in principle from ordinary warrants." Are they different in practice? Note Justice Scalia's observation that the probable cause determination for a conditioned anticipatory warrant requires two findings: (1) that if the triggering condition occurs, there is a fair probability of finding evidence in a particular place; and (2) that there is probable cause to believe the triggering condition will occur. Granted that in the normal case, a court finding probable cause to believe evidence will be found in a given location is also implicitly determining that it will likely still be there when agents promptly execute the warrant. But doesn't an anticipatory warrant require a qualitatively different sort of assessment as to the likelihood of some future "triggering" event? If so, should this make a difference to the assessment of such warrants in terms of their compliance with the Fourth Amendment? You may wish to consider this question again after more closely considering the Fourth Amendment's application to electronic surveillance—a context in which courts regularly issue warrants to "seize" conversations that have not yet taken place.

2. The Fourth Amendment's Warrant Clause specifies in full that "no Warrants shall issue, but upon probable cause, supported by Oath or affirmation, and particularly describing the place to be searched, and the persons or things to be seized." In rejecting the Ninth Circuit's position in *Grubbs*, the Court makes much of the fact that the text says nothing about particularly describing any conditions precedent to authorization to execute an anticipatory warrant in the warrant itself. Should this be the end of the matter? Or do you agree with Justice Souter that the very notion of issuing a "warrant" implies that the warrant should contain a statement of authority "set[ting]out the time at which (or, in the case of anticipatory warrants, the condition on which) the authorization begins"? What is more important to proper resolution of a case like *Grubbs*? The Fourth Amendment's text? Historical practice—which may not have encompassed things like anticipatory warrants? Should judges look at the underlying values served by the particularity requirement?

What about policy considerations related to the warrant process as it exists today?

3. Return to the Court's approach to probable cause in *Grubbs*. Why should the magistrate issuing the warrant have to find probable cause to believe the "triggering condition" will actually happen? Suppose the police have reason to believe that a quantity of illegal drugs will be delivered by a particular suspect at a particular time to one of a half-dozen houses on a suburban cul-de-sac. The police do not know which house. Under *Grubbs*, a warrant to search the house to which the drugs are delivered is improper — even if the police witness the delivery. Is that right?

On page 452, replace the first paragraph of text under the heading, The Execution of Warrants, with the following:

Not only do warrants and warrant applications raise Fourth Amendment issues; so does the manner in which warrants are "executed." That is, the Fourth Amendment regulates the *character* of warrant-based searches, not just the question whether those searches may happen.

This point requires some explanation. Nearly all the cases you have read in this chapter — and the large majority of the cases that follow — address one of two questions: First, does the Fourth Amendment apply to this encounter? *Katz* doctrine and the cases defining "seizures" deal with this question. Second, did the police have a sufficient justification for searching the relevant place or seizing the relevant person? The cases defining "probable cause" address this question. Remarkably few Fourth Amendment cases deal with a third question: Did the police carry out the search or seizure in an unreasonably intrusive manner?

The exclusionary rule explains that strange fact. Because most Fourth Amendment claims are raised by motions to suppress physical evidence, judges are regularly required to ask whether the police had sufficiently good reason for looking in this place or listening to that conversation. But when officers carry out searches in an unusually violent or degrading manner, the violence and degradation rarely lead to the discovery of evidence. So motions to suppress rarely challenge those kinds of police conduct, and judges have few opportunities to define the legal standards that protect against such harms.

What little Fourth Amendment law exists on the subject tends to fall into two categories: doctrines that restrict police violence — the use of deadly and non-deadly force — and doctrines that govern the execution of warrants to search private homes. The cases on police use of force are covered below, at pages 658-668. The cases below deal with the second category. We begin with the "knock and announce" requirement, which may be unique in Fourth Amendment jurisprudence: All four of the Supreme Court decisions that established and defined it were unanimous.

Insert the following material at the end of Note 4 on page 457:

Note that in March 2006, Congress passed the USA PATRIOT Act Improvement and Reauthorization Act of 2005. The legislation set out a presumptive limit of 30 days on the initial period of delay of notice with regard to the execution of a warrant and also provided for 90-day extensions. The new law also removed "unduly delaying a trial" as an adverse result that may justify a "sneak-and-peek" warrant. The Justice Department noted at the time that "[t]he ability to obtain court permission to delay notice has proved invaluable in a wide range of cases, including major drug trafficking investigations." Dep't of Justice, Fact Sheet: USA PATRIOT Act Improvement and Reauthorization Act of 2005 (March, 2006).

Insert the following notes and main case after Note 4 on page 457:

4a. The execution of a warrant often requires the detention of people found at the scene and the use of force with regard not only to suspects, but also bystanders. In Graham v. Connor, 490 U.S. 386 (1989), the Supreme Court determined that claims that law enforcement officers have used excessive force in the course of an arrest, investigatory stop, or other "seizure" should be analyzed under the Fourth Amendment's "reasonableness" standard. *Graham* and its general approach to the constitutional regulation of use of force are taken up at page 663. For now, consider a recent discussion of the reasonableness of police officers' detention and handcuffing of persons present at the scene of the execution of a search warrant:

MUEHLER v. MENA

Certiorari to the United States Court of Appeals for the Ninth Circuit
544 U.S. 93 (2005)

CHIEF JUSTICE REHNQUIST delivered the opinion of the Court.

Respondent Iris Mena was detained in handcuffs during a search of the premises that she and several others occupied. Petitioners were lead members of a police detachment executing a search warrant of these premises. She sued the officers under Rev. Stat. § 1979, 42 U.S.C. § 1983, and the District Court found in her favor. The Court of Appeals affirmed the judgment. . . . We hold that Mena's detention in handcuffs for the length of the search was consistent with our opinion in Michigan v. Summers, 452 U.S. 692 (1981), and that the officers' questioning during that detention did not violate her Fourth Amendment rights.

* * *

Based on information gleaned from the investigation of a gang-related, driveby shooting, petitioners Muehler and Brill had reason to believe at least one member of a gang—the West Side Locos—lived at 1363 Patricia Avenue. They also suspected that the individual was armed and dangerous, since he had recently been involved in the driveby shooting. As a result, Muehler obtained a search warrant for 1363 Patricia Avenue that authorized a broad search of the house and premises for, among other things, deadly weapons and evidence of gang membership. In light of the high degree of risk involved in searching a house suspected of housing at least one, and perhaps multiple, armed gang members, a Special Weapons and Tactics (SWAT) team was used to secure the residence and grounds before the search.

At 7 a.m. on February 3, 1998, petitioners, along with the SWAT team and other officers, executed the warrant. Mena was asleep in her bed when the SWAT team, clad in helmets and black vests adorned with badges and the word "POLICE," entered her bedroom and placed her in handcuffs at gunpoint. The SWAT team also handcuffed three other individuals found on the property. The SWAT team then took those individuals and Mena into a converted garage, which contained several beds and some other bedroom furniture. While the search proceeded, one or two officers guarded the four detainees, who were allowed to move around the garage but remained in handcuffs.

Aware that the West Side Locos gang was composed primarily of illegal immigrants, the officers had notified the Immigration and Naturalization Service (INS) that they would be conducting the search, and an INS officer accompanied the officers executing the warrant. During their detention in the garage, an officer asked for each detainee's name, date of birth, place of birth, and immigration status. The INS officer later asked the detainees for their immigration documentation. Mena's status as a permanent resident was confirmed by her papers.

The search of the premises yielded a .22 caliber handgun with .22 caliber ammunition, a box of .25 caliber ammunition, several baseball bats with gang writing, various additional gang paraphernalia, and a bag of marijuana. Before the officers left the area, Mena was released.

In her § 1983 suit against the officers she alleged that she was detained "for an unreasonable time and in an unreasonable manner" in violation of the Fourth Amendment. App. 19. In addition, she claimed that the warrant and its execution were overbroad, that the officers failed to comply with the "knock and announce" rule, and that the officers had needlessly destroyed property during the search. The officers moved for summary judgment, asserting that they were entitled to qualified immunity, but the District Court denied their motion. The Court of Appeals affirmed that denial, *except* for Mena's claim that the warrant was overbroad; on this claim the Court of Appeals held that the officers were entitled to qualified immunity. Mena v. Simi Valley, 226 F.3d 1031 (C.A.9 2000). After a trial, a jury, pursuant to a special verdict form, found that Officers Muehler and Brill violated Mena's Fourth Amendment right to be free from unreasonable seizures by detaining her both with force greater than that which was reasonable and for a longer period than that which was reasonable. The jury awarded Mena $10,000 in actual damages and $20,000 in punitive damages against each petitioner for a total of $60,000.

The Court of Appeals affirmed the judgment on two grounds. 332 F.3d 1255 (C.A.9 2003). Reviewing the denial of qualified immunity *de novo, id.*, at 1261, n. 2, it first held that the officers' detention of Mena violated the Fourth Amendment because it was objectively unreasonable to confine her in the converted garage and keep her in handcuffs during the search, id., at 1263-1264. In the Court of Appeals' view, the officers should have released Mena as soon as it became clear that she posed no immediate threat. *Id.*, at 1263. The court additionally held that the questioning of Mena about her immigration status constituted an independent Fourth Amendment violation. *Id.*, at 1264-1266. The Court of Appeals went on to hold that those rights were clearly established at the time of Mena's questioning, and thus the officers were not entitled to qualified immunity. *Id.*, at 1266-1267. We granted certiorari and now vacate and remand.

* * *

In Michigan v. Summers, 452 U.S. 692 (1981), we held that officers executing a search warrant for contraband have the authority "to detain the occupants of the premises while a proper search is conducted." *Id.,* at 705. Such detentions are appropriate, we explained, because the character of the additional intrusion caused by detention is slight and because the justifications for detention are substantial. *Id.,* at 701-705. We made clear that the detention of an occupant is "surely less intrusive than the search itself," and the presence of a warrant assures that a neutral magistrate has determined that probable cause exists to search the home. Id., at 701. Against this incremental intrusion, we posited three legitimate law enforcement interests that provide substantial justification for detaining an occupant: "preventing flight in the event that incriminating evidence is found"; "minimizing the risk of harm to the officers"; and facilitating "the orderly completion of the search," as detainees' "self-interest may induce them to open locked doors or locked containers to avoid the use of force." *Id.,* at 702-703.

Mena's detention was, under *Summers,* plainly permissible. An officer's authority to detain incident to a search is categorical; it does not depend on the "quantum of proof justifying detention or the extent of the intrusion to be imposed by the seizure." *Id.,* at 705, n. 19. Thus, Mena's detention for the duration of the search was reasonable under *Summers* because a warrant existed to search 1363 Patricia Avenue and she was an occupant of that address at the time of the search.

Inherent in *Summers'* authorization to detain an occupant of the place to be searched is the authority to use reasonable force to effectuate the detention. See Graham v. Connor, 490 U.S. 386, 396 (1989) ("Fourth Amendment jurisprudence has long recognized that the right to make an arrest or investigatory stop necessarily carries with it the right to use some degree of physical coercion or threat thereof to effect it"). Indeed, *Summers* itself stressed that the risk of harm to officers and occupants is minimized "if the officers routinely exercise unquestioned command of the situation." 452 U.S., at 703.

The officers' use of force in the form of handcuffs to effectuate Mena's detention in the garage, as well as the detention of the three other occupants, was reasonable because the governmental interests outweigh the marginal intrusion. See *Graham, supra,* at 396-397. The imposition of correctly applied handcuffs on Mena, who was already being lawfully detained during a search of the house, was undoubtedly a separate intrusion in addition to detention in the converted garage. The detention was thus more intrusive than that which we upheld in *Summers*. See 452 U.S., at 701-702 (concluding that the additional intrusion in the form of a detention was less than that of the warrant-sanctioned search); Maryland v. Wilson, 519 U.S. 408, 413-414 (1997) (concluding that the additional intrusion from ordering passengers out of a car, which was already stopped, was minimal).

But this was no ordinary search. The governmental interests in not only detaining, but using handcuffs, are at their maximum when, as here, a warrant authorizes a search for weapons and a wanted gang member resides on the premises. In such inherently dangerous situations, the use of handcuffs minimizes the risk of harm to both officers and occupants. Cf. *Summers, supra,* at 702-703 (recognizing the execution of a warrant to search for drugs "may give rise to sudden violence or frantic efforts to conceal or destroy evidence"). Though this safety risk inherent in executing a search warrant for weapons was sufficient to justify the use of handcuffs, the need to detain multiple occupants made the use of handcuffs all the more reasonable. Cf. Maryland v. Wilson, *supra,* at 414 (noting that "danger to an officer from a traffic stop is likely to be greater when there are passengers in addition to the driver in the stopped car").

Mena argues that, even if the use of handcuffs to detain her in the garage was reasonable as an initial matter, the duration of the use of handcuffs made the detention unreasonable. The duration of a detention can, of course, affect the balance of interests under *Graham*. However, the 2- to 3-hour detention in handcuffs in this case does not outweigh the government's continuing safety interests. . . .

The Court of Appeals also determined that the officers violated Mena's Fourth Amendment rights by questioning her about her immigration status during the detention. 332 F.3d, at 1264-1266. This holding, it appears, was premised on the assumption that the officers were required to have independent reasonable suspicion in order to question Mena concerning her immigration status because the questioning constituted a discrete Fourth Amendment event. But the premise is faulty. We have "held repeatedly that mere police questioning does not constitute a seizure." Florida v. Bostick, 501 U.S. 429, 434 (1991); see also INS v. Delgado, 466 U.S. 210, 212 (1984). "[E]ven when officers have no basis for suspecting a particular individual, they may generally ask questions of that individual; ask to examine the individual's identification; and request consent to search his or her luggage." *Bostick, supra,* at 434-435 (citations omitted). As the Court of Appeals did not hold that the detention was prolonged by the questioning, there was no additional seizure within the meaning of the Fourth Amendment. . . .

. . . Mena has advanced in this Court, as she did before the Court of Appeals, an alternative argument for affirming the judgment below. She asserts that her detention extended beyond the time the police completed the tasks incident to the search. Because the Court of Appeals did not address this contention, we too decline to address it.

The judgment of the Court of Appeals is therefore vacated, and the case is remanded for further proceedings consistent with this opinion.

[The concurring opinion of JUSTICE KENNEDY is omitted.]

JUSTICE STEVENS, with whom JUSTICE SOUTER, JUSTICE GINSBURG, and JUSTICE BREYER join, concurring in the judgment. . . .

In its opinion affirming the judgment, the Court of Appeals made two mistakes. First, as the Court explains, ante, at 1471, it erroneously held that the immigration officers' questioning of Iris Mena about her immigration status was an independent violation of the Fourth Amendment. Second, instead of merely deciding whether there was sufficient evidence in the record to support the jury's verdict, the Court of Appeals appears to have ruled as a matter of law that the officers should have released her from the handcuffs sooner than they did. I agree that it is appropriate to remand the case to enable the Court of Appeals to consider whether the evidence supports Iris Mena's contention that she was held longer than the search actually lasted. . . .

In my judgment, however, the Court's discussion of the amount of force used to detain Iris pursuant to Michigan v. Summers, 452 U.S. 692 (1981), is analytically unsound. Although the Court correctly purports to apply the "objective reasonableness" test announced in Graham v. Connor, 490 U.S. 386 (1989), it misapplies that test. Given the facts of this case — and the presumption that a reviewing court must draw all reasonable inferences in favor of supporting the verdict — I think it clear that the jury could properly have found that this 5-foot-2-inch young lady posed no threat to the officers at the scene, and that they used excessive force in keeping her in handcuffs for up to three hours. Although *Summers* authorizes the detention of any individual who is present when a valid search warrant is being executed, that case does not give officers *carte blanche* to keep individuals who pose no threat in handcuffs throughout a search, no matter how long it may last. On remand, I would therefore instruct the Court of Appeals to consider whether the evidence supports Mena's contention that the petitioners used excessive force in detaining her when it considers the length of the *Summers* detention.

I

As the Court notes, the warrant in this case authorized the police to enter the Mena home to search for a gun belonging to Raymond Romero that may have been used in a gang-related driveby shooting. Romero, a known member of the West Side Locos gang, rented a room from the Mena family. The house, described as a "'poor house,'" was home to several unrelated individuals who rented from the Menas. Brief for Petitioners 4. Each resident had his or her own bedroom, which could be locked with a padlock on the outside, and each had access to the living room and kitchen. In addition, several individuals lived in trailers in the back yard and also had access to the common spaces in the Mena home. Id., at 5.

In addition to Romero, police had reason to believe that at least one other West Side Locos gang member had lived at the residence, although Romero's brother told police that the individual had returned to Mexico. . . .

In light of the fact that the police believed that Romero possessed a gun and that there might be other gang members at the residence, petitioner Muehler decided to use a Special Weapons and Tactics (SWAT) team to execute the warrant. As described in the majority opinion, eight members of the SWAT team forcefully entered the home at 7 a. m. In fact, Iris Mena was the only occupant of the house and she was asleep in her bedroom. The police woke her up at gunpoint, and immediately handcuffed her. At the same time, officers served another search warrant at the home of Romero's mother, where Romero was known to stay several nights each week. In part because Romero's mother had previously cooperated with police officers, they did not use a SWAT team to serve that warrant. Romero was found at his mother's house; after being cited for possession of a small amount of marijuana, he was released.

Meanwhile, after the SWAT team secured the Mena residence and gave the "all clear," police officers transferred Iris and three other individuals (who had been in trailers in the back yard) to a converted garage.[3] To get to the garage, Iris, who was still in her bedclothes, was forced to walk barefoot through the pouring rain. The officers kept her and the other three individuals in the garage for up to three hours while they searched the home. Although she requested them to remove the handcuffs, they refused to do so. For the duration of the search, two officers guarded Iris and the other three detainees. A .22 caliber handgun, ammunition, and gang-related paraphernalia were found in Romero's bedroom, and other gang-related paraphernalia was found in the living room. Officers found nothing of significance in Iris' bedroom.[4] *Id.*, at 6-9.

3. The other individuals were a 55-year-old Latina female, a 40-year-old Latino male who was removed from the scene by the Immigration and Naturalization Service (INS), and a white male who appears to be in his early thirties and who was cited for possession of a small amount of marijuana.

4. One of the justifications for our decision in Michigan v. Summers, 452 U.S. 692 (1981), was the fact that the occupants may be willing to "open locked doors or locked containers to avoid the use of force that is not only damaging to property but may also delay the completion of the task at hand." *Id.*, at 703. Iris, however, was never asked to assist the officers, although she testified that she was willing to do so. See 3 Tr. 42 (June 14, 2001). Instead, officers broke the locks on several cabinets and dressers to which Iris possessed the keys.

II

In analyzing the quantum of force used to effectuate the *Summers* detention, the Court rightly employs the "objective reasonableness" test of *Graham*. Under *Graham*, the trier of fact must balance "'the nature and quality of the intrusion on the individual's Fourth Amendment interests' against the countervailing governmental interests at stake." 490 U.S., at 396. The District Court correctly instructed the jury to take into consideration such factors as "'the severity of the suspected crime, whether the person being detained is the subject of the investigation, whether such person poses an immediate threat to the security of the police or others or to the ability of the police to conduct the search, and whether such person is actively resisting arrest or attempting to flee.'" See n.2, *supra*. The District Court also correctly instructed the jury to consider whether the detention was prolonged and whether Iris was detained in handcuffs after the search had ended. *Ibid.* . . .

Considering those factors, it is clear that the SWAT team's initial actions were reasonable. When officers undertake a dangerous assignment to execute a warrant to search property that is presumably occupied by violence-prone gang members, it may well be appropriate to use both overwhelming force and surprise in order to secure the premises as promptly as possible. . . . At the time they first encountered Iris, the officers had no way of knowing her relation to Romero, whether she was affiliated with the West Side Locos, or whether she had any weapons on her person. Further, the officers needed to use overwhelming force to immediately take command of the situation; by handcuffing Iris they could more quickly secure her room and join the other officers. . . .

Whether the well-founded fears that justified the extraordinary entry into the house should also justify a prolonged interruption of the morning routine of a presumptively innocent person, however, is a separate question and one that depends on the specific facts of the case. This is true with respect both to how the handcuffs were used, and to the totality of the circumstances surrounding the detention, including whether Mena was detained in handcuffs after the search had concluded. With regard to the handcuffs, police may use them in different ways.[5] Here, the cuffs kept Iris' arms behind her for two to three hours. She testified that they were "'real uncomfortable'" and that she had asked the officers to remove

5. For instance, a suspect may be handcuffed to a fixed object, to a custodian, or her hands may simply be linked to one another. The cuffs may join the wrists either in the front or the back of the torso. They can be so tight that they are painful, particularly when applied for prolonged periods. While they restrict movement, they do not necessarily preclude flight if the prisoner is not kept under constant surveillance.

them, but that they had refused. App. 105. Moreover, she was continuously guarded by two police officers who obviously made flight virtually impossible even if the cuffs had been removed.

A jury could reasonably have found a number of facts supporting a conclusion that the prolonged handcuffing was unreasonable. No contraband was found in Iris' room or on her person. There were no indications suggesting she was or ever had been a gang member. . . . She fully cooperated with the officers and the INS agent, answering all their questions. She was unarmed, and given her small size, was clearly no match for either of the two armed officers who were guarding her. . . .

The justifications offered by the officers are not persuasive. They have argued that at least six armed officers were required to guard the four detainees, even though all of them had been searched for weapons. Since there were 18 officers at the scene, and since at least 1 officer who at one point guarded Mena and the other three residents was sent home after offering to assist in the search, it seems unlikely that lack of resources was really a problem. . . .

The jury may also have been skeptical of testimony that the officers in fact feared for their safety given that the actual suspect of the shooting had been found at the other location and promptly released. Additionally, while the officers testified that as a general matter they would not release an individual from handcuffs while searching a residence, the SWAT team's tactical plan for this particular search arguably called for them to do just that, since it directed that "[a]ny subjects encountered will be handcuffed and detained until they can be patted down, their location noted, [field identified], and released by Office Muehler or Officer R. Brill." 2 Record 53. . . . The SWAT team leader testified that handcuffs are not always required when executing a search.

In short, under the factors listed in *Graham* and those validly presented to the jury in the jury instructions, a jury could have reasonably found from the evidence that there was no apparent need to handcuff Iris for the entire duration of the search and that she was detained for an unreasonably prolonged period. . . . Viewing the facts in the light most favorable to the jury's verdict, as we are required to do, there is certainly no obvious factual basis for rejecting the jury's verdict that the officers acted unreasonably, and no obvious basis for rejecting the conclusion that, on these facts, the quantum of force used was unreasonable as a matter of law. . . .

NOTES AND QUESTIONS

1. Was there any basis for suspecting Mena of involvement in the driveby shooting? If not, why does the majority conclude that her two- to three-hour handcuffed detention was reasonable? Is the Court overly solicitous of the safety interests of police executing warrants? On the other hand, how fine-grained should the analysis of reasonableness in the execution of search warrants be? As the majority notes, the police officers in this case had reason to believe that an armed and dangerous gang member who had recently been involved in a driveby shooting lived at 1363 Patricia Avenue. In searching the premises, should police be required to worry whether a jury might find the two- or three-hour handcuffing of an occupant unreasonable, as Justice Stevens' approach might suggest?

2. The warrant execution in this case was no doubt violent. Mena was roused from sleep by eight armed SWAT team members. She was handcuffed. But all the Justices seem to agree that the violence of the initial entry and Mena's immediate handcuffing were reasonable, given concerns for the safety of the officers and the efficacy of the search. In his concurring opinion, which is omitted here, Justice Kennedy asserts that the use of handcuffs is a use of force and that the reasonableness calculation for this use of force must be in part a function of the "expected and actual duration of the search." He continues:

> If the search extends to the point when the handcuffs can cause real pain or serious discomfort, provision must be made to alter the conditions of detention at least long enough to attend to the needs of the detainee. This is so even if there is no question that the initial handcuffing was objectively reasonable. The restraint should also be removed if, at any point during the search, it would be readily apparent to any objectively reasonable officer that removing the handcuffs would not compromise the officers' safety or risk interference or substantial delay in the execution of the search. The time spent in the search here, some two to three hours, certainly approaches, and may well exceed, the time beyond which a detainee's Fourth Amendment interests require revisiting the necessity of handcuffing in order to ensure the restraint, even if permissible as an initial matter, has not become excessive.
>
> That said, under these circumstances I do not think handcuffing the detainees for the duration of the search was objectively unreasonable. As I understand the record, during much of this search 2 armed officers were available to watch over the 4 unarmed detainees, while the other 16 officers on the scene conducted an extensive search of a suspected gang safe house. Even if we accept as true—as we must—the factual assertions that these detainees posed no readily apparent danger and that keeping them handcuffed deviated from standard police procedure, it does not follow that the handcuffs were unreasonable. Where the detainees outnumber those supervising

> them, and this situation could not be remedied without diverting officers from an extensive, complex, and time-consuming search, the continued use of handcuffs after the initial sweep may be justified, subject to adjustments or temporary release under supervision to avoid pain or excessive physical discomfort. [O]n this record it does not appear the restraints were excessive. . . .

544 U.S. at 103-104. Do you agree? Who is likely to make wiser judgments about the objective reasonableness of the force used in executing search warrants—juries determining whether to award damages, or appellate courts reviewing their decisions? Note that, in light of the discomfort over police handcuffing plainly evident in Justice Stevens's opinion concurring in the judgment (an opinion joined by three other Justices), Justice Kennedy's concurring opinion may be the one that ends up defining the position of the Court on the issue.

3. Los Angeles County v. Rettele, 550 U.S. 609 (2007) (per curiam), offers an interesting counterpoint to *Mena*. The Los Angeles County Sheriff's office was conducting an investigation of fraud and identity theft; one of the suspects had a registered handgun, a fact that plainly affected the nature of the subsequent search. Deputies obtained a warrant to search two houses where various public records indicated the suspects lived. Unbeknownst to the police, one of the two houses had recently been sold to plaintiff Max Rettele, who lived there with his girlfriend and her teenage son.

When the police arrived at Rettele's door at 7:15 A.M., here is what transpired:

> Watters and six other deputies knocked on the door and announced their presence. Chase Hall [the teenage son] answered. The deputies entered the house after ordering Hall to lie face down on the ground.
>
> The deputies' announcement awoke Rettele and Sadler. The deputies entered their bedroom with guns drawn and ordered them to get out of their bed and to show their hands. They protested that they were not wearing clothes. Rettele stood up and attempted to put on a pair of sweatpants, but deputies told him not to move. Sadler also stood up and attempted, without success, to cover herself with a sheet. Rettele and Sadler were held at gunpoint for one to two minutes before Rettele was allowed to retrieve a robe for Sadler. He was then permitted to dress. Rettele and Sadler left the bedroom within three to four minutes to sit on the couch in the living room.
>
> By that time the deputies realized they had made a mistake. They apologized to Rettele and Sadler, thanked them for not becoming upset, and left within five minutes. They proceeded to the other house the warrant authorized them to search, where they found three suspects. Those suspects were arrested and convicted.

550 U.S. at 611-612. Rettele sued, claiming that, even if the warrant was legally valid, the search was conducted in an unreasonable manner. The Supreme Court disagreed, unanimously:

> The orders by the police to the occupants, in the context of this lawful search, were permissible, and perhaps necessary, to protect the safety of the deputies. Blankets and bedding can conceal a weapon, and one of the suspects was known to own a firearm, factors which underscore this point. The Constitution does not require an officer to ignore the possibility that an armed suspect may sleep with a weapon within reach. The reports are replete with accounts of suspects sleeping close to weapons. . . .
>
> The deputies needed a moment to secure the room and ensure that other persons were not close by or did not present a danger. Deputies were not required to turn their backs to allow Rettele and Sadler to retrieve clothing or to cover themselves with the sheets. Rather, "the risk of harm to both the police and the occupants is minimized if the officers routinely exercise unquestioned command of the situation." [Michigan v. Summers, 452 U.S. 692, 702-703 (1981).]
>
> This is not to say, of course, that the deputies were free to force Rettele and Sadler to remain motionless and standing for any longer than necessary. We have recognized that "special circumstances, or possibly a prolonged detention" might render a search unreasonable. See *id.,* at 705 n. 21. There is no accusation that the detention here was prolonged. The deputies left the home less than 15 minutes after arriving. The detention was shorter and less restrictive than the 2- to 3-hour handcuff detention upheld in *Mena*. And there is no allegation that the deputies prevented Sadler and Rettele from dressing longer than necessary to protect their safety. Sadler was unclothed for no more than two minutes, and Rettele for only slightly more time than that. Sadler testified that once the police were satisfied that no immediate threat was presented, "they wanted us to get dressed and they were pressing us really fast to hurry up and get some clothes on."
>
> The Fourth Amendment allows warrants to issue on probable cause, a standard well short of absolute certainty. Valid warrants will issue to search the innocent, and people like Rettele and Sadler unfortunately bear the cost. Officers executing search warrants on occasion enter a house when residents are engaged in private activity; and the resulting frustration, embarrassment, and humiliation may be real, as was true here. When officers execute a valid warrant and act in a reasonable manner to protect themselves from harm, however, the Fourth Amendment is not violated.

550 U.S. at 614-616.

The plaintiffs in *Rettele* argued that the police should have recognized their mistake sooner — the suspects identified in the warrant were African American, and the plaintiffs were white. The Court dismissed this argument in a peremptory paragraph:

> Because respondents were of a different race than the suspects the deputies were seeking, the Court of Appeals held that "after taking one look at [respondents], the deputies should have realized that [respondents] were not the subjects of the search warrant and did not pose a threat to the deputies' safety." We need not pause long in rejecting this unsound proposition. When the deputies ordered respondents from their bed, they had no way of knowing whether the African-American suspects were elsewhere in the house. The presence of some Caucasians in the residence did not eliminate the possibility that the suspects lived there as well. As the deputies stated in their affidavits, it is not uncommon in our society for people of different races to live together. Just as people of different races live and work together, so too might they engage in joint criminal activity. The deputies, who were searching a house where they believed a suspect might be armed, possessed authority to secure the premises before deciding whether to continue with the search.

550 U.S. at 613.

Did the Court adequately value the interests at stake in *Rettele*? In *Mena*?

3. "Exceptions" to the Warrant "Requirement"

a. Exigent Circumstances

Insert the following notes and main case after note 5 on page 470:

5a. Consider the preceding question again in light of the following case, in which the Court unanimously opted for the objective approach:

BRIGHAM CITY v. STUART

Certiorari to the Utah Supreme Court
547 U.S. 398 (2006)

CHIEF JUSTICE ROBERTS delivered the opinion of the Court.

In this case we consider whether police may enter a home without a warrant when they have an objectively reasonable basis for believing that an occupant is seriously injured or imminently threatened with such injury. We conclude that they may.

I

This case arises out of a melee that occurred in a Brigham City, Utah, home in the early morning hours of July 23, 2000. At about 3 a.m., four police officers responded to a call regarding a loud party at a residence. Upon arriving at the house, they heard shouting from inside, and proceeded down the driveway to investigate. There, they observed two juveniles drinking beer in the backyard. They entered the backyard, and saw—through a screen door and windows—an altercation taking place in the kitchen of the home. According to the testimony of one of the officers, four adults were attempting, with some difficulty, to restrain a juvenile. The juvenile eventually "broke free, swung a fist and struck one of the adults in the face." 2005 UT 13, ¶ 2. The officer testified that he observed the victim of the blow spitting blood into a nearby sink. App. 40. The other adults continued to try to restrain the juvenile, pressing him up against a refrigerator with such force that the refrigerator began moving across the floor. At this point, an officer opened the screen door and announced the officers' presence. Amid the tumult, nobody noticed. The officer entered the kitchen and again cried out, and as the occupants slowly became aware that the police were on the scene, the altercation ceased.

The officers subsequently arrested respondents and charged them with contributing to the delinquency of a minor, disorderly conduct, and intoxication. In the trial court, respondents filed a motion to suppress all evidence obtained after the officers entered the home, arguing that the warrantless entry violated the Fourth Amendment. The court granted the motion, and the Utah Court of Appeals affirmed.

Before the Supreme Court of Utah, Brigham City argued that although the officers lacked a warrant, their entry was nevertheless reasonable on either of two grounds. The court rejected both contentions and, over two dissenters, affirmed. First, the court held that the injury caused by the juvenile's punch was insufficient to trigger the so-called "emergency aid doctrine" because it did not give rise to an "objectively reasonable belief that an unconscious, semi-conscious, or missing person feared injured or dead [was] in the home." 122 P.3d, at 513 (internal quotation marks omitted). Furthermore, the court suggested that the doctrine was inapplicable because the officers had not sought to assist the injured adult, but instead had acted "exclusively in their law enforcement capacity." *Ibid.*

The court also held that the entry did not fall within the exigent circumstances exception to the warrant requirement. This exception applies, the court explained, where police have probable cause and where "a reasonable person [would] believe that the entry was necessary to prevent physical harm to the officers or other persons." *Id.,* at 514 (internal quotation marks omitted). Under this standard, the court stated, the potential harm need not be as serious as that required to invoke the emergency aid exception. Although it found the case "a close and difficult call," the court nevertheless concluded that the officers' entry was not justified by exigent circumstances. *Id.,* at 515.

We granted certiorari in light of differences among state courts and the Courts of Appeals concerning the appropriate Fourth Amendment standard governing warrantless entry by law enforcement in an emergency situation.

II

It is a "'basic principle of Fourth Amendment law that searches and seizures inside a home without a warrant are presumptively unreasonable.'" Groh v. Ramirez, 540 U.S. 551, 559 (2004) (quoting Payton v. New York, 445 U.S. 573, 586 (1980) (some internal quotation marks omitted)). Nevertheless, because the ultimate touchstone of the Fourth Amendment is "reasonableness," the warrant requirement is subject to certain exceptions. Flippo v. West Virginia, 528 U.S. 11, 13 (1999) (per curiam); Katz v. United States, 389 U.S. 347, 357 (1967). We have held, for example, that law enforcement officers may make a warrantless entry onto private property to fight a fire and investigate its cause, Michigan v. Tyler, 436 U.S. 499, 509 (1978), to prevent the imminent destruction of evidence, Ker v. California, 374 U.S. 23, 40 (1963), or to engage in "hot pursuit" of a fleeing suspect, United States v. Santana, 427 U.S. 38, 42-43 (1976). "[W]arrants are generally required to search a person's home or his person unless 'the exigencies of the situation' make the needs of law enforcement so compelling that the warrantless search is objectively reasonable under the Fourth Amendment." Mincey v. Arizona, 437 U.S. 385, 393-394 (1978).

One exigency obviating the requirement of a warrant is the need to assist persons who are seriously injured or threatened with such injury. "'The need to protect or preserve life or avoid serious injury is justification for what would be otherwise illegal absent an exigency or emergency.'" *Id.,* at 392 (quoting Wayne v. United States, 318 F.2d 205, 212 (C.A.D.C.1963) (Burger, J.)); see also *Tyler, supra,* at 509. Accordingly, law enforcement officers may enter a home without a warrant to render emergency assistance to an injured occupant or to protect an occupant from imminent injury. *Mincey, supra,* at 392.

Respondents do not take issue with these principles, but instead advance two reasons why the officers' entry here was unreasonable. First, they argue that the officers were more interested in making arrests than quelling violence. They urge us to consider, in assessing the reasonableness of the entry, whether the officers were "indeed motivated primarily by a desire to save lives and property." Brief for Respondents 3; see also Brief for National Association of Criminal Defense Lawyers as Amicus Curiae 6 (entry to render emergency assistance justifies a search "only when the searching officer is acting outside his traditional law-enforcement capacity"). The Utah Supreme Court also considered the officers' subjective motivations relevant. See 122 P.3d, at 513 (search under the "emergency aid doctrine" may not be "primarily motivated by intent to arrest and seize evidence" (internal quotation marks omitted)).

Our cases have repeatedly rejected this approach. An action is "reasonable" under the Fourth Amendment, regardless of the individual officer's state of mind, "as long as the circumstances, viewed *objectively*, justify [the] action." Scott v. United States, 436 U.S. 128, 138 (1978) (emphasis added). The officer's subjective motivation is irrelevant. See Bond v. United States, 529 U.S. 334, 338, n. 2 (2000) ("The parties properly agree that the subjective intent of the law enforcement officer is irrelevant in determining whether that officer's actions violate the Fourth Amendment . . . ; the issue is not his state of mind, but the objective effect of his actions"); Whren v. United States, 517 U.S. 806, 813 ("[W]e have been unwilling to entertain Fourth Amendment challenges based on the actual motivations of individual officers"); Graham v. Connor, 490 U.S. 386, 397 (1989) ("[O]ur prior cases make clear" that "the subjective motivations of the individual officers . . . ha[ve] no bearing on whether a particular seizure is 'unreasonable' under the Fourth Amendment"). It therefore does not matter here—even if their subjective motives could be so neatly unraveled—whether the officers entered the kitchen to arrest respondents and gather evidence against them or to assist the injured and prevent further violence.

As respondents note, we have held in the context of programmatic searches conducted without individualized suspicion—such as checkpoints to combat drunk driving or drug trafficking—that "an inquiry into *programmatic* purpose" is sometimes appropriate. Indianapolis v. Edmond, 531 U.S. 32, 46 (2000) (emphasis added); see also Florida v. Wells, 495 U.S. 1, 4 (1990) (an inventory search must be regulated by "standardized criteria" or "established routine" so as not to "be a ruse for a general rummaging in order to discover incriminating evidence"). But this inquiry is directed at ensuring that the purpose behind the program is not "ultimately indistinguishable from the general interest in crime control." Edmond, 531 U.S., at 44. It has nothing to do with discerning what is in the mind of the individual officer conducting the search. *Id.*, at 48.

Respondents further contend that their conduct was not serious enough to justify the officers' intrusion into the home. They rely on Welsh v. Wisconsin, 466 U.S. 740, 753 (1984), in which we held that "an important factor to be considered when determining whether any exigency exists is the gravity of the underlying offense for which the arrest is being made." This contention, too, is misplaced. *Welsh* involved a warrantless entry by officers to arrest a suspect for driving while intoxicated. There, the "only potential emergency" confronting the officers was the need to preserve evidence (i.e., the suspect's blood-alcohol level)—an exigency that we held insufficient under the circumstances to justify entry into the suspect's home. *Ibid.* Here, the officers were confronted with ongoing violence occurring within the home. *Welsh* did not address such a situation.

We think the officers' entry here was plainly reasonable under the circumstances. The officers were responding, at 3 o'clock in the morning, to complaints about a loud party. As they approached the house, they could hear from within "an altercation occurring, some kind of a fight." App. 29. "It was loud and it was tumultuous." *Id.*, at 33. The officers heard "thumping and crashing" and people yelling "stop, stop" and "get off me." *Id.*, at 28, 29. As the trial court found, "it was obvious that . . . knocking on the front door" would have been futile. *Id.*, at 92. The noise seemed to be coming from the back of the house; after looking in the front window and seeing nothing, the officers proceeded around back to investigate further. They found two juveniles drinking beer in the backyard. From there, they could see that a fracas was taking place inside the kitchen. A juvenile, fists clenched, was being held back by several adults. As the officers watch, he breaks free and strikes one of the adults in the face, sending the adult to the sink spitting blood.

In these circumstances, the officers had an objectively reasonable basis for believing both that the injured adult might need help and that the violence in the kitchen was just beginning. Nothing in the Fourth Amendment required them to wait until another blow rendered someone "unconscious" or "semi-conscious" or worse before entering. The role of a peace officer includes preventing violence and restoring order, not simply rendering first aid to casualties; an officer is not like a boxing (or hockey) referee, poised to stop a bout only if it becomes too one-sided.

The manner of the officers' entry was also reasonable. After witnessing the punch, one of the officers opened the screen door and "yelled in police." *Id.*, at 40. When nobody heard him, he stepped into the kitchen and announced himself again. Only then did the tumult subside. The officer's announcement of his presence was at least equivalent to a knock on the screen door. Indeed, it was probably the only option that had even a chance of rising above the din. Under these circumstances, there was no violation of the Fourth Amendment's knock-and-announce rule. Furthermore, once the announcement was made, the officers were free to enter; it would serve no purpose to require them to stand dumbly at the door awaiting a response while those within brawled on, oblivious to their presence.

Accordingly, we reverse the judgment of the Supreme Court of Utah, and remand the case for further proceedings not inconsistent with this opinion.

It is so ordered.

[JUSTICE STEVENS' concurring opinion is omitted.]

NOTES ON PUNITIVE AND PROTECTIVE POLICING

1. In a concurring opinion, Justice Stevens observed as follows:

> This is an odd flyspeck of a case. The charges that have been pending against respondents for the past six years are minor offenses — intoxication, contributing to the delinquency of a minor, and disorderly conduct — two of which could have been proved by evidence that was gathered by the responding officers before they entered the home. The maximum punishment for these crimes ranges between 90 days and 6 months in jail. And the Court's unanimous opinion restating well-settled rules of federal law is so clearly persuasive that it is hard to imagine the outcome was ever indoubt.
>
> Under these circumstances, the only difficult question is which of the following is the most peculiar: (1) that the Utah trial judge, the intermediate state appellate court, and the Utah Supreme Court all found a Fourth Amendment violation on these facts; (2) that the prosecution chose to pursue this matter all the way to the United States Supreme Court; or (3) that this Court voted to grant the petition for a writ of certiorari.

Brigham City, 547 U.S., at 407 (Stevens, J., dissenting).

Do you agree? Justice Stevens noted that a possible explanation for the Utah state court rulings was that suppression was deemed correct as a matter of Utah law, and that neither trial counsel nor the trial judge bothered to identify the Utah Constitution as an independent basis for decision. Assume Justice Stevens is correct. Should police motive be considered in deciding on the reasonableness of a warrantless entry in cases like this—as a matter of federal or state constitutional law? Whether or not it should, it often is: A number of state courts have elaborated emergency doctrines that do take police motive into account in settings like the one in *Stuart*.

2. The Chief Justice is careful not to say that the police entry was legal because the officers' intent was to protect victims, not to punish offenders. Likewise, the Court's opinion characterizes the case as an easy one, calling the police conduct "plainly reasonable." But while the bottom line may be clear, the rationale is not. Here is the key sentence in Chief Justice Roberts' opinion: "In these circumstances, the officers had an objectively reasonable basis for believing both that the injured adult might need help and that the violence in the kitchen was just beginning." Notice what is missing from that sentence. There is no mention of probable cause or reasonable suspicion—more to the point, there is no mention of *crime*. As Roberts puts it, "[t]he role of a peace officer includes preventing violence and restoring order, not simply rendering first aid to casualties." The idea that the officers had good reason to suspect that they would find evidence of crime inside the house, and that the evidence might be destroyed if they sought a warrant—the core justification for warrantless entries into private homes—is nowhere to be found in *Stuart*.

Presumably Chief Justice Roberts avoided the words "probable cause" in the sentences just quoted for a reason. If probable cause isn't the standard, what is? How should the Court answer that question?

3. *Stuart* is a particular instance of a more general problem. Nearly all Fourth Amendment law was designed for situations in which the police and search targets are adversaries—the police are trying to gather evidence that can be used in court to convict suspects of crimes. But, as *Stuart* illustrates, the police and those whose privacy they infringe often are *not* adversaries. Police officers often enter private homes in order to protect people, not in order to punish them. It would seem strange to say that officers must not protect citizens from harm unless they have good reason to suspect those same citizens of wrongdoing.

It seems obvious, then, that different rules should apply to protective policing than to the punitive kind. If one accepts that proposition, two questions follow. What limits should be placed on police exercise of their protective function? And how should the line between protective and punitive policing be drawn?

4. The answers to both questions may turn on intent—either the intent of the private citizens involved, or the intent of the officers.

Consider first the limits on police authority to protect. There is obviously a danger in the idea that police can enter any dwelling anytime so long as they claim to be offering help rather than trying to bring the law's hammer down on those inside. The idea is a good deal less dangerous if one important limit is added: The party being protected *wanted* the police assistance. Sometimes, as in *Stuart,* it isn't possible to freeze the situation and ask everyone involved whether they wish to invite police officers inside. But it seems reasonable to assume that, if asked, victims of domestic violence would say "yes." That alone seems to make the entry in this case reasonable.

Or does it? Often protecting one person may mean arresting and punishing another. It's a fair guess that while those victimized by violence in private homes might want outside intervention, those doing the violence don't. Whose wishes should control? *Stuart* hints that the answer is that victims' wishes control. In another case decided the same Term, the Court held—over a strong dissent by Chief Justice Roberts—that the consent of one spouse to police entry was not enough to override the non-consent of the other. See Georgia v. Randolph, 547 U.S. 103 (2006). (*Randolph* is excerpted *infra,* at supplement page 129.) Which answer is right?

5. Assuming that the law places appropriate limits on protective policing, there is still a need to separate it from more traditional, and more adversarial, kinds of policing. One obvious way to do that is to look to police officers' intent: if the officers were trying to gather evidence, the usual rules apply; if they were trying to assist those in need of assistance, different rules apply. The Court rejects that approach in *Stuart,* but it has not always done so—as the Chief Justice's opinion acknowledges. Indianapolis v. Edmond, 531 U.S. 32 (2000), barred a police roadblock designed to catch and punish drug crime. But the Court left standing precedents permitting police roadblocks with a "primary purpose" that was something other than "detect[ing] evidence of ordinary criminal wrongdoing." *Id.* at 37.

6. In both cases—both with respect to private citizens' desire for assistance and police officers' desire to provide it—the law may consider intent without having cases turn on the thoughts of particular police officers or litigants. In a case like *Stuart,* one might ask whether a reasonable person in the circumstances of the adult spitting blood in the kitchen sink would welcome police intervention. Similarly, one might ask whether a reasonable officer would have believed the need for assistance was strong enough to justify entry without express permission. Such objective indicators of intent may be what the Court is describing

when it says that "'an inquiry into *programmatic* purpose' is sometimes appropriate."

7. Judicial power to define the bounds of police searches and seizures is sometimes justified by the need to protect the interests of those unable to protect themselves through politics. Criminal suspects are not exactly a powerful political lobby—one might fear that, if courts do not look out for their interests, no one will. Does the same proposition hold true of people in need of police protection? Are there good reasons why Supreme Court Justices should define the boundaries of police authority in settings like *Stuart*? Perhaps Justice Stevens was right to complain that the Court chose to hear and decide the case—not because it was "a flyspeck," but because it deals with issues that other institutions can resolve better than the Justices can.

e. *Searches Incident to Arrest*

Insert the following note and main case after Note 4 on page 549:

4a. The composition of the Court changed after the decision in *Thornton*, but the prediction that five votes would exist to revisit searches incident to arrest, at least in the context of car searches, proved accurate. Consider the following case:

ARIZONA v. GANT

Certiorari to the Arizona Supreme Court
129 S. Ct. 1710 (2009)

JUSTICE STEVENS delivered the opinion of the Court.

After Rodney Gant was arrested for driving with a suspended license, handcuffed, and locked in the back of a patrol car, police officers searched his car and discovered cocaine in the pocket of a jacket on the backseat. Because Gant could not have accessed his car to retrieve weapons or evidence at the time of the search, the Arizona Supreme Court held that the search-incident-to-arrest exception to the Fourth Amendment's warrant requirement, as defined in Chimel v. California, 395 U.S. 752 (1969), and applied to vehicle searches in New York v. Belton, 453 U.S. 454 (1981), did not justify the search in this case. We agree with that conclusion.

Under *Chimel,* police may search incident to arrest only the space within an arrestee's "'immediate control,'" meaning "the area from within which he might gain possession of a weapon or destructible evidence."

395 U.S., at 763. The safety and evidentiary justifications underlying *Chimel*'s reaching-distance rule determine *Belton*'s scope. Accordingly, we hold that *Belton* does not authorize a vehicle search incident to a recent occupant's arrest after the arrestee has been secured and cannot access the interior of the vehicle. Consistent with the holding in Thornton v. United States, 541 U.S. 615, and following the suggestion in JUSTICE SCALIA's opinion concurring in the judgment in that case, *id.*, at 632, we also conclude that circumstances unique to the automobile context justify a search incident to arrest when it is reasonable to believe that evidence of the offense of arrest might be found in the vehicle.

I

On August 25, 1999, acting on an anonymous tip that the residence at 2524 North Walnut Avenue was being used to sell drugs, Tucson police officers Griffith and Reed knocked on the front door and asked to speak to the owner. Gant answered the door and, after identifying himself, stated that he expected the owner to return later. The officers left the residence and conducted a records check, which revealed that Gant's driver's license had been suspended and there was an outstanding warrant for his arrest for driving with a suspended license.

When the officers returned to the house that evening, they found a man near the back of the house and a woman in a car parked in front of it. After a third officer arrived, they arrested the man for providing a false name and the woman for possessing drug paraphernalia. Both arrestees were handcuffed and secured in separate patrol cars when Gant arrived. The officers recognized his car as it entered the driveway, and Officer Griffith confirmed that Gant was the driver by shining a flashlight into the car as it drove by him. Gant parked at the end of the driveway, got out of his car, and shut the door. Griffith, who was about 30 feet away, called to Gant, and they approached each other, meeting 10-to-12 feet from Gant's car. Griffith immediately arrested Gant and handcuffed him.

Because the other arrestees were secured in the only patrol cars at the scene, Griffith called for backup. When two more officers arrived, they locked Gant in the backseat of their vehicle. After Gant had been handcuffed and placed in the back of a patrol car, two officers searched his car: One of them found a gun, and the other discovered a bag of cocaine in the pocket of a jacket on the backseat.

Gant was charged with two offenses-possession of a narcotic drug for sale and possession of drug paraphernalia (*i.e.*, the plastic bag in which the cocaine was found). . . .

After protracted state-court proceedings, the Arizona Supreme Court concluded that the search of Gant's car was unreasonable within the meaning of the Fourth Amendment. . . .

The chorus that has called for us to revisit *Belton* includes courts, scholars, and Members of this Court who have questioned that decision's clarity and its fidelity to Fourth Amendment principles. We therefore granted the State's petition for certiorari. . . .

II

In *Chimel,* we held that a search incident to arrest may only include "the arrestee's person and the area 'within his immediate control'—construing that phrase to mean the area from within which he might gain possession of a weapon or destructible evidence." *Ibid.* That limitation, which continues to define the boundaries of the exception, ensures that the scope of a search incident to arrest is commensurate with its purposes of protecting arresting officers and safeguarding any evidence of the offense of arrest that an arrestee might conceal or destroy. . . .

In *Belton,* we considered *Chimel*'s application to the automobile context, . . .

[W]e held that when an officer lawfully arrests "the occupant of an automobile, he may, as a contemporaneous incident of that arrest, search the passenger compartment of the automobile" and any containers therein. *Belton,* 453 U.S., at 460 (footnote omitted). That holding was based in large part on our assumption "that articles inside the relatively narrow compass of the passenger compartment of an automobile are in fact generally, even if not inevitably, within 'the area into which an arrestee might reach.'" *Ibid.*

The Arizona Supreme Court read our decision in *Belton* as merely delineating "the proper scope of a search of the interior of an automobile" incident to an arrest, *id.,* at 459. That is, *when* the passenger compartment is within an arrestee's reaching distance, *Belton* supplies the generalization that the entire compartment and any containers therein may be reached. On that view of *Belton,* the state court concluded that the search of Gant's car was unreasonable because Gant clearly could not have accessed his car at the time of the search. . . .

III

Despite the textual and evidentiary support for the Arizona Supreme Court's reading of *Belton,* our opinion has been widely understood to allow a vehicle search incident to the arrest of a recent occupant even if there is no possibility the arrestee could gain access to the vehicle at the time of the search. . . .

Under this broad reading of *Belton,* a vehicle search would be authorized incident to every arrest of a recent occupant notwithstanding that in most cases the vehicle's passenger compartment will not be within the arrestee's reach at the time of the search. To read *Belton* as authorizing a vehicle search incident to every recent occupant's arrest would thus untether the rule from the justifications underlying the *Chimel* exception—a result clearly incompatible with our statement in *Belton* that it "in no way alters the fundamental principles established in the *Chimel* case regarding the basic scope of searches incident to lawful custodial arrests." 453 U.S., at 460, n. 3. Accordingly, we reject this reading of *Belton* and hold that the *Chimel* rationale authorizes police to search a vehicle incident to a recent occupant's arrest only when the arrestee is unsecured and within reaching distance of the passenger compartment at the time of the search.

Although it does not follow from *Chimel,* we also conclude that circumstances unique to the vehicle context justify a search incident to a lawful arrest when it is "reasonable to believe evidence relevant to the crime of arrest might be found in the vehicle." *Thornton,* 541 U.S., at 632 (SCALIA, J., concurring in judgment). In many cases, as when a recent occupant is arrested for a traffic violation, there will be no reasonable basis to believe the vehicle contains relevant evidence. See, *e.g.,* Atwater v. Lago Vista, 532 U.S. 318, 324 (2001); Knowles v. Iowa, 525 U.S. 113, 118 (1998). But in others, including *Belton* and *Thornton,* the offense of arrest will supply a basis for searching the passenger compartment of an arrestee's vehicle and any containers therein.

Neither the possibility of access nor the likelihood of discovering offense-related evidence authorized the search in this case. . . . Because police could not reasonably have believed either that Gant could have accessed his car at the time of the search or that evidence of the offense for which he was arrested might have been found therein, the search in this case was unreasonable.

IV

The State does not seriously disagree with the Arizona Supreme Court's conclusion that Gant could not have accessed his vehicle at the time of the search, but it nevertheless asks us to uphold the search of his vehicle under the broad reading of *Belton* discussed above. The State argues that *Belton* searches are reasonable regardless of the possibility of access in a given case because that expansive rule correctly balances law enforcement interests, including the interest in a bright-line rule, with an arrestee's limited privacy interest in his vehicle.

For several reasons, we reject the State's argument. First, the State seriously undervalues the privacy interests at stake. Although we have recognized that a motorist's privacy interest in his vehicle is less substantial than in his home, see New York v. Class, 475 U.S. 106, 112-113 (1986), the former interest is nevertheless important and deserving of constitutional protection, see *Knowles,* 525 U.S., at 117. It is particularly significant that *Belton* searches authorize police officers to search not just the passenger compartment but every purse, briefcase, or other container within that space. A rule that gives police the power to conduct such a search whenever an individual is caught committing a traffic offense, when there is no basis for believing evidence of the offense might be found in the vehicle, creates a serious and recurring threat to the privacy of countless individuals. Indeed, the character of that threat implicates the central concern underlying the Fourth Amendment-the concern about giving police officers unbridled discretion to rummage at will among a person's private effects.

At the same time as it undervalues these privacy concerns, the State exaggerates the clarity that its reading of *Belton* provides. Courts that have read *Belton* expansively are at odds regarding how close in time to the arrest and how proximate to the arrestee's vehicle an officer's first contact with the arrestee must be to bring the encounter within *Belton*'s purview and whether a search is reasonable when it commences or continues after the arrestee has been removed from the scene. . . .

Contrary to the State's suggestion, a broad reading of *Belton* is also unnecessary to protect law enforcement safety and evidentiary interests. Under our view, *Belton* and *Thornton* permit an officer to conduct a vehicle search when an arrestee is within reaching distance of the vehicle or it is reasonable to believe the vehicle contains evidence of the offense of arrest. Other established exceptions to the warrant requirement authorize a vehicle search under additional circumstances when safety or evidentiary concerns demand. . . .

V

Our dissenting colleagues argue that the doctrine of *stare decisis* requires adherence to a broad reading of *Belton* even though the justifications for searching a vehicle incident to arrest are in most cases absent. The doctrine of *stare decisis* is of course "essential to the respect accorded to the judgments of the Court and to the stability of the law," but it does not compel us to follow a past decision when its rationale no longer withstands "careful analysis." Lawrence v. Texas, 539 U.S. 558, 577 (2003). . . .

The experience of the 28 years since we decided *Belton* has shown that the generalization underpinning the broad reading of that decision is unfounded. We now know that articles inside the passenger compartment are rarely "within 'the area into which an arrestee might reach,'" 453 U.S., at 460, and blind adherence to *Belton* 's faulty assumption would authorize myriad unconstitutional searches. The doctrine of *stare decisis* does not require us to approve routine constitutional violations.

VI

Police may search a vehicle incident to a recent occupant's arrest only if the arrestee is within reaching distance of the passenger compartment at the time of the search or it is reasonable to believe the vehicle contains evidence of the offense of arrest. When these justifications are absent, a search of an arrestee's vehicle will be unreasonable unless police obtain a warrant or show that another exception to the warrant requirement applies. The Arizona Supreme Court correctly held that this case involved an unreasonable search. Accordingly, the judgment of the State Supreme Court is affirmed.

JUSTICE SCALIA, concurring.

To determine what is an "unreasonable" search within the meaning of the Fourth Amendment, we look first to the historical practices the Framers sought to preserve; if those provide inadequate guidance, we apply traditional standards of reasonableness. Since the historical scope of officers' authority to search vehicles incident to arrest is uncertain, see Thornton v. United States, 541 U.S. 615, 629-631 (SCALIA, J., concurring in judgment), traditional standards of reasonableness govern. It is abundantly clear that those standards do not justify what I take to be the rule set forth in New York v. Belton, 453 U.S. 454 (1981), and *Thornton:* that arresting officers may always search an arrestee's vehicle in order to protect themselves from hidden weapons. When an arrest is made in connection with a roadside stop, police virtually always have a less intrusive and more effective means of ensuring their safety-and a means that is virtually always employed: ordering the arrestee away from the vehicle, patting him down in the open, handcuffing him, and placing him in the squad car. . . .

JUSTICE STEVENS acknowledges that an officer-safety rationale cannot justify all vehicle searches incident to arrest, but asserts that that is not the rule *Belton* and *Thornton* adopted. (As described above, I read those cases differently). JUSTICE STEVENS would therefore retain the application of Chimel v. California, 395 U.S. 752 (1969), in the car-search context but would apply in the future what he believes our cases held in the past: that officers making a roadside stop may search the vehicle so long as the "arrestee is within reaching distance of the passenger compartment at the time of the search." I believe that this standard fails to provide the needed guidance to arresting officers and also leaves much room for manipulation, inviting officers to leave the scene unsecured (at least where dangerous suspects are not involved) in order to conduct a vehicle search. In my view we should simply abandon the *Belton-Thornton* charade of officer safety and overrule those cases. I would hold that a vehicle search incident to arrest is *ipso facto* "reasonable" only when the object of the search is evidence of the crime for which the arrest was made, or of another crime that the officer has probable cause to believe occurred. Because respondent was arrested for driving without a license (a crime for which no evidence could be expected to be found in the vehicle), I would hold in the present case that the search was unlawful. . . .

JUSTICE ALITO argues that there is no reason to adopt a rule limiting automobile-arrest searches to those cases where the search's object is evidence of the crime of arrest. I disagree. This formulation of officers' authority both preserves the outcomes of our prior cases and tethers the scope and rationale of the doctrine to the triggering event. *Belton,* by contrast, allowed searches precisely when its exigency-based rationale was least applicable: The fact of the arrest in the automobile context makes searches on exigency grounds *less* reasonable, not more. . . .

No other Justice, however, shares my view that application of *Chimel* in this context should be entirely abandoned. It seems to me unacceptable for the Court to come forth with a 4-to-1-to-4 opinion that leaves the governing rule uncertain. I am therefore confronted with the choice of either leaving the current understanding of *Belton* and *Thornton* in effect, or acceding to what seems to me the artificial narrowing of those cases adopted by JUSTICE STEVENS. The latter, as I have said, does not provide the degree of certainty I think desirable in this field; but the former opens the field to what I think are plainly unconstitutional searches-which is the greater evil. I therefore join the opinion of the Court.

[JUSTICE BREYER's dissenting opinion is omitted.]

JUSTICE ALITO, with whom CHIEF JUSTICE ROBERTS and JUSTICE KENNEDY join, and with whom JUSTICE BREYER joins except as to Part II-E, dissenting.

Twenty-eight years ago, in New York v. Belton, 453 U.S. 454, 460 (1981), this Court held that "when a policeman has made a lawful custodial arrest of the occupant of an automobile, he may, as a contemporaneous incident of that arrest, search the passenger compartment of that automobile." (Footnote omitted.) Five years ago, in Thornton v. United States, 541 U.S. 615 (2004)-a case involving a situation not materially distinguishable from the situation here-the Court not only reaffirmed but extended the holding of *Belton,* making it applicable to recent occupants. Today's decision effectively overrules those important decisions. . . .

II

Because the Court has substantially overruled *Belton* and *Thornton,* the Court must explain why its departure from the usual rule of *stare decisis* is justified. . . . [T]he Court has said that a constitutional precedent should be followed unless there is a "'special justification'" for its abandonment. Dickerson v. United States, 530 U.S. 428, 443 (2000). Relevant factors identified in prior cases include whether the precedent has engendered reliance, *id.*, at 442, whether there has been an important change in circumstances in the outside world, Randall v. Sorrell, 548 U.S. 230, 244 (2006) (plurality opinion); Burnet v. Coronado Oil & Gas Co., 285 U.S. 393, 412 (1932) (Brandeis, J., dissenting), whether the precedent has proved to be unworkable, Vieth v. Jubelirer, 541 U.S. 267, 306 (2004) (plurality opinion) (citing *Payne, supra,* at 827), whether the precedent has been undermined by later decisions, see, *e.g.*, Patterson v. McLean Credit Union, 491 U.S. 164, 173-174 (1989), and whether the decision was badly reasoned. *Vieth, supra,* at 306 (plurality opinion). These factors weigh in favor of retaining the rule established in *Belton.*

A

Reliance. . . . The opinion of the Court recognizes that "*Belton* has been widely taught in police academies and that law enforcement officers have relied on the rule in conducting vehicle searches during the past 28 years." But for the Court, this seemingly counts for nothing. The Court states that "[w]e have never relied on *stare decisis* to justify the continuance of an unconstitutional police practice," but of course the Court routinely relies on decisions sustaining the constitutionality of police practices without doing what the Court has done here-*sua sponte* considering whether those decisions should be overruled. And the Court cites no authority for the proposition that *stare decisis* may be disregarded or provides only lesser protection when the precedent that is challenged is one that sustained the constitutionality of a law enforcement practice. . . .

B

Changed circumstances. Abandonment of the *Belton* rule cannot be justified on the ground that the dangers surrounding the arrest of a vehicle occupant are different today than they were 28 years ago. The Court claims that "[w]e now know that articles inside the passenger compartment are rarely within "the area into which an arrestee might reach,"" but surely it was well known in 1981 that a person who is taken from a vehicle, handcuffed, and placed in the back of a patrol car is unlikely to make it back into his own car to retrieve a weapon or destroy evidence.

C

Workability. The *Belton* rule has not proved to be unworkable. On the contrary, the rule was adopted for the express purpose of providing a test that would be relatively easy for police officers and judges to apply. The Court correctly notes that even the *Belton* rule is not perfectly clear in all situations. Specifically, it is sometimes debatable whether a search is or is not contemporaneous with an arrest, but that problem is small in comparison with the problems that the Court's new two-part rule will produce.

The first part of the Court's new rule-which permits the search of a vehicle's passenger compartment if it is within an arrestee's reach at the time of the search-reintroduces the same sort of case-by-case, fact-specific decisionmaking that the *Belton* rule was adopted to avoid. . . .

Even more serious problems will also result from the second part of the Court's new rule, which requires officers making roadside arrests to determine whether there is reason to believe that the vehicle contains evidence of the crime of arrest. What this rule permits in a variety of situations is entirely unclear.

D

Consistency with later cases. The *Belton* bright-line rule has not been undermined by subsequent cases. On the contrary, that rule was reaffirmed and extended just five years ago in *Thornton.*

E

Bad reasoning. The Court is harshly critical of *Belton* 's reasoning, but the problem that the Court perceives cannot be remedied simply by overruling *Belton. Belton* represented only a modest-and quite defensible-extension of *Chimel,* as I understand that decision.

Prior to *Chimel,* the Court's precedents permitted an arresting officer to search the area within an arrestee's "possession" and "control" for the purpose of gathering evidence. See 395 U.S., at 759-760. Based on this "abstract doctrine," *id.*, at 760, n. 4, the Court had sustained searches that extended far beyond an arrestee's grabbing area. See United States v. Rabinowitz, 339 U.S. 56 (1950) (search of entire office); Harris v. United States, 331 U.S. 145 (1947) (search of entire apartment).

The *Chimel* Court, in an opinion written by Justice Stewart, overruled these cases. Concluding that there are only two justifications for a warrantless search incident to arrest-officer safety and the preservation of evidence-the Court stated that such a search must be confined to "the arrestee's person" and "the area from within which he might gain possession of a weapon or destructible evidence." 395 U.S., at 762-763.

Unfortunately, *Chimel* did not say whether "the area from within which [an arrestee] might gain possession of a weapon or destructible evidence" is to be measured at the time of the arrest or at the time of the search, but unless the *Chimel* rule was meant to be a specialty rule, applicable to only a few unusual cases, the Court must have intended for this area to be measured at the time of arrest.

This is so because the Court can hardly have failed to appreciate the following two facts. First, in the great majority of cases, an officer making an arrest is able to handcuff the arrestee and remove him to a secure place before conducting a search incident to the arrest. Second, because it is safer for an arresting officer to secure an arrestee before searching, it is likely that this is what arresting officers do in the great majority of cases. (And it appears, not surprisingly, that this is in fact the prevailing practice.) Thus, if the area within an arrestee's reach were assessed, not at the time of arrest, but at the time of the search, the *Chimel* rule would rarely come into play.

Moreover, if the applicability of the *Chimel* rule turned on whether an arresting officer chooses to secure an arrestee prior to conducting a search, rather than searching first and securing the arrestee later, the rule would "create a perverse incentive for an arresting officer to prolong the period during which the arrestee is kept in an area where he could pose a danger to the officer." United States v. Abdul-Saboor, 85 F.3d 664, 669 (C.A.D.C.1996). If this is the law, the D.C. Circuit observed, "the law would truly be, as Mr. Bumble said, 'a ass.'" *Ibid.*

I do not think that this is what the *Chimel* Court intended. Handcuffs were in use in 1969. The ability of arresting officers to secure arrestees before conducting a search–and their incentive to do so–are facts that can hardly have escaped the Court's attention. I therefore believe that the

Chimel Court intended that its new rule apply in cases in which the arrestee is handcuffed before the search is conducted.

The *Belton* Court, in my view, proceeded on the basis of this interpretation of *Chimel*. Again speaking through Justice Stewart, the *Belton* Court reasoned that articles in the passenger compartment of a car are "generally, even if not inevitably" within an arrestee's reach. 453 U.S., at 460. This is undoubtedly true at the time of the arrest of a person who is seated in a car but plainly not true when the person has been removed from the car and placed in handcuffs. Accordingly, the *Belton* Court must have proceeded on the assumption that the *Chimel* rule was to be applied at the time of arrest. And that is why the *Belton* Court was able to say that its decision "in no way alter[ed] the fundamental principles established in the *Chimel* case regarding the basic scope of searches incident to lawful custodial arrests." 453 U.S., at 460, n. 3.Viewing *Chimel* as having focused on the time of arrest, *Belton* 's only new step was to eliminate the need to decide on a case-by-case basis whether a particular person seated in a car actually could have reached the part of the passenger compartment where a weapon or evidence was hidden. For this reason, if we are going to reexamine *Belton,* we should also reexamine the reasoning in *Chimel* on which *Belton* rests.

F

The Court, however, does not reexamine *Chimel* and thus leaves the law relating to searches incident to arrest in a confused and unstable state. The first part of the Court's new two-part rule—which permits an arresting officer to search the area within an arrestee's reach at the time of the search—applies, at least for now, only to vehicle occupants and recent occupants, but there is no logical reason why the same rule should not apply to all arrestees.

The second part of the Court's new rule, which the Court takes uncritically from JUSTICE SCALIA's separate opinion in *Thornton,* raises doctrinal and practical problems that the Court makes no effort to address. Why, for example, is the standard for this type of evidence-gathering search "reason to believe" rather than probable cause? And why is this type of search restricted to evidence of the offense of arrest? It is true that an arrestee's vehicle is probably more likely to contain evidence of the crime of arrest than of some other crime, but if reason-to-believe is the governing standard for an evidence-gathering search incident to arrest, it is not easy to see why an officer should not be able to search when the officer has reason to believe that the vehicle in question possesses evidence of a crime other than the crime of arrest.

Nor is it easy to see why an evidence-gathering search incident to arrest should be restricted to the passenger compartment. The *Belton* rule was limited in this way because the passenger compartment was considered to be the area that vehicle occupants can generally reach, 453 U.S., at 460, but since the second part of the new rule is not based on officer safety or the preservation of evidence, the ground for this limitation is obscure.

III

. . . In this case, I would simply apply *Belton* and reverse the judgment below.

NOTES AND QUESTIONS

1. How is *Gant* consistent with the holding in *Thornton*, as the majority proclaims? Presumably because in *Thornton*, unlike *Gant*, the officer who performed the search had reason to believe that additional contraband or other evidence relevant to Thornton's drug offense might be found in the car. But what is the Fourth Amendment rationale for permitting *any* search of the car's interior, once an arrestee has been secured? In *Thornton*, Justice Scalia, who started this whole thing, suggested that it is reasonable to permit searches for evidence related to the crime for which a car's occupant has been arrested, due in part to the reduced expectation of privacy associated with cars. But the majority takes pains to emphasize the importance of our privacy interest in vehicles. So what is the rationale?

2. Does the absence of one suggest, as the dissent contends, that *Gant* has unsettled not just *Belton* and *Thornton*, but also *Chimel*?

3. Does the dissent have a broader point? *Thornton* was decided only five years before *Gant*. Even if the holdings in the two cases are consistent, the reasoning is certainly not. Should the Court have considered *stare decisis* principles more carefully? Or is it an adequate answer to Justice Alito that "[t]he doctrine of *stare decisis* does not require [the Court] to approve routine constitutional violations"?

4. Who has the better argument with regard to the workability of the new rule, as opposed to the old? Do you agree with Justice Alito that while *Belton* and *Thornton* produced some uncertainty as to whether a passenger compartment search is incident to an arrest, *Gant* is likely to produce considerably more uncertainty?

5. What about the second part of the Court's new rule? In *Thornton*, Justice Scalia concluded that because Thornton had been arrested for a drug offense, "it was reasonable for Officer Nichols to believe that further contraband or similar evidence relevant to the crime for which he had been arrested might be found in the vehicle. . . . " Thornton was carrying drugs on his person when arrested. Should the same passenger compartment search rule apply when a drug kingpin is arrested after a four-month investigation, and he happens to be driving his car? Would it be reasonable to believe that an investment advisor who has been defrauding clients might be carrying relevant evidence in his briefcase when he is arrested in his car?

6. Now consider Note 5 on page 549. Does the inventory search doctrine render all of this a little beside the point? If the car is going into impound, why must we carefully calibrate the appropriate scope of the search incident to arrest? Isn't this a fundamental point distinguishing cars from houses, and the *Belton-Thornton-Gant* line of cases from *Chimel*?

Insert the following material after the commentary following Knowles v. Iowa on page 552:

Perhaps the problem in *Knowles* (if, in fact, there is a problem) lies in the scope that state law afforded to police in that case to pick and choose whether to arrest. (Remember Atwater v. Lago Vista, 532 U.S. 318 (2001), on page 518?) The following case deals with a situation in which the state had acted to constrain officers' arrest discretion. But this raises a different question. What happens when the relevant state law is violated? Does this mean the Fourth Amendment is violated as well?

VIRGINIA v. MOORE

Certiorari to the Virginia Supreme Court
553 U.S. 164 (2008)

Justice Scalia delivered the opinion of the Court.

We consider whether a police officer violates the Fourth Amendment by making an arrest based on probable cause but prohibited by state law.

I

On February 20, 2003, two City of Portsmouth police officers stopped a car driven by David Lee Moore. They had heard over the police radio that a person known as "Chubs" was driving with a suspended license, and one of the officers knew Moore by that nickname. The officers determined that Moore's license was in fact suspended, and arrested him for the misdemeanor of driving on a suspended license, which is punishable under Virginia law by a year in jail and a $2,500 fine. The officers subsequently searched Moore and found that he was carrying 16 grams of crack cocaine and $516 in cash.

Under state law, the officers should have issued Moore a summons instead of arresting him. Driving on a suspended license, like some other misdemeanors, is not an arrestable offense except as to those who "fail or refuse to discontinue" the violation, and those whom the officer reasonably believes to be likely to disregard a summons, or likely to harm themselves or others. Va. Code Ann. § 19.2-74 (Lexis 2004). The intermediate appellate court found none of these circumstances applicable, and Virginia did not appeal that determination. Virginia also permits arrest for driving on a suspended license in jurisdictions where "prior general approval has been granted by order of the general district court," Va. Code Ann. § 46.2-936; Virginia has never claimed such approval was in effect in the county where Moore was arrested.

Moore was charged with possessing cocaine with the intent to distribute it in violation of Virginia law. He filed a pretrial motion to suppress the evidence from the arrest search. Virginia law does not, as a general matter, require suppression of evidence obtained in violation of state law. Moore argued, however, that suppression was required by the Fourth Amendment. The trial court denied the motion, and after a bench trial found Moore guilty of the drug charge and sentenced him to a 5-year prison term, with one year and six months of the sentence suspended. The conviction was reversed by a panel of Virginia's intermediate court on Fourth Amendment grounds, reinstated by the intermediate court sitting en banc, and finally reversed again by the Virginia Supreme Court. The Court reasoned that since the arresting officers should have issued Moore a citation under state law, and the Fourth Amendment does not permit search incident to citation, the arrest search violated the Fourth Amendment. We granted certiorari.

II

The Fourth Amendment protects "against unreasonable searches and seizures" of (among other things) the person. In determining whether a search or seizure is unreasonable, we begin with history. We look to the statutes and common law of the founding era to determine the norms that the Fourth Amendment was meant to preserve. See Wyoming v. Houghton, 526 U.S. 295, 299 (1999).

We are aware of no historical indication that those who ratified the Fourth Amendment understood it as a redundant guarantee of whatever limits on search and seizure legislatures might have enacted. The immediate object of the Fourth Amendment was to prohibit the general warrants and writs of assistance that English judges had employed against the colonists. That suggests, if anything, that founding-era citizens were skeptical of using the rules for search and seizure set by government actors as the index of reasonableness.

Joseph Story, among others, saw the Fourth Amendment as "little more than the affirmance of a great constitutional doctrine of the common law," 3 Commentaries on the Constitution of the United States § 1895, p. 748 (1833), which Story defined in opposition to statutes, see Codification of the Common Law in The Miscellaneous Writings of Joseph Story 698, 699, 701 (W. Story ed. 1852). No early case or commentary, to our knowledge, suggested the Amendment was intended to incorporate subsequently enacted statutes. None of the early Fourth Amendment cases that scholars have identified sought to base a constitutional claim on a violation of a state or federal statute concerning arrest. See Davies, Recovering the Original Fourth Amendment, 98 Mich. L. Rev. 547, 613-614 (1999); see also T. Taylor, Two Studies in Constitutional Interpretation 44-45 (1969).

Of course such a claim would not have been available against state officers, since the Fourth Amendment was a restriction only upon federal power. But early Congresses tied the arrest authority of federal officers to state laws of arrest. See United States v. Di Re, 332 U.S. 581, 589 (1948). Moreover, even though several state constitutions also prohibited unreasonable searches and seizures, citizens who claimed officers had violated state restrictions on arrest did not claim that the violations also ran afoul of the state constitutions. The apparent absence of such litigation is particularly striking in light of the fact that searches incident to warrantless arrests (which is to say arrests in which the officer was not insulated from private suit) were, as one commentator has put it, "taken for granted" at the founding, Taylor, *supra,* at 45, as were warrantless arrests themselves, Amar, Fourth Amendment First Principles, 107 Harv. L. Rev. 757, 764 (1994).

There are a number of possible explanations of why such constitutional claims were not raised. Davies, for example, argues that actions taken in violation of state law could not qualify as state action subject to

Fourth Amendment constraints, 98 Mich. L. Rev., at 660-663. Be that as it may, as Moore adduces neither case law nor commentaries to support his view that the Fourth Amendment was intended to incorporate statutes, this is "not a case in which the claimant can point to 'a clear answer [that] existed in 1791 and has been generally adhered to by the traditions of our society ever since.'" Atwater v. Lago Vista, 532 U.S. 318, 345 (2001) (alteration in original).

III

A

When history has not provided a conclusive answer, we have analyzed a search or seizure in light of traditional standards of reasonableness "by assessing, on the one hand, the degree to which it intrudes upon an individual's privacy and, on the other, the degree to which it is needed for the promotion of legitimate governmental interests." *Houghton*, 526 U.S., at 300. That methodology provides no support for Moore's Fourth Amendment claim. In a long line of cases, we have said that when an officer has probable cause to believe a person committed even a minor crime in his presence, the balancing of private and public interests is not in doubt. The arrest is constitutionally reasonable.

Our decisions counsel against changing this calculus when a State chooses to protect privacy beyond the level that the Fourth Amendment requires. We have treated additional protections exclusively as matters of state law. . . .

In California v. Greenwood, 486 U.S. 35 (1988), we held that search of an individual's garbage forbidden by California's Constitution was not forbidden by the Fourth Amendment. "[W]hether or not a search is reasonable within the meaning of the Fourth Amendment," we said, has never "depend[ed] on the law of the particular State in which the search occurs." *Id.*, at 43. While "[i]ndividual States may surely construe their own constitutions as imposing more stringent constraints on police conduct than does the Federal Constitution," *ibid.*, state law did not alter the content of the Fourth Amendment.

We have applied the same principle in the seizure context. Whren v. United States, 517 U.S. 806 (1996), held that police officers had acted reasonably in stopping a car, even though their action violated regulations limiting the authority of plainclothes officers in unmarked vehicles. We thought it obvious that the Fourth Amendment's meaning did not change with local law enforcement practices—even practices set by rule. While those practices "vary from place to place and from time to time,"

Fourth Amendment protections are not "so variable" and cannot "be made to turn upon such trivialities." *Id.*, at 815. . . .

B

We are convinced that the approach of our prior cases is correct, because an arrest based on probable cause serves interests that have long been seen as sufficient to justify the seizure. Arrest ensures that a suspect appears to answer charges and does not continue a crime, and it safeguards evidence and enables officers to conduct an in-custody investigation. See W. LaFave, Arrest: The Decision to Take a Suspect into Custody 177-202 (1965).

Moore argues that a State has no interest in arrest when it has a policy against arresting for certain crimes. That is not so, because arrest will still ensure a suspect's appearance at trial, prevent him from continuing his offense, and enable officers to investigate the incident more thoroughly. State arrest restrictions are more accurately characterized as showing that the State values its interests in forgoing arrests more highly than its interests in making them, *see, e.g.*, Dept. of Justice, National Institute of Justice, D. Whitcomb, B. Lewin, & M. Levine, Issues and Practices: Citation Release 17 (Mar.1984) (describing cost savings as a principal benefit of citation-release ordinances); or as showing that the State places a higher premium on privacy than the Fourth Amendment requires. A State is free to prefer one search-and-seizure policy among the range of constitutionally permissible options, but its choice of a more restrictive option does not render the less restrictive ones unreasonable, and hence unconstitutional.

If we concluded otherwise, we would often frustrate rather than further state policy. Virginia chooses to protect individual privacy and dignity more than the Fourth Amendment requires, but it also chooses not to attach to violations of its arrest rules the potent remedies that federal courts have applied to Fourth Amendment violations. Virginia does not, for example, ordinarily exclude from criminal trials evidence obtained in violation of its statutes. Moore would allow Virginia to accord enhanced protection against arrest only on pain of accompanying that protection with federal remedies for Fourth Amendment violations, which often include the exclusionary rule. States unwilling to lose control over the remedy would have to abandon restrictions on arrest altogether. This is an odd consequence of a provision designed to protect against searches and seizures.

Even if we thought that state law changed the nature of the Commonwealth's interests for purposes of the Fourth Amendment, we would adhere to the probable-cause standard. In determining what is reasonable under the Fourth Amendment, we have given great weight to the "essential interest in readily administrable rules." *Atwater*, 532 U.S., at 347. In *Atwater*, we acknowledged that nuanced judgments about the need for warrantless arrest were desirable, but we nonetheless declined to limit to felonies and disturbances of the peace the Fourth Amendment rule allowing arrest based on probable cause to believe a law has been broken in the presence of the arresting officer. *Id.*, at 346-347. The rule extends even to minor misdemeanors, we concluded, because of the need for a bright-line constitutional standard. If the constitutionality of arrest for minor offenses turned in part on inquiries as to risk of flight and danger of repetition, officers might be deterred from making legitimate arrests. *Id.*, at 351. We found little to justify this cost, because there was no "epidemic of unnecessary minor-offense arrests," and hence "a dearth of horribles demanding redress." *Id.*, at 353.

Incorporating state-law arrest limitations into the Constitution would produce a constitutional regime no less vague and unpredictable than the one we rejected in *Atwater*. The constitutional standard would be only as easy to apply as the underlying state law, and state law can be complicated indeed. The Virginia statute in this case, for example, calls on law enforcement officers to weigh just the sort of case-specific factors that *Atwater* said would deter legitimate arrests if made part of the constitutional inquiry. . . . *Atwater* differs from this case in only one significant respect: It considered (and rejected) federal constitutional remedies for *all* minor-misdemeanor arrests; Moore seeks them in only that *subset* of minor-misdemeanor arrests in which there is the least to be gained—that is, where the State has already acted to constrain officers' discretion and prevent abuse. Here we confront fewer horribles than in *Atwater*, and less of a need for redress.

Finally, linking Fourth Amendment protections to state law would cause them to "vary from place to place and from time to time," *Whren*, 517 U.S., at 815. Even at the same place and time, the Fourth Amendment's protections might vary if federal officers were not subject to the same statutory constraints as state officers. In Elkins v. United States, 364 U.S. 206, 210-212 (1960), we noted the practical difficulties posed by the "silver-platter doctrine," which had imposed more stringent limitations on federal officers than on state police acting independent of them. It would be strange to construe a constitutional provision that did not apply to the States at all when it was adopted to now restrict state officers more than federal officers, solely because the States have passed search-and-seizure laws that are the prerogative of independent sovereigns.

We conclude that warrantless arrests for crimes committed in the presence of an arresting officer are reasonable under the Constitution, and that while States are free to regulate such arrests however they desire, state restrictions do not alter the Fourth Amendment's protections.

IV

Moore argues that even if the Constitution allowed his arrest, it did not allow the arresting officers to search him. We have recognized, however, that officers may perform searches incident to constitutionally permissible arrests in order to ensure their safety and safeguard evidence. United States v. Robinson, 414 U.S. 218 (1973). We have described this rule as covering any "lawful arrest," *id.*, at 235, with constitutional law as the reference point. That is to say, we have equated a lawful arrest with an arrest based on probable cause: "A custodial arrest of a suspect based on probable cause is a reasonable intrusion under the Fourth Amendment; *that intrusion being lawful,* a search incident to the arrest requires no additional justification." *Ibid.* (emphasis added). . . .

The interests justifying search are present whenever an officer makes an arrest. A search enables officers to safeguard evidence, and, most critically, to ensure their safety during "the extended exposure which follows the taking of a suspect into custody and transporting him to the police station." *Robinson, supra,* at 234-235. Officers issuing citations do not face the same danger, and we therefore held in Knowles v. Iowa, 525 U.S. 113 (1998), that they do not have the same authority to search. We cannot agree with the Virginia Supreme Court that *Knowles* controls here. The state officers *arrested* Moore, and therefore faced the risks that are "an adequate basis for treating all custodial arrests alike for purposes of search justification." *Robinson, supra,* at 235.

The Virginia Supreme Court may have concluded that *Knowles* required the exclusion of evidence seized from Moore because, under state law, the officers who arrested Moore should have issued him a citation instead. This argument might have force if the Constitution forbade Moore's arrest, because we have sometimes excluded evidence obtained through unconstitutional methods in order to deter constitutional violations. See Wong Sun v. United States, 371 U.S. 471, 484-485, 488 (1963). But the arrest rules that the officers violated were those of state law alone, and as we have just concluded, it is not the province of the Fourth Amendment to enforce state law. That Amendment does not require the exclusion of evidence obtained from a constitutionally permissible arrest.

* * *

We reaffirm against a novel challenge what we have signaled for more than half a century. When officers have probable cause to believe that a person has committed a crime in their presence, the Fourth Amendment permits them to make an arrest, and to search the suspect in order to safeguard evidence and ensure their own safety. The judgment of the Supreme Court of Virginia is reversed, and the case is remanded for further proceedings not inconsistent with this opinion.

[The opinion of JUSTICE GINSBURG concurring in the judgment is omitted.]

NOTES AND QUESTIONS

1. *Moore* makes sense, doesn't it? An officer's violation of state law isn't necessarily a violation of the Fourth Amendment. On the other hand, what does an arrest based on probable cause mean except for an arrest based on a fair probability that the arrestee has violated a law—a *state* law, in the case of Moore? And if the relevant state holds that it is not reasonable to arrest based simply on cause to believe that one of its laws has been violated, what sense does it make for Fourth Amendment doctrine to hold that an arrest is nonetheless reasonable? Doesn't Moore also have a point? He should have been issued a citation, and *Knowles* says that a search incident is not constitutionally permissible in this circumstance.

2. Perhaps this is another case best understood in light of the remedy at issue, rather than the right. Does it make sense to suppress the evidence found on Moore in the face of Virginia's general position that suppression is *not* required for violations of state law? If not, is there any rationale for concluding here that the officer's conduct violated the Fourth Amendment, but exclusion is *not* the necessary result?

3. What if Virginia did require exclusion of evidence as a general consequence of violation of its arrest rules? Does this mean that in this case, Moore could not be prosecuted in state court, because the evidence found on his person would be suppressed, but he could be prosecuted in federal court? What are the "practical difficulties," if any, associated with this reverse "silver platter doctrine"?

4. Let's return to the first question for just a moment. Doesn't *Moore* mean that it is constitutionally reasonable to perform a search incident to

arrest in connection with an arrest that is not authorized by law? How can that make sense?

D. *Reasonableness*

1. Stops and Frisks

Insert the following note after Note 2, page 576:

2a. At any rate, the Court has continued to acknowledge that officer safety concerns are of considerable importance in the context of traffic encounters. In Arizona v. Johnson, 129 S. Ct. 781 (2009), for instance, the Court considered the authority of police officers to frisk the passenger in a car temporarily detained because of the driver's traffic infraction.

In *Johnson*, three members of Arizona's gang task force on patrol in Tucson stopped a car after a license plate check revealed that the car's registration had been suspended for an insurance-related civil violation. The officers were patrolling near a neighborhood associated with Crips activity, but they had no reason to suspect anyone in the car of gang-related conduct. As the other officers approached the driver and the front seat passenger, Officer Trevizo engaged Johnson, who was in the backseat. Trevizo had noticed that Johnson looked back and kept his eyes on the officers when they approached. She observed that Johnson was wearing clothing consistent with Crips membership and that he carried a scanner that could be used to evade police. Johnson had no identification, but volunteered that he had served time in prison for burglary and that he was from Eloy, Arizona, which the officer knew to be the home of a Crips gang.

Officer Trevizo, who wanted to pose some questions to Johnson about gang membership, asked him to get out of the car and patted him down. During the patdown, she discovered a gun near Johnson's waist. The Arizona Court of Appeals concluded that while Johnson was lawfully detained as a passenger in connection with the original stop, once Officer Trevizo decided to question him on a unrelated matter, the detention evolved into a consensual encounter so that the authority to frisk required not only reasonable suspicion that Johnson was armed and dangerous, but also reasonable suspicion that he had engaged, or was about to engage, in criminal activity.

The Supreme Court disagreed, unanimously concluding that when a driver or a passenger is lawfully detained in connection with a traffic stop, the police may pat down the person whenever police have reasonable suspicion that the person is armed and dangerous, regardless whether police also have cause to believe the vehicle's occupant is involved in criminal activity:

> A lawful roadside stop begins when a vehicle is pulled over for investigation of a traffic violation. The temporary seizure of driver and passengers ordinarily continues, and remains reasonable, for the duration of the stop. Normally, the stop ends when the police have no further need to control the scene, and inform the driver and passengers they are free to leave. An officer's inquiries into matters unrelated to the justification for the traffic stop . . . do not convert the encounter into something other than a lawful seizure, so long as those inquiries do not measurably extend the duration of the stop.
>
> In sum . . . a traffic stop of a car communicates to a reasonable passenger that he or she is not free to terminate the encounter with the police and move about at will. Nothing occurred in this case that would have conveyed to Johnson that, prior to the frisk, the traffic stop had ended or that he was otherwise free "to depart without police permission." Officer Trevizo surely was not constitutionally required to give Johnson an opportunity to depart the scene after he exited the vehicle without first ensuring that, in so doing, she was not permitting a dangerous person to get behind her.

Assuming *Wilson* was correctly decided, doesn't *Johnson* follow? If a police officer may lawfully detain a passenger in connection with a traffic violation, isn't a frisk necessary in circumstances where the officer has reason to believe the passenger is armed and dangerous? Do you think Officer Trevizo had adequate reason to believe that Johnson might be carrying a weapon?

3. "Special Needs"

b. Non-Police Searches

Insert the following note after Note 5, page 657:

5a. In Ontario v. Quon, ___ S.Ct. ___ (2010), the Supreme Court took up the question of what Fourth Amendment standards should apply when a government employer asserts the right to read text messages sent and received on a pager the employer owns and issues to an employee. Jeff Quon was a sergeant with the Ontario Police Department in California and in that capacity he was issued a pager by the City of Ontario. Pursuant to the City's service contract with its wireless service company, each of the pagers it issued was allotted a limited number of characters to be sent or received each month, after which usage would result in an additional fee. When a number of officers incurred overage fees for their pager usage, the Department reviewed transcripts of text messages sent or received in a two-month period by Quon and another employee for the purpose of determining whether the existing character limit was too low—that is, whether the overages were for work-related or personal messages. A review of the transcripts associated with Quon's pager revealed that many of the messages sent and received were not work related, and some were sexually explicit. Quon was allegedly disciplined. He thereafter brought suit, alleging, *inter alia*, violation of his Fourth Amendment rights.

The record before the Supreme Court established that the Ontario Police Department had a computer policy that made clear that users should have no expectation of privacy or confidentiality with regard to pager messages. Quon contended that he nevertheless reasonably expected that the contents of his pager messages would remain private based on a supervisor's statement to him that an audit of his usage would be unnecessary so long as Quon paid for the overage incurred in any month, which Quon had, in fact, done. The Supreme Court at the start declined to address the question of employees' privacy expectations *vis-à-vis* employer-provided technological equipment, determining that it was best in the circumstances of the case before it simply to assume that Quon had a reasonable expectation of privacy in the text messages:

> The Court must proceed with care when considering the whole concept of privacy expectations in communications made on electronic equipment owned by a government employer. The judiciary risks error by elaborating too fully on the Fourth Amendment implications of emerging technology before its role in society has become clear. *See, e.g.*, Olmstead v. United States, 277 U.S. 438 (1928), *overruled by* Katz v. United States, 389 U.S. 347, 353 (1967). In *Katz*, the Court relied on its own knowledge and experience to conclude that there is a reasonable expectation of privacy in a telephone booth. *See id.*, at 360-361 (Harlan, J., concurring). It is not so clear that courts at present are on so sure a ground. Prudence counsels caution before the facts in the instant case are used to establish far-reaching premises that define the existence, and extent, of privacy expectations enjoyed by employees when using employer-provided communication devices.

Id., at ___.

The Court reiterated that while individuals do not lose their Fourth Amendment rights merely because they work for the government instead of a private employer, special needs dictate that the Fourth Amendment standards in this context will be applied differently than in the context of ordinary police investigation. The Court then determined, assuming that

Quon had a reasonable expectation of privacy in the content of his pager messages, that because the search in this case was motivated by a legitimate, work-related purpose and because it was not overly intrusive in light of this justification, the search did not violate Quon's Fourth Amendment rights. The Court noted that the search was undertaken to determine whether the character limit in the City's wireless service contract was sufficient to meet its needs. "As for the scope of the search, reviewing the transcripts was reasonable because it was an efficient and expedient way to determine whether Quon's overages were the result of work-related messaging or personal use." The Court also noted that even assuming Quon had a reasonable expectation of privacy, a reasonable employee in his situation "would be aware that sound management principles might require the audit of messages to determine whether the pager was being appropriately used." *Id.*, at ___.

Insert the following material after Note 7, page 657:

8. Return to the facts of *Ferguson*. In that case, the Supreme Court found non-consensual searches by hospital personnel improper when there was at least some suspicion justifying the searches. In Samson v. California, 547 U.S. 843 (2006), the Court approved searches *by police officers* with *no* individualized suspicion. The decisive fact in *Samson* was the identity of the search targets: former prisoners released on parole.

California requires, as a condition of release, that parolees agree in writing to submit to warrantless and suspicionless searches. In an opinion by Justice Thomas, the Court found the searches constitutionally reasonable:

> . . . As the recidivism rate demonstrates, most parolees are ill prepared to handle the pressures of reintegration. Thus, most parolees require intense supervision. The California Legislature has concluded that, given the number of inmates the State paroles and its high recidivism rate, a requirement that searches be based on individualized suspicion would undermine the State's ability to effectively supervise parolees and protect the public from criminal acts by reoffenders. This conclusion makes eminent sense. Imposing a reasonable suspicion requirement, as urged by petitioner, would give parolees greater opportunity to anticipate searches and conceal criminality. This Court concluded that the incentive-to-conceal concern justified an "intensive" system for supervising probationers in Griffin [v. Wisconsin, 483 U.S. 868, 875 (1987)]. That concern applies with even greater force to a system of supervising parolees. See United States v. Reyes, 283 F.3d 446, 461 (2d Cir. 2002) (observing that the *Griffin* rationale "applies a fortiori" to "federal supervised release, which, in contrast to probation, is 'meted out in addition to, not in lieu of, incareration'"); United States v. Crawford, 372

F.3d 1048, 1077 (CA9 2004) (en banc) (Kleinfeld, J., concurring) (explaining that parolees, in contrast to probationers, "have been sentenced to prison for felonies and released before the end of their prison terms" and are "deemed to have acted more harmfully than anyone except those felons not released on parole"). . . .

Petitioner observes that the majority of States and the Federal Government have been able to further similar interests in reducing recidivism and promoting reintegration, despite having systems that permit parolee searches based upon some level of suspicion. Thus, petitioner contends, California's system is constitutionally defective by comparison. Petitioner's reliance on the practices of jurisdictions other than California, however, is misplaced. That some States and the Federal Government require a level of individualized suspicion is of little relevance to our determination whether California's supervisory system is drawn to meet its needs and is reasonable, taking into account a parolee's substantially diminished expectation of privacy.[4]

Nor is there merit to the argument that California's parole search law permits "a blanket grant of discretion untethered by any procedural safeguards," (STEVENS, J., dissenting). The concern that California's suspicionless search system gives officers unbridled discretion to conduct searches, thereby inflicting dignitary harms that arouse strong resentment in parolees and undermine their ability to reintegrate into productive society, is belied by California's prohibition on "arbitrary, capricious or harassing" searches. See [People v. Reyes, 968 P.2d 445, 450, 451 (Calif. 1998); see also Cal. Penal Code Ann. § 3067(d) (West 2000) ("It is not the intent of the Legislature to authorize law enforcement officers to conduct searches for the sole purpose of harassment"). The dissent's claim that parolees under California law are subject to capricious searches conducted at the unchecked "whim" of law enforcement officers, post, at 3, ignores this prohibition. Likewise, petitioner's concern that California's suspicionless search law frustrates reintegration efforts by permitting intrusions into the privacy interests of third parties is also unavailing because that concern would arise under a suspicion-based regime as well.

Justice Stevens' dissent, joined by Justices Souter and Breyer, contended that "our Fourth Amendment jurisprudence does not permit the conclusion, reached by the Court here for the first time, that a search

4. The dissent argues that, "once one acknowledges that parolees do have legitimate expectations of privacy beyond those of prisoners, our Fourth Amendment jurisprudence does not permit the conclusion, reached by the Court here for the first time, that a search supported by neither individualized suspicion nor 'special needs' is nonetheless 'reasonable.'" That simply is not the case. The touchstone of the Fourth Amendment is reasonableness, not individualized suspicion. Thus, while this Court's jurisprudence has often recognized that "to accommodate public and private interests some quantum of individualized suspicion is usually a prerequisite to a constitutional search or seizure," United States v. Martinez-Fuerte, 428 U.S. 543, 560 (1976), we have also recognized that the "Fourth Amendment imposes no irreducible requirement of such suspicion," id., at 561. Therefore, although this Court has only sanctioned suspicionless searches in limited circumstances, namely programmatic and special needs searches, we have never held that these are the only limited circumstances in which searches absent individualized suspicion could be "reasonable" under the Fourth Amendment. . . .

supported by neither individualized suspicion nor 'special needs' is nonetheless 'reasonable.'" *Id.*, at 858 (Stevens, J., dissenting). The dissenters found *Samson* flatly inconsistent with "special needs" cases like *Ferguson*:

> The suspicionless search is the very evil the Fourth Amendment was intended to stamp out. See Boyd v. United States, 116 U.S. 616, 625-630 (1886); see also, e.g., Indianapolis v. Edmond, 531 U.S. 32, 37 (2000). The pre-Revolutionary "writs of assistance," which permitted roving searches for contraband, were reviled precisely because they "placed 'the liberty of every man in the hands of every petty officer.'" *Boyd*, 116 U.S., at 625. While individualized suspicion "is not an irreducible component of reasonableness" under the Fourth Amendment, *Edmond*, 531 U.S., at 37, the requirement has been dispensed with only when programmatic searches were required to meet a "'special need' . . . divorced from the State's general interest in law enforcement." Ferguson v. Charleston, 532 U.S. 67, 79 (2001).
>
> Not surprisingly, the majority does not seek to justify the search of petitioner on "special needs" grounds. Although the Court has in the past relied on special needs to uphold warrantless searches of probationers, it has never gone so far as to hold that a probationer or parolee may be subjected to full search at the whim of any law enforcement officer he happens to encounter, whether or not the officer has reason to suspect him of wrongdoing. *Griffin*, after all, involved a search by a probation officer that was supported by reasonable suspicion. The special role of probation officers was critical to the analysis; "we deal with a situation," the Court explained, "in which there is an ongoing supervisory relationship—and one that is not, or at least not entirely, adversarial—between the object of the search and the decisionmaker." [483 U.S. at 879]. The State's interest or "special need," as articulated in *Griffin*, was an interest in supervising the wayward probationer's reintegration into society—not, or at least not principally, the general law enforcement goal of detecting crime.

Who has the better of the argument? Does *Samson* rest on the proposition that parolees have no constitutionally protected privacy? Or does it rest on the proposition that, so long as the *system* of searching parolees is reasonable—as California's bar on arbitrary or harassing searches might suggest—individual searches must be? If the latter, why didn't the Court require some evidence that such searches are carefully regulated? If *Samson* isn't a "special needs" case, what is its core justification?

4. Reasonableness and Police Use of Force

Insert the following material at the end of note 5 on page 668:

Note that the state announced shortly after the en banc decision that it would no longer pursue its case against Horiuchi, and both the panel opinion and the opinion of the en banc court were subsequently vacated as moot. See Ninth Circuit Vacates En Banc Ruling Allowing Trial in Ruby Ridge Shooting, Metropolitan News-Enterprise, Sept. 17, 2001, at 3; Idaho v. Horiuchi, 266 F.3d 979 (9th Cir. 2001)(en banc order).

SCOTT v. HARRIS

Certiorari to the United States Court of Appeals for the Eleventh Circuit
550 U.S. 372 (2007)

JUSTICE SCALIA delivered the opinion of the Court.

We consider whether a law enforcement official can, consistent with the Fourth Amendment, attempt to stop a fleeing motorist from continuing his public-endangering flight by ramming the motorist's car from behind. Put another way: Can an officer take actions that place a fleeing motorist at risk of serious injury or death in order to stop the motorist's flight from endangering the lives of innocent bystanders?

I

In March 2001, a Georgia county deputy clocked respondent's vehicle traveling at 73 miles per hour on a road with a 55-mile-per-hour speed limit. The deputy activated his blue flashing lights indicating that respondent should pull over. Instead, respondent sped away, initiating a chase down what is in most portions a two-lane road, at speeds exceeding 85 miles per hour. The deputy radioed his dispatch to report that he was pursuing a fleeing vehicle, and broadcast its license plate number. Petitioner, Deputy Timothy Scott, heard the radio communication and joined the pursuit along with other officers. In the midst of the chase, respondent pulled into the parking lot of a shopping center and was nearly boxed in by the various police vehicles. Respondent evaded the trap by making a sharp turn, colliding with Scott's police car, exiting the parking lot, and speeding off once again down a two-lane highway.

Following respondent's shopping center maneuvering, which resulted in slight damage to Scott's police car, Scott took over as the lead pursuit vehicle. Six minutes and nearly 10 miles after the chase had begun, Scott decided to attempt to terminate the episode by employing a "Precision Intervention Technique ('PIT') maneuver, which causes the fleeing vehicle to spin to a stop." Brief for Petitioner 4. Having radioed his supervisor for permission, Scott was told to "go ahead and take him out." Harris v. Coweta County, 433 F.3d 807, 811 (CA11 2005). Instead, Scott applied his push bumper to the rear of respondent's vehicle.[1] As a result, respondent lost control of his vehicle, which left the roadway, ran down an embankment, overturned, and crashed. Respondent was badly injured and was rendered a quadriplegic.

Respondent filed suit against Deputy Scott and others under 42 U.S.C. § 1983, alleging . . . use of excessive force resulting in an unreasonable seizure under the Fourth Amendment. In response, Scott filed a motion for summary judgment based on an assertion of qualified immunity. The District Court denied the motion. . . . On interlocutory appeal,[2] the United States Court of Appeals for the Eleventh Circuit affirmed the District Court's decision to allow respondent's Fourth Amendment claim against Scott to proceed to trial. Taking respondent's view of the facts as given, the Court of Appeals concluded that Scott's actions could constitute "deadly force" under Tennessee v. Garner, 471 U.S. 1 (1985), and that the use of such force in this context "would violate [respondent's] constitutional right to be free from excessive force during a seizure. Accordingly, a reasonable jury could find that Scott violated [respondent's] Fourth Amendment rights." 433 F.3d at 816. The Court of Appeals further concluded that "the law as it existed [at the time of the incident], was sufficiently clear to give reasonable law enforcement officers 'fair notice' that ramming a vehicle under these circumstances was unlawful." *Id.,* at 817. The Court of Appeals thus concluded that Scott was not entitled to qualified immunity. We granted certiorari, and now reverse.

II

In resolving questions of qualified immunity, courts are required to resolve a "threshold question: Taken in the light most favorable to the party asserting the injury, do the facts alleged show the officer's conduct violated a constitutional right? This must be the initial inquiry." Saucier v. Katz, 533 U.S. 194, 201 (2001). If, and only if, the court finds a violation

1. Scott says he decided not to employ the PIT maneuver because he was "concerned that the vehicles were moving too quickly to safely execute the maneuver." Brief for Petitioner 4. Respondent agrees that the PIT maneuver could not have been safely employed. See Brief for Respondent 9. It is irrelevant to our analysis whether Scott had permission to take the precise actions he took.

2. Qualified immunity is "an *immunity from suit* rather than a mere defense to liability; and like an absolute immunity, it is effectively lost if a case is erroneously permitted to go to trial." Mitchell v. Forsyth, 472 U.S. 511, 526 (1985). Thus, we have held that an order denying qualified immunity is immediately appealable even though it is interlocutory; otherwise, it would be "effectively unreviewable." *Id.,* at 527. . . .

of a constitutional right, "the next, sequential step is to ask whether the right was clearly established . . . in light of the specific context of the case." *Ibid.* Although this ordering contradicts "our policy of avoiding unnecessary adjudication of constitutional issues," United States v. Treasury Employees, 513 U.S. 454, 478 (1995), we have said that such a departure from practice is "necessary to set forth principles which will become the basis for a [future] holding that a right is clearly established." *Saucier, supra,* at 201.[4] We therefore turn to the threshold inquiry: whether Deputy Scott's actions violated the Fourth Amendment.

III

The first step in assessing the constitutionality of Scott's actions is to determine the relevant facts. As this case was decided on summary judgment, there have not yet been factual findings by a judge or jury, and respondent's version of events (unsurprisingly) differs substantially from Scott's version. When things are in such a posture, courts are required to view the facts and draw reasonable inferences "in the light most favorable to the party opposing the [summary judgment] motion." United States v. Diebold, Inc., 369 U.S. 654, 655 (1962) (per curiam). In qualified immunity cases, this usually means adopting (as the Court of Appeals did here) the plaintiff's version of the facts.

There is, however, an added wrinkle in this case: existence in the record of a videotape capturing the events in question. There are no allegations or indications that this videotape was doctored or altered in any way, nor any contention that what it depicts differs from what actually happened. The videotape quite clearly contradicts the version of the story told by respondent and adopted by the Court of Appeals.[5] For example, the Court of Appeals adopted respondent's assertions that, during the chase, "there was little, if any, actual threat to pedestrians or other motorists, as the roads were mostly empty and [respondent] remained in control of his vehicle." 433 F.3d at 815. Indeed, reading

4. . . . There has been doubt expressed regarding the wisdom of *Saucier's* decision to make the threshold inquiry mandatory, especially in cases where the constitutional question is relatively difficult and the qualified immunity question relatively straightforward. We need not address the wisdom of *Saucier* in this case, however, because the constitutional question with which we are presented is, as discussed *infra,* easily decided. Deciding that question first is thus the "better approach," [County of Sacramento v. Lewis, 523 U.S. 833, 841 n. 5 (1998)], regardless of whether it is required.

5. JUSTICE STEVENS suggests that our reaction to the videotape is somehow idiosyncratic, and seems to believe we are misrepresenting its contents. We are happy to allow the videotape to speak for itself. See Record 36, Exh. A, available at *http://www.supremecourtus.gov/opinions/video/scott_v_harris.rmvb* and in Clerk of Court's case file.

the lower court's opinion, one gets the impression that respondent, rather than fleeing from police, was attempting to pass his driving test:

> "Taking the facts from the non-movant's viewpoint, [respondent] remained in control of his vehicle, slowed for turns and intersections, and typically used his indicators for turns. He did not run any motorists off the road. Nor was he a threat to pedestrians in the shopping center parking lot, which was free from pedestrian and vehicular traffic as the center was closed. Significantly, by the time the parties were back on the highway and Scott rammed [respondent], the motorway had been cleared of motorists and pedestrians allegedly because of police blockades of the nearby intersections." *Id.*, at 815-816 (citations omitted).

The videotape tells quite a different story. There we see respondent's vehicle racing down narrow, two-lane roads in the dead of night at speeds that are shockingly fast. We see it swerve around more than a dozen other cars, cross the double-yellow line, and force cars traveling in both directions to their respective shoulders to avoid being hit. We see it run multiple red lights and travel for considerable periods of time in the occasional center left-turn-only lane, chased by numerous police cars forced to engage in the same hazardous maneuvers just to keep up. Far from being the cautious and controlled driver the lower court depicts, what we see on the video more closely resembles a Hollywood-style car chase of the most frightening sort, placing police officers and innocent bystanders alike at great risk of serious injury.

At the summary judgment stage, facts must be viewed in the light most favorable to the nonmoving party only if there is a "genuine" dispute as to those facts. Fed. Rule Civ. Proc. 56(c). As we have emphasized, "when the moving party has carried its burden under Rule 56(c), its opponent must do more than simply show that there is some metaphysical doubt as to the material facts . . . . Where the record taken as a whole could not lead a rational trier of fact to find for the nonmoving party, there is no genuine issue for trial." Matsushita Elec. Industrial Co. v. Zenith Radio Corp., 475 U.S. 574, 586-587 (1986) (footnote omitted). . . . When opposing parties tell two different stories, one of which is blatantly contradicted by the record, so that no reasonable jury could believe it, a court should not adopt that version of the facts for purposes of ruling on a motion for summary judgment.

That was the case here with regard to the factual issue whether respondent was driving in such fashion as to endanger human life. Respondent's version of events is so utterly discredited by the record that no reasonable jury could have believed him. The Court of Appeals should not have relied on such visible fiction; it should have viewed the facts in the light depicted by the videotape.

Judging the matter on that basis, we think it is quite clear that Deputy Scott did not violate the Fourth Amendment. Scott does not contest that his decision to terminate the car chase by ramming his bumper into respondent's vehicle constituted a "seizure." "[A] Fourth Amendment seizure [occurs] . . . when there is a governmental termination of freedom of movement through means intentionally applied." Brower v. County of Inyo, 489 U.S. 593, 596-597 (1989) (emphasis deleted). See also *id.*, at 597 ("If . . . the police cruiser had pulled alongside the fleeing car and sideswiped it, producing the crash, then the termination of the suspect's freedom of movement would have been a seizure"). It is also conceded, by both sides, that a claim of "excessive force in the course of making [a] . . . 'seizure' of [the] person . . . [is] properly analyzed under the Fourth Amendment's 'objective reasonableness' standard." Graham v. Connor, 490 U.S. 386, 388 (1989). The question we need to answer is whether Scott's actions were objectively reasonable.

Respondent urges us to analyze this case as we analyzed *Garner*. We must first decide, he says, whether the actions Scott took constituted "deadly force." . . . If so, respondent claims that *Garner* prescribes certain preconditions that must be met before Scott's actions can survive Fourth Amendment scrutiny: (1) The suspect must have posed an immediate threat of serious physical harm to the officer or others; (2) deadly force must have been necessary to prevent escape;[9] and (3) where feasible, the officer must have given the suspect some warning. See Brief for Respondent 17-18 (citing *Garner*, 471 U.S., at 9-12). Since these *Garner* preconditions for using deadly force were not met in this case, Scott's actions were *per se* unreasonable.

Respondent's argument falters at its first step; *Garner* did not establish a magical on/off switch that triggers rigid preconditions whenever an officer's actions constitute "deadly force." *Garner* was simply an application of the Fourth Amendment's "reasonableness" test, *Graham, supra,* at

9. Respondent, like the Court of Appeals, defines this second precondition as "'necessary to prevent escape,'" Harris v. Coweta County, 433 F.3d 807, 813 (CA11 2005), quoting *Garner*, 471 U.S., at 11. But that quote from *Garner* is taken out of context. The necessity described in *Garner* was, in fact, the need to prevent "serious physical harm, either to the officer or to others." *Ibid.* By way of example only, *Garner* hypothesized that deadly force may be used "if necessary to prevent escape" when the suspect is known to have "committed a crime involving the infliction or threatened infliction of serious physical harm," *ibid.*, so that his mere being at large poses an inherent danger to society. Respondent did not pose that type of inherent threat to society, since (prior to the car chase) he had committed only a minor traffic offense and, as far as the police were aware, had no prior criminal record. But in this case, unlike in *Garner*, it was respondent's flight itself (by means of a speeding automobile) that posed the threat of "serious physical harm . . . to others." *Ibid.*

388, to the use of a particular type of force in a particular situation. *Garner* held that it was unreasonable to kill a "young, slight, and unarmed" burglary suspect, 471 U.S., at 21, by shooting him "in the back of the head" while he was running away on foot, *id.,* at 4, and when the officer "could not reasonably have believed that [the suspect] . . . posed any threat," and "never attempted to justify his actions on any basis other than the need to prevent an escape," *id.,* at 21. Whatever *Garner* said about the factors that *might have* justified shooting the suspect in that case, such "preconditions" have scant applicability to this case, which has vastly different facts. "*Garner* had nothing to do with one car striking another or even with car chases in general . . . . A police car's bumping a fleeing car is, in fact, not much like a policeman's shooting a gun so as to hit a person." Adams v. St. Lucie County Sheriff's Dep't, 962 F.2d 1563, 1577 (CA11 1992) (Edmondson, J., dissenting), adopted by 998 F.2d 923 (CA11 1993) (en banc). Nor is the threat posed by the flight on foot of an unarmed suspect even remotely comparable to the extreme danger to human life posed by respondent in this case. Although respondent's attempt to craft an easy-to-apply legal test in the Fourth Amendment context is admirable, in the end we must still slosh our way through the factbound morass of "reasonableness." Whether or not Scott's actions constituted application of "deadly force," all that matters is whether Scott's actions were reasonable.

In determining the reasonableness of the manner in which a seizure is effected, "we must balance the nature and quality of the intrusion on the individual's Fourth Amendment interests against the importance of the governmental interests alleged to justify the intrusion." United States v. Place, 462 U.S. 696, 703 (1983). Scott defends his actions by pointing to the paramount governmental interest in ensuring public safety . . . . Thus, in judging whether Scott's actions were reasonable, we must consider the risk of bodily harm that Scott's actions posed to respondent in light of the threat to the public that Scott was trying to eliminate. Although there is no obvious way to quantify the risks on either side, it is clear from the videotape that respondent posed an actual and imminent threat to the lives of any pedestrians who might have been present, to other civilian motorists, and to the officers involved in the chase. It is equally clear that Scott's actions posed a high likelihood of serious injury or death to respondent—though not the near *certainty* of death posed by, say, shooting a fleeing felon in the back of the head, see *Garner, supra,* at 4 . . . . So how does a court go about weighing the perhaps lesser probability of injuring or killing numerous bystanders against the perhaps larger probability of injuring or killing a single person? We think it appropriate in this process to take into account not only the number of lives at risk, but also their relative culpability. It was respondent, after all, who intentionally placed himself and the public in danger by unlawfully engaging in the reckless, high-speed flight that ultimately produced the choice between two evils that Scott confronted. Multiple police cars, with blue lights flashing and sirens blaring, had been chasing respondent for nearly 10 miles, but he ignored their warning to stop. By contrast, those who might have been harmed had Scott not taken the action he did were entirely innocent. We have little difficulty in concluding it was reasonable for Scott to take the action that he did.[10]

But wait, says respondent: Couldn't the innocent public equally have been protected, and the tragic accident entirely avoided, if the police had simply ceased their pursuit? We think the police need not have taken that chance and hoped for the best. Whereas Scott's action—ramming respondent off the road—was *certain* to eliminate the risk that respondent posed to the public, ceasing pursuit was not. First of all, there would have been no way to convey convincingly to respondent that the chase was off, and that he was free to go. Had respondent looked in his rear-view mirror and seen the police cars deactivate their flashing lights and turn around, he would have had no idea whether they were truly letting him get away, or simply devising a new strategy for capture. Perhaps the police knew a shortcut he didn't know, and would reappear down the road to intercept him; or perhaps they were setting up a roadblock in his path. Given such uncertainty, respondent might have been just as likely to respond by continuing to drive recklessly as by slowing down and wiping his brow.

Second, we are loath to lay down a rule requiring the police to allow fleeing suspects to get away whenever they drive *so recklessly* that they put other people's lives in danger. It is obvious the perverse incentives such a rule would create: Every fleeing motorist would know that escape is within his grasp, if only he accelerates to 90 miles per hour, crosses the double-yellow line a few times, and runs a few red lights. The Constitution assuredly does not impose this invitation to impunity-earned-by-recklessness. Instead, we lay down a more sensible rule: A police officer's

10. The Court of Appeals cites Brower v. County of Inyo, 489 U.S. 593, 595 (1989), for its refusal to "countenance the argument that by continuing to flee, a suspect absolves a pursuing police officer of any possible liability for all ensuing actions during the chase," 433 F.3d at 816. The only question in *Brower* was whether a police roadblock constituted a *seizure* under the Fourth Amendment. In deciding that question, the relative culpability of the parties is, of course, irrelevant; a seizure occurs whenever the police are "responsible for the termination of [a person's] movement," 433 F.3d at 816, regardless of the reason for the termination. Culpability *is* relevant, however, to the *reasonableness* of the seizure—to whether preventing possible harm to the innocent justifies exposing to possible harm the person threatening them.

attempt to terminate a dangerous high-speed car chase that threatens the lives of innocent bystanders does not violate the Fourth Amendment, even when it places the fleeing motorist at risk of serious injury or death.

* * *

The car chase that respondent initiated in this case posed a substantial and immediate risk of serious physical injury to others; no reasonable jury could conclude otherwise. Scott's attempt to terminate the chase by forcing respondent off the road was reasonable, and Scott is entitled to summary judgment. The Court of Appeals' decision to the contrary is reversed.

It is so ordered.

JUSTICE GINSBURG, concurring.

I join the Court's opinion and would underscore two points. First, I do not read today's decision as articulating a mechanical, *per se* rule. The inquiry described by the Court is situation specific. Among relevant considerations: Were the lives and well-being of others (motorists, pedestrians, police officers) at risk? Was there a safer way, given the time, place, and circumstances, to stop the fleeing vehicle? "Admirable" as "[an] attempt to craft an easy-to-apply legal test in the Fourth Amendment context [may be]," the Court explains, "in the end we must still slosh our way through the factbound morass of 'reasonableness.'"

Second, were this case suitable for resolution on qualified immunity grounds, without reaching the constitutional question, JUSTICE BREYER's discussion would be engaging. In joining the Court's opinion, however, JUSTICE BREYER apparently shares the view that, in the appeal before us, the constitutional question warrants an answer. The video footage of the car chase, he agrees, demonstrates that the officer's conduct did not transgress Fourth Amendment limitations. Confronting [Saucier v. Katz, 533 U.S. 194 (2001)], therefore, is properly reserved for another day and case.

JUSTICE BREYER, concurring.

I join the Court's opinion with one suggestion and two qualifications. Because watching the video footage of the car chase made a difference to my own view of the case, I suggest that the interested reader take advantage of the link in the Court's opinion, ante, at 1775, n. 5, and watch it. Having done so, I do not believe a reasonable jury could, in this instance, find that Officer Timothy Scott (who joined the chase late in the day and did not know the specific reason why the respondent was being pursued) acted in violation of the Constitution.

Second, the video makes clear the highly fact-dependent nature of this constitutional determination. And that fact-dependency supports the argument that we should overrule the requirement, announced in Saucier v. Katz, 533 U.S. 194 (2001), that lower courts must first decide the "constitutional question" before they turn to the "qualified immunity question." See *id.*, at 200 ("The first inquiry must be whether a constitutional right would have been violated on the facts alleged"). Instead, lower courts should be free to decide the two questions in whatever order makes sense in the context of a particular case. Although I do not object to our deciding the constitutional question in this particular case, I believe that in order to lift the burden from lower courts we can and should reconsider *Saucier*'s requirement as well.

Sometimes (*e.g.*, where a defendant is clearly entitled to qualified immunity) *Saucier*'s fixed order-of-battle rule wastes judicial resources in that it may require courts to answer a difficult constitutional question unnecessarily. Sometimes (*e.g.*, where the defendant loses the constitutional question but wins on qualified immunity) that order-of-battle rule may immunize an incorrect constitutional ruling from review. Sometimes, as here, the order-of-battle rule will spawn constitutional rulings in areas of law so fact dependent that the result will be confusion rather than clarity. And frequently the order-of-battle rule violates that older, wiser judicial counsel "not to pass on questions of constitutionality . . . unless such adjudication is unavoidable." Spector Motor Service, Inc. v. McLaughlin, 323 U.S. 101, 105 (1944). . . .

Third, I disagree with the Court insofar as it articulates a *per se* rule. The majority states: "A police officer's attempt to terminate a dangerous high-speed car chase that threatens the lives of innocent bystanders does not violate the Fourth Amendment, even when it places the fleeing motorist at risk of serious injury or death." This statement is too absolute. As JUSTICE GINSBURG points out, whether a high-speed chase violates the Fourth Amendment may well depend upon more circumstances than the majority's rule reflects. With these qualifications, I join the Court's opinion.

JUSTICE STEVENS, dissenting.

. . . [E]ven though respondent's original speeding violation on a four-lane highway was rather ordinary, his refusal to stop and subsequent flight was a serious offense that merited severe punishment. It was not, however, a capital offense, or even an offense that justified the use of deadly force rather than an abandonment of the chase. The Court's concern about the "imminent threat to the lives of any pedestrians who might have been present," while surely valid in an appropriate case, should be discounted in a case involving a nighttime chase in an area where no pedestrians were present.

What would have happened if the police had decided to abandon the chase? We now know that they could have apprehended respondent later because they had his license plate number. Even if that were not true, and even if he would have escaped any punishment at all, the use of deadly force in this case was no more appropriate than the use of a deadly weapon against a fleeing felon in Tennessee v. Garner, 471 U.S. 1 (1985). In any event, any uncertainty about the result of abandoning the pursuit has not prevented the Court from basing its conclusions on its own factual assumptions. The Court attempts to avoid the conclusion that deadly force was unnecessary by speculating that if the officers had let him go, respondent might have been "just as likely" to continue to drive recklessly as to slow down and wipe his brow. That speculation is unconvincing as a matter of common sense and improper as a matter of law. . . . Indeed, rules adopted by countless police departments throughout the country are based on a judgment that differs from the Court's. See, e.g., App. to Brief for Georgia Association of Chiefs of Police, Inc., as Amicus Curiae A-52 ("During a pursuit, the need to apprehend the suspect should always outweigh the level of danger created by the pursuit. When the immediate danger to the public created by the pursuit is greater than the immediate or potential danger to the public should the suspect remain at large, then the pursuit should be discontinued or terminated . . . . Pursuits should usually be discontinued when the violator's identity has been established to the point that later apprehension can be accomplished without danger to the public"). . . .

The Court today sets forth a *per se* rule that presumes its own version of the facts: "A police officer's attempt to terminate a dangerous high-speed car chase *that threatens the lives of innocent bystanders* does not violate the Fourth Amendment, even when it places the fleeing motorist at risk of serious injury or death." Ante, at 1779 (emphasis added). Not only does that rule fly in the face of the flexible and case-by-case "reasonableness" approach applied in *Garner* and Graham v. Connor, 490 U.S. 386 (1989), but it is also arguably inapplicable to the case at hand, given that it is not clear that this chase threatened the life of any "innocent bystander." In my view, the risks inherent in justifying unwarranted police conduct on the basis of unfounded assumptions are unacceptable, particularly when less drastic measures—in this case, the use of stop sticks[9] or a simple warning issued from a loudspeaker—could have

9. "Stop sticks" are a device which can be placed across the roadway and used to flatten a vehicle's tires slowly to safely terminate a pursuit.

avoided such a tragic result. . . . [J]urors in Georgia should be allowed to evaluate the reasonableness of the decision to ram respondent's speeding vehicle in a manner that created an obvious risk of death and has in fact made him a quadriplegic at the age of 19.

I respectfully dissent.

NOTES AND QUESTIONS

1. Unlike most search and seizure doctrines, constitutional limits on police use of force are litigated in damages suits, not in suppression motions in criminal cases. Those damages suits are generally brought under 42 U.S.C. § 1983, which creates a federal cause of action against state and local officials for constitutional violations. Section 1983 doctrine gives police officers a qualified immunity from damages liability; the immunity applies unless the officer violated clearly established constitutional rules. In effect, qualified immunity means that legal close calls go to the police, not to civil plaintiffs. Cases like Scott v. Harris might be decided solely on qualified immunity grounds—the Justices might conclude that, whatever else the governing constitutional standard might be, it wasn't clearly established; it follows that Scott is immune from liability. Saucier v. Katz, 533 U.S. 194 (2001), rules out that approach: Appellate courts are instructed to determine the relevant constitutional law first, and only then to decide whether that law was or wasn't clearly established. In *Scott*, Justice Breyer takes issue with that approach to judicial decisionmaking.

2. Like *Scott*, County of Sacramento v. Lewis, 523 U.S. 833 (1998) involved a high-speed police chase of a fleeing vehicle (in *Lewis*, the fleeing vehicle was a motorcycle). As in *Scott*, the chase ended badly: The fleeing motorcyclist attempted a sharp left turn, the pursuing police car hit the brakes, and the car struck and killed a passenger who had been on the motorcycle. The Court held that the dead passenger had not been "seized," because the pursuing officer did not acquire physical control over him "through means intentionally applied"—the test defined by Brower v. Country of Inyo, 489 U.S. 593 (1989). Consequently, the relevant source of constitutional regulation in *Lewis* was the Fourteenth Amendment's due process clause, not the Fourth Amendment's ban on unreasonable searches and seizures. The *Lewis* Court relied on a line of cases barring police conduct that "shocks the conscience." See Rochin v. California, 342 U.S. 165 (1954). The key language follows:

> Just as a purpose to cause harm is needed for Eighth Amendment liability in a [case arising from a prison riot], so it ought to be needed for Due Process

> liability in a pursuit case. Accordingly, we hold that high-speed chases with no intent to harm suspects physically or to worsen their legal plight do not give rise to liability under the Fourteenth Amendment . . . . Regardless whether [the officer's] behavior offended the reasonableness held up by tort law or the balance struck in law enforcement's own codes of sound practice, it does not shock the conscience, and petitioners are not called upon to answer for it under § 1983.

Lewis, 523 U.S. at 854-855.

3. In *Scott*, the fleeing motorist *was* seized. The governing legal standard is thus different than in *Lewis*. Or is it? Justice Scalia describes the majority's "sensible rule" (note: a "rule," not a standard) as follows: "A police officer's attempt to terminate a dangerous high-speed car chase that threatens the lives of innocent bystanders does not violate the Fourth Amendment, even when it places the fleeing motorist at risk of serious injury or death." That test appears to turn on the officer's intent: Because Scott was "attempt[ing] to terminate a dangerous high-speed car chase," Scott's conduct is categorically reasonable. Good motives are all the Fourth Amendment requires in the context of high-speed chases, whether or not a "seizure" occurs.

Maybe. But the majority's description of its holding seems in tension, and maybe at odds, with the reasoning that supports that holding. Recall Justice Scalia's injunction to "slosh our way through the factbound morass of 'reasonableness.'" So which is it—does *Scott* define a rule, or a standard? Justice Ginsburg seems to think it's a standard. Justice Breyer apparently fears it's a rule. Stay tuned.

4. Notice that both *Lewis* and *Scott* emphasize police officers' intent—contrary to usual Fourth Amendment "reasonableness" analysis. Why? It would seem logical to focus on subjective intent in cases in which such intent varies from case to case, and in which the variations correlate with the reasonableness of the police conduct. Those conditions do not appear satisfied in high-speed chase cases. In those cases, the police intent is always the same: to apprehend the fleeing offender. The factors that differentiate reasonable from unreasonable police conduct are objective: the speed of the vehicles, the number and location of other vehicles on the roads, the presence or absence of pedestrians, and so on. Fourth Amendment analysis typically turns on such factors; the Court usually goes out of its way to bar consideration of police intent. Why are high-speed chases different?

5. Does *Scott* change the standard to be applied in more ordinary deadly force cases? Tennessee v. Garner, 471 U.S. 1 (1985), is not usually seen as an instance of the Court "slosh[ing] [its] way through the factbound morass

of 'reasonableness.'" But that is the way Justice Scalia describes it. After *Scott*, the *Garner* test (is there such a thing anymore?) seems more "fact-bound" than it did before.

6. At the heart of the Court's decision in *Scott* is a disagreement with the Court of Appeals about the facts. And at the heart of that disagreement is the now-famous videotape, the web address for which appears in footnote 5 in the majority opinion. How would *Scott* have been decided without the videotape? What does this case teach about the quality of appellate decisionmaking in the many cases with written records but no tape recordings?

E. Consent Searches

Insert the following notes and main case after Note 5 on page 678:

5a. In the following case the Court took up the question whether one occupant can consent to the search of a home as against the objection of another occupant who is present at the scene and expressly refuses to consent. Has the refusing party assumed the risk that the person with whom he lives might grant access to his home over his objection? Is it reasonable under these circumstances for police to proceed? The Court divided on these and other questions. Do the opinions below reveal a common approach to consent searches?

GEORGIA v. RANDOLPH

Certiorari to the Georgia Supreme Court
547 U.S. 103 (2006)

JUSTICE SOUTER delivered the opinion of the Court.

The Fourth Amendment recognizes a valid warrantless entry and search of premises when police obtain the voluntary consent of an occupant who shares, or is reasonably believed to share, authority over the area in common with a co-occupant who later objects to the use of evidence so obtained. Illinois v. Rodriguez, 497 U.S. 177 (1990); United States v. Matlock, 415 U.S. 164 (1974). The question here is whether such an evidentiary seizure is likewise lawful with the permission of one occupant when the other, who later seeks to suppress the evidence, is present at the scene and expressly refuses to consent. We hold that, in the circumstances here at issue, a physically present co-occupant's stated refusal to permit entry prevails, rendering the warrantless search unreasonable and invalid as to him.

I

Respondent Scott Randolph and his wife, Janet, separated in late May 2001, when she left the marital residence in Americus, Georgia, and went to stay with her parents in Canada, taking their son and some belongings. In July, she returned to the Americus house with the child, though the record does not reveal whether her object was reconciliation or retrieval of remaining possessions.

On the morning of July 6, she complained to the police that after a domestic dispute her husband took their son away, and when officers reached the house she told them that her husband was a cocaine user whose habit had caused financial troubles. She mentioned the marital problems and said that she and their son had only recently returned after a stay of several weeks with her parents. Shortly after the police arrived, Scott Randolph returned and explained that he had removed the child to a neighbor's house out of concern that his wife might take the boy out of the country again; he denied cocaine use, and countered that it was in fact his wife who abused drugs and alcohol.

One of the officers, Sergeant Murray, went with Janet Randolph to reclaim the child, and when they returned she not only renewed her complaints about her husband's drug use, but also volunteered that there were "'items of drug evidence'" in the house. Brief for Petitioner 3. Sergeant Murray asked Scott Randolph for permission to search the house, which he unequivocally refused.

The sergeant turned to Janet Randolph for consent to search, which she readily gave. She led the officer upstairs to a bedroom that she identified as Scott's, where the sergeant noticed a section of a drinking straw with a powdery residue he suspected was cocaine. He then left the house to get an evidence bag from his car and to call the district attorney's office, which instructed him to stop the search and apply for a warrant. When Sergeant Murray returned to the house, Janet Randolph withdrew her consent. The police took the straw to the police station, along with the Randolphs. After getting a search warrant, they returned to the house and seized further evidence of drug use, on the basis of which Scott Randolph was indicted for possession of cocaine.

He moved to suppress the evidence . . . . The trial court denied the motion, ruling that Janet Randolph had common authority to consent to the search. The Court of Appeals of Georgia reversed, and was itself sustained by the State Supreme Court . . . .

We granted certiorari to resolve a split of authority on whether one occupant may give law enforcement effective consent to search shared premises, as against a co-tenant who is present and states a refusal to permit the search. We now affirm.

II

To the Fourth Amendment rule ordinarily prohibiting the warrantless entry of a person's house as unreasonable *per se*, one "jealously and carefully drawn" exception, Jones v. United States, 357 U.S. 493, 499 (1958), recognizes the validity of searches with the voluntary consent of an individual possessing authority, *Rodriguez*, 497 U.S., at 181. . . . [T]he exception for consent extends even to entries and searches with the permission of a co-occupant whom the police reasonably, but erroneously, believe to possess shared authority as an occupant, *Rodriguez, supra,* at 186. None of our co-occupant consent-to-search cases, however, has presented the further fact of a second occupant physically present and refusing permission to search, and later moving to suppress evidence so obtained. The significance of such a refusal turns on the underpinnings of the co-occupant consent rule, as recognized since *Matlock*.

A

The defendant in that case was arrested in the yard of a house where he lived with a Mrs. Graff and several of her relatives, and was detained in a squad car parked nearby. When the police went to the door, Mrs. Graff admitted them and consented to a search of the house. 415 U.S., at 166. In resolving the defendant's objection to use of the evidence taken in the warrantless search, we said that "the consent of one who possesses common authority over premises or effects is valid as against the absent, nonconsenting person with whom that authority is shared." *Id.,* at 170. Consistent with our prior understanding that Fourth Amendment rights are not limited by the law of property, cf. Katz v. United States, 389 U.S. 347, 352-353 (1967), we explained that the third party's "common authority" is not synonymous with a technical property interest:

> "The authority which justified the third-party consent does not rest upon the law of property, with its attendant historical and legal refinement, but rests rather on mutual use of the property by persons generally having joint access

> or control for most purposes, so that it is reasonable to recognize that any of the co-inhabitants has the right to permit the inspection in his own right and that the others have assumed the risk that one of their number might permit the common area to be searched." 415 U.S., at 171, n. 7 (citations omitted).

The common authority that counts under the Fourth Amendment may thus be broader than the rights accorded by property law, although its limits, too, reflect specialized tenancy arrangements apparent to the police, see Chapman v. United States, 365 U.S. 610 (1961) (landlord could not consent to search of tenant's home).

The constant element in assessing Fourth Amendment reasonableness in the consent cases, then, is the great significance given to widely shared social expectations, which are naturally enough influenced by the law of property, but not controlled by its rules. *Matlock* accordingly not only holds that a solitary co-inhabitant may sometimes consent to a search of shared premises, but stands for the proposition that the reasonableness of such a search is in significant part a function of commonly held understanding about the authority that co-inhabitants may exercise in ways that affect each other's interests.

B

Matlock's example of common understanding is readily apparent. When someone comes to the door of a domestic dwelling with a baby at her hip, as Mrs. Graff did, she shows that she belongs there, and that fact standing alone is enough to tell a law enforcement officer or any other visitor that if she occupies the place along with others, she probably lives there subject to the assumption tenants usually make about their common authority when they share quarters. They understand that any one of them may admit visitors, with the consequence that a guest obnoxious to one may nevertheless be admitted in his absence by another. . . .

It is also easy to imagine different facts on which, if known, no common authority could sensibly be suspected. A person on the scene who identifies himself, say, as a landlord or a hotel manager calls up no customary understanding of authority to admit guests without the consent of the current occupant. . . . In these circumstances, neither state-law property rights, nor common contractual arrangements, nor any other source points to a common understanding of authority to admit third parties generally without the consent of a person occupying the premises. And when it comes to searching through bureau drawers, there will be instances in which even a person clearly belonging on premises as an occupant may lack any perceived authority to consent; "a child of eight might well be considered to have the power to consent to the police crossing the threshold into that part of the house where any caller, such as a pollster or salesman, might well be admitted," 4 LaFave § 8.4(c), at 207 (4th ed. 2004), but no one would reasonably expect such a child to be in a position to authorize anyone to rummage through his parents' bedroom.

C

Although we have not dealt directly with the reasonableness of police entry in reliance on consent by one occupant subject to immediate challenge by another, we took a step toward the issue in an earlier case dealing with the Fourth Amendment rights of a social guest arrested at premises the police entered without a warrant or the benefit of any exception to the warrant requirement. Minnesota v. Olson, 495 U.S. 91 (1990), held that overnight houseguests have a legitimate expectation of privacy in their temporary quarters because "it is unlikely that [the host] will admit someone who wants to see or meet with the guest over the objection of the guest," *id.*, at 99. If that customary expectation of courtesy or deference is a foundation of Fourth Amendment rights of a houseguest, it presumably should follow that an inhabitant of shared premises may claim at least as much, and it turns out that the co-inhabitant naturally has an even stronger claim.

To begin with, it is fair to say that a caller standing at the door of shared premises would have no confidence that one occupant's invitation was a sufficiently good reason to enter when a fellow tenant stood there saying, "stay out." Without some very good reason, no sensible person would go inside under those conditions. . . .

The visitor's reticence . . . would show not timidity but a realization that when people living together disagree over the use of their common quarters, a resolution must come through voluntary accommodation, not by appeals to authority. Unless the people living together fall within some recognized hierarchy, like a household of parent and child or barracks housing military personnel of different grades, there is no societal understanding of superior and inferior, a fact reflected in a standard formulation of domestic property law, that "[e]ach cotenant . . . has the right to use and enjoy the entire property as if he or she were the sole owner, limited only by the same right in the other cotenants." 7 R. Powell, Powell on Real Property § 50.03[1], p. 50-14 (M. Wolf gen. ed. 2005). . . .

D

Since the co-tenant wishing to open the door to a third party has no recognized authority in law or social practice to prevail over a present and objecting co-tenant, his disputed invitation, without more, gives a police officer no better claim to reasonableness in entering than the officer would have in the absence of any consent at all. . . .

[W]e recognize the consenting tenant's interest as a citizen in bringing criminal activity to light. And we understand a co-tenant's legitimate self-interest in siding with the police to deflect suspicion raised by sharing quarters with a criminal.

But society can often have the benefit of these interests without relying on a theory of consent that ignores an inhabitant's refusal to allow a warrantless search. The co-tenant acting on his own initiative may be able to deliver evidence to the police, and can tell the police what he knows, for use before a magistrate in getting a warrant. The reliance on a co-tenant's information instead of disputed consent accords with the law's general partiality toward "police action taken under a warrant [as against] searches and seizures without one," United States v. Ventresca, 380 U.S. 102, 107 (1965) . . . .

Nor should this established policy of Fourth Amendment law be undermined by the principal dissent's claim that it shields spousal abusers and other violent co-tenants who will refuse to allow the police to enter a dwelling when their victims ask the police for help. It is not that the dissent exaggerates violence in the home; we recognize that domestic abuse is a serious problem in the United States.

But this case has no bearing on the capacity of the police to protect domestic victims. . . . No question has been raised, or reasonably could be, about the authority of the police to enter a dwelling to protect a resident from domestic violence; so long as they have good reason to believe such a threat exists, it would be silly to suggest that the police would commit a tort by entering, say, to give a complaining tenant the opportunity to collect belongings and get out safely, or to determine whether violence (or threat of violence) has just occurred or is about to (or soon will) occur, however much a spouse or other co-tenant objected. . . . Thus, the question whether the police might lawfully enter over objection in order to provide any protection that might be reasonable is easily answered yes. The undoubted right of the police to enter in order to protect a victim, however, has nothing to do with the question in this case, whether a search with the consent of one co-tenant is good against another, standing at the door and expressly refusing consent. . . .

The dissent's red herring aside, we know, of course, that alternatives to disputed consent will not always open the door to search for evidence that the police suspect is inside. The consenting tenant may simply not disclose enough information, or information factual enough, to add up to a showing of probable cause, and there may be no exigency to justify fast action. But nothing in social custom or its reflection in private law argues for placing a higher value on delving into private premises to search for evidence in the face of disputed consent, than on requiring clear justification before the government searches private living quarters over a resident's objection. We therefore hold that a warrantless search of a shared dwelling for evidence over the express refusal of consent by a physically present resident cannot be justified as reasonable as to him on the basis of consent given to the police by another resident.

E

There are two loose ends, the first being the explanation given in *Matlock* for the constitutional sufficiency of a co-tenant's consent to enter and search: it "rests . . . on mutual use of the property by persons generally having joint access or control for most purposes, so that it is reasonable to recognize that any of the co-inhabitants has the right to permit the inspection in his own right . . . . " 415 U.S., at 171, n. 7. If *Matlock*' s co-tenant is giving permission "in his own right," how can his "own right" be eliminated by another tenant's objection? The answer appears in the very footnote from which the quoted statement is taken: the "right" to admit the police to which *Matlock* refers is not an enduring and enforceable ownership right as understood by the private law of property, but is instead the authority recognized by customary social usage as having a substantial bearing on Fourth Amendment reasonableness in specific circumstances. . . .

The second loose end is the significance of *Matlock* and *Rodriguez* after today's decision. Although the *Matlock* defendant was not present with the opportunity to object, he was in a squad car not far away; the *Rodriguez* defendant was actually asleep in the apartment, and the police might have roused him with a knock on the door before they entered with only the consent of an apparent co-tenant. If those cases are not to be undercut by today's holding, we have to admit that we are drawing a fine line; if a potential defendant with self-interest in objecting is in fact at the door and objects, the co-tenant's permission does not suffice for a reasonable search, whereas the potential objector, nearby but not invited to take part in the threshold colloquy, loses out.

This is the line we draw, and we think the formalism is justified. So long as there is no evidence that the police have removed the potentially objecting tenant from the entrance for the sake of avoiding a possible objection, there is practical value in the simple clarity of complementary rules, one recognizing the co-tenant's permission when there is no fellow occupant on hand, the other according dispositive weight to the fellow occupant's contrary indication when he expresses it.

III

This case invites a straightforward application of the rule that a physically present inhabitant's express refusal of consent to a police search is dispositive as to him, regardless of the consent of a fellow occupant. Scott Randolph's refusal is clear, and nothing in the record justifies the search on grounds independent of Janet Randolph's consent. The State does not argue that she gave any indication to the police of a need for protection inside the house that might have justified entry into the portion of the premises where the police found the powdery straw (which, if lawfully seized, could have been used when attempting to establish probable cause for the warrant issued later). Nor does the State claim that the entry and search should be upheld under the rubric of exigent circumstances, owing to some apprehension by the police officers that Scott Randolph would destroy evidence of drug use before any warrant could be obtained.

The judgment of the Supreme Court of Georgia is therefore affirmed.

It is so ordered.

JUSTICE ALITO took no part in the consideration or decision of this case.

JUSTICE BREYER, concurring.

If Fourth Amendment law forced us to choose between two bright-line rules, (1) a rule that always found one tenant's consent sufficient to justify a search without a warrant and (2) a rule that never did, I believe we should choose the first. That is because, as the Chief Justice's dissent points out, a rule permitting such searches can serve important law enforcement needs (for example, in domestic abuse cases) and the consenting party's joint tenancy diminishes the objecting party's reasonable expectation of privacy.

But the Fourth Amendment does not insist upon bright-line rules. Rather, it recognizes that no single set of legal rules can capture the ever changing complexity of human life. It consequently uses the general terms "unreasonable searches and seizures." And this Court has continuously emphasized that "reasonableness . . . is measured . . . by examining the totality of the circumstances." Ohio v. Robinette, 519 U.S. 33, 39 (1996).

The circumstances here include the following: The search at issue was a search solely for evidence. The objecting party was present and made his objection known clearly and directly to the officers seeking to enter the house. The officers did not justify their search on grounds of possible evidence destruction. And, as far as the record reveals, the officers might easily have secured the premises and sought a warrant permitting them to enter. See Illinois v. McArthur, 531 U.S. 326 (2001). Thus, the "totality of the circumstances" present here do not suffice to justify abandoning the Fourth Amendment's traditional hostility to police entry into a home without a warrant.

I stress the totality of the circumstances, however, because, were the circumstances to change significantly, so should the result. . . .

. . . Consider, for example, instances of domestic abuse. . . . If a possible abuse victim invites a responding officer to enter a home or consents to the officer's entry request, that invitation (or consent) itself could reflect the victim's fear about being left alone with an abuser. It could also indicate the availability of evidence, in the form of an immediate willingness to speak, that might not otherwise exist. In that context, an invitation (or consent) would provide a special reason for immediate, rather than later, police entry. And, entry following invitation or consent by one party ordinarily would be reasonable even in the face of direct objection by the other. That being so, contrary to the the Chief Justice's suggestion, today's decision will not adversely affect ordinary law enforcement practices.

Given the case-specific nature of the Court's holding, and with these understandings, I join the Court's holding and its opinion.

[JUSTICE STEVENS' concurring opinion is omitted.]

CHIEF JUSTICE ROBERTS, with whom JUSTICE SCALIA joins, dissenting.

The Court creates constitutional law by surmising what is typical when a social guest encounters an entirely atypical situation. The rule the majority fashions does not implement the high office of the Fourth Amendment to protect privacy, but instead provides protection on a random and happenstance basis, protecting, for example, a co-occupant who happens to be at the front door when the other occupant consents to a search, but not one napping or watching television in the next room.

And the cost of affording such random protection is great, as demonstrated by the recurring cases in which abused spouses seek to authorize police entry into a home they share with a nonconsenting abuser.

The correct approach to the question presented is clearly mapped out in our precedents: The Fourth Amendment protects privacy. If an individual shares information, papers, *or places* with another, he assumes the risk that the other person will in turn share access to that information or those papers *or places* with the government. And just as an individual who has shared illegal plans or incriminating documents with another cannot interpose an objection when that other person turns the information over to the government, just because the individual happens to be present at the time, so too someone who shares a place with another cannot interpose an objection when that person decides to grant access to the police, simply because the objecting individual happens to be present.

A warrantless search is reasonable if police obtain the voluntary consent of a person authorized to give it. Co-occupants have "assumed the risk that one of their number might permit [a] common area to be searched." United States v. Matlock, 415 U.S. 164, 171, n. 7 (1974). Just as Mrs. Randolph could walk upstairs, come down, and turn her husband's cocaine straw over to the police, she can consent to police entry and search of what is, after all, her home, too.

I

In Illinois v. Rodriguez, 497 U.S. 177 (1990), this Court stated that "[w] hat [a person] is assured by the Fourth Amendment . . . is not that no government search of his house will occur unless he consents; but that no such search will occur that is 'unreasonable.'" *Id.,* at 183. One element that can make a warrantless government search of a home "'reasonable'" is voluntary consent. *Id.,* at 184. Proof of voluntary consent "is not limited to proof that consent was given by the defendant," but the government "may show that permission to search was obtained from a third party who possessed common authority over or other sufficient relationship to the premises." *Matlock, supra,* at 171. Today's opinion creates an exception to this otherwise clear rule: A third-party consent search is unreasonable, and therefore constitutionally impermissible, if the co-occupant against whom evidence is obtained was present and objected to the entry and search.

This exception is based on what the majority describes as "widely shared social expectations" that "when people living together disagree over the use of their common quarters, a resolution must come through voluntary accommodation." But this fundamental predicate to the majority's analysis gets us nowhere: Does the objecting cotenant accede to the consenting cotenant's wishes, or the other way around? The majority's assumption about voluntary accommodation simply leads to the common stalemate of two gentlemen insisting that the other enter a room first.

Nevertheless, the majority is confident in assuming—confident enough to incorporate its assumption into the Constitution—that an invited social guest who arrives at the door of a shared residence, and is greeted by a disagreeable co-occupant shouting "'stay out,'" would simply go away. . . .

The fact is that a wide variety of differing social situations can readily be imagined, giving rise to quite different social expectations. A relative or good friend of one of two feuding roommates might well enter the apartment over the objection of the other roommate. The reason the invitee appeared at the door also affects expectations: A guest who came to celebrate an occupant's birthday, or one who had traveled some distance for a particular reason, might not readily turn away simply because of a roommate's objection. The nature of the place itself is also pertinent: Invitees may react one way if the feuding roommates share one room, differently if there are common areas from which the objecting roommate could readily be expected to absent himself. Altering the numbers might well change the social expectations: Invitees might enter if two of three co-occupants encourage them to do so, over one dissenter.

The possible scenarios are limitless, and slight variations in the fact pattern yield vastly different expectations about whether the invitee might be expected to enter or to go away. Such shifting expectations are not a promising foundation on which to ground a constitutional rule . . . .

And in fact the Court has not looked to such expectations to decide questions of consent under the Fourth Amendment, but only to determine when a search has occurred and whether a particular person has standing to object to a search. . . . [T]he social expectations concept has not been applied to all questions arising under the Fourth Amendment, least of all issues of consent. A criminal might have a strong expectation that his longtime confidant will not allow the government to listen to their private conversations, but however profound his shock might be upon betrayal, government monitoring with the confidant's consent is reasonable under the Fourth Amendment. See United States v. White, 401 U.S. 745, 752 (1971).

The majority suggests that "widely shared social expectations" are a "constant element in assessing Fourth Amendment reasonableness," *ante*, at 1521 (citing Rakas v. Illinois, 439 U.S. 128, 144, n. 12 (1978)), but that is not the case; the Fourth Amendment precedents the majority cites refer instead to a "legitimate expectation of *privacy*." *Ibid.* (emphasis added; internal quotation marks omitted). Whatever social expectation the majority seeks to protect, it is not one of privacy. The very predicate giving rise to the question in cases of shared information, papers, containers, or places is that privacy has been shared with another. Our common social expectations may well be that the other person will not, in turn, share what we have shared with them with another—including the police—but that is the risk we take in sharing. . . .

II

Our cases reflect this understanding. In United States v. White, we held that one party to a conversation can consent to government eavesdropping, and statements made by the other party will be admissible at trial. 401 U.S., at 752. This rule is based on privacy: "Inescapably, one contemplating illegal activities must realize and risk that his companions may be reporting to the police . . . . [I]f he has no doubts, or allays them, or risks what doubt he has, the risk is his." *Ibid.*

The Court has applied this same analysis to objects and places as well. In Frazier v. Cupp, 394 U.S. 731 (1969), a duffel bag "was being used jointly" by two cousins. *Id.*, at 740. The Court held that the consent of one was effective to result in the seizure of evidence used against both: "[I]n allowing [his cousin] to use the bag and in leaving it in his house, [the defendant] must be taken to have assumed the risk that [his cousin] would allow someone else to look inside." *Ibid.* . . .

The same analysis applies to the question whether our privacy can be compromised by those with whom we share common living space. If a person keeps contraband in common areas of his home, he runs the risk that his co-occupants will deliver the contraband to the police. In Coolidge v. New Hampshire, 403 U.S. 443 (1971), Mrs. Coolidge retrieved four of her husband's guns and the clothes he was wearing the previous night and handed them over to police. We held that these items were properly admitted at trial because "when Mrs. Coolidge of her own accord produced the guns and clothes for inspection, . . . it was not incumbent on the police to stop her or avert their eyes." *Id.*, at 489.

Even in our most private relationships, our observable actions and possessions are private at the discretion of those around us. A husband can request that his wife not tell a jury about contraband that she observed in their home or illegal activity to which she bore witness, but it is she who decides whether to invoke the testimonial marital privilege. Trammel v. United States, 445 U.S. 40, 53 (1980). . . .

There is no basis for evaluating physical searches of shared space in a manner different from how we evaluated the privacy interests in the foregoing cases, and in fact the Court has proceeded along the same lines in considering such searches. In *Matlock,* police arrested the defendant in the front yard of a house and placed him in a squad car, and then obtained permission from Mrs. Graff to search a shared bedroom for evidence of Matlock's bank robbery. 415 U.S., at 166. Police certainly could have assumed that Matlock would have objected were he consulted as he sat handcuffed in the squad car outside. And in *Rodriguez,* where Miss Fischer offered to facilitate the arrest of her sleeping boyfriend by admitting police into an apartment she apparently shared with him, 497 U.S., at 179, police might have noted that this entry was undoubtedly contrary to Rodriguez's social expectations. Yet both of these searches were reasonable under the Fourth Amendment because Mrs. Graff had authority, and Miss Fischer apparent authority, to admit others into areas over which they exercised control, despite the almost certain wishes of their present co-occupants.

The common thread in our decisions upholding searches conducted pursuant to third-party consent is an understanding that a person "assume[s] the risk" that those who have access to and control over his shared property might consent to a search. *Matlock,* 415 U.S., at 171, n. 7. . . .

In this sense, the risk assumed by a joint occupant is comparable to the risk assumed by one who reveals private information to another. If a person has incriminating information, he can keep it private in the face of a request from police to share it, because he has that right under the Fifth Amendment. If a person occupies a house with incriminating information in it, he can keep that information private in the face of a request from police to search the house, because he has that right under the Fourth Amendment. But if he shares the information—or the house—with another, that other can grant access to the police in each instance.

To the extent a person wants to ensure that his possessions will be subject to a consent search only due to his own consent, he is free to place these items in an area over which others do not share access and control, be it a private room or a locked suitcase under a bed. . . .

The law acknowledges that although we might not expect our friends and family to admit the government into common areas, sharing space entails risk. A person assumes the risk that his co-occupants—just as they might report his illegal activity or deliver his contraband to the government—might consent to a search of areas over which they have access and control.

III

The majority states its rule as follows: "[A] warrantless search of a shared dwelling for evidence over the express refusal of consent by a physically present resident cannot be justified as reasonable as to him on the basis of consent given to the police by another resident."

Just as the source of the majority's rule is not privacy, so too the interest it protects cannot reasonably be described as such. That interest is not protected if a co-owner happens to be absent when the police arrive, in the backyard gardening, asleep in the next room, or listening to music through earphones so that only his co-occupant hears the knock on the door. That the rule is so random in its application confirms that it bears no real relation to the privacy protected by the Fourth Amendment. . . . We should not embrace a rule at the outset that its *sponsors* appreciate will result in drawing fine, formalistic lines. . . .

The scope of the majority's rule is not only arbitrary but obscure as well. The majority repeats several times that a present co-occupant's refusal to permit entry renders the search unreasonable and invalid "as to him." This implies entry and search would be reasonable "as to" someone else, presumably the consenting co-occupant and any other absent co-occupants. The normal Fourth Amendment rule is that items discovered in plain view are admissible if the officers were legitimately on the premises; if the entry and search were reasonable "as to" Mrs. Randolph, based on her consent, it is not clear why the cocaine straw should not be admissible "as to" Mr. Randolph, as discovered in plain view during a legitimate search "as to" Mrs. Randolph. The majority's differentiation between entry focused on discovering whether domestic violence has occurred (and the consequent authority to seize items in plain view), and entry focused on searching for evidence of other crime, is equally puzzling. This Court has rejected subjective motivations of police officers in assessing Fourth Amendment questions, see Whren v. United States, 517 U.S. 806, 812-813 (1996), with good reason: The police do not need a particular reason to ask for consent to search, whether for signs of domestic violence or evidence of drug possession.

While the majority's rule protects something random, its consequences are particularly severe. The question presented often arises when innocent cotenants seek to disassociate or protect themselves from ongoing criminal activity. See, e.g., United States v. Hendrix, 595 F.2d 883, 884

(C.A.D.C. 1979) (wife asked police "to get her baby and take [a] sawed-off shotgun out of her house"); People v. Cosme, 48 N.Y.2d 286, 288-289, 293 (1979) (woman asked police to remove cocaine and a gun from a shared closet). Under the majority's rule, there will be many cases in which a consenting co-occupant's wish to have the police enter is overridden by an objection from another present co-occupant. What does the majority imagine will happen, in a case in which the consenting co-occupant is concerned about the other's criminal activity, once the door clicks shut? . . .

Perhaps the most serious consequence of the majority's rule is its operation in domestic abuse situations, a context in which the present question often arises. While people living together might typically be accommodating to the wishes of their cotenants, requests for police assistance may well come from coinhabitants who are having a disagreement. The Court concludes that because "no sensible person would go inside" in the face of disputed consent, and the consenting cotenant thus has "no recognized authority" to insist on the guest's admission, a "police officer [has] no better claim to reasonableness in entering than the officer would have in the absence of any consent at all." But the police officer's superior claim to enter is obvious: Mrs. Randolph did not invite the police to join her for dessert and coffee; the officer's precise purpose in knocking on the door was to assist with a dispute between the Randolphs — one in which Mrs. Randolph felt the need for the protective presence of the police. The majority's rule apparently forbids police from entering to assist with a domestic dispute if the abuser whose behavior prompted the request for police assistance objects.

The majority acknowledges these concerns, but dismisses them on the ground that its rule can be expected to give rise to exigent situations, and police can then rely on an exigent circumstances exception to justify entry. This is a strange way to justify a rule, and the fact that alternative justifications for entry might arise does not show that entry pursuant to consent is unreasonable. In addition, it is far from clear that an exception for emergency entries suffices to protect the safety of occupants in domestic disputes. See, e.g., United States v. Davis, 290 F.3d 1239, 1240- 1241 (C.A.10 2002) (finding no exigent circumstances justifying entry when police responded to a report of domestic abuse, officers heard no noise upon arrival, defendant told officers that his wife was out of town, and wife then appeared at the door seemingly unharmed but resisted husband's efforts to close the door).

Rather than give effect to a consenting spouse's authority to permit entry into her house to avoid such situations, the majority again alters established Fourth Amendment rules to defend giving veto power to the objecting spouse. In response to the concern that police might be turned away under its rule before entry can be justified based on exigency, the majority creates a new rule: A "good reason" to enter, coupled with one occupant's consent, will ensure that a police officer is "lawfully in the premises." As support for this "consent plus a good reason" rule, the majority cites a treatise, which itself refers only to emergency entries. *Ante,* at 1525- 1526 (citing 4 W. LaFave, Search and Seizure § 8.3(d), p. 161 (4th ed. 2004)). For the sake of defending what it concedes are fine, formalistic lines, the majority spins out an entirely new framework for analyzing exigent circumstances. Police may now enter with a "good reason" to believe that "violence (or threat of violence) has just occurred or is about to (or soon will) occur." *Ante,* at 1525. And apparently a key factor allowing entry with a "good reason" short of exigency is the very consent of one co-occupant the majority finds so inadequate in the first place. . . .

Considering the majority's rule is solely concerned with protecting a person who happens to be present at the door when a police officer asks his co-occupant for consent to search, but not one who is asleep in the next room or in the backyard gardening, the majority has taken a great deal of pain in altering Fourth Amendment doctrine, for precious little (if any) gain in privacy. Perhaps one day, as the consequences of the majority's analytic approach become clearer, today's opinion will be treated the same way the majority treats our opinions in *Matlock* and *Rodriguez*—as a "loose end" to be tied up. . . .

* * *

Our third-party consent cases have recognized that a person who shares common areas with others "assume[s] the risk that one of their number might permit the common area to be searched." *Matlock,* 415 U.S., at 171, n. 7. The majority reminds us, in high tones, that a man's home is his castle, but even under the majority's rule, it is not his castle if he happens to be absent, asleep in the keep, or otherwise engaged when the constable arrives at the gate. Then it is his co-owner's castle. And, of course, it is not his castle if he wants to consent to entry, but his co-owner objects. Rather than constitutionalize such an arbitrary rule, we should acknowledge that a decision to share a private place, like a decision to share a secret or a confidential document, necessarily entails the risk that those with whom we share may in turn choose to share—for their own protection or for other reasons—with the police.

I respectfully dissent.

[The dissenting opinions of JUSTICE SCALIA and JUSTICE THOMAS are omitted.]

NOTES AND QUESTIONS

1. Don't the dissenters have a point here? What interest is served by safeguarding the right of a home's occupant to override any consent to search given by his co-occupant—if, but only if, the objecting party happens to be at the door when the search is to take place? Is there any principled way to square the result in *Randolph* with the Court's decision in United States v. Matlock, 415 U.S. 164 (1974)? Suppose the two cases had arisen in the opposite order: Imagine that the Court had decided in *Randolph* that the search target's objection was decisive, notwithstanding his spouse's consent—and some years later, *Matlock* arose, forcing the Court to decide whether the police could evade *Randolph* by taking the search target to a nearby police car and only *then* asking the consent of another occupant of the target's house. Could one persuasively argue that the police conduct in *Matlock* was constitutionally reasonable?

If the answer is no—if these two decisions are contradictory—why didn't the Court simply overrule *Matlock*?

2. What do you think of the dissent's argument that the Court's decision will seriously complicate police responses to domestic violence? Police are often called to a home by one or more of the home's occupants, usually in circumstances that lead some members of the household to fear violence from other members of the household. Naturally, in such circumstances, some residents want to invite the police inside the home, and other residents object to any police entry. How are police officers supposed to respond? Is it reasonable to expect accurate on-the-spot assessments of the threat of violence in such situations? Might *Randolph* lead officers to underrate that threat?

3. Are you persuaded by the majority's evaluation of our widely shared social expectations regarding settings in which roommates, spouses, or family members disagree about admitting a visitor? Are you persuaded that this is the right way to define the contours of consent search doctrine?

4. Chief Justice Roberts argues that search targets assume the risk that those who share their homes may allow police to enter those homes when the targets would prefer that they chose differently. Is *that* the right way to define the contours of consent search doctrine? The defendant in United States v. White, 401 U.S. 745 (1971), assumed the risk that the informant in that case was an informant, just as the defendant in California v. Greenwood, 486 U.S. 35 (1988), assumed the risk that sanitation workers would

turn over his garbage to the police. Are those risks more readily assumable? Is *Randolph* consistent with *White* and *Greenwood*?

5. One way to address the issues in *Randoph* would be to combine consent analysis with, say, reasonable suspicion of the sort required to justify *Terry* frisks. Perhaps police searches based on co-occupants' consent should be permitted if, but only if, the police have some reasonable grounds to suspect criminal activity. Would that be a better standard than the one the Court applies in *Randolph*?

6. Reread the last paragraph of Justice Breyer's concurring opinion. Suppose the goal of the searching officer in Randolph was not to find evidence of crime but to protect a possible victim of domestic violence. Would Justice Breyer change his vote? Should he? See Brigham City v. Stuart, 547 U.S. 398 (2006), and the notes following, *supra,* at supplement pages 98-106.

Insert the following material after Note 4, page 682:

5. In at least one context, advance waivers of Fourth Amendment rights are enforceable. In California, parolees must agree in writing, as a condition of release, to permit warrantless and suspicionless searches. In Samson v. California, 547 U.S. 843 (2006), the Supreme Court upheld that requirement—though the Court noted that California law bars "arbitrary, capricious, or harassing" searches of parolees. In *Samson*, the bulk of the Court's opinion was devoted to explaining why parolees have less substantial Fourth Amendment privacy interests than most of the population. Does it follow that waivers executed in advance are improper when the waiving parties haven't already been convicted and imprisoned? Why do you suppose California law requires parolees' written consent?

F. Remedies

1. Limits on the Exclusionary Remedy

a. The "Good Faith" Exception

Insert the following notes and main case after Note 6 on page 695:

6a. Perhaps the Court has answered these questions, at least with regard to the negligent bookkeeping errors of police employees. Consider the following case:

HERRING v. UNITED STATES

Certiorari to the United States Court of Appeals for the Eleventh Circuit
129 S. Ct. 695 (2009)

CHIEF JUSTICE ROBERTS delivered the opinion of the Court.

The Fourth Amendment forbids "unreasonable searches and seizures," and this usually requires the police to have probable cause or a warrant before making an arrest. What if an officer reasonably believes there is an outstanding arrest warrant, but that belief turns out to be wrong because of a negligent bookkeeping error by another police employee? The parties here agree that the ensuing arrest is still a violation of the Fourth Amendment, but dispute whether contraband found during a search incident to that arrest must be excluded in a later prosecution.

Our cases establish that such suppression is not an automatic consequence of a Fourth Amendment violation. Instead, the question turns on the culpability of the police and the potential of exclusion to deter wrongful police conduct. Here the error was the result of isolated negligence attenuated from the arrest. We hold that in these circumstances the jury should not be barred from considering all the evidence.

I

On July 7, 2004, Investigator Mark Anderson learned that Bennie Dean Herring had driven to the Coffee County Sheriff's Department to retrieve something from his impounded truck. Herring was no stranger to law enforcement, and Anderson asked the county's warrant clerk, Sandy Pope, to check for any outstanding warrants for Herring's arrest. When she found none, Anderson asked Pope to check with Sharon Morgan, her counterpart in neighboring Dale County. After checking Dale County's computer database, Morgan replied that there was an active arrest warrant for Herring's failure to appear on a felony charge. Pope relayed the information to Anderson and asked Morgan to fax over a copy of the warrant as confirmation. Anderson and a deputy followed Herring as he left the impound lot, pulled him over, and arrested him. A search incident to the arrest revealed methamphetamine in Herring's pocket, and a pistol (which as a felon he could not possess) in his vehicle.

There had, however, been a mistake about the warrant. The Dale County sheriff's computer records are supposed to correspond to actual arrest warrants, which the office also maintains. But when Morgan went to the files to retrieve the actual warrant to fax to Pope, Morgan was unable to find it. She called a court clerk and learned that the warrant had been recalled five months earlier. Normally when a warrant is recalled the court clerk's office or a judge's chambers calls Morgan, who enters the information in the sheriff's computer database and disposes of the physical copy. For whatever reason, the information about the recall of the warrant for Herring did not appear in the database. Morgan immediately called Pope to alert her to the mixup, and Pope contacted Anderson over a secure radio. This all unfolded in 10 to 15 minutes, but Herring had already been arrested and found with the gun and drugs, just a few hundred yards from the sheriff's office.

Herring was indicted in the District Court for the Middle District of Alabama for illegally possessing the gun and drugs. . . . He moved to suppress the evidence. . . . The Magistrate Judge recommended denying the motion because the arresting officers had acted in a good-faith belief that the warrant was still outstanding. . . . The District Court adopted the Magistrate Judge's recommendation, and the Court of Appeals for the Eleventh Circuit affirmed. . . .

We now affirm the Eleventh Circuit's judgment. . . .

II

. . . For purposes of deciding this case . . . we accept the parties' assumption that there was a Fourth Amendment violation. The issue is whether the exclusionary rule should be applied.

A

The Fourth Amendment protects "[t]he right of the people to be secure in their persons, houses, papers, and effects, against unreasonable searches and seizures," but "contains no provision expressly precluding the use of evidence obtained in violation of its commands," Arizona v. Evans, 514 U.S. 1, 10 (1995). Nonetheless, our decisions establish an exclusionary rule that, when applicable, forbids the use of improperly obtained evidence at trial. See, *e.g.*, Weeks v. United States, 232 U.S. 383, 398 (1914). We have stated that this judicially created rule is "designed to safeguard Fourth Amendment rights generally through its deterrent effect." United States v. Calandra, 414 U.S. 338, 348 (1974). . . .

The Coffee County officers did nothing improper. Indeed, the error was noticed so quickly because Coffee County requested a faxed confirmation of the warrant.

The Eleventh Circuit concluded, however, that somebody in Dale County should have updated the computer database to reflect the recall of the arrest warrant. The court also concluded that this error was negligent, but did not find it to be reckless or deliberate. That fact is crucial to our holding that this error is not enough by itself to require "the extreme sanction of exclusion." [United States v. Leon, 468 U.S. 897, 916 (1984)].

B

1. The fact that a Fourth Amendment violation occurred—*i.e.*, that a search or arrest was unreasonable—does not necessarily mean that the exclusionary rule applies. Illinois v. Gates, 462 U.S. 213, 223 (1983). Indeed, exclusion "has always been our last resort, not our first impulse," Hudson v. Michigan, 547 U.S. 586, 591 (2006) . . . .

First, the exclusionary rule is not an individual right and applies only where it "'result[s] in appreciable deterrence.'" *Leon, supra,* at 909, (quoting *United States v. Janis,* 428 U.S. 433, 454 (1976)). . . .

In addition, the benefits of deterrence must outweigh the costs. *Leon, supra,* at 910. . . . The principal cost of applying the rule is, of course, letting guilty and possibly dangerous defendants go free—something that "offends basic concepts of the criminal justice system." *Leon, supra,* at 908. . . .

2. The extent to which the exclusionary rule is justified by these deterrence principles varies with the culpability of the law enforcement conduct. . . .

An error that arises from nonrecurring and attenuated negligence is . . . far removed from the core concerns that led us to adopt the rule in the first place. And in fact since *Leon,* we have never applied the rule to exclude evidence obtained in violation of the Fourth Amendment, where the police conduct was no more intentional or culpable than this.

3. To trigger the exclusionary rule, police conduct must be sufficiently deliberate that exclusion can meaningfully deter it, and sufficiently culpable that such deterrence is worth the price paid by the justice system. As laid out in our cases, the exclusionary rule serves to deter deliberate, reckless, or grossly negligent conduct, or in some circumstances recurring or systemic negligence. The error in this case does not rise to that level. . . .

4. We do not suggest that all recordkeeping errors by the police are immune from the exclusionary rule. In this case, however, the conduct at issue was not so objectively culpable as to require exclusion. . . .

If the police have been shown to be reckless in maintaining a warrant system, or to have knowingly made false entries to lay the groundwork for future false arrests, exclusion would certainly be justified under our cases should such misconduct cause a Fourth Amendment violation. We said as much in *Leon,* explaining that an officer could not "obtain a warrant on the basis of a 'bare bones' affidavit and then rely on colleagues who are ignorant of the circumstances under which the warrant was obtained to conduct the search." *Id.,* at 923, n. 24 (citing Whiteley v. Warden, Wyo. State Penitentiary, 401 U.S. 560, 568 (1971)). . . .

In a case where systemic errors were demonstrated, it might be reckless for officers to rely on an unreliable warrant system. See *Evans,* 514 U.S., at 17 (O'Connor, J., concurring) ("Surely it would *not* be reasonable for the police to rely ... on a recordkeeping system ... that *routinely* leads to false arrests" (second emphasis added)); *Hudson,* 547 U.S., at 604 (KENNEDY, J., concurring) ("If a *widespread pattern* of violations were shown ... there would be reason for grave concern" (emphasis added)). But there is no evidence that errors in Dale County's system are routine or widespread. . . .

Petitioner's claim that police negligence automatically triggers suppression cannot be squared with the principles underlying the exclusionary rule, as they have been explained in our cases. In light of our repeated holdings that the deterrent effect of suppression must be substantial and outweigh any harm to the justice system, *e.g., Leon,* 468 U.S., at 909-910, we conclude that when police mistakes are the result of negligence such as that described here, rather than systemic error or reckless disregard of constitutional requirements, any marginal deterrence does not "pay its way." *Id.,* at 907-908, n. 6 (internal quotation marks omitted). In such a case, the criminal should not "go free because the constable has blundered." People v. Defore, 242 N.Y. 13, 21 (1926) (opinion of the Court by Cardozo, J.).

The judgment of the Court of Appeals for the Eleventh Circuit is affirmed.

JUSTICE GINSBURG, with whom JUSTICE STEVENS, JUSTICE SOUTER, and JUSTICE BREYER join, dissenting.

. . . The exclusionary rule provides redress for Fourth Amendment violations by placing the government in the position it would have been in had there been no unconstitutional arrest and search. The rule thus strongly encourages police compliance with the Fourth Amendment in the future. The Court, however, holds the rule inapplicable because careless recordkeeping by the police—not flagrant or deliberate misconduct—accounts for Herring's arrest. . . .

I would not so constrict the domain of the exclusionary rule and would hold the rule dispositive of this case . . . .

The Court's discussion invokes a view of the exclusionary rule famously held by renowned jurists Henry J. Friendly and Benjamin Nathan Cardozo. Over 80 years ago, Cardozo, then seated on the New York Court of Appeals, commented critically on the federal exclusionary rule, which had not yet been applied to the States. He suggested that in at least some cases the rule exacted too high a price from the criminal justice system. See People v. Defore, 242 N.Y. 13, 24-25. In words often quoted, Cardozo questioned whether the criminal should "go free because the constable has blundered." *Id.*, at 21.

Judge Friendly later elaborated on Cardozo's query. "The sole reason for exclusion," Friendly wrote, "is that experience has demonstrated this to be the only effective method for deterring the police from violating the Constitution." The Bill of Rights as a Code of Criminal Procedure, 53 Calif. L. Rev. 929, 951 (1965). He thought it excessive, in light of the rule's aim to deter police conduct, to require exclusion when the constable had merely "blundered"—when a police officer committed a technical error in an on-the-spot judgment, *id.*, at 952, or made a "slight and unintentional miscalculation," *id.*, at 953 . . .

Others have described "a more majestic conception" of the Fourth Amendment and its adjunct, the exclusionary rule. [Arizona v. Evans, 514 U.S. 1, 18 (1995)] (STEVENS, J., dissenting). . . . I share that vision of the Amendment. . . .

Beyond doubt, a main objective of the rule "is to deter—to compel respect for the constitutional guaranty in the only effectively available way—by removing the incentive to disregard it." Elkins v. United States, 364 U.S. 206, 217 (1960). But the rule also serves other important purposes: It "enabl[es] the judiciary to avoid the taint of partnership in official lawlessness," and it "assur[es] the people—all potential victims of unlawful government conduct—that the government would not profit from its lawless behavior, thus minimizing the risk of seriously undermining popular trust in government." United States v. Calandra, 414 U.S. 338, 357 (1974) (Brennan, J., dissenting). . . .

The Court maintains that Herring's case is one in which the exclusionary rule could have scant deterrent effect and therefore would not "pay its way." *Ante*, at 704 (internal quotation marks omitted). I disagree. . . .

Electronic databases form the nervous system of contemporary criminal justice operations. In recent years, their breadth and influence have dramatically expanded. Police today can access databases that include not only the updated National Crime Information Center (NCIC), but also terrorist watchlists, the Federal Government's employee eligibility system, and various commercial databases. Moreover, States are actively expanding information sharing between jurisdictions. As a result, law enforcement has an increasing supply of information within its easy electronic reach.

The risk of error stemming from these databases is not slim. . . .

Inaccuracies in expansive, interconnected collections of electronic information raise grave concerns for individual liberty. "The offense to the dignity of the citizen who is arrested, handcuffed, and searched on a public street simply because some bureaucrat has failed to maintain an accurate computer data base" is evocative of the use of general warrants that so outraged the authors of our Bill of Rights. *Evans,* 514 U.S., at 23 (STEVENS, J., dissenting).

The Court assures that "exclusion would certainly be justified" if "the police have been shown to be reckless in maintaining a warrant system, or to have knowingly made false entries to lay the groundwork for future false arrests." This concession provides little comfort.

First, by restricting suppression to bookkeeping errors that are deliberate or reckless, the majority leaves Herring, and others like him, with no remedy for violations of their constitutional rights. There can be no serious assertion that relief is available under 42 U.S.C. § 1983. The arresting officer would be sheltered by qualified immunity, see Harlow v. Fitzgerald, 457 U.S. 800 (1982), and the police department itself is not liable for the negligent acts of its employees, see Monell v. New York City Dept. of Social Servs., 436 U.S. 658 (1978). Moreover, identifying the department employee who committed the error may be impossible.

Second, I doubt that police forces already possess sufficient incentives to maintain up-to-date records. The Government argues that police have no desire to send officers out on arrests unnecessarily, because arrests consume resources and place officers in danger. The facts of this case do not fit that description of police motivation. Here the officer wanted to arrest Herring and consulted the Department's records to legitimate his predisposition.

Third, even when deliberate or reckless conduct is afoot, the Court's assurance will often be an empty promise: How is an impecunious defendant to make the required showing? . . .

Negligent recordkeeping errors by law enforcement threaten individual liberty, are susceptible to deterrence by the exclusionary rule, and cannot be remedied effectively through other means. Such errors present no occasion to further erode the exclusionary rule. The rule "is needed to make the Fourth Amendment something real; a guarantee that does not carry with it the exclusion of evidence obtained by its violation is a chimera." *Calandra,* 414 U.S., at 361 (Brennan, J., dissenting). . . .

For the reasons stated, I would reverse the judgment of the Eleventh Circuit.

[JUSTICE BREYER's dissenting opinion, in which JUSTICE SOUTER joined, is omitted.]

NOTES AND QUESTIONS

1. Are you persuaded by the majority's analysis? In a portion of the dissent not excerpted here, Justice Ginsburg charged that the majority was ignoring a "foundational premise of tort law—that liability for negligence, *i.e.*, lack of due care, creates an incentive to act with greater care." Do you agree that by suppressing evidence in circumstances such as this, courts encourage police policymakers and systems managers better to monitor their recordkeeping systems and the people who operate them? Is there any reason to question this assumption? Do we need the exclusionary rule to make sure police forces have adequate incentives to keep their recordkeeping systems up to date?

2. As you will see, more than one doctrine limits application of the exclusionary rule. *Leon* and its progeny focus on the blameworthiness of police conduct and the need for deterrence. From a blameworthiness perspective, *Herring* looks like an easy case—in that this is not a situation where an overzealous officer has willfully trampled on Fourth Amendment rights. But to the extent that the majority is interested in reckless and grossly negligent recordkeeping, and also in providing the requisite amount of deterrence, is this case so easy? For one thing, will a future criminal defendant in Herring's situation be entitled to discovery into a department's recordkeeping system, so that he might establish that the injury he suffered was the result of recklessness or grossly negligent conduct? Is there a reason to think civil plaintiffs might be better positioned to pursue such matters?

3. Setting deterrence aside, Justice Ginsburg suggests that there is a more majestic conception of the exclusionary rule's purposes—that the rule provides a means for the judiciary to avoid the taint of official lawlessness and assures the public that the Government will not profit from its lawless behavior. But how are such concerns implicated in this case—where, as Chief Justice Roberts says, the officer involved did noth-

ing improper? Does Justice Ginsburg have a stronger argument based on deterrence or based on this majestic conception of the exclusionary rule?

4. Now consider Note 7 on page 695. Assume that the police officer on the street makes an isolated, negligent mistake, resulting in a search or seizure that would not otherwise have taken place. Should we treat such a mistake by a line officer in the same manner as the recordkeeping mistake of a non-uniformed police employee?

c. *"Fruit of the Poisonous Tree" Doctrine*

Insert the following notes and main case after Note 5 on page 724:

6. The Court wrestled with the meaning of attenuation, independent source, and other related matters in the following case, which addresses the proper remedy for a violation of the knock-and-announce rule. Recall that the Court was unanimous in each of the four decisions defining this Fourth Amendment rule. See *infra,* at 452. The question of remedy proved to be significantly more divisive:

HUDSON v. MICHIGAN

Certiorari to the Michigan Court of Appeals
547 U.S. 586 (2006)

JUSTICE SCALIA delivered the opinion of the Court with respect to Parts I, II, and III, and an opinion with respect to Part IV, in which CHIEF JUSTICE ROBERTS, JUSTICE THOMAS, and JUSTICE ALITO joined.

We decide whether violation of the "knock-and-announce" rule requires the suppression of all evidence found in the search.

I

Police obtained a warrant authorizing a search for drugs and firearms at the home of petitioner Booker Hudson. They discovered both. Large quantities of drugs were found, including cocaine rocks in Hudson's pocket. A loaded gun was lodged between the cushion and armrest of the chair in which he was sitting. Hudson was charged under Michigan law with unlawful drug and firearm possession.

This case is before us only because of the method of entry into the house. When the police arrived to execute the warrant, they announced their presence, but waited only a short time — perhaps "three to five seconds" — before turning the knob of the unlocked front door and entering Hudson's home. Hudson moved to suppress all the inculpatory evidence, arguing that the premature entry violated his Fourth Amendment rights.

The Michigan trial court granted his motion. On interlocutory review, the Michigan Court of Appeals reversed . . . . The Michigan Supreme Court denied leave to appeal. Hudson was convicted of drug possession. He renewed his Fourth Amendment claim on appeal, but the Court of Appeals rejected it and affirmed the conviction. The Michigan Supreme Court again declined review. We granted certiorari.

II

The common-law principle that law enforcement officers must announce their presence and provide residents an opportunity to open the door is an ancient one. See Wilson v. Arkansas, 514 U.S. 927, 931-932 (1995). Since 1917, when Congress passed the Espionage Act, this traditional protection has been part of federal statutory law, and is currently codified at 18 U.S.C. § 3109. . . . [I]in *Wilson*, we were asked whether the rule was also a command of the Fourth Amendment. Tracing its origins in our English legal heritage, we concluded that it was.

We recognized that the new constitutional rule we had announced is not easily applied. *Wilson* and cases following it have noted the many situations in which it is not necessary to knock and announce. It is not necessary when "circumstances presen[t] a threat of physical violence," or if there is "reason to believe that evidence would likely be destroyed if advance notice were given," *id.*, at 936, or if knocking and announcing would be "futile," Richards v. Wisconsin, 520 U.S. 385, 394 (1997). We require only that police "have a reasonable suspicion . . . under the particular circumstances" that one of these grounds for failing to knock and announce exists, and we have acknowledged that "[t]his showing is not high." *Ibid.*

When the knock-and-announce rule does apply, it is not easy to determine precisely what officers must do. How many seconds' wait are too few? Our "reasonable wait time" standard, see United States v. Banks, 540 U.S. 31, 41 (2003), is necessarily vague. . . . [I]t is unsurprising that, *ex ante*, police officers about to encounter someone who may try to harm them will be uncertain how long to wait.

Happily, these issues do not confront us here. From the trial level onward, Michigan has conceded that the entry was a knock-and-announce violation. The issue here is remedy. . . .

III

A

Suppression of evidence . . . has always been our last resort, not our first impulse. The exclusionary rule generates "substantial social costs," United States v. Leon, 468 U.S. 897, 907 (1984), which sometimes include setting the guilty free and the dangerous at large. . . . We have rejected "[i]ndiscriminate application" of the rule, *Leon, supra,* at 908, and have held it to be applicable only "where its remedial objectives are thought most efficaciously served," United States v. Calandra, 414 U.S. 338, 348 (1974)—that is, "where its deterrence benefits outweigh its 'substantial social costs,'" [Pennsylvania Bd. of Probation and Parole v.] Scott, [524 U.S. 357,] 363 [1998](quoting *Leon, supra,* at 907).

We did not always speak so guardedly. Expansive dicta in Mapp [v. Ohio, 367 U.S. 643 (1961)], for example, suggested wide scope for the exclusionary rule. See, e.g., 367 U.S., at 655 ("[A]ll evidence obtained by searches and seizures in violation of the Constitution is, by that same authority, inadmissible in a state court"). . . . But we have long since rejected that approach. . . .

[E]xclusion may not be premised on the mere fact that a constitutional violation was a "but-for" cause of obtaining evidence. Our cases show that but-for causality is only a necessary, not a sufficient, condition for suppression. In this case, of course, the constitutional violation of an illegal manner of entry was not a but-for cause of obtaining the evidence. Whether that preliminary misstep had occurred or not, the police would have executed the warrant they had obtained, and would have discovered the gun and drugs inside the house. But even if the illegal entry here could be characterized as a but-for cause of discovering what was inside, we have "never held that evidence is 'fruit of the poisonous tree' simply because 'it would not have come to light but for the illegal actions of the police.'" Segura v. United States, 468 U.S. 796, 815 (1984). Rather, but-for cause, or "causation in the logical sense alone," United States v. Ceccolini, 435 U.S. 268, 274 (1978), can be too attenuated to justify exclusion, *id.*, at 274-275. . . .

Attenuation can occur, of course, when the causal connection is remote. See, e.g., Nardone v. United States, 308 U.S. 338, 341 (1939). Attenuation also occurs when, even given a direct causal connection, the interest protected by the constitutional guarantee that has been violated would not be served by suppression of the evidence obtained. . . .

For this reason, cases excluding the fruits of unlawful warrantless searches say nothing about the appropriateness of exclusion to vindicate the interests protected by the knock-and-announce requirement. Until a valid warrant has issued, citizens are entitled to shield "their persons, houses, papers, and effects," U.S. Const., Amdt. 4, from the government's scrutiny. Exclusion of the evidence obtained by a warrantless search vindicates that entitlement. The interests protected by the knock-and-announce requirement are quite different—and do not include the shielding of potential evidence from the government's eyes.

One of those interests is the protection of human life and limb, because an unannounced entry may provoke violence in supposed self-defense by the surprised resident. See, e.g., McDonald v. United States, 335 U.S. 451, 460-461 (1948) (JACKSON, J., concurring). Another interest is the protection of property. . . . The knock-and-announce rule gives individuals "the opportunity to comply with the law and to avoid the destruction of property occasioned by a forcible entry." *Richards,* 520 U.S., at 393, n. 5. And thirdly, the knock-and-announce rule protects those elements of privacy and dignity that can be destroyed by a sudden entrance. . . . In other words, it assures the opportunity to collect oneself before answering the door.

What the knock-and-announce rule has never protected, however, is one's interest in preventing the government from seeing or taking evidence described in a warrant. Since the interests that were violated in this case have nothing to do with the seizure of the evidence, the exclusionary rule is inapplicable.

B

Quite apart from the requirement of unattenuated causation, the exclusionary rule has never been applied except "where its deterrence benefits outweigh its 'substantial social costs,'" *Scott,* 524 U.S., at 363 (quoting *Leon,* 468 U.S., at 907). The costs here are considerable. In addition to the grave adverse consequence that exclusion of relevant incriminating evidence always entails (viz., the risk of releasing dangerous criminals into society), imposing that massive remedy for a knock-and-announce violation would generate a constant flood of alleged failures to observe the rule, and claims that any asserted *Richards* justification for a no-knock entry, see 520 U.S., at 394, had inadequate support. The cost of entering this lottery would be small, but the jackpot enormous: suppression of all evidence, amounting in many cases to a get-out-of-jail-free card. Courts would experience as never before the reality that "[t]he exclusionary rule frequently requires extensive litigation to determine whether particular evidence must be excluded." *Scott, supra,* at 366.

Unlike the warrant or *Miranda* requirements, compliance with which is readily determined (either there was or was not a warrant; either the *Miranda* warning was given, or it was not), what constituted a "reasonable wait time" in a particular case, *Banks, supra,* at 41 (or, for that matter, how many seconds the police in fact waited), or whether there was "reasonable suspicion" of the sort that would invoke the *Richards* exceptions, is difficult for the trial court to determine and even more difficult for an appellate court to review.

Another consequence of the incongruent remedy Hudson proposes would be police officers' refraining from timely entry after knocking and announcing. As we have observed, the amount of time they must wait is necessarily uncertain. If the consequences of running afoul of the rule were so massive, officers would be inclined to wait longer than the law requires—producing preventable violence against officers in some cases, and the destruction of evidence in many others. . . .

Next to these "substantial social costs" we must consider the deterrence benefits, existence of which is a necessary condition for exclusion. . . . To begin with, the value of deterrence depends upon the strength of the incentive to commit the forbidden act. Viewed from this perspective, deterrence of knock-and-announce violations is not worth a lot. Violation of the warrant requirement sometimes produces incriminating evidence that could not otherwise be obtained. But ignoring knock-and-announce can realistically be expected to achieve absolutely nothing except the prevention of destruction of evidence and the avoidance of life-threatening resistance by occupants of the premises—dangers which, if there is even "reasonable suspicion" of their existence, suspend the knock-and-announce requirement anyway. Massive deterrence is hardly required.

It seems to us not even true, as Hudson contends, that without suppression there will be no deterrence of knock-and-announce violations at all. Of course even if this assertion were accurate, it would not necessarily justify suppression. Assuming (as the assertion must) that civil suit is not an effective deterrent, one can think of many forms of police misconduct that are similarly "undeterred." When, for example, a confessed suspect in the killing of a police officer, arrested (along with incriminating evidence) in a lawful warranted search, is subjected to physical abuse at the station house, would it seriously be suggested that the evidence must be excluded, since that is the only "effective deterrent"? And what, other than civil suit, is the "effective deterrent" of police violation of an already-confessed suspect's Sixth Amendment rights by denying him prompt access to counsel? Many would regard these violated rights as more significant than the right not to be intruded upon in one's nightclothes—and yet nothing but "ineffective" civil suit is available as a deterrent. . . .

We cannot assume that exclusion in this context is necessary deterrence simply because we found that it was necessary deterrence in different contexts and long ago. That would be forcing the public today to pay for the sins and inadequacies of a legal regime that existed almost half a century ago. Dollree Mapp could not turn to 42 U.S.C. § 1983 for meaningful relief; Monroe v. Pape, 365 U.S. 167 (1961), which began the slow but steady expansion of that remedy, was decided the same Term as *Mapp*. . . .

Hudson complains that "it would be very hard to find a lawyer to take a case such as this," Tr. of Oral Arg. 7, but 42 U.S.C. §1988(b) answers this objection. Since some civil-rights violations would yield damages too small to justify the expense of litigation, Congress has authorized attorney's fees for civil-rights plaintiffs. This remedy was unavailable in the heydays of our exclusionary-rule jurisprudence, because it is tied to the availability of a cause of action. . . .

Hudson points out that few published decisions to date announce huge awards for knock-and-announce violations. But this is an unhelpful statistic. Even if we thought that only large damages would deter police misconduct (and that police somehow are deterred by "damages" but indifferent to the prospect of large § 1988 attorney's fees), we do not know how many claims have been settled, or indeed how many violations have occurred that produced anything more than nominal injury. It is clear, at least, that the lower courts are allowing colorable knock-and-announce suits to go forward, unimpeded by assertions of qualified immunity. As far as we know, civil liability is an effective deterrent here, as we have assumed it is in other contexts.

Another development over the past half-century that deters civil-rights violations is the increasing professionalism of police forces, including a new emphasis on internal police discipline. . . . There have been "wide-ranging reforms in the education, training, and supervision of police officers." S. Walker, Taming the System: The Control of Discretion in Criminal Justice 1950-1990, p. 51 (1993). Numerous sources are now available to teach officers and their supervisors what is required of them under this Court's cases, how to respect constitutional guarantees in various situations, and how to craft an effective regime for internal discipline. Failure to teach and enforce constitutional requirements exposes municipalities to financial liability. Moreover, modern police forces are staffed with professionals; it is not credible to assert that internal discipline, which can limit successful careers, will not have a deterrent effect. There is also evidence that the increasing use of various forms of citizen review can enhance police accountability.

In sum, the social costs of applying the exclusionary rule to knock-and-announce violations are considerable; the incentive to such violations is minimal to begin with, and the extant deterrences against them are substantial—incomparably greater than the factors deterring warrantless entries when *Mapp* was decided. Resort to the massive remedy of suppressing evidence of guilt is unjustified.

IV

A trio of cases—Segura v. United States, 468 U.S. 796 (1984); New York v. Harris, 495 U.S. 14 (1990); and United States v. Ramirez, 523 U.S. 65 (1998)—confirms our conclusion that suppression is unwarranted in this case.

Like today's case, *Segura* involved a concededly illegal entry. Police conducting a drug crime investigation waited for Segura outside an apartment building; when he arrived, he denied living there. The police arrested him and brought him to the apartment where they suspected illegal activity. An officer knocked. When someone inside opened the door, the police entered, taking Segura with them. They had neither a warrant nor consent to enter, and they did not announce themselves as police—an entry as illegal as can be. Officers then stayed in the apartment for 19 hours awaiting a search warrant. Once alerted that the search warrant had been obtained, the police—still inside, having secured the premises so that no evidence could be removed—conducted a search. We refused to exclude the resulting evidence. We recognized that only the evidence gained from the particular violation could be excluded, and therefore distinguished the effects of the illegal entry from the effects of the legal search: "None of the information on which the warrant was secured was derived from or related in any way to the initial entry into petitioners' apartment. . . . " *Id.*, at 814. It was therefore "beyond dispute that the information possessed by the agents before they entered the apartment constituted an independent source for the discovery and seizure of the evidence now challenged." *Ibid.*

If the search in *Segura* could be "wholly unrelated to the prior entry," *ibid.*, when the only entry was warrantless, it would be bizarre to treat more harshly the actions in this case, where the only entry was with a warrant. . . .

In the second case, *Harris*, the police violated the defendant's Fourth Amendment rights by arresting him at home without a warrant, contrary to Payton v. New York, 445 U.S. 573 (1980). Once taken to the station house, he gave an incriminating statement. We refused to exclude it. Like the illegal entry which led to discovery of the evidence in today's case, the illegal arrest in *Harris* began a process that culminated in acquisition of the evidence sought to be excluded. While Harris's statement was "the product of an arrest and being in custody," it "was not the fruit of the fact that the arrest was made in the house rather than someplace else." *Id.*, at 20. Likewise here: While acquisition of the gun and drugs was the product of a search pursuant to warrant, it was not the fruit of the fact that the entry was not preceded by knock and announce.

United States v. Ramirez, *supra*, involved a claim that police entry violated the Fourth Amendment because it was effected by breaking a window. We ultimately concluded that the property destruction was, under all the circumstances, reasonable, but in the course of our discussion we unanimously said the following: "[D]estruction of property in the course of a search may violate the Fourth Amendment, even though the entry itself is lawful and the fruits of the search are not subject to suppression." *Id.*, at 71. Had the breaking of the window been unreasonable, the Court said, it would have been necessary to determine whether there had been a "sufficient causal relationship between the breaking of the window and the discovery of the guns to warrant suppression of the evidence." *Id.*, at 72, n. 3. What clearer expression could there be of the proposition that an impermissible manner of entry does not necessarily trigger the exclusionary rule?

For the foregoing reasons we affirm the judgment of the Michigan Court of Appeals.

JUSTICE KENNEDY, concurring in part and concurring in the judgment.

. . . Under our precedents the causal link between a violation of the knock-and-announce requirement and a later search is too attenuated to allow suppression. When, for example, a violation results from want of a 20-second pause but an ensuing, lawful search lasting five hours discloses evidence of criminality, the failure to wait at the door cannot properly be described as having caused the discovery of evidence.

Today's decision does not address any demonstrated pattern of knock-and-announce violations. If a widespread pattern of violations were shown, and particularly if those violations were committed against persons who lacked the means or voice to mount an effective protest, there would be reason for grave concern. Even then, however, the Court would have to acknowledge that extending the remedy of exclusion to all the evidence seized following a knock-and-announce violation would mean revising the requirement of causation that limits our discretion in applying the exclusionary rule. That type of extension also would have significant practical implications, adding to the list of issues requiring resolution at the criminal trial questions such as whether police officers entered a home after waiting 10 seconds or 20.

In this case the relevant evidence was discovered not because of a failure to knock-and-announce, but because of a subsequent search pursuant to a lawful warrant. The Court in my view is correct to hold that suppression was not required. While I am not convinced that Segura v. United States, 468 U.S. 796 (1984), and New York v. Harris, 495 U.S. 14 (1990), have as much relevance here as JUSTICE SCALIA appears to conclude, the Court's holding is fully supported by Parts I through III of its opinion. I accordingly join those Parts and concur in the judgment.

JUSTICE BREYER, with whom JUSTICE STEVENS, JUSTICE SOUTER, and JUSTICE GINSBURG join, dissenting. . . .

Reading our knock-and-announce cases in light of . . . foundational Fourth Amendment case law, it is clear that the exclusionary rule should apply. For one thing, elementary logic leads to that conclusion. We have held that a court must "conside[r]" whether officers complied with the knock-and-announce requirement "in assessing the reasonableness of a search or seizure." Wilson [v. Arkansas, 514 U.S. 927, 934 (1995)]. The Fourth Amendment insists that an unreasonable search or seizure is, constitutionally speaking, an illegal search or seizure. And ever since [Weeks v. United States, 232 U.S. 383 (1914)] (in respect to federal prosecutions) and [Mapp v. Ohio, 367 U.S. 643 (1961)] (in respect to state prosecutions), "the use of evidence secured through an illegal search and seizure" is "barred" in criminal trials. Wolf [v. Colorado, 338 U.S. 25, 28 (1949)] (citing *Weeks*); see *Mapp, supra,* at 655.

For another thing, the driving legal purpose underlying the exclusionary rule, namely, the deterrence of unlawful government behavior, argues strongly for suppression. . . . Without such a rule, as in *Mapp*, police know that they can ignore the Constitution's requirements without risking suppression of evidence discovered after an unreasonable entry. . . .

Of course, the State or the Federal Government may provide alternative remedies for knock-and-announce violations. But that circumstance was true of *Mapp* as well. . . .

The cases reporting knock-and-announce violations are legion. . . . Yet the majority . . . has failed to cite a single reported case in which a plaintiff has collected more than nominal damages solely as a result of a knock-and-announce violation. . . .

To argue, as the majority does, that new remedies, such as 42 U.S.C. § 1983 actions or better trained police, make suppression unnecessary is to argue that *Wolf*, not *Mapp*, is now the law. . . . Neither can the majority justify its failure to respect the need for deterrence . . . through its claim of "substantial social costs"—at least if it means that those "social costs" are somehow special here. The only costs it mentions are those that typically accompany any use of the Fourth Amendment's exclusionary principle: (1) that where the constable blunders, a guilty defendant may be set free (consider *Mapp* itself); (2) that defendants may assert claims where Fourth Amendment rights are uncertain . . . , and (3) that sometimes it is difficult to decide the merits of those uncertain claims. In fact, the "no-knock" warrants that are provided by many States, by diminishing uncertainty, may make application of the knock-and-announce principle less "cost[ly]" on the whole than application of comparable Fourth Amendment principles. . . .

The majority . . . argues that "the constitutional violation of an illegal manner of entry was not a but-for cause of obtaining the evidence." But taking causation as it is commonly understood in the law, I do not see how that can be so. Although the police might have entered Hudson's home lawfully, they did not in fact do so. Their unlawful behavior inseparably characterizes their actual entry; that entry was a necessary condition of their presence in Hudson's home; and their presence in Hudson's home was a necessary condition of their finding and seizing the evidence. . . .

The Court nonetheless accepts Michigan's argument that the requisite but-for causation is not satisfied in this case because, whether or not the constitutional violation occurred (what the Court refers to as a "preliminary misstep"), "the police would have executed the warrant they had obtained, and would have discovered the gun and drugs inside the house." As support for this proposition, Michigan rests on this Court's inevitable discovery cases.

This claim, however, misunderstands the inevitable discovery doctrine. Justice Holmes in [Silverthorne Lumber Co. v. United States, 251 U.S. 385 (1920)], in discussing an "independent source" exception, set forth the principles underlying the inevitable discovery rule. That rule does not refer to discovery that would have taken place if the police behavior in question had (contrary to fact) been lawful. The doctrine does not treat as critical what hypothetically could have happened had the police acted lawfully in the first place. Rather, "independent" or "inevitable" discovery refers to discovery that did occur or that would have occurred (1) despite (not simply in the absence of) the unlawful behavior and (2) independently of that unlawful behavior. The government cannot, for example, avoid suppression of evidence seized without a warrant (or pursuant to a defective warrant) simply by showing that it could have obtained a valid warrant had it sought one. . . .

[T]he Court's opinion reflects a misunderstanding of what "inevitable discovery" means when it says, "[i]n this case, of course, the constitutional violation of an illegal manner of entry was not a but-for cause of obtaining the evidence." The majority rests this conclusion on its next statement: "Whether that preliminary misstep has occurred or not, the police . . . would have discovered the gun and the drugs inside the house." Despite the phrase "of course," neither of these statements is correct. It is not true that, had the illegal entry not occurred, "police would have discovered the guns and drugs inside the house." Without that unlawful entry they would not have been inside the house; so there would have been no discovery.

Of course, had the police entered the house lawfully, they would have found the gun and drugs. But that fact is beside the point. The question is not what police might have done had they not behaved unlawfully. The question is what they did do. Was there set in motion an independent chain of events that would have inevitably led to the discovery and seizure of the evidence despite, and independent of, that behavior? The answer here is "no."

The majority . . . point[s] out that the officers here possessed a warrant authorizing a search. . . . The warrant in question was not a "no-knock" warrant . . . .

. . . It is difficult for me to see how the presence of a warrant that does not authorize the entry in question has anything to do with the "inevitable discovery" exception or otherwise diminishes the need to enforce the knock-and-announce requirement through suppression. . . .

The majority . . . says that evidence should not be suppressed once the causal connection between unlawful behavior and discovery of the evidence becomes too "attenuated." But the majority then makes clear that it is not using the word "attenuated" to mean what this Court's precedents have typically used that word to mean, namely, that the discovery of the evidence has come about long after the unlawful behavior or in an independent way . . . .

Rather, the majority gives the word "attenuation" a new meaning . . . . "Attenuation," it says, "also occurs when, even given a direct causal connection, the interest protected by the constitutional guarantee that has been violated would not be served by suppression of the evidence obtained." . . .

There are three serious problems with this argument. First, it does not fully describe the constitutional values, purposes, and objectives underlying the knock-and-announce requirement. That rule does help to protect homeowners from damaged doors; it does help to protect occupants from surprise. But it does more than that. It protects the occupants' privacy by assuring them that government agents will not enter their home without complying with those requirements . . . that diminish the offensive nature of any such intrusion. . . .

Second, whether the interests underlying the knock-and-announce rule are implicated in any given case is, in a sense, beside the point. As we have explained, failure to comply with the knock-and-announce rule renders the related search unlawful. And where a search is unlawful, the law insists upon suppression of the evidence consequently discovered . . . .

Third, the majority's interest-based approach departs from prior law. Ordinarily a court will simply look to see if the unconstitutional search produced the evidence. . . .

The United States, in its brief and at oral argument, has argued that suppression is "an especially harsh remedy given the nature of the violation in this case." Brief for United States as *Amicus Curiae* 28; see also *id.,* at 24. This argument focuses upon the fact that entering a house after knocking and announcing can, in some cases, prove dangerous to a police officer. Perhaps someone inside has a gun . . . . The majority adds that police officers about to encounter someone who may try to harm them will be "uncertain" as to how long to wait. *Ante,* at 9. It says that, "[i]f the consequences of running afoul" of the knock-and-announce "rule were so massive," i.e., would lead to the exclusion of evidence, then "officers would be inclined to wait longer than the law requires — producing preventable violence against officers in some cases." *Ante,* at 8-9.

To argue that police efforts to assure compliance with the rule may prove dangerous, however, is not to argue against evidence suppression. It is to argue against the validity of the rule itself. Similarly, to argue that enforcement means uncertainty, which in turn means the potential for dangerous and longer-than-necessary delay, is (if true) to argue against meaningful compliance with the rule.

The answer to the first argument is that the rule itself does not require police to knock or to announce their presence where police have a "reasonable suspicion" that doing so "would be dangerous or futile" or "would inhibit the effective investigation of the crime by, for example, allowing the destruction of evidence." Richards [v. Wisconsin, 520 U.S. 385, 394 (1997)].

The answer to the second argument is that States can, and many do, reduce police uncertainty while assuring a neutral evaluation of concerns about risks to officers or the destruction of evidence by permitting police to obtain a "no-knock" search warrant from a magistrate judge, thereby assuring police that a prior announcement is not necessary. . . .

Of course, even without such a warrant, police maintain the backup "authority to exercise independent judgment concerning the wisdom of a no-knock entry at the time the warrant is being executed." *Ibid.* "[I]f circumstances support a reasonable suspicion of exigency when the officers arrive at the door, they may go straight in." [United States v. Banks, 540 U.S. 31, 37 (2003)]. . . .

Consider this very case. The police obtained a search warrant that authorized a search, not only for drugs, but also for guns. If probable cause justified a search for guns, why would it not also have justified a no-knock warrant, thereby diminishing any danger to the officers? Why (in a State such as Michigan that lacks no-knock warrants) would it not have justified the very no-knock entry at issue here? Indeed, why did the prosecutor not argue in this very case that, given the likelihood of guns, the no-knock entry was lawful? From what I have seen in the record, he would have won. And had he won, there would have been no suppression here.

That is the right way to win. The very process of arguing the merits of the violation would help to clarify the contours of the knock-and-announce rule, contours that the majority believes are too fuzzy. . . .

It should be apparent by now that the three cases upon which JUSTICE SCALIA relies—Segura v. United States, 468 U.S. 796; New York v. Harris, 495 U.S. 14; and *Ramirez,* 523 U.S. 65—do not support his conclusion. . . .

[T]he timing of the warrant in *Segura* made no difference to the case. The relevant fact about the warrant there was that it was lawfully obtained and arguably set off an independent chain of events that led the police to seize the evidence. As noted, there is no such independent event, or intervening chain of events that would purge the taint of the illegal entry, present here. The search that produced the relevant evidence here is the very search that the knock-and-announce violation rendered unlawful. There simply is no "independent source." . . .

Neither does New York v. Harris, *supra,* support the Court's result. In *Harris,* police officers arrested the defendant at his home without a warrant, in violation of Payton v. New York, 445 U.S. 573 (1980). Harris made several incriminating statements: a confession in his home, a written inculpatory statement at the stationhouse, and a videotaped interview conducted by the district attorney at the stationhouse. 495 U.S., at 16. The trial court suppressed the statements given by Harris in the house and on the videotape, and the State did not challenge either of those rulings. The sole question in the case was whether the written statement given later at the stationhouse should also have been suppressed. The Court held that this later, outside-the-home statement "was admissible because Harris was in legal custody . . . and because the statement, while the product of an arrest and being in custody, was not the fruit of the fact that the arrest was made in the house rather than someplace else." *Id.*, at 20. . . .

How can JUSTICE SCALIA maintain that the evidence here—a gun and drugs seized in the home—is "'not the fruit'" of the illegal entry? The officers' failure to knock and announce rendered the entire search unlawful, and that unlawful search led to the discovery of evidence in petitioner's home. Thus, *Harris* compels the opposite result than that reached by the Court today. . . . Like the confession that was "excluded, as it should have been," in *Harris, id.*, at 20, the evidence in this case was seized in the home, immediately following the illegal entry. And like *Harris*, nothing in petitioner's argument would require the suppression of evidence obtained outside the home following a knock-and-announce violation . . . , precisely because officers have a remaining incentive to follow the rule to avoid the suppression of any evidence obtained from the very place they are searching.

I concede that United States v. Ramirez, 523 U.S. 65, offers the majority its last best hope. But not even that case can offer the majority significant support. The majority focuses on the Court's isolated statement that "destruction of property in the course of a search may violate the Fourth Amendment, even though the entry itself is lawful and the fruits of the search are not subject to suppression." *Ramirez, supra*, at 71. But even if I accept this dictum, the entry here is unlawful, not lawful. It is one thing to say (in an appropriate case) that destruction of property after proper entry has nothing to do with discovery of the evidence, and to refuse to suppress. It would be quite another thing to say that improper entry had nothing to do with discovery of the evidence in this case. . . .

There is perhaps one additional argument implicit in the majority's approach. . . . Leaving aside what I believe are invalid arguments based on precedent or the majority's own estimate that suppression is not necessary to deter constitutional violations, one is left with a simple unvarnished conclusion, namely, that in this kind of case, a knock-and-announce case, "[r]esort to the massive remedy of suppressing evidence of guilt is unjustified." Why is that judicial judgment, taken on its own, inappropriate? Could it not be argued that the knock-and-announce rule, a subsidiary Fourth Amendment rule, is simply not important enough to warrant a suppression remedy? Could the majority not simply claim that the suppression game is not worth the candle?

The answer, I believe, is "no." That "no" reflects history, a history that shows the knock-and-announce rule is important. That "no" reflects precedent, precedent that shows there is no pre-existing legal category of exceptions to the exclusionary rule into which the knock-and-announce cases might fit. That "no" reflects empirical fact, experience that provides confirmation of what common sense suggests: Without suppression there is little to deter knock-and-announce violations.

There may be instances in the law where text or history or tradition leaves room for a judicial decision that rests upon little more than an unvarnished judicial instinct. But this is not one of them. Rather, our Fourth Amendment traditions place high value upon protecting privacy in the home. They emphasize the need to assure that its constitutional protections are effective, lest the Amendment 'sound the word of promise to the ear but break it to the hope.' They include an exclusionary principle, which since *Weeks* has formed the centerpiece of the criminal law's effort to ensure the practical reality of those promises. That is why the Court should assure itself that any departure from that principle is firmly grounded in logic, in history, in precedent, and in empirical fact. It has not done so. That is why, with respect, I dissent.

NOTES AND QUESTIONS

1. Is *Hudson* primarily about remedies, or is it primarily about rights? The majority notes that the knock-and-announce rule is a recent addition to Fourth Amendment doctrine — the Court confirmed its existence only in 1995 — and that the rule is both vague and costly to apply. Those might be seen as reasons not to enforce the rule. Are they good reasons?

Maybe so. One might plausibly argue that the knock-and-announce principle should be folded into the broader requirement that searches be carried out reasonably: the same requirement that yields limits on police use of force against criminal suspects. Or, one might say that the rule amounts to a wise principle of policing that is best left out of Fourth Amendment litigation — because courts are poorly equipped to decide when no-knock entries are appropriate, and how long police should wait for a response when they aren't. But those arguments aren't obviously right. Fourth Amendment law focuses a great deal of attention on small distinctions involving what police officers saw and heard: Think of Arizona v. Hicks, 480 U.S. 321 (1987), which turned on the fact that a police officer had to turn over a piece of stereo equipment to see its serial number, or New York v. Belton, 453 U.S. 454 (1981), which authorized police searches of the passenger compartments of arrestees' cars but not the trunks. Perhaps that is as it should be: A detailed constitutional law of privacy is bound to draw fine lines. But if the law is to pay such close attention to what officers see and hear, it may be all the more important to pay close attention to what officers *do*—to the fear and indignity and violence that sometimes accompany police searches. That is what knock-and-announce doctrine is about. Why should that doctrine merit less stringent enforcement than other Fourth Amendment doctrines? Maybe it merits *more* stringent enforcement.

2. Is that how the Justices should think about the issue in *Hudson*? Should they ask themselves which doctrines require strict enforcement and which ones don't, and adjust the scope of the exclusionary rule accordingly?

3. As an application of existing doctrine, *Hudson* seems fairly straightforward. "Fruit of the poisonous tree" doctrine requires the suppression of all evidence the police obtained because of an unconstitutional search or seizure. Aside from a few unusual fact situations, violation of the knock-and-announce rule cannot possibly cause the police to discover evidence, unless the suspect is in the process of destroying that evidence at the time of police entry. There is no constitutional right to get rid of evidence—on the contrary: Police are permitted to enter homes without warrants when they have good reason to believe evidence might soon be destroyed. So unless the Fourth Amendment is to privilege behavior that amounts to criminal obstruction of justice, knock-and-announce violations should never be enforced by suppression of evidence found in the subsequent search.

Actually, there is one other circumstance in which a knock-and-announce violation might be the but-for cause of discovering evidence. *Hudson* itself is an example. Recall that a gun was stuffed between the cushion and armrest of Hudson's chair. It's far from inconceivable that a delayed entry might have led Hudson to grab the gun and, when the police entered, try to kill the arresting officer. Once again, a no-knock violation causes discovery of evidence only in cases in which the police behavior was reasonable—because the suspect either was eager to destroy evidence or posed a serious threat to police safety.

4. What does Justice Scalia mean by the claim that "civil liability is an effective deterrent here, as we have assumed it is in other contexts"? Does it seem the Court is applying the same standards when assessing the deterrent force of damages liability that it applies when assessing the deterrent value of the exclusionary rule? Should it?

5. A lot has changed in the forty-five years since the Justices held that the exclusionary rule applies in state-court criminal cases. The level of police training and professionalism is much higher. Victims of police misconduct have much more generous damages claims available to them. And political checks on police misbehavior are much more substantial: Congress has enacted federal statutes granting attorneys' fees to successful plaintiffs in police misconduct cases, 42 U.S.C. § 1988, and authorizing the Justice Department to seek injunctions against departments that show a pattern of misconduct. See 42 U.S.C. § 14141. Meanwhile, two dozen state legislatures have enacted laws banning racial profiling by police patrolling state roadways. See Police Foundation, Racial Profiling: The State of the Law, available at *http://www.policefoundation.org/pdf/racialprofiling.pdf*. Given these developments, is a broad exclusionary rule still necessary?

6. Causation-based analysis is not the only way Fourth Amendment law governs the scope of the exclusionary rule. Another approach focuses not on whether the police conduct in question caused discovery of the evidence, but on whether that conduct was blameworthy. The classic example of this approach is United States v. Leon, 468 U.S. 897 (1984). Is *Leon* the right model for a case like *Hudson*? Should the exclusionary rule apply if, but only if, the officers behaved in bad faith? If so, what would constitute bad faith in this context?

Chapter 6

The Fifth Amendment

B. The Contours of the Privilege Against Self-Incrimination

1. "No Person . . . Shall Be Compelled": The Meaning of Compulsion

Add the following paragraph at the conclusion of this subsection, at page 775:

At least one lower court has held, notwithstanding *McKune,* that a probation condition requiring disclosure of prior sex crimes (without a grant of immunity from prosecution for those crimes) cannot be enforced. In United States v. Antelope, 395 F.3d 1128 (9th Cir. 2005), the Ninth Circuit concluded that revocation of the defendant's probation was "more than merely hypothetical" (the government actually had pursued such revocation twice, based on Antelope's repeated refusal to disclose), and effectively "extend[ed the defendant's] term of incarceration," thus distinguishing the case from *McKune* on both counts. The court went on to state in dictum that Antelope should be entitled to immunity from prosecution based on any statements he might make in response to the "compulsion" of the probation revocation. The court rejected the government's argument that Chavez v. Martinez, 538 U.S. 760 (2003), see *infra* at pages 920 and 1033–1034, left the defendant without Fifth Amendment protection unless and until actually prosecuted based on his statements; according to the court, "the holding of *Chavez* is tightly bound to its § 1983 context," and does not alter the scope or application of immunity in the context of a criminal proceeding.

D. *Police Interrogation*

1. Police Interrogation and the *Miranda* Revolution

Insert the following note after Note 6 on page 839:

6a. *Miranda* is not the only doctrine that requires police officers to warn detained suspects of their rights prior to questioning them. Under Article 36 of the Vienna Convention on Consular Relations, which the United States ratified in 1969, police must notify officials in the relevant foreign consulate when they arrest a foreign national, and must inform the arrestee that he has a right to have officials in his consulate notified of his detention.

The key question in Sanchez-Llamas v. Oregon, 548 U.S. 331 (2006), was whether violation of these requirements would trigger a *Miranda*-style exclusionary rule. By a 6-3 vote, the Court answered that question in the negative. Chief Justice Roberts wrote for five of the six Justices in the majority:

> It would be startling if the Convention were read to require suppression. The exclusionary rule as we know it is an entirely American legal creation. More than 40 years after the drafting of the Convention, the automatic exclusionary rule applied in our courts is still "universally rejected" by other countries. Bradley, *Mapp* Goes Abroad, 52 Case W. Res. L. Rev. 375, 399-400 (2001). It is implausible that other signatories to the Convention thought it to require a remedy that nearly all refuse to recognize as a matter of domestic law. There is no reason to suppose that Sanchez-Llamas would be afforded the relief he seeks here in any of the other 169 countries party to the Vienna Convention.[3] . . .
>
> . . . Sanchez-Llamas argues that the language of the Convention implicitly requires a judicial remedy because it states that the laws and regulations governing the exercise of Article 36 rights "must enable *full effect* to be given to the purposes for which the rights . . . are intended," Art. 36(2), 21 U.S. T., at 101 (emphasis added). In his view, although "full effect" may not automatically require an exclusionary rule, it does require an appropriate judicial remedy of some kind . . . .

3. See Declaration of Ambassador Maura A. Harty, Annex 4 to Counter-Memorial of the United States in Case Concerning Avena and other Mexican Nationals (Mex. v. U.S.), 2004 I. C. J. No. 128, p. A386, P41 (Oct. 25, 2003) (Harty Declaration) ("With the possible exception of Brazil, we are not aware of a single country that has a law, regulation or judicial decision requiring that a statement taken before consular notification and access automatically must be excluded from use at trial" (footnote omitted)) . . . .

In a few cases, as several amici point out, the United Kingdom and Australia appear to have applied a discretionary rule of exclusion for violations of domestic statutes implementing the Vienna Convention . . . .

. . . [E]ven if Sanchez-Llamas is correct that Article 36 implicitly requires a judicial remedy, the Convention equally states that Article 36 rights "shall be exercised in conformity with the laws and regulations of the receiving State." Art. 36(2), 21 U.S. T., at 101. Under our domestic law, the exclusionary rule is not a remedy we apply lightly. . . . Because the rule's social costs are considerable, suppression is warranted only where the rule's "'remedial objectives are thought most efficaciously served.'" United States v. Leon, 468 U.S. 897, 908 (1984) (quoting United States v. Calandra, 414 U.S. 338, 348 (1974)). . . .

The few cases in which we have suppressed evidence for statutory violations do not help Sanchez-Llamas. In those cases, the excluded evidence arose directly out of statutory violations that implicated important Fourth and Fifth Amendment interests. McNabb [v. United States, 318 U.S. 332 (1943)], for example, involved the suppression of incriminating statements obtained during a prolonged detention of the defendants, in violation of a statute requiring persons arrested without a warrant to be promptly presented to a judicial officer. We noted that the statutory right was intended to "avoid all the evil implications of secret interrogation of persons accused of crime," 318 U.S., at 344, and later stated that *McNabb* was "responsive to the same considerations of Fifth Amendment policy that . . . faced us . . . as to the states" in *Miranda*, 384 U.S. at 463 . . . .

The violation of the right to consular notification, in contrast, is at best remotely connected to the gathering of evidence. Article 36 has nothing whatsoever to do with searches or interrogations. Indeed, Article 36 does not guarantee defendants any assistance at all. The provision secures only a right of foreign nationals to have their consulate informed of their arrest or detention—not to have their consulate intervene, or to have law enforcement authorities cease their investigation pending any such notice or intervention. In most circumstances, there is likely to be little connection between an Article 36 violation and evidence or statements obtained by police.

Moreover, the reasons we often require suppression for Fourth and Fifth Amendment violations are entirely absent from the consular notification context. We require exclusion of coerced confessions both because we disapprove of such coercion and because such confessions tend to be unreliable. We exclude the fruits of unreasonable searches on the theory that without a strong deterrent, the constraints of the Fourth Amendment might be too easily disregarded by law enforcement. The situation here is quite different. The failure to inform a defendant of his Article 36 rights is unlikely, with any frequency, to produce unreliable confessions. And unlike the search-and-seizure context—where the need to obtain valuable evidence may tempt authorities to transgress Fourth Amendment limitations—police win little, if any, practical advantage from violating Article 36. Suppression would be a vastly disproportionate remedy for an Article 36 violation.

548 U.S. at 343-349. Justice Breyer's dissent conceded that "a *Miranda*-style automatic exclusionary rule" is inappropriate, but insisted that "*sometimes* suppression could prove the only effective remedy."

Based on his opinion in *Sanchez-Llamas*, Chief Justice Roberts does not seem enamored of the exclusionary rule, either in its Fourth or Fifth Amendment incarnation. But the Chief Justice's claim of American exceptionalism—"the automatic exclusionary rule applied in our courts is still 'universally rejected' by other countries"—is a little misleading. The key word is "automatic." As footnote 3 acknowledges and as Justice Breyer's dissent elaborates, a *discretionary* exclusionary rule is far from unknown elsewhere in the world.

The popularity of discretionary suppression relative to automatic suppression is not hard to understand. Exclusionary rules have an obvious downside: They sometimes make guilty defendants unconvictable. That downside is especially large when the crime charged is especially serious—note that Sanchez-Llamas was charged with attempted murder, and many of the defendants in the Supreme Court's police interrogation cases have faced homicide charges. But discretionary suppression has its own downside: Only a rare judge will suppress a murderer's confession when the law gives her another option. The law of police interrogation would mean something—but only for low-level (or perhaps mid-level) crimes. Not in homicide cases.

Is that sensible? Is it just? Would *Miranda* be fairer if courts had discretion to overlook police violations? Which violations should be overlooked?

2. The Scope of *Miranda*

c. *What Constitutes a Valid* Miranda *Waiver?*

Warnings

Insert the following new material at the end of the section, at page 860:

A similar situation led to a similar result in Florida v. Powell, 130 S.Ct. 1195 (2010). Powell was warned by police in Tampa, Florida, as follows:

> "You have the right to remain silent. If you give up the right to remain silent, anything you say can be used against you in court. You have the right to talk to a lawyer before answering any of our questions. If you cannot afford to hire a lawyer, one will be appointed for you without cost and before any questioning. You have the right to use any of these rights at any time you want during this interview."

The Court, in a 7-2 decision authored by Justice Ginsburg, held that the warnings given were constitutionally adequate:

> The four warnings *Miranda* requires are invariable, but this Court has not dictated the words in which the essential information must be conveyed. . . .
>
> . . . The Tampa officers did not "entirely omi[t]," post, at 9, any information *Miranda* required them to impart. They informed Powell that he had "the right to talk to a lawyer before answering any of [their] questions" and "the right to use any of [his] rights at any time [he] want[ed] during th[e] interview." App. 3. The first statement communicated that Powell could consult with a lawyer before answering any particular question, and the second statement confirmed that he could exercise that right while the interrogation was underway. In combination, the two warnings reasonably conveyed Powell's right to have an attorney present, not only at the outset of interrogation, but at all times.
>
> To reach the opposite conclusion, i.e., that the attorney would not be present throughout the interrogation, the suspect would have to imagine an unlikely scenario: To consult counsel, he would be obliged to exit and reenter the interrogation room between each query. A reasonable suspect in a custodial setting who has just been read his rights, we believe, would not come to the counterintuitive conclusion that he is obligated, or allowed, to hop in and out of the holding area to seek his attorney's advice. Instead, the suspect would likely assume that he must stay put in the interrogation room and that his lawyer would be there with him the entire time.
>
> The Florida Supreme Court found the warning misleading because it believed the temporal language—that Powell could "talk to a lawyer before answering any of [the officers'] questions"—suggested Powell could consult with an attorney only before the interrogation started. In context, however, the term "before" merely conveyed when Powell's right to an attorney became effective—namely, before he answered any questions at all. Nothing in the words used indicated that counsel's presence would be restricted after the questioning commenced. Instead, the warning communicated that the right to counsel carried forward to and through the interrogation: Powell could seek his attorney's advice before responding to "*any* of [the officers'] questions" and "*at any time . . . during* th[e] interview." App. 3 (emphasis added). Although the warnings were not the *clearest possible* formulation of *Miranda*'s right-to-counsel advisement, they were sufficiently comprehensive and comprehensible when given a commonsense reading.
>
> Pursuing a different line of argument, Powell points out that most jurisdictions in Florida and across the Nation expressly advise suspects of the right to have counsel present both before and during interrogation. Brief for Respondent 41-44. If we find the advice he received adequate, Powell suggests, law enforcement agencies, hoping to obtain uninformed waivers, will be tempted to end-run *Miranda* by amending their warnings to introduce ambiguity. Brief for Respondent 50-53. But as the United States explained as *amicus curiae* in support of the State of Florida, "law enforcement agencies have little reason to assume the litigation risk of experimenting with novel *Miranda* formulations," Brief for United States as *Amicus Curiae* 6; instead, it is

> "desirable police practice" and "in law enforcement's own interest" to state warnings with maximum clarity, *id.*, at 12. See also *id.*, at 11 ("By using a conventional and precise formulation of the warnings, police can significantly reduce the risk that a court will later suppress the suspect's statement on the ground that the advice was inadequate.").
>
> For these reasons, "all . . . federal law enforcement agencies explicitly advise . . . suspect[s] of the full contours of each [*Miranda*] right, including the right to the presence of counsel during questioning." *Id.*, at 12. The standard warnings used by the Federal Bureau of Investigation are exemplary. They provide, in relevant part: "You have the right to talk to a lawyer for advice before we ask you any questions. You have the right to have a lawyer with you during questioning." *Ibid.*, n. 3 (internal quotation marks omitted). This advice is admirably informative, but we decline to declare its precise formulation necessary to meet *Miranda*'s requirements. Different words were used in the advice Powell received, but they communicated the same essential message.

Id., at 1204-06. In a footnote, Justice Ginsburg responded directly to the dissenting opinion of Justice Stevens, which was joined by Justice Breyer:

> JUSTICE STEVENS asserts that the Court today approves, for "the first time [,] . . . a warning which, if given its natural reading, entirely omitted an essential element of a suspect's rights." Post, at 9. See also post, at 12 ("[T]he warning entirely failed to inform [Powell] of the separate and distinct right 'to have counsel present during any questioning.'"). We find the warning in this case adequate, however, only because it communicated just what *Miranda* prescribed. JUSTICE STEVENS ascribes a different meaning to the warning Powell received, but he cannot credibly suggest that the Court regards the warning to have omitted a vital element of Powell's rights.

Id., at 1205 n. 5.

Invocations

Delete Note 7, page 871; renumber Note 8, page 872, as Note 7; and insert the following note after the renumbered Note 7:

8. The prophylactic protection provided by *Edwards* to suspects who have invoked their right to counsel may be absolute, but it is absolute only for so long as it lasts. In Maryland v. Shatzer, 130 S.Ct. 1213 (2010), the Supreme Court held that the *Edwards* protection may, under certain circumstances, last for only 14 days.

In *Shatzer*, the defendant was interrogated on August 7, 2003, about allegations that he had sexually abused his three-year-old son. At the time, Shatzer was already serving a prison sentence for an unrelated crime of sexual abuse of a child. Shatzer was read, and signed a waiver of, his *Miranda* rights. Shortly thereafter, Shatzer told the interrogating officer that he did not want to speak without an attorney. The officer ended the interrogation, and Shatzer was returned to the general prison population.

On March 2, 2006, more than two-and-a-half years later, a different detective obtained new information from Shatzer's son about the sexual abuse he had suffered. The detective went to the prison where Shatzer had since been transferred and sought to interview Shatzer. Shatzer expressed surprise because he thought the investigation had been closed, but the detective explained that they had reopened it. The detective read Shatzer his *Miranda* warnings, and obtained a written waiver. Shatzer then admitted to performing sexual acts in front of his son. Five days later, on March 7, Shatzer—after again receiving and again waiving his *Miranda* rights—confessed to sexual abuse of his son. Shatzer was convicted at trial of sexual child abuse.

The issue before the Court was whether *Edwards* rendered Shatzer's March 2006 statements inadmissible. All nine Justices agreed that it did not. Justice Scalia, writing for seven Justices, engaged in an explicit cost-benefit analysis to conclude that *Edwards* should not reach so far:

> When, unlike what happened in [*Edwards*, *Roberson*, and *Minnick*], a suspect has been released from his pretrial custody and has returned to his normal life for some time before the later attempted interrogation, there is little reason to think that his change of heart regarding interrogation without counsel has been coerced. He has no longer been isolated. He has likely been able to seek advice from an attorney, family members, and friends. And he knows from his earlier experience that he need only demand counsel to bring the interrogation to a halt; and that investigative custody does not last indefinitely. In these circumstances, it is far fetched to think that a police officer's asking the suspect whether he would like to waive his *Miranda* rights will any more "wear down the accused," *Smith* v. *Illinois*, 469 U.S. 91, 98 (1984) *(per curiam)*, than did the first such request at the original attempted interrogation—which is of course not deemed coercive. His change of heart is less likely attributable to "badgering" than it is to the fact that further deliberation in familiar surroundings has caused him to believe (rightly or wrongly) that cooperating with the investigation is in his interest. Uncritical extension of *Edwards* to this situation would not significantly increase the number of genuinely coerced confessions excluded. . . .
>
> At the same time that extending the *Edwards* rule yields diminished benefits, extending the rule also increases its costs: the in-fact voluntary confessions it excludes from trial, and the voluntary confessions it deters law

> enforcement officers from even trying to obtain. Voluntary confessions are not merely "a proper element in law enforcement," *Miranda, supra*, at 478, they are an "unmitigated good," *McNeil*, 501 U.S., at 181, "'essential to society's compelling interest in finding, convicting, and punishing those who violate the law,'" *ibid.* (quoting *Moran* v. *Burbine*, 475 U.S. 412, 426 (1986)).
>
> The only logical endpoint of *Edwards* disability is termination of *Miranda* custody and any of its lingering effects. Without that limitation—and barring some purely arbitrary time-limit—every *Edwards* prohibition of custodial interrogation of a particular suspect would be eternal. The prohibition applies, of course, when the subsequent interrogation pertains to a different crime, *Roberson, supra*, when it is conducted by a different law enforcement authority, *Minnick*, 498 U.S. 146, and even when the suspect has met with an attorney after the first interrogation, *ibid.* And it not only prevents questioning *ex ante;* it would render invalid *ex post*, confessions invited and obtained from suspects who (unbeknownst to the interrogators) have acquired *Edwards* immunity previously in connection with any offense in any jurisdiction. In a country that harbors a large number of repeat offenders, this consequence is disastrous.

Id., at 1221-22. In a separate part of the opinion joined by eight of the Justices, Justice Scalia also concluded that Shatzer's return to the general prison population after the August 2003 invocation of his right to counsel represented a break in "custody," noting that it placed Shatzer back into his usual prison routine and removed him from the direct control of the interrogating officer.

Finally, Justice Scalia declared it "impractical" to leave "for clarification in future case-by-case adjudication" the issue of just how long a break in custody might be required to terminate the *Edwards* protection:

> [L]aw enforcement officers need to know, with certainty and beforehand, when renewed interrogation is lawful. . . .
>
> . . . We think it appropriate to specify a period of time . . . . It seems to us that period is 14 days. That provides plenty of time for the suspect to get reacclimated to his normal life, to consult with friends and counsel, and to shake off any residual coercive effects of his prior custody.
>
> The 14-day limitation meets Shatzer's concern that a break-in-custody rule lends itself to police abuse. He envisions that once a suspect invokes his *Miranda* right to counsel, the police will release the suspect briefly (to end the *Edwards* presumption) and then promptly bring him back into custody for reinterrogation. But once the suspect has been out of custody long enough (14 days) to eliminate its coercive effect, there will be nothing to gain by such gamesmanship—nothing, that is, except the entirely appropriate gain of being able to interrogate a suspect who has made a valid waiver of his *Miranda* rights.

Id., at 1222-23. Justice Scalia reserved, for another day, the question whether mere passage of time, without a break in custody, might likewise end the *Edwards* protection. *Id.*, at 1222 n. 4.

Justice Thomas concurred in the judgment because he believed that *Edwards*'s protection should not necessarily last for even 14 days after a break in "custody," and Justice Stevens concurred in the judgment because he believed that *Edwards*'s protection should not necessarily expire at the end of 14 days after a break in "custody."

Keep in mind — for whatever it's worth — that the *Shatzer* ruling affects only the prophylactic protection of *Edwards*. Suspects like Shatzer may still argue that their subsequent *Miranda* waivers are involuntary in fact and thus invalid.

Does *Shatzer*'s reasoning (and especially the statement, "he knows from his earlier experience that he need only demand counsel to bring the interrogation to a halt") suggest that the Court might soon move to a simple duration requirement for the cessation of questioning following an invocation of the *Miranda* right to counsel? Would such a duration requirement also likely apply to an invocation of the right to silence?

Waivers Without Invocations

Insert the following new material at the end of the paragraph that starts on page 872 and carries over to the top of page 873:

Butler was reprised, and perhaps expanded, in Berghuis v. Thompkins, 130 S.Ct. 2250 (2010). The defendant, Thompkins, was arrested on suspicion of murder. A police detective named Helgert first confirmed that Thompkins understood English, then read him the *Miranda* warnings. Helgert asked Thompkins to sign a *Miranda* waiver form, but Thompkins declined. There was conflicting evidence about whether or not Helgert specifically confirmed that Thompkins understood his *Miranda* rights. Picking up the story from the Supreme Court's summary of the facts:

> Officers began an interrogation. At no point during the interrogation did Thompkins say that he wanted to remain silent, that he did not want to talk with the police, or that he wanted an attorney. *Id.*, at 10a. Thompkins was "[l]argely" silent during the interrogation, which lasted about three hours. *Id.*, at 19a. He did give a few limited verbal responses, however, such as "yeah," "no," or "I don't know." And on occasion he communicated by nodding his head. *Id.*, at 23a. Thompkins also said that he "didn't want a peppermint" that was offered to him by the police and that the chair he was "sitting in was hard." *Id.*, at 152a.

> About 2 hours and 45 minutes into the interrogation, Helgert asked Thompkins, "Do you believe in God?" *Id.*, at 11a, 153a. Thompkins made eye contact with Helgert and said "Yes," as his eyes "well[ed] up with tears." *Id.*, at 11a. Helgert asked, "Do you pray to God?" Thompkins said "Yes." *Id.*, at 11a, 153a. Helgert asked, "Do you pray to God to forgive you for shooting that boy down?" *Id.*, at 153a. Thompkins answered "Yes" and looked away. *Ibid.* Thompkins refused to make a written confession, and the interrogation ended about 15 minutes later. *Id.*, at 11a.

Id., at 2256-57.

At trial, Thompkins moved to suppress his statements to Helgert on the grounds that he had invoked his right to remain silent under *Miranda* and *Mosley*, that he had not validly waived his *Miranda* rights, and that his statements were involuntary. The motion was denied, Thompkins was convicted of first-degree murder, and he was sentenced to life in prison without parole.

The Court, in a 5-4 decision, held that the statements were properly admitted. The Court, per Justice Kennedy, first concluded that Thompkins did not invoke his *Miranda* right to silence:

> In the context of invoking the *Miranda* right to counsel, the Court in Davis v. United States, 512 U.S. 452, 459 (1994), held that a suspect must do so "unambiguously." If an accused makes a statement concerning the right to counsel "that is ambiguous or equivocal" or makes no statement, the police are not required to end the interrogation, *ibid.*, or ask questions to clarify whether the accused wants to invoke his or her *Miranda* rights, 512 U.S., at 461-462.
>
> The Court has not yet stated whether an invocation of the right to remain silent can be ambiguous or equivocal, but there is no principled reason to adopt different standards for determining when an accused has invoked the *Miranda* right to remain silent and the *Miranda* right to counsel at issue in *Davis*. . . .
>
> There is good reason to require an accused who wants to invoke his or her right to remain silent to do so unambiguously. A requirement of an unambiguous invocation of *Miranda* rights results in an objective inquiry that "avoid[s] difficulties of proof and . . . provide[s] guidance to officers" on how to proceed in the face of ambiguity. *Davis*, 512 U.S., at 458-459. If an ambiguous act, omission, or statement could require police to end the interrogation, police would be required to make difficult decisions about an accused's unclear intent and face the consequence of suppression "if they guess wrong." *Id.*, at 461. Suppression of a voluntary confession in these circumstances would place a significant burden on society's interest in prosecuting criminal activity. See *id.*, at 459-461; Moran v. Burbine, 475 U.S. 412, 427 (1986). Treating an ambiguous or equivocal act, omission, or statement as an invocation of *Miranda* rights "might add marginally to *Miranda*'s goal of dispelling the compulsion inherent in custodial interrogation." *Burbine*, 475 U.S., at 425. But "as *Miranda* holds, full comprehension of the rights to remain silent and

> request an attorney are sufficient to dispel whatever coercion is inherent in the interrogation process." *Id.*, at 427; see *Davis*, *supra*, at 460.
>
> Thompkins did not say that he wanted to remain silent or that he did not want to talk with the police. Had he made either of these simple, unambiguous statements, he would have invoked his "'right to cut off questioning.'" *Mosley*, *supra*, at 103 (quoting *Miranda*, *supra*, at 474). Here he did neither, so he did not invoke his right to remain silent.

Id. at 2259-60.

The Court then ruled that Thompkins validly waived his *Miranda* rights by his course of conduct, and also that he made a voluntary statement to Helgert:

> . . . *Butler* made clear that a waiver of *Miranda* rights may be implied through "the defendant's silence, coupled with an understanding of his rights and a course of conduct indicating waiver." 441 U.S., at 373. The Court in *Butler* therefore "retreated" from the "language and tenor of the *Miranda* opinion," which "suggested that the Court would require that a waiver . . . be 'specifically made.'" Connecticut v. Barrett, 479 U.S. 523, 531-532 (1987) (Brennan, J., concurring in judgment).
>
> If the State establishes that a *Miranda* warning was given and the accused made an uncoerced statement, this showing, standing alone, is insufficient to demonstrate "a valid waiver" of *Miranda* rights. *Miranda*, *supra*, at 475. The prosecution must make the additional showing that the accused understood these rights. See Colorado v. Spring, 479 U.S. 564, 573-575 (1987). Where the prosecution shows that a *Miranda* warning was given and that it was understood by the accused, an accused's uncoerced statement establishes an implied waiver of the right to remain silent.
>
> Although *Miranda* imposes on the police a rule that is both formalistic and practical when it prevents them from interrogating suspects without first providing them with a *Miranda* warning, . . . it does not impose a formalistic waiver procedure that a suspect must follow to relinquish those rights. As a general proposition, the law can presume that an individual who, with a full understanding of his or her rights, acts in a manner inconsistent with their exercise has made a deliberate choice to relinquish the protection those rights afford. See, *e.g.*, *Butler*, *supra*, at 372-376. The Court's cases have recognized that a waiver of *Miranda* rights need only meet the standard of Johnson v. Zerbst, 304 U.S. 458, 464 (1938). As *Butler* recognized, 441 U.S., at 375-376, *Miranda* rights can therefore be waived through means less formal than a typical waiver on the record in a courtroom, cf. Fed. Rule Crim. Proc. 11, given the practical constraints and necessities of interrogation and the fact that *Miranda*'s main protection lies in advising defendants of their rights. . . .
>
> The record in this case shows that Thompkins waived his right to remain silent. There is no basis in this case to conclude that he did not understand his rights; and on these facts it follows that he chose not to invoke or rely on those rights when he did speak. First, there is no contention that Thompkins did not understand his rights; and from this it follows that he knew what he gave

up when he spoke. . . . There was more than enough evidence in the record to conclude that Thompkins understood his *Miranda* rights. Thompkins received a written copy of the *Miranda* warnings; Detective Helgert determined that Thompkins could read and understand English; and Thompkins was given time to read the warnings. Thompkins, furthermore, read aloud the fifth warning, which stated that "you have the right to decide at any time before or during questioning to use your right to remain silent and your right to talk with a lawyer while you are being questioned." Brief for Petitioner 60 (capitalization omitted). He was thus aware that his right to remain silent would not dissipate after a certain amount of time and that police would have to honor his right to be silent and his right to counsel during the whole course of interrogation. Those rights, the warning made clear, could be asserted at any time. Helgert, moreover, read the warnings aloud.

Second, Thompkins's answer to Detective Helgert's question about whether Thompkins prayed to God for forgiveness for shooting the victim is a "course of conduct indicating waiver" of the right to remain silent. *Butler*, *supra*, at 373. If Thompkins wanted to remain silent, he could have said nothing in response to Helgert's questions, or he could have unambiguously invoked his *Miranda* rights and ended the interrogation. The fact that Thompkins made a statement about three hours after receiving a *Miranda* warning does not overcome the fact that he engaged in a course of conduct indicating waiver. Police are not required to rewarn suspects from time to time. Thompkins's answer to Helgert's question about praying to God for forgiveness for shooting the victim was sufficient to show a course of conduct indicating waiver. This is confirmed by the fact that before then Thompkins had given sporadic answers to questions throughout the interrogation.

Third, there is no evidence that Thompkins's statement was coerced. . . . Thompkins does not claim that police threatened or injured him during the interrogation or that he was in any way fearful. The interrogation was conducted in a standard-sized room in the middle of the afternoon. It is true that apparently he was in a straight-backed chair for three hours, but there is no authority for the proposition that an interrogation of this length is inherently coercive. Indeed, even where interrogations of greater duration were held to be improper, they were accompanied, as this one was not, by other facts indicating coercion, such as an incapacitated and sedated suspect, sleep and food deprivation, and threats. . . . The fact that Helgert's question referred to Thompkins's religious beliefs also did not render Thompkins's statement involuntary. . . . In these circumstances, Thompkins knowingly and voluntarily made a statement to police, so he waived his right to remain silent.

Thompkins next argues that, even if his answer to Detective Helgert could constitute a waiver of his right to remain silent, the police were not allowed to question him until they obtained a waiver first. *Butler* forecloses this argument. The *Butler* Court held that courts can infer a waiver of *Miranda* rights "from the actions and words of the person interrogated." 441 U.S., at 373. This principle would be inconsistent with a rule that requires a waiver at the outset. The *Butler* Court thus rejected the rule proposed by the *Butler* dissent, which would have "requir[ed] the police to obtain an express waiver of

> [*Miranda* rights] before proceeding with interrogation." *Id.*, at 379 (Brennan, J., dissenting). . . .
>
> Interrogation provides the suspect with additional information that can put his or her decision to waive, or not to invoke, into perspective. As questioning commences and then continues, the suspect has the opportunity to consider the choices he or she faces and to make a more informed decision, either to insist on silence or to cooperate. When the suspect knows that *Miranda* rights can be invoked at any time, he or she has the opportunity to reassess his or her immediate and long-term interests. Cooperation with the police may result in more favorable treatment for the suspect; the apprehension of accomplices; the prevention of continuing injury and fear; beginning steps towards relief or solace for the victims; and the beginning of the suspect's own return to the law and the social order it seeks to protect.

Id., at 2261-64.

Justice Sotomayor, joined by Justices Stevens, Ginsburg, and Breyer, dissented:

> The Court concludes today that a criminal suspect waives his right to remain silent if, after sitting tacit and uncommunicative through nearly three hours of police interrogation, he utters a few one-word responses. The Court also concludes that a suspect who wishes to guard his right to remain silent against such a finding of "waiver" must, counterintuitively, speak—and must do so with sufficient precision to satisfy a clear-statement rule that construes ambiguity in favor of the police. Both propositions mark a substantial retreat from the protection against compelled self-incrimination that Miranda v. Arizona, 384 U.S. 436 (1966), has long provided during custodial interrogation. . . .
>
> Today's dilution of the prosecution's burden of proof to the bare fact that a suspect made inculpatory statements after *Miranda* warnings were given and understood takes an unprecedented step away from the "high standards of proof for the waiver of constitutional rights" this Court has long demanded. *Miranda, supra*, at 475; *Zerbst*, 304 U.S., at 464. When waiver is to be inferred during a custodial interrogation, there are sound reasons to require evidence beyond inculpatory statements themselves. *Miranda* and our subsequent cases are premised on the idea that custodial interrogation is inherently coercive. Requiring proof of a course of conduct beyond the inculpatory statements themselves is critical to ensuring that those statements are voluntary admissions and not the dubious product of an overborne will.
>
> Today's decision thus ignores the important interests *Miranda* safeguards. The underlying constitutional guarantee against self-incrimination reflects "many of our fundamental values and most noble aspirations," our society's "preference for an accusatorial rather than an inquisitorial system of criminal justice"; a "fear that self-incriminating statements will be elicited by inhumane treatment and abuses" and a resulting "distrust of self-deprecatory statements"; and a realization that while the privilege is "sometimes a shelter to the guilty, [it] is often a protection to the innocent." Withrow v. Williams,

> 507 U.S. 680, 692 (1993) (internal quotation marks omitted). For these reasons, we have observed, a criminal law system "which comes to depend on the 'confession' will, in the long run, be less reliable and more subject to abuses than a system relying on independent investigation." *Ibid.* (some internal quotation marks omitted). "By bracing against 'the possibility of unreliable statements in every instance of in-custody interrogation,'" *Miranda*'s prophylactic rules serve to "'protect the fairness of the trial itself.'" 507 U.S., at 692 (quoting Johnson v. New Jersey, 384 U.S. 719, 730 (1966); Schneckloth v. Bustamonte, 412 U.S. 218, 240 (1973)). Today's decision bodes poorly for the fundamental principles that *Miranda* protects.

Id., at 2266, 2272-73.

4. The Right to Counsel Reconsidered

Insert the following note after Note 4 on page 931:

4a. In Kansas v. Ventris, 129 S. Ct. 1841 (2009), the Court held by 7-2 that statements obtained in violation of *Massiah* and its progeny nevertheless can be used at trial for impeachment purposes. Justice Scalia, writing for the majority, explained:

> Our opinion in *Massiah*, to be sure, was equivocal on what precisely constituted the violation. It quoted various authorities indicating that the violation occurred at the moment of the postindictment interrogation because such questioning "'contravenes the basic dictates of fairness in the conduct of criminal causes.'" 377 U.S., at 205. But the opinion later suggested that the violation occurred only when the improperly obtained evidence was "used against [the defendant] at his trial." 377 U.S., at 206-207. That question was irrelevant to the decision in *Massiah* in any event. Now that we are confronted with the question, we conclude that the *Massiah* right is a right to be free of uncounseled interrogation, and is infringed at the time of the interrogation. That, we think, is when the "Assistance of Counsel" is denied.
>
> This case does not involve, therefore, the prevention of a constitutional violation, but rather the scope of the remedy for a violation that has already occurred. Our precedents make clear that the game of excluding tainted evidence for impeachment purposes is not worth the candle. . . .
>
> Once the defendant testifies in a way that contradicts prior statements, denying the prosecution use of "the traditional truth-testing devices of the adversary process" . . . is a high price to pay for vindication of the right to counsel at the prior stage.
>
> On the other side of the scale, preventing impeachment use of statements taken in violation of *Massiah* would add little appreciable deterrence. Officers have significant incentive to ensure that they and their informants comply with the Constitution's demands, since statements lawfully obtained can be

used for all purposes rather than simply for impeachment. And the *ex ante* probability that evidence gained in violation of *Massiah* would be of use for impeachment is exceedingly small. An investigator would have to anticipate both that the defendant would choose to testify at trial (an unusual occurrence to begin with) *and* that he would testify inconsistently despite the admissibility of his prior statement for impeachment. Not likely to happen—or at least not likely enough to risk squandering the opportunity of using a properly obtained statement for the prosecution's case in chief.

Starting at page 931, replace the second paragraph of Note 5, the main case of Michigan v. Jackson, *the textual material immediately following* Jackson, *and Notes 1 and 2 following* Jackson, *with the following note:*

6. Perhaps the best answer to the question posed at the end of the preceding Note is that the Fifth Amendment and Sixth Amendment are concerned with different matters, even if their concerns overlap in the confession area. In Michigan v. Jackson, 475 U.S. 625 (1986), however, the Court temporarily lost sight of this. The *Jackson* Court held that, once a defendant's Sixth Amendment right to counsel has attached and has been "asserted" by the defendant, the authorities can no longer approach that defendant to seek a waiver of the right to counsel—even if *Miranda* warnings are properly given and the defendant responds by clearly expressing the desire to waive counsel. *Jackson* was based on a simple (or should we say simplistic?) analogy to *Edwards*; as with the Fifth Amendment right at issue in *Edwards*, the Court concluded that the Sixth Amendment right to counsel in *Jackson* requires protection by the same kind of prophylactic, "bright-line" rule prohibiting any further police-initiated interrogations.

The *Jackson* decision managed to survive for 23 years before being overruled. In Montejo v. Louisiana, 129 S. Ct. 2079 (2009), the Court, per Justice Scalia, finally saw the light:

> What does the *Jackson* rule actually achieve by way of preventing unconstitutional conduct? Recall that the purpose of the rule is to preclude the State from badgering defendants into waiving their previously asserted rights. . . . The effect of this badgering might be to coerce a waiver, which would render the subsequent interrogation a violation of the Sixth Amendment. . . . [But] the Court has already taken substantial other, overlapping measures toward the same end. Under *Miranda*'s prophylactic protection of the right against compelled self-incrimination, any suspect subject to custodial interrogation has the right to have a lawyer present if he so requests, and to be advised of that right. . . . Under *Edwards*' prophylactic protection of the *Miranda* right, once such a defendant "has invoked his right to have counsel present," interrogation must stop. . . . And under *Minnick*'s prophylactic protection of the

Edwards right, no subsequent interrogation may take place until counsel is present, "whether or not the accused has consulted with his attorney." . . . These three layers of prophylaxis are sufficient. Under the *Miranda-Edwards-Minnick* line of cases (which is not in doubt), a defendant who does not want to speak to the police without counsel present need only say as much when he is first approached and given the *Miranda* warnings. At that point, not only must the immediate contact end, but "badgering" by later requests is prohibited. If that regime suffices to protect the integrity of "a suspect's voluntary choice not to speak outside his lawyer's presence," . . . it is hard to see why it would not also suffice to protect that same choice after arraignment, when Sixth Amendment rights have attached. And if so, then *Jackson* is simply superfluous.

It is true, as Montejo points out in his supplemental brief, that the doctrine established by *Miranda* and *Edwards* is designed to protect Fifth Amendment, not Sixth Amendment, rights. But that is irrelevant. What matters is that these cases, like *Jackson,* protect the right to have counsel during custodial interrogation—which right happens to be guaranteed (once the adversary judicial process has begun) by *two* sources of law. Since the right under both sources is waived using the same procedure, . . . doctrines ensuring voluntariness of the Fifth Amendment waiver simultaneously ensure the voluntariness of the Sixth Amendment waiver.

Montejo also correctly observes that the *Miranda-Edwards* regime is narrower than *Jackson* in one respect: The former applies only in the context of custodial interrogation. If the defendant is not in custody then those decisions do not apply; nor do they govern other, noninterrogative types of interactions between the defendant and the State (like pretrial lineups). However, those uncovered situations are the *least* likely to pose a risk of coerced waivers. When a defendant is not in custody, he is in control, and need only shut his door or walk away to avoid police badgering. And noninterrogative interactions with the State do not involve the "inherently compelling pressures," *Miranda, supra,* at 467, that one might reasonably fear could lead to involuntary waivers.

Jackson was policy driven, and if that policy is being adequately served through other means, there is no reason to retain its rule. *Miranda* and the cases that elaborate upon it already guarantee not simply noncoercion in the traditional sense, but what Justice Harlan referred to as "voluntariness with a vengeance," 384 U.S., at 505 (dissenting opinion). There is no need to take *Jackson*'s further step of requiring voluntariness on stilts.

Renumber Note 3 on page 942 as Note 7; insert the following at the end of the renumbered Note 7:

In 2009, in *Montejo*, the Court remanded so that the defendant could litigate whether he had in fact asserted his *Miranda* rights, which would (if true) have triggered protection against police-initiated interrogation under *Edwards*. The Court then added:

> Montejo may also seek on remand to press any claim he might have that his Sixth Amendment waiver was not knowing and voluntary, *e.g.*, his argument that the waiver was invalid because it was based on misrepresentations by police as to whether he had been appointed a lawyer, cf. *Moran*, 475 U.S., at 428-429. These matters have heightened importance in light of our opinion today.

129 S. Ct. at 2092 Does this mean that the Court—in light of its rejection of the *Jackson* rule—might now be willing to reconsider whether, at least in some cases, the fact of representation alone might be of constitutional significance? If the Court were to overturn this aspect of *Moran*, what kind of new approach might it substitute?

Chapter 7

Investigating Complex Crimes

A. Electronic Surveillance and the Search of Electronic Data

1. Wiretapping and Related Electronic Surveillance

Insert the following note after Note 5 on page 958:

5a. The Electronic Privacy Information Center (EPIC), which monitors civil liberties and privacy issues, reported in January 2005 that it appears that the FBI is no longer using the DCS-1000 system. The FBI reported to Congress that from 2001 through 2003, it has instead used commercially available software to conduct court-ordered electronic surveillances. See U.S. Carnivore Surveillance Consigned to the Doghouse, Privacy Alert (Feb. 9, 2005). Does this solve the problem?

Insert the following after note 6 on page 959:

Note that in March 2006, Congress passed the USA PATRIOT Act Improvement and Reauthorization Act of 2005, which made permanent these provisions related to information sharing.

2. Grand Jury Secrecy

Replace the text of Federal Rules of Criminal Procedure 6(d) and 6(e), at pages 1000-1002, with the following amended text:

FEDERAL RULES OF CRIMINAL PROCEDURE
Rule 6. The Grand Jury

(d) Who May Be Present.

(1) While the Grand Jury Is in Session. The following persons may be present while the grand jury is in session: attorneys for

the government, the witness being questioned, interpreters when needed, and a court reporter or an operator of a recording device.

(2) During Deliberations and Voting. No person other than the jurors, and any interpreter needed to assist a hearing-impaired or speech-impaired juror, may be present while the grand jury is deliberating or voting.

(e) Recording and Disclosing the Proceedings.

(1) Recording the Proceedings. Except while the grand jury is deliberating or voting, all proceedings must be recorded by a court reporter or by a suitable recording device. But the validity of a prosecution is not affected by the unintentional failure to make a recording. Unless the court orders otherwise, an attorney for the government will retain control of the recording, the reporter's notes, and any transcript prepared from those notes.

(2) Secrecy.

(A) No obligation of secrecy may be imposed on any person except in accordance with Rule 6(e)(2)(B).

(B) Unless these rules provide otherwise, the following persons must not disclose a matter occurring before the grand jury:

(i) a grand juror;

(ii) an interpreter;

(iii) a court reporter;

(iv) an operator of a recording device;

(v) a person who transcribes recorded testimony;

(vi) an attorney for the government; or

(vii) a person to whom disclosure is made under Rule 6(e)(3)(A)(ii) or (iii).

(3) Exceptions.

(A) Disclosure of a grand-jury matter—other than the grand jury's deliberations or any grand juror's vote—may be made to:

(i) an attorney for the government for use in performing that attorney's duty;

(ii) any government personnel—including those of a state, state subdivision, Indian tribe, or foreign government—that an attorney for the government considers necessary to assist in performing that attorney's duty to enforce federal criminal law; or

(iii) a person authorized by 18 U.S.C. § 3322.

(B) A person to whom information is disclosed under Rule 6(e)(3)(A)(ii) may use that information only to assist an attorney for the government in performing that attorney's duty to enforce federal criminal law. An attorney for the government must promptly provide the court that impaneled the grand jury with the names of all persons to whom a disclosure has been made, and must certify that the attorney has advised those persons of their obligation of secrecy under this rule.

(C) An attorney for the government may disclose any grand-jury matter to another federal grand jury.

(D) An attorney for the government may disclose any grand-jury matter involving foreign intelligence, counterintelligence (as defined in 50 U.S.C. § 401a), or foreign intelligence information (as defined in Rule 6(e)(3)(D)(iii)) to any federal law enforcement, intelligence, protective, immigration, national defense, or national security official to assist the official receiving the information in the performance of that official's duties. An attorney for the government may also disclose any grand-jury matter involving, within the United States or elsewhere, a threat of attack or other grave hostile acts of a foreign power or its agent, a threat of domestic or international sabotage or terrorism, or clandestine intelligence gathering activities by an intelligence service or network of a foreign power or by its agent, to any appropriate federal, state, state subdivision, Indian tribal, or foreign government official, for the purpose of preventing or responding to such threat or activities.

(i) Any official who receives information under Rule 6(e)(3)(D) may use the information only as necessary in the conduct of that person's official duties subject to any limitations on the unauthorized disclosure of such information. Any state, state subdivision, Indian tribal, or foreign government official who receives information under Rule 6(e)(3)(D) may use the information only in a manner consistent with any guidelines issued by the Attorney General and the Director of National Intelligence.

(ii) Within a reasonable time after disclosure is made under Rule 6(e)(3)(D), an attorney for the government must file, under seal, a notice with the court in the district where the grand jury convened stating that such information was disclosed and the departments, agencies, or entities to which the disclosure was made.

(iii) As used in Rule 6(e)(3)(D), the term "foreign intelligence information" means:

(a) information, whether or not it concerns a United States person, that relates to the ability of the United States to protect against—

- actual or potential attack or other grave hostile acts of a foreign power or its agent;
- sabotage or international terrorism by a foreign power or its agent; or
- clandestine intelligence activities by an intelligence service or network of a foreign power or by its agent; or

(b) information, whether or not it concerns a United States person, with respect to a foreign power or foreign territory that relates to—

- the national defense or the security of the United States; or
- the conduct of the foreign affairs of the United States.

(E) The court may authorize disclosure—at a time, in a manner, and subject to any other conditions that it directs—of a grand-jury matter:

(i) preliminarily to or in connection with a judicial proceeding;

(ii) at the request of a defendant who shows that a ground may exist to dismiss the indictment because of a matter that occurred before the grand jury;

(iii) at the request of the government, when sought by a foreign court or prosecutor for use in an official criminal investigation;

(iv) at the request of the government if it shows that the matter may disclose a violation of State, Indian tribal, or foreign criminal law, as long as the disclosure is to an appropriate state, state-subdivision, Indian tribal, or foreign government official for the purpose of enforcing that law; or

(v) at the request of the government if it shows that the matter may disclose a violation of military criminal law under the Uniform Code of Military Justice, as long as the disclosure is to an appropriate military official for the purpose of enforcing that law.

(F) A petition to disclose a grand-jury matter under Rule 6(e)(3)(E)(i) must be filed in the district where the grand jury convened. Unless the hearing is ex parte—as it may be when the government is the petitioner—the petitioner must serve the petition on, and the court must afford a reasonable opportunity to appear and be heard to:

(i) an attorney for the government;
(ii) the parties to the judicial proceeding; and
(iii) any other person whom the court may designate.

(G) If the petition to disclose arises out of a judicial proceeding in another district, the petitioned court must transfer the petition to the other court unless the petitioned court can reasonably determine whether disclosure is proper. If the petitioned court decides to transfer, it must send to the transferee court the material sought to be disclosed, if feasible, and a written evaluation of the need for continued grand-jury secrecy. The transferee court must afford those persons identified in Rule 6(e)(3)(F) a reasonable opportunity to appear and be heard.

(4) Sealed Indictment. The magistrate judge to whom an indictment is returned may direct that the indictment be kept secret until the defendant is in custody or has been released pending trial. The clerk must then seal the indictment, and no person may disclose the indictment's existence except as necessary to issue or execute a warrant or summons.

(5) Closed Hearing. Subject to any right to an open hearing in a contempt proceeding, the court must close any hearing to the extent necessary to prevent disclosure of a matter occurring before a grand jury.

(6) Sealed Records. Records, orders, and subpoenas relating to grand-jury proceedings must be kept under seal to the extent and as long as necessary to prevent the unauthorized disclosure of a matter occurring before a grand jury.

(7) Contempt. A knowing violation of Rule 6, or of any guidelines jointly issued by the Attorney General and the Director of National Intelligence under Rule 6, may be punished as a contempt of court.

D. *Law Enforcement and Counterterrrorism*

Insert the following after Note 4 on page 1037:

The USA PATRIOT Improvement and Reauthorization Act of 2005, enacted in March 2006, made some changes to Section 215 but extended it for an additional four years. The reauthorizing legislation also amended the provision to require that with respect to certain sensitive categories of documents, including library, bookstore, medical, tax return, and gun sale records, applications to the FISA court seeking such records must be signed by either the Director or Deputy Director of the FBI. In addition, the Attorney General is now required to develop and implement minimization procedures limiting the retention and dissemination of information obtained through Section 215 orders and concerning U.S. persons.

The law further directed the Department of Justice Office of the Inspector General to prepare a comprehensive audit as to the effective use, including illegal use, of Section 215. To that end, the DOJ has issued two reports on Section 215, in March 2007 and 2008, respectively. The first report examined the years 2002-2005, and the second report reviewed Section 215 orders in 2006. See U.S. Dep't of Justice, Office of the Inspector Gen., Review of the FBI's Use of Section 215 Orders for Business Records in 2006, March 2008; U.S. Dep't of Justice, Office of the Inspector Gen., Review of the Federal Bureau of Investigation's Use of Section 215 Orders for Business Records [in 2002-2005], March 2007. Both reports are available at *www.usdoj.gov/oig/special*.

While neither report identified any illegal use of Section 215 authority, the reports did identify a number of "noteworthy" issues relating to problematic procedural safeguards in the employment of Section 215 and a small number of potentially inappropriate uses of Section 215 authority.

Insert the following addition to footnote 5 on page 1038:

On October 17, 2006, President George W. Bush signed into law the Military Commissions Act of 2006, Pub. L. No. 109-366 ("MCA"). (The Act is codified at Chapter 47A of Title 10 of the U.S. Code.) In a related case, Boumediene v. Bush, 553 U.S. 723 (2008), the Supreme Court built on its holding in *Rasul*, determining that detainees at Guantanamo Bay have a right to challenge their detentions by means of a federal habeas corpus petition, and that Section 7 of the MCA, which purported to strip habeas jurisdiction from the federal courts for petitions filed by Guantanamo aliens who had been determined by the military to be enemy combatants, did not provide an effective and adequate substitute for habeas, thus operating as an unconstitutional suspension of the habeas writ.

Insert the following note after Note 5 on page 1041:

5a. Padilla filed a habeas petition in the District of South Carolina on July 2, 2004. The District Court granted the petition in February 2005 and ordered Padilla's release:

> It is true that there may be times during which it is necessary to give the Executive Branch greater power than at other times. Such a granting of power, however, is in the province of the legislature and no one else—not the Court and not the President. . . .
>
> Simply stated, this is a law enforcement matter, not a military matter. The civilian authorities captured Petitioner just as they should have. At the time that Petitioner was arrested pursuant to the material arrest warrant, any alleged terrorist plans that he harbored were thwarted. From then on, he was available to be questioned—and was indeed questioned—just like any other citizen accused of criminal conduct. This is as it should be. . . .
>
> If the law in its current state is found by the President to be insufficient to protect this country from terrorist plots, such as the one alleged here, then the President should prevail upon Congress to remedy the problem.

Padilla v. Hanft, 389 F. Supp. 2d 678, 691-92 (D.S.C. 2005). The Fourth Circuit reversed. Writing for a unanimous panel, Judge Luttig reasoned:

> As the AUMF authorized Hamdi's detention by the President, so also does it authorize Padilla's detention. Under the facts as presented here, Padilla unquestionably qualifies as an "enemy combatant" as that term was defined for purposes of the controlling opinion in *Hamdi*. Indeed, under the definition of "enemy combatant" employed in *Hamdi*, we can discern no difference in principle between Hamdi and Padilla. Like Hamdi, Padilla associated with forces hostile to the United States in Afghanistan. And, like Hamdi, Padilla took up arms against United States forces in that country in the same way and to the same extent as did Hamdi. Because, like Hamdi, Padilla is an enemy combatant, and because his detention is no less necessary than was Hamdi's in order to prevent his return to the battlefield, the President is authorized by the AUMF to detain Padilla as a fundamental incident to the conduct of war.

Padilla v. Hanft, 423 F.3d 386, 391 (4th Cir. 2005). Shortly after that opinion was filed, the government transferred Padilla to the custody of civilian law enforcement authorities—a move Judge Luttig harshly criticized, on the ground that it created "an appearance that the government may be attempting to avoid consideration of our decision by the Supreme Court." Padilla v. Hanft, 432 F.3d 582 (4th Cir. 2005).

On August 16, 2007, Padilla and his two co-defendants were convicted in federal court of one count of conspiracy to murder, kidnap, and maim people overseas, one count of conspiracy to provide material support for terrorists, and one count of material support for terrorists, following a criminal jury trial in Miami. See Peter Whoriskey, Jury Convicts Jose Padilla of Terror Charges, Wash. Post, Aug. 17, 2007, at A01. Despite the government's request that he receive the maximum allowable sentence—life imprisonment—he was sentenced on January 22, 2008, to

17 years and 4 months in prison. In explaining the lenient sentence, the judge noted that there was no evidence linking Padilla and his co-defendants to specific acts of terrorism, and that no deaths or injuries had resulted from their actions. See Kirk Semple, Padilla Sentenced to 17 Years in Prison, N.Y. Times, Jan. 22, 2008, available at *http://www.nytimes.com/2008/01/22/us/22cnd-padilla.html?ref=us*.

As for Yaser Esam Hamdi, subsequent to the Supreme Court's decision in Hamdi v. Rumsfeld, 542 U.S. 507 (2004), Hamdi was returned to Saudi Arabia and released pursuant to an agreement with the Government. In exchange for his freedom, Hamdi agreed to renounce his U.S. citizenship and to live in Saudi Arabia for five years. The agreement also requires that Hamdi not sue the U.S. over his detention, that he renounce terrorism, and that he never travel to Afghanistan, Iraq, Israel, Pakistan, or Syria. See Former Saudi-American Detainee Says He's Innocent, The Star-Ledger (Oct. 15, 2004).

PART FOUR

THE ADJUDICATION PROCESS

Chapter 8

The Charging Decision

A. Prosecutorial Discretion

2. Enforcement Discretion for Low-Level Crimes

Insert the following note after Note 2, page 1071:

2a. Given the figures discussed in *Wayte*, it should come as no surprise that many millions of crimes go unprosecuted each year. Prosecutors are probably unaware of most of those crimes, but they clearly know about some, and nevertheless choose not to prosecute. Keep that fact in mind, and think about the following scenario. Defendant does something to irritate some influential government official. That official in turn lobbies police and prosecutors to undertake an investigation, to try to find some crime they can pin on Defendant. After some investigation, Defendant is charged with the kind of crime that often goes unenforced. At some point, the charges are dropped or dismissed, or Defendant wins an acquittal. Now Defendant wants to sue—after all, he has been criminally prosecuted because he irritated a powerful government official: not the sort of thing that is supposed to happen in a just criminal justice system. What happens?

That scenario describes Hartman v. Moore, 547 U.S. 250 (2006). Moore ran a firm that had developed multi-line scanning technology for sorting mail—machines that could read addresses on letters and sort the letters properly. Moore lobbied the Postal Service to buy his technology; instead, the Postal Service temporarily adopted nine-digit zip codes, because those longer zip codes could be read without the equipment Moore was selling. Moore responded by turning his lobbying efforts to members of Congress and other government agencies. Eventually, in part because of Moore's efforts, the nine-digit zip code program was abandoned, and the Postal Service decided to purchase the multi-line scanning technology—but from one of Moore's competitors. To add insult to injury, postal inspectors began a criminal investigation of

Moore and his company; both were charged with criminal fraud. After a six-week trial, a federal district judge dismissed the charges, see United States v. Recognition Equipment Inc., 725 F. Supp. 587 (D. D.C. 1989), Moore sued six postal inspectors and one federal prosecutor, claiming he had been charged in retaliation for embarrassing the Postal Service.

After a litigation of Dickensian length—Justice Souter called it "a procedural history portending another Jarndyce v. Jarndyce"—the postal inspectors successfully moved for summary judgment, on the ground that the underlying criminal charges were supported by probable cause. By a vote of 5-2, the Supreme Court agreed. Here is the key passage from Justice Souter's majority opinion:

> In sum, the complexity of causation in a claim that prosecution was induced by an official bent on retaliation should be addressed specifically in defining the elements of the tort. Probable cause or its absence will be at least an evidentiary issue in practically all such cases. Because showing an absence of probable cause will have high probative force, and can be made mandatory with little or no added cost, it makes sense to require such a showing as an element of a plaintiff's case, and we hold that it must be pleaded and proven.

Justice Ginsburg's dissent, joined by Justice Breyer, began by stating:

> The Court of Appeals, reviewing the record so far made, determined that "the evidence of retaliatory motive [came] close to the proverbial smoking gun." The record also indicated that the postal inspectors engaged in "unusual prodding," strenuously urging a reluctant U.S. Attorney's Office to press charges against Moore.

The dissenters went on to argue that plaintiffs like Moore should prevail if they could show that, but for the retaliatory motive, they would not have been prosecuted—a showing it appeared Moore could easily make.

Who has the better of the argument? Is the probable-cause requirement, as Justice Souter contends, little more than a matter of legal bookkeeping that will have only slight effects on case outcomes? Or does the Court's decision amount to a blank check for government officials inclined to use criminal charges to harass their critics? If state and federal criminal codes covered only core crimes—major thefts, violent felonies, plus prohibitions of distributing "hard" drugs like cocaine or heroin—*Hartman* would make little difference. Given how broad criminal codes really are, however, it comes close to absolute immunity not just for prosecutors, but for other government officials who may exert influence over them as well.

Chapter 9

Bail, Detention, and the Right to a Speedy Trial

B. The Right to a Speedy Trial

Add the following material to Note 2, at the end of the second paragraph on page 1144:

However, delay resulting from a continuance granted to allow the defendant to prepare for pretrial motions is *not* automatically excludable; such delay can be excluded *only* if the judge specifically finds that the "ends of justice" warrant the continuance. See Bloate v. United States, 130 S.Ct. 1345 (2010).

Add the following new paragraph to Note 2, which starts on page 1143, between the second and third full paragraphs on page 1144:

In Zedner v. United States, 547 U.S. 489 (2006), in the midst of prolonged pretrial proceedings, the defendant agreed to waive "for all time" the application of the Speedy Trial Act. (He did so, in part, to buy himself time to try to prove that alleged counterfeit U.S. bonds, on which the charges against him were based, were actually authentic.) Thereafter, a 91-day delay ensued, and the defendant moved to dismiss the indictment for failure to comply with the Act. The district court denied the motion based on the earlier waiver, and the Second Circuit affirmed. The Supreme Court, however, reversed. According to the Court, the Act "comprehensively regulates the time within which a trial must begin," and makes no allowance for a "prospective" waiver of the kind purportedly signed by the defendant. Although the Act itself provides that a defendant may waive a completed violation of the Act by failing to move for dismissal prior to the start of the trial (or the entry of a guilty plea), the Court noted that "prospective" and "retrospective" waivers raise quite different concerns:

> [T]here is no reason to think that Congress wanted to treat prospective and retrospective waivers similarly. Allowing prospective waivers would seriously undermine the Act because there are many cases — like the case at hand — in which the prosecution, the defense, and the court would all be happy to opt out of the Act, to the detriment of the public interest. The sort of retrospective waiver allowed by [the Act] does not pose a comparable danger because the prosecution and the court cannot know until the trial actually starts or the guilty plea is actually entered whether the defendant will forgo moving to dismiss. As a consequence, the prosecution and the court retain a strong incentive to make sure that the trial begins on time.

Id., at 502. The Court rejected the government's alternative arguments that: (1) the defendant was estopped, by his purported waiver, from complaining about the Act's violation; (2) the trial court could still exclude the challenged 91-day delay, on remand, by making a *post hoc* finding that the "ends of justice" supported the delay; and (3) the violation of the Act could still be found, on remand, to be "harmless error." The Court held, therefore, that dismissal was required under the Act, and remanded the case solely for the purpose of allowing the trial court to determine whether the dismissal should be with or without prejudice.

Insert the following note after Note 2 on page 1144:

2a. In Vermont v. Brillon, 129 S. Ct. 1283 (2009), the Court dealt with how to determine whether the length of time from arrest to trial violated the speedy trial clause. Brillon was apparently a difficult client. According to the Court:

> During the time between his arrest and his trial, at least six different attorneys were appointed to represent him. Brillon "fired" his first attorney, who served from July 2001 to February 2002. His third lawyer, who served from March 2002 until June 2002, was allowed to withdraw when he reported that Brillon had threatened his life. His fourth lawyer served from June 2002 until November 2002, when the trial court released him from the case. His fifth lawyer, assigned two months later, withdrew in April 2003. Four months thereafter, his sixth lawyer was assigned, and she took the case to trial in June 2004.

The Vermont Supreme Court concluded that the three-year delay from arrest to trial was "extreme" and that actions of several of Brillon's appointed counsel were to be attributed to the state. The Court reversed. The Court concluded that the Vermont Supreme Court was wrong to look at each time period associated with each new counsel discretely, and by doing so neglected that, had Brillon not behaved toward his first and third counsel as he did, there would have been no speedy trial problem. Moreover, the Court concluded, merely because those counsel were appointed by the state does not mean their actions can be attributed to the state. Appointed counsel are analogous to retained counsel in this regard, and for the most part their actions in delaying proceedings are to be analyzed accordingly. As the Court noted, "A contrary conclusion could encourage appointed counsel to delay proceedings by seeking unreasonable continuances, hoping thereby to obtain a dismissal of the indictment on speedy-trial grounds."

Chapter 10

Guilty Pleas and Plea Bargaining

A. *Guilty Pleas as a Substitute for Trials*

1. The Plea Process

Insert the following note after Note 5, on page 1180:

6. Actually, there is one more way around a procedurally defaulted challenge to a guilty plea: the defendant may assert his defaulted claim, without showing "cause" and "prejudice," if he can "establish that the constitutional error . . . has probably resulted in the conviction of one who is actually innocent. To establish actual innocence, petitioner must demonstrate that, in light of all the evidence, it is more likely than not that no reasonable juror would have convicted him." Bousley v. United States, 523 U.S. 614 (1998) (citations omitted). The constitutional error in *Bousley* was the same as in Henderson v. Morgan: the defendant was misinformed about the elements of the crime to which he pled guilty. Bousley pled guilty to "using" a firearm "during and in relation to a drug trafficking crime." He was told that "using" meant essentially the same thing as possessing; later, the Supreme Court construed the relevant statute to require proof that the defendant had actively employed the weapon, which Bousley claimed he had not done. Even though neither Bousley nor his lawyer objected at the plea proceeding (or appealed his conviction afterward), the Court held that he could raise his Henderson v. Morgan claim if he could prove his innocence.

The defendant in Bradshaw v. Stumpf, 545 U.S. 175 (2005), raised a similar claim but with less success. Stumpf and an accomplice named Wesley robbed and shot an elderly couple, leaving the husband wounded and the wife dead. Both men were charged with capital murder. Stumpf pled guilty. At his sentencing proceeding, the government argued that he had fired the shot that killed the victim; Stumpf maintained that Wesley had fired the fatal shot. In the alternative, the government contended that Stumpf deserved execution even if Wesley was the triggerman.

Stumpf was sentenced to death. When Wesley was later tried for the same murder, the prosecution argued that *he* had fired the fatal shot, not Stumpf. Wesley was allowed to introduce evidence that the government had taken an inconsistent position in his accomplice's case; the jury convicted, but imposed a life sentence. Stumpf then sought relief on habeas corpus, maintaining that he had pled guilty under a false understanding of Ohio's capital murder statute, and that the government's use of inconsistent arguments in the two cases invalidated both his guilty plea and sentence.

The Supreme Court rejected Stumpf's challenge to his guilty plea, and remanded for consideration of the challenge to his death sentence. Justice O'Connor's opinion for a unanimous Court noted that, even if the trial judge in the plea colloquy had failed to describe the intent term of the crime to which Stumpf pled guilty, defense counsel had correctly described that term in previous conversations with the defendant. Due process required no more, the Court held. As for the government's inconsistent arguments in the two cases: The Court noted that it was difficult to see how the government's subsequent argument could undermine Stumpf's prior plea. Moreover, the accuracy of Stumpf's guilty plea did not depend on his having fired the fatal shot; the relevant state statute provides for liability for an accomplice who intends to kill but does not commit the act that directly causes the victim's death. And the requisite intent could be inferred from the defendant's other actions—including shooting the husband.

After *Bousley* and *Stumpf*, it is not clear how much additional work "actual innocence" actually does. If a defendant can show he is probably innocent of the crime to which he pled guilty, he can likely also show that his lawyer was constitutionally ineffective for advising him to so plead. Thus, in most cases, ineffective assistance and actual innocence will travel together. Actual innocence adds something only in the rare case, like *Bousley*, in which the legal definition of the relevant crime has changed. In all other cases, the defendant is, basically, stuck with having to show ineffective assistance if he wishes to undo his guilty plea.

Chapter 11

Discovery and Disclosure

A. Disclosure by the Government

2. The Prosecutor's Constitutional Disclosure Obligations

Add the following material to the end of Note 3 on page 1281:

If prosecutors must be the initial judges of *Brady* materiality, how likely are they to judge fairly? Recall Justice Souter's twin statements that prosecutors are supposed to be concerned not with winning cases but with doing justice, and that "the criminal trial, as distinct from the prosecutor's private deliberations" should be "the chosen forum for ascertaining the truth about criminal accusations." In other words, in close cases, prosecutors should err on the side of disclosure, and let the judge and jury decide how significant the evidence in question is.

Perhaps they should, but they often won't, as a recent Supreme Court decision in a First Amendment case makes clear. The plaintiff in Garcetti v. Ceballos, 547 U.S. 410 (2006), was a long-time prosecutor in the Los Angeles County D.A.'s office who sued his bosses. Ceballos claimed he was punished for constitutionally protected speech—including speech that he believed *Brady* doctrine required. After reviewing the file in a pending criminal case and visiting the crime scene, Ceballos decided that the police affidavit supporting a key search warrant in the case was false, and might be dishonest. Ceballos wrote a memo to that effect to his superiors, and testified for the defense in a suppression hearing in the relevant case. (The trial judge denied the suppression motion. Does that matter?) After his memo and testimony, Ceballos was denied promotion, removed from a pending murder case, and reassigned to misdemeanors. He sued, claiming that his superiors had, in effect, punished him for his speech—and for trying in good faith to comply with *Brady*. Ceballos lost in the Supreme Court: By a 5-4 vote, the Justices held that Ceballos's speech was not constitutionally protected because it was made "pursuant to [his] official duties"—that is, Ceballos's memo and testimony were offered as a public official, not as a private citizen.

Consider the implications of *Garcetti* for *Brady* doctrine. A prosecutor deciding whether a particular piece of evidence is sufficiently "material" to justify disclosure has (at least) two reasons to err on the side of secrecy. First, disclosure might raise the odds of losing the case. While prosecutors no doubt do seek justice, they also like to win—and once the prosecutor has decided to go forward with criminal charges, winning and doing justice will appear to be congruent goals. Second, as *Garcetti* illustrates, the prosecutor's career might suffer. Having climbed the office ladder, no one wants to be shoved back down to the bottom rung. Of course, the prosecutor must also worry about the risk that, sometime down the road, the evidence will be uncovered and lead to a judicial finding that disclosure was constitutionally required. But such a finding requires only that the criminal case be retried, not that the prosecutor suffer any penalty personally. And the likelihood of an adverse *Brady* decision is usually small—most nondisclosures never come to light. It's easy to understand why prosecutors might resolve doubts in favor of keeping quiet.

How should the law combat that tendency? One possible answer is to broaden the scope of *Brady* doctrine. Perhaps due process—not the First Amendment—should protect prosecutors from any employment-related sanctions based on actions they believe, in good faith, are compelled by *Brady*. If it existed, that protection might better advance the goal of ensuring disclosure of exculpatory evidence than decisions like *Kyles*.

What do you think? Should the law of criminal procedure govern not just criminal litigation but the administration of prosecutors' offices as well? Are judges likely to do that job well? What is the alternative?

Delete Note 5, pages 1282-1283, and insert the following main case and notes at the end of Note 14 on page 1290:

UNITED STATES v. RUIZ

Certiorari to the United States Court of Appeals for the Ninth Circuit
536 U.S. 622 (2002)

JUSTICE BREYER delivered the opinion of the Court.

In this case we primarily consider whether the Fifth and Sixth Amendments require federal prosecutors, before entering into a binding plea agreement with a criminal defendant, to disclose "impeachment information relating to any informants or other witnesses." App. to Pet. for Cert. 46a. We hold that the Constitution does not require that disclosure.

After immigration agents found 30 kilograms of marijuana in Angela Ruiz's luggage, federal prosecutors offered her what is known in the Southern District of California as a "fast track" plea bargain. That bargain—standard in that district—asks a defendant to waive indictment, trial, and an appeal. In return, the Government agrees to recommend to the sentencing judge a two-level departure downward from the otherwise applicable United States Sentencing Guidelines sentence. In Ruiz's case, a two-level departure downward would have shortened the ordinary Guidelines-specified 18-to-24-month sentencing range by 6 months, to 12-to-18 months. 241 F.3d 1157, 1161 (2001).

The prosecutors' proposed plea agreement contains a set of detailed terms. Among other things, it specifies that "any [known] information establishing the factual innocence of the defendant" "has been turned over to the defendant," and it acknowledges the Government's "continuing duty to provide such information." App. to Pet. for Cert. 45a-46a. At the same time it requires that the defendant "waive the right" to receive "impeachment information relating to any informants or other witnesses" as well as the right to receive information supporting any affirmative defense the defendant raises if the case goes to trial. *Id.*, at 46a. Because Ruiz would not agree to this last-mentioned waiver, the prosecutors withdrew their bargaining offer. The Government then indicted Ruiz for unlawful drug possession. And despite the absence of any agreement, Ruiz ultimately pleaded guilty.

At sentencing, Ruiz asked the judge to grant her the same two-level downward departure that the Government would have recommended had she accepted the "fast track" agreement. The Government opposed her request, and the District Court denied it, imposing a standard Guideline sentence instead.

. . . Ruiz appealed her sentence to the United States Court of Appeals for the Ninth Circuit. The Ninth Circuit vacated the District Court's sentencing determination. The Ninth Circuit pointed out that the Constitution requires prosecutors to make certain impeachment information available to a defendant before trial. It decided that this obligation entitles defendants to receive that same information before they enter into a plea agreement. [241 F.3d, at 1164.] The Ninth Circuit also decided that the Constitution prohibits defendants from waiving their right to that information. *Id.*, at 1165-66. And it held that the prosecutors' standard "fast track" plea agreement was unlawful because it insisted upon that waiver. *Id.*, at 1167. . . .

The constitutional question concerns a federal criminal defendant's waiver of the right to receive from prosecutors exculpatory impeachment material — a right that the Constitution provides as part of its basic "fair trial" guarantee. See U.S. Const., Amdts. 5, 6. See also Brady v. Maryland, 373 U.S. 83, 87 (1963) (Due process requires prosecutors to "avoid . . . an unfair trial" by making available "upon request" evidence "favorable to an accused . . . where the evidence is material either to guilt or to punishment"); United States v. Agurs, 427 U.S. 97, 112-113 (1976) (defense request unnecessary); Kyles v. Whitley, 514 U.S. 419, 435 (1995) (exculpatory evidence is evidence the suppression of which would "undermine confidence in the verdict"); Giglio v. United States, 405 U.S. 150, 154 (1972) (exculpatory evidence includes "evidence affecting" witness "credibility," where the witness' "reliability" is likely "determinative of guilt or innocence").

When a defendant pleads guilty, he or she, of course, forgoes not only a fair trial, but also other accompanying constitutional guarantees. Given the seriousness of the matter, the Constitution insists, among other things, that the defendant enter a guilty plea that is "voluntary" and that the defendant must make related waivers "knowingly, intelligently, [and] with sufficient awareness of the relevant circumstances and likely consequences." Brady v. United States, 397 U.S. 742, 748 (1970).

In this case, the Ninth Circuit in effect held that a guilty plea is not "voluntary" (and that the defendant could not, by pleading guilty, waive his right to a fair trial) unless the prosecutors first made the same disclosure of material impeachment information that the prosecutors would have had to make had the defendant insisted upon a trial. We must decide whether the Constitution requires that preguilty plea disclosure of impeachment information. We conclude that it does not.

First, impeachment information is special in relation to the fairness of a trial, not in respect to whether a plea is voluntary ("knowing," "intelligent," and "sufficiently aware"). Of course, the more information the defendant has, the more aware he is of the likely consequences of a plea, waiver, or decision, and the wiser that decision will likely be. But the Constitution does not require the prosecutor to share all useful information with the defendant. And the law ordinarily considers a waiver knowing, intelligent, and sufficiently aware if the defendant fully understands the nature of the right and how it would likely apply in general in the circumstances — even though the defendant may not know the specific detailed consequences of invoking it. A defendant, for example, may waive his right to remain silent, his right to a jury trial, or his right to counsel even if the defendant does not know the specific questions the authorities intend to ask, who will likely serve on the jury, or the particular lawyer the State might otherwise provide.

It is particularly difficult to characterize impeachment information as critical information of which the defendant must always be aware prior to pleading guilty given the random way in which such information may, or may not, help a particular defendant. The degree of help that impeachment information can provide will depend upon the defendant's own independent knowledge of the prosecution's potential case — a matter that the Constitution does not require prosecutors to disclose.

Second, we have found no legal authority embodied either in this Court's past cases or in cases from other circuits that provide significant support for the Ninth Circuit's decision. To the contrary, this Court has found that the Constitution, in respect to a defendant's awareness of relevant circumstances, does not require complete knowledge of the relevant circumstances, but permits a court to accept a guilty plea, with its accompanying waiver of various constitutional rights, despite various forms of misapprehension under which a defendant might labor. See Brady v. United States, 397 U.S. at 757 (defendant "misapprehended the quality of the State's case"); ibid. (defendant misapprehended "the likely penalties"); ibid. (defendant failed to "anticipate a change in the law regarding" relevant "punishments"); McMann v. Richardson, 397 U.S. 759, 770 (1970) (counsel "misjudged the admissibility" of a "confession"); United States v. Broce, 488 U.S. 563, 573 (1989) (counsel failed to point out a potential defense); Tollett v. Henderson, 411 U.S. 258, 267 (1973) (counsel failed to find a potential constitutional infirmity in grand jury proceedings). It is difficult to distinguish, in terms of importance, a defendant's ignorance of grounds for impeachment of potential witnesses at a possible future trial from the varying forms of ignorance at issue in these cases.

Third, due process considerations, the very considerations that led this Court to find trial-related rights to exculpatory and impeachment information in *Brady* and *Giglio,* argue against the existence of the "right" that the Ninth Circuit found here. This Court has said that due process considerations include not only (1) the nature of the private interest at stake, but also (2) the value of the additional safeguard, and (3) the adverse impact of the requirement upon the Government's interests. Ake v. Oklahoma, 470 U.S. 68, 77 (1985). Here, as we have just pointed out, the added value of the Ninth Circuit's "right" to a defendant is often limited, for it depends upon the defendant's independent awareness of the details of the Government's case. And in any case, as the proposed plea agreement at issue here specifies, the Government will provide "any information establishing the factual innocence of the defendant" regardless. That fact, along with other guilty-plea safeguards, see Fed. Rule

Crim. Proc. 11, diminishes the force of Ruiz's concern that, in the absence of impeachment information, innocent individuals, accused of crimes, will plead guilty.

At the same time, a constitutional obligation to provide impeachment information during plea bargaining, prior to entry of a guilty plea, could seriously interfere with the Government's interest in securing those guilty pleas that are factually justified, desired by defendants, and help to secure the efficient administration of justice. The Ninth Circuit's rule risks premature disclosure of Government witness information, which, the Government tells us, could "disrupt ongoing investigations" and expose prospective witnesses to serious harm. Brief for United States 25. And the careful tailoring that characterizes most legal Government witness disclosure requirements suggests recognition by both Congress and the Federal Rules Committees that such concerns are valid. See, e.g., 18 U.S.C. § 3432 (witness list disclosure required in capital cases three days before trial with exceptions); § 3500 (Government witness statements ordinarily subject to discovery only after testimony given); Fed. Rule Crim. Proc. 16(a)(2) (embodies limitations of 18 U.S.C. § 3500).

Consequently, the Ninth Circuit's requirement could force the Government to abandon its "general practice" of not "disclosing to a defendant pleading guilty information that would reveal the identities of cooperating informants, undercover investigators, or other prospective witnesses." Brief for United States 25. It could require the Government to devote substantially more resources to trial preparation prior to plea bargaining, thereby depriving the plea-bargaining process of its main resource-saving advantages. Or it could lead the Government instead to abandon its heavy reliance upon plea bargaining in a vast number — 90% or more — of federal criminal cases. We cannot say that the Constitution's due process requirement demands so radical a change in the criminal justice process in order to achieve so comparatively small a constitutional benefit.

These considerations, taken together, lead us to conclude that the Constitution does not require the Government to disclose material impeachment evidence prior to entering a plea agreement with a criminal defendant.

In addition, we note that the "fast track" plea agreement requires a defendant to waive her right to receive information the Government has regarding any "affirmative defense" she raises at trial. Pet. for Cert. 46a. We do not believe the Constitution here requires provision of this information to the defendant prior to plea bargaining — for most (though not all) of the reasons previously stated. That is to say, in the context of this agreement, the need for this information is more closely related to the fairness of a trial than to the voluntariness of the plea; the value in terms of the defendant's added awareness of relevant circumstances is ordinarily limited; yet the added burden imposed upon the Government by requiring its provision well in advance of trial (often before trial preparation begins) can be serious, thereby significantly interfering with the administration of the plea bargaining process.

For these reasons the decision of the Court of Appeals for the Ninth Circuit is reversed.

JUSTICE THOMAS, concurring in the judgment.

I agree with the Court that the Constitution does not require the Government to disclose either affirmative defense information or impeachment information relating to informants or other witnesses before entering into a binding plea agreement with a criminal defendant. The Court, however, suggests that the constitutional analysis turns in some part on the "degree of help" such information would provide to the defendant at the plea stage, a distinction that is neither necessary nor accurate. To the extent that the Court is implicitly drawing a line based on a flawed characterization about the usefulness of certain types of information, I can only concur in the judgment. The principle supporting *Brady* was "avoidance of an unfair trial to the accused." Brady v. Maryland, 373 U.S. 83, 87 (1963). That concern is not implicated at the plea stage. . . .

NOTES AND QUESTIONS

1. Is *Ruiz* consistent with *Kyles*? Recall that in *Kyles,* the Court drew no distinction between information that might impeach government witnesses and other sorts of exculpatory evidence. Justice Thomas apparently thinks no such distinction should be drawn in *Ruiz* either. Is he right?

2. After *Ruiz,* is the *Brady* right to discovery of material exculpatory evidence waivable? It would appear that the answer is yes. Should it be? Consider: Most rights that defendants waive when pleading guilty fall into one of two categories. The first category consists of rights to some future benefit—say, a jury trial—about which the defendant is informed at the plea colloquy. The second category consists of rights to litigate some claim of past government misconduct—say, an improper police search—about which the defendant already knows. Even when the defendant doesn't know the particulars of the claim, as with claims that the grand jury was discriminatorily selected, he generally knows that

some such claim is possible, for he knows whether or not a grand jury has indicted him. *Brady* claims are different. The defendant does not know about material exculpatory evidence in the government's possession unless and until such evidence is disclosed to him. And *Brady* violations are ongoing—the violation lasts as long as the government fails to disclose the evidence. Thus, a *Brady* waiver amounts to an entitlement to the government to engage in an ongoing constitutional violation. Is that appropriate? If, as the Court likes to say, *Brady* protects the fundamental fairness of criminal litigation, can one really consent to a fundamentally unfair litigation process?

3. *Brady*'s materiality standard is roughly analogous to the prejudice standard the Court uses when deciding ineffective assistance claims under Strickland v. Washington, 466 U.S. 668 (1984). Could a defendant validly waive his right to raise a *Strickland* claim? Could the government condition a plea bargain on such a waiver? In practice, such waivers are common in cases in which defendants represent themselves. Would they be enforceable when the defendant is represented by counsel? Should they be?

4. Suppose the Court had ruled in *Ruiz* that *Brady* requires disclosure, in advance of guilty pleas, of any material exculpatory evidence in the government's possession, and that the requirement cannot be waived. What effect would that ruling have on government evidence-gathering? One possibility is that the *Brady* right would make pre-plea investigation more expensive for the government; police or prosecutors might find evidence that would be helpful to the defense, in which case the evidence would have to be disclosed, possibly destroying any chance at reaching a plea bargain. At the margin, the government might decide to do less evidence-gathering prior to plea bargaining in order to reduce that risk. That does not sound like good news for innocent defendants. How should the law solve this problem?

5. *Ruiz* does not resolve the broader question whether *Brady* applies to guilty pleas; only Justice Thomas takes a clear position on that question. The issue has received surprisingly little attention in lower federal and state courts, but the dominant view is not Justice Thomas's. Most courts have concluded that a defendant is entitled to know about material exculpatory evidence—including impeachment evidence—when deciding whether to plead guilty. See, e.g., United States v. Avellino, 136 F.3d 249, 255 (2d Cir. 1998). Is that view sound? What should one make of all the language in the Supreme Court's *Brady* decisions to the effect that the right to discovery of exculpatory evidence is part of the defendant's right to a fair *trial*? Note, too, that in all but a tiny fraction of guilty pleas, the

defendant acknowledges in open court that he committed the crime charged. Extending *Brady* to guilty pleas seems like nothing more than a means by which guilty defendants can strike better bargains with the government. Or is that analysis too simplistic?

6. Assuming that, at least in some cases, *Brady* does require pre-guilty plea disclosure, what does materiality mean in guilty plea cases? In *Strickland* cases, defendants who plead guilty must show that there is a reasonable probability that, but for defense counsel's errors, the defendant would not have pled guilty but would have insisted on going to trial. See Hill v. Lockhart, 474 U.S. 52 (1985). Should a similar standard apply to *Brady* claims? What if the nondisclosure affected the terms of the defendant's sentence?

Insert the following note after Note 13 on page 1286:

13a. In April 2005, Moussaoui pled guilty to all six counts of the indictment while continuing to insist that, although he is a member of al Qaeda and had trained to fly planes into buildings in preparation for a future attack, he was not part of the 9/11 attacks. See David Johnston and Neil A. Lewis, Officials Say There Is No Evidence to Back Moussaoui's Story, The New York Times, April 27, 2005, at A14. A jury recommended against the death penalty for Moussaoui, and on May 4, 2006, he was sentenced to life in prison without possibility of parole.

Chapter 12

The Jury and the Criminal Trial

B. Jury Composition

Insert the following material at the end of the first full paragraph on page 1327:

See also Uttecht v. Brown, 551 U.S. 1 (2007), where the Court, by 5-4, held that the *Witt* standard must be applied by federal habeas courts with a kind of "double" deference: deference to the trial court that had the chance to judge the demeanor of the prospective juror in the first instance, as well as the mandatory deference owed to state courts by all federal habeas courts.

Insert the following at the end of Note 3(B) on page 1351:

What if a defendant seeks to exercise a peremptory challenge against a juror who would not be subject to a for-cause challenge, and the peremptory challenge is erroneously denied by the trial judge based on *Batson* and *McCollum*? Does the seating of such a challenged juror violate the constitutional rights of the defendant, and if so, does it require automatic reversal of the resulting conviction? In Rivera v. Illinois, 129 S. Ct. 1446 (2009), the Court unanimously held that such an error does not require automatic reversal as a matter of federal law. The Court noted that peremptory challenges are not themselves of constitutional status; moreover, because the challenged juror was unbiased, there was no violation of the defendant's constitutional right to an impartial jury. In the end, the Court held that it was up to each state to decide—as a matter of state law—whether the erroneous denial of a peremptory challenge should lead to automatic reversal or be subjected to harmless error analysis.

Renumber Note 4, at pages 1352-53, as Note 2a, and move it to follow Note 2 at page 1350. Replace the first sentence of Note 3(C), at page 1351, with the following new material:

C. Perhaps the key issue, in terms of *Batson*'s significance to the real world of criminal jury trials, is how the lower courts should interpret and apply the *Batson* standard to prosecutorial (and, after *McCollum*, defense) peremptory challenges. Justice Marshall, in his *Batson* dissent, argued that the standard would not limit prosecutors who wished to discriminate because it would be all too easy to come up with "race-neutral" explanations for any contested challenges. The *Batson* majority, however, placed its faith in the lower courts to police the prosecutorial abuse of peremptories.

Subsequent developments seemed to indicate that perhaps Marshall was right.

Replace the third paragraph of Note 3(C), at page 1352, with the following new material:

After *Hernandez* and *Purkett*, many believed that *Batson*'s promise would go unfulfilled. If it was really so easy for prosecutors to explain their peremptories in race-neutral terms, and thereby avoid a *Batson* reversal, then what was the point of the whole exercise in the first place?

Possibly for this reason, some lower courts began to screen *Batson* claims more aggressively at the initial stage of the three-stage inquiry, eliminating many claims before ever reaching the second, "race-neutral explanation" stage. These courts (utilizing the flexibility that the Supreme Court appeared to grant them in implementing *Batson*'s mandate) held that, at the initial stage of the inquiry, the defendant must meet a prima facie burden of proving, by a preponderance of the evidence, that the prosecutor's use of peremptories gives rise to an inference of racial discrimination. Otherwise, there is nothing for the prosecutor to rebut at the second stage.

In (Jay Shawn) Johnson v. California, 545 U.S. 162 (2005), the Supreme Court, by 8-1, soundly rejected this interpretation of *Batson*. According to the Court:

> [W]e assumed in *Batson* that the trial judge would have the benefit of all relevant circumstances, including the prosecutor's explanation, before deciding whether it was more likely than not that the challenge was improperly motivated. We did not intend the first step to be so onerous that a defendant would have to persuade the judge—on the basis of all the facts, some of which are impossible for the defendant to know with certainty—that the challenge was more likely than not the product of purposeful discrimination. Instead, a defendant satisfies the requirements of *Batson*'s first step by producing evidence sufficient to permit the trial judge to draw an inference that discrimination has occurred.
>
> . . . *Batson*, of course, explicitly stated that the defendant ultimately carries the "burden of persuasion" to "prove the existence of purposeful

> discrimination." 476 U.S., at 93. . . . This burden of persuasion "rests with, and never shifts from, the opponent of the strike." *Purkett*, 514 U.S., at 768. Thus, even if the State produces only a frivolous or utterly nonsensical justification for its strike, the case does not end—it merely proceeds to step three. The first two *Batson* steps govern the production of evidence that allows the trial court to determine the persuasiveness of the defendant's constitutional claim. "It is not until the *third* step that the persuasiveness of the justification becomes relevant—the step in which the trial court determines whether the opponent of the strike has carried his burden of proving purposeful discrimination." *Purkett, supra,* at 768. . . .
>
> The *Batson* framework is designed to produce actual answers to suspicions and inferences that discrimination may have infected the jury selection process. See 476 U.S., at 97-98, and n. 20. The inherent uncertainty present in inquiries of discriminatory purpose counsels against engaging in needless and imperfect speculation when a direct answer can be obtained by asking a simple question. See Paulino v. Castro, 371 F.3d 1083, 1090 (CA9 2004) ("It does not matter that the prosecutor might have had good reasons . . . what matters is the real reason they were stricken" (emphasis deleted)); Holloway v. Horn, 355 F.3d 707, 725 (CA3 2004) (speculation "does not aid our inquiry into the reasons the prosecutor actually harbored" for a peremptory strike). The three-step process thus simultaneously serves the public purposes *Batson* is designed to vindicate and encourages "prompt rulings on objections to peremptory challenges without substantial disruption of the jury selection process." Hernandez v. New York, 500 U.S. 352, 358-359 (1991) (opinion of Kennedy, J.).

In a footnote, the Court pointed out what perhaps should have been obvious—that even if a defendant's *Batson* claim is relatively weak, there might nevertheless be some value in requiring the prosecution to respond:

> In the unlikely hypothetical in which the prosecutor declines to respond to a trial judge's inquiry regarding his justification for making a strike, the evidence before the judge would consist not only of the original facts from which the prima facie case was established, but also the prosecutor's refusal to justify his strike in light of the court's request. Such a refusal would provide additional support for the inference of discrimination raised by a defendant's prima facie case.

The clear message of *Johnson* seems to be that most *Batson* claims (i.e., all those that are not facially implausible) should survive the first stage of the *Batson* analysis and proceed to the second and third stages. But that may still beg the question. What happens when those claims get to the later stages of the analysis? How aggressive should the lower courts be, in reviewing the prosecutor's asserted race-neutral reasons for the challenged peremptory strikes?

Two recent Supreme Court decisions—in the same case—seem, at least on the surface, to suggest that such review should be fairly aggressive. In the first decision, Miller-El v. Cockrell, 537 U.S. 322 (2003), the Court (with only Justice Thomas dissenting) overturned the Fifth Circuit's denial of a "certificate of appealability" to review a *Batson* claim made by a Dallas County, Texas, death-row inmate in a federal habeas corpus petition. The Court concluded that Miller-El's evidence was more than adequate to raise an inference of prosecutorial race discrimination, and thus met the test of habeas appealability, which requires a "substantial showing of the denial of a constitutional right." The Court also found the lower court's reliance on the prosecution's alleged race-neutral reasons unwarranted, especially given that "the application of these rationales to the venire might have been selective and based on racial considerations." *Id.*, at 343.

The Fifth Circuit, on remand, issued the "certificate of appealability," but then (somewhat inexplicably, given the Supreme Court's tone in *Miller-El* v. *Cockrell*) rejected Miller-El's underlying *Batson* claim on the merits. The case then returned to the Supreme Court.

MILLER-EL v. DRETKE

Certiorari to the U.S. Court of Appeals for the Fifth Circuit
545 U.S. 231 (2005)

JUSTICE SOUTER delivered the opinion of the Court.

Two years ago, we ordered that a certificate of appealability, under 28 U.S.C. § 2253(c), be issued to habeas petitioner Miller-El, affording review of the District Court's rejection of the claim that prosecutors in his capital murder trial made peremptory strikes of potential jurors based on race. Today we find Miller-El entitled to prevail on that claim and order relief under § 2254.

I

In the course of robbing a Holiday Inn in Dallas, Texas in late 1985, Miller-El and his accomplices bound and gagged two hotel employees, whom Miller-El then shot, killing one and severely injuring the other. During jury selection in Miller-El's trial for capital murder, prosecutors used peremptory strikes against 10 qualified black venire members. Miller-El objected that the strikes were based on race and could not be presumed legitimate, given a history of excluding black members from criminal juries by the Dallas County District Attorney's Office. The trial court received evidence of the practice alleged but found no "systematic exclusion of blacks as a matter of policy" by that office, and therefore no entitlement to relief under Swain v. Alabama, 380 U.S. 202 (1965), the case then defining and marking the limits of relief from racially biased jury selection. The court denied Miller-El's request to pick a new jury, and the trial ended with his death sentence for capital murder.

While an appeal was pending, this Court decided Batson v. Kentucky, 476 U.S. 79 (1986), which replaced *Swain*'s threshold requirement to prove systemic discrimination under a Fourteenth Amendment jury claim, with the rule that discrimination by the prosecutor in selecting the defendant's jury sufficed to establish the constitutional violation. The Texas Court of Criminal Appeals then remanded the matter to the trial court to determine whether Miller-El could show that prosecutors in his case peremptorily struck prospective black jurors because of race. Miller-El v. State, 748 S.W.2d 459 (1988).

The trial court found no such demonstration. After reviewing the *voir dire* record of the explanations given for some of the challenged strikes, and after hearing one of the prosecutors, Paul Macaluso, give his justification for those previously unexplained, the trial court accepted the stated race-neutral reasons for the strikes, which the judge called "completely credible [and] sufficient" as the grounds for a finding of "no purposeful discrimination." The Court of Criminal Appeals affirmed, stating it found "ample support" in the *voir dire* record for the race-neutral explanations offered by prosecutors for the peremptory strikes.

Miller-El then sought habeas relief under 28 U.S.C. § 2254, again pressing his *Batson* claim, among others not now before us. The District Court denied relief, and the Court of Appeals for the Fifth Circuit precluded appeal by denying a certificate of appealability, Miller-El v. Johnson, 261 F.3d 445 (2001). We granted certiorari to consider whether Miller-El was entitled to review on the *Batson* claim, Miller-El v. Cockrell, 534 U.S. 1122 (2002), and reversed the Court of Appeals. After examining the record of Miller-El's extensive evidence of purposeful discrimination by the Dallas County District Attorney's Office before and during his trial, we found an appeal was in order, since the merits of the *Batson* claim were, at the least, debatable by jurists of reason. Miller-El v. Cockrell, 537 U.S. 322 (2003). After granting a certificate of appealability, the Fifth Circuit rejected Miller-El's *Batson* claim on the merits. 361 F.3d 849 (2004). We again granted certiorari, and again we reverse.

II

A

"It is well known that prejudices often exist against particular classes in the community, which sway the judgment of jurors, and which, therefore, operate in some cases to deny to persons of those classes the full enjoyment of that protection which others enjoy." Strauder v. West Virginia,

100 U.S. 303, 309 (1880). Defendants are harmed, of course, when racial discrimination in jury selection compromises the right of trial by impartial jury, but racial minorities are harmed more generally, for prosecutors drawing racial lines in picking juries establish "state-sponsored group stereotypes rooted in, and reflective of, historical prejudice," J. E. B. v. Alabama ex rel. T. B., 511 U.S. 127, 128 (1994).

Nor is the harm confined to minorities. When the government's choice of jurors is tainted with racial bias, that "overt wrong . . . casts doubt over the obligation of the parties, the jury, and indeed the court to adhere to the law throughout the trial. . . ." Powers v. Ohio, 499 U.S. 400, 412 (1991). That is, the very integrity of the courts is jeopardized when a prosecutor's discrimination "invites cynicism respecting the jury's neutrality," *id.*, at 412, and undermines public confidence in adjudication, Georgia v. McCollum, 505 U.S. 42, 49 (1992); Edmonson v. Leesville Concrete Co., 500 U.S. 614, 628 (1991); Batson v. Kentucky, *supra,* at 87. So, "for more than a century, this Court consistently and repeatedly has reaffirmed that racial discrimination by the State in jury selection offends the Equal Protection Clause." Georgia v. McCollum, *supra,* at 44; see Strauder v. West Virginia, *supra,* at 308, 310; Norris v. Alabama, 294 U.S. 587, 596 (1935); Swain v. Alabama, *supra,* at 223-224; Batson v. Kentucky, *supra,* at 84; Powers v. Ohio, *supra,* at 404.

The rub has been the practical difficulty of ferreting out discrimination in selections discretionary by nature, and choices subject to myriad legitimate influences, whatever the race of the individuals on the panel from which jurors are selected. . . . The *Swain* court tried to relate peremptory challenge to equal protection by presuming the legitimacy of prosecutors' strikes except in the face of a longstanding pattern of discrimination. . . . [380 U.S.,] at 223-224.

Swain's demand to make out a continuity of discrimination over time, however, turned out to be difficult to the point of unworkable, and in Batson v. Kentucky, we . . . held that a defendant could make out a prima facie case of discriminatory jury selection by "the totality of the relevant facts" about a prosecutor's conduct during the defendant's own trial. 476 U.S., at 94, 96. "Once the defendant makes a prima facie showing, the burden shifts to the State to come forward with a neutral explanation for challenging . . . jurors" within an arguably targeted class. *Id.*, at 97. Although there may be "any number of bases on which a prosecutor reasonably [might] believe that it is desirable to strike a juror who is not excusable for cause . . . , the prosecutor must give a clear and reasonably specific explanation of his legitimate reasons for exercising the challenge." *Id.*, at 98, n. 20 (internal quotation marks omitted). "The trial court then will have the duty to determine if the defendant has established purposeful discrimination." *Id.*, at 98.

Although the move from *Swain* to *Batson* left a defendant free to challenge the prosecution without having to cast *Swain*'s wide net, the net was not entirely consigned to history, for *Batson*'s individualized focus came with a weakness of its own, owing to its very emphasis on the particular reasons a prosecutor might give. If any facially neutral reason sufficed to answer a *Batson* challenge, then *Batson* would not amount to much more than *Swain*. Some stated reasons are false, and although some false reasons are shown up within the four corners of a given case, sometimes a court may not be sure unless it looks beyond the case at hand. Hence *Batson*'s explanation that a defendant may rely on "all relevant circumstances" to raise an inference of purposeful discrimination. 476 U.S., at 96-97.

B

This case comes to us on review of a denial of habeas relief sought under 28 U.S.C. § 2254, following the Texas trial court's prior determination of fact that the State's race-neutral explanations were true, see Purkett v. Elem, 514 U.S. 765, 769 (1995) *(per curiam);* Batson v. Kentucky, *supra*, at 98, n. 21.

Under the Antiterrorism and Effective Death Penalty Act of 1996, Miller-El may obtain relief only by showing the Texas conclusion to be "an unreasonable determination of the facts in light of the evidence presented in the State court proceeding." 28 U.S.C. § 2254(d)(2). Thus we presume the Texas court's factual findings to be sound unless Miller-El rebuts the "presumption of correctness by clear and convincing evidence." § 2254(e)(1). The standard is demanding but not insatiable; as we said the last time this case was here, "deference does not by definition preclude relief." Miller-El v. Cockrell, 537 U.S., at 340.

III

A

The numbers describing the prosecution's use of peremptories are remarkable. Out of 20 black members of the 108-person venire panel for Miller-El's trial, only 1 served. Although 9 were excused for cause or by agreement, 10 were peremptorily struck by the prosecution. *Id.*, at 331. "The prosecutors used their peremptory strikes to exclude 91% of the eligible African-American venire members. . . . Happenstance is unlikely to produce this disparity." *Id.*, at 342.

More powerful than these bare statistics, however, are side-by-side comparisons of some black venire panelists who were struck and white panelists allowed to serve. If a prosecutor's proffered reason for striking a black panelist applies just as well to an otherwise similar nonblack who is permitted to serve, that is evidence tending to prove purposeful discrimination to be considered at *Batson*'s third step. . . . While we did not develop a comparative juror analysis last time, we did note that the prosecution's reasons for exercising peremptory strikes against some black panel members appeared equally on point as to some white jurors who served. Miller-El v. Cockrell, *supra*, at 343. The details of two panel member comparisons bear this out.

The prosecution used its second peremptory strike to exclude Billy Jean Fields, a black man who expressed unwavering support for the death penalty. On the questionnaire filled out by all panel members before individual examination on the stand, Fields said that he believed in capital punishment, and during questioning he disclosed his belief that the State acts on God's behalf when it imposes the death penalty. "Therefore, if the State exacts death, then that's what it should be." App. 174. He testified that he had no religious or philosophical reservations about the death penalty and that the death penalty deterred crime. *Id.*, at 174-175. He twice averred, without apparent hesitation, that he could sit on Miller-El's jury and make a decision to impose this penalty. *Id.*, at 176-177.

Although at one point in the questioning, Fields indicated that the possibility of rehabilitation might be relevant to the likelihood that a defendant would commit future acts of violence, *id.*, at 183, he responded to ensuing questions by saying that although he believed anyone could be rehabilitated, this belief would not stand in the way of a decision to impose the death penalty:

> "Based on what you [the prosecutor] said as far as the crime goes, there are only two things that could be rendered, death or life in prison. If for some reason the testimony didn't warrant death, then life imprisonment would give an individual an opportunity to rehabilitate. But, you know, you said that the jurors didn't have the opportunity to make a personal decision in the matter with reference to what I thought or felt, but it was just based on the questions according to the way the law has been handed down." *Id.*, at 185 (alteration omitted).

Fields also noted on his questionnaire that his brother had a criminal history. During questioning, the prosecution went into this, too:

> "*Q* Could you tell me a little bit about that?
>
> "*A* He was arrested and convicted on [a] number of occasions for possession of a controlled substance.
>
> "*Q* Was that here in Dallas?

"*A* Yes.

"*Q* Was he involved in any trials or anything like that?

"*A* I suppose of sorts. I don't really know too much about it.

"*Q* Was he ever convicted?

"*A* Yeah, he served time.

"*Q* Do you feel that that would in any way interfere with your service on this jury at all?

"*A* No." App. 190.

Fields was struck peremptorily by the prosecution, with prosecutor James Nelson offering a race-neutral reason:

> "We . . . have concern with reference to some of his statements as to the death penalty in that he said that he could only give death if he thought a person could not be rehabilitated and he later made the comment that any person could be rehabilitated if they find God or are introduced to God and the fact that we have a concern that his religious feelings may affect his jury service in this case." *Id.*, at 197 (alteration omitted).

Thus, Nelson simply mischaracterized Fields's testimony. He represented that Fields said he would not vote for death if rehabilitation was possible, whereas Fields unequivocally stated that he could impose the death penalty regardless of the possibility of rehabilitation. Perhaps Nelson misunderstood, but unless he had an ulterior reason for keeping Fields off the jury we think he would have proceeded differently. In light of Fields's outspoken support for the death penalty, we expect the prosecutor would have cleared up any misunderstanding by asking further questions before getting to the point of exercising a strike.

If, indeed, Fields's thoughts on rehabilitation did make the prosecutor uneasy, he should have worried about a number of white panel members he accepted with no evident reservations. Sandra Hearn said that she believed in the death penalty "if a criminal cannot be rehabilitated and continues to commit the same type of crime." *Id.*, at 429. Hearn went so far as to express doubt that at the penalty phase of a capital case she could conclude that a convicted murderer "would probably commit some criminal acts of violence in the future." *Id.*, at 440. "People change," she said, making it hard to assess the risk of someone's future dangerousness. "The evidence would have to be awful strong." *Ibid.* But the prosecution did not respond to Hearn the way it did to Fields, and without delving into her views about rehabilitation with any further question, it raised no objection to her serving on the jury. White panelist Mary Witt said she would take the possibility of rehabilitation into account in deciding at the penalty phase of the trial about a defendant's probability of future dangerousness, 6 Record of *Voir Dire* 2433 (hereinafter Record), but the prosecutors asked her no further question about her views on reformation, and they accepted her as a juror. *Id.*, at 2464-2465.[4] Latino venireman Fernando Gutierrez, who served on the jury, said that he would consider the death penalty for someone who could not be rehabilitated, App. 777, but the prosecutors did not question him further about this view. In sum, nonblack jurors whose remarks on rehabilitation could well have signaled a limit on their willingness to impose a death sentence were not questioned further and drew no objection, but the prosecution expressed apprehension about a black juror's belief in the possibility of reformation even though he repeatedly stated his approval of the death penalty and testified that he could impose it according to state legal standards even when the alternative sentence of life imprisonment would give a defendant (like everyone else in the world) the opportunity to reform.[5]

The unlikelihood that his position on rehabilitation had anything to do with the peremptory strike of Fields is underscored by the prosecution's response after Miller-El's lawyer pointed out that the prosecutor had misrepresented Fields's responses on the subject. A moment earlier the prosecutor had finished his misdescription of Fields's views on potential rehabilitation with the words, "Those are our reasons for exercising our . . . strike at this time." *Id.*, at 197. When defense counsel called him on his misstatement, he neither defended what he said nor withdrew the strike. *Id.*, at 198. Instead, he suddenly came up with Fields's brother's prior conviction as another reason for the strike. *Id.*, at 199.

It would be difficult to credit the State's new explanation, which reeks of afterthought. While the Court of Appeals tried to bolster it with the observation that no seated juror was in Fields's position with respect to his brother, 361 F.3d at 859-860, the court's readiness to accept the State's substitute reason ignores not only its pretextual timing but the other reasons rendering it implausible. Fields's testimony indicated he was not close to his brother, App. 190 ("I don't really know too much about it"), and

4. Witt ultimately did not serve because she was peremptorily struck by the defense. 6 Record 2465. The fact that Witt and other venire members discussed here were peremptorily struck by the defense is not relevant to our point. For each of them, the defense did not make a decision to exercise a peremptory until after the prosecution decided whether to accept or reject, so each was accepted by the prosecution before being ultimately struck by the defense. . . .

5. Prosecutors did exercise peremptory strikes on Penny Crowson and Charlotte Whaley, who expressed views about rehabilitation similar to those of Witt and Gutierrez. App. 554, 715.

the prosecution asked nothing further about the influence his brother's history might have had on Fields, as it probably would have done if the family history had actually mattered. See, e.g., Ex parte Travis, 776 So. 2d 874, 881 (Ala. 2000) ("The State's failure to engage in any meaningful voir dire examination on a subject the State alleges it is concerned about is evidence suggesting that the explanation is a sham and a pretext for discrimination"). There is no good reason to doubt that the State's afterthought about Fields's brother was anything but makeweight.

The Court of Appeals's judgment on the Fields strike is unsupportable for the same reason the State's first explanation is itself unsupportable. The Appeals Court's description of Fields's *voir dire* testimony mentioned only his statements that everyone could be rehabilitated, failing to note that Fields affirmed that he could give the death penalty if the law and evidence called for it, regardless of the possibility of divine grace. The Court of Appeals made no mention of the fact that the prosecution mischaracterized Fields as saying he could not give death if rehabilitation were possible. 361 F.3d at 856.

In sum, when we look for nonblack jurors similarly situated to Fields, we find strong similarities as well as some differences.[6] But the differences seem far from significant, particularly when we read Fields's *voir dire* testimony in its entirety. Upon that reading, Fields should have been an ideal juror in the eyes of a prosecutor seeking a death sentence, and the prosecutors' explanations for the strike cannot reasonably be accepted. See Miller-El v. Cockrell, 537 U.S., at 339 (the credibility of reasons given can be measured by "how reasonable, or how improbable, the explanations are; and by whether the proffered rationale has some basis in accepted trial strategy").

The prosecution's proffered reasons for striking Joe Warren, another black venireman, are comparably unlikely. Warren gave this answer when he was asked what the death penalty accomplished:

> "I don't know. It's really hard to say because I know sometimes you feel that it might help to deter crime and then you feel that the person is not really suffering. You're taking the suffering away from him. So it's like I said, sometimes you have mixed feelings about whether or not this is punishment or, you know, you're relieving personal punishment." App. 205; 3 Record 1532.

6. The dissent contends that there are no white panelists similarly situated to Fields and to panel member Joe Warren because "'similarly situated' does not mean matching any one of several reasons the prosecution gave for striking a potential juror — it means matching *all* of them.'" *Post*, at 19 (quoting Miller-El v. Cockrell, 537 U.S., at 362-363 (THOMAS, J., dissenting)). None of our cases announces a rule that no comparison is probative unless the situation of the individuals compared is identical in all respects, and there is no reason to accept one. Nothing in the combination of Fields's statements about rehabilitation and his brother's history discredits our grounds for inferring that these purported reasons were pretextual. A *per se* rule that a defendant cannot win a *Batson* claim unless there is an exactly identical white juror would leave *Batson* inoperable; potential jurors are not products of a set of cookie cutters.

The prosecution said nothing about these remarks when it struck Warren from the panel, but prosecutor Paul Macaluso referred to this answer as the first of his reasons when he testified at the later *Batson* hearing:

> "I thought [Warren's statements on *voir dire*] were inconsistent responses. At one point he says, you know, on a case-by-case basis and at another point he said, well, I think—I got the impression, at least, that he suggested that the death penalty was an easy way out, that they should be made to suffer more." App. 909.

On the face of it, the explanation is reasonable from the State's point of view, but its plausibility is severely undercut by the prosecution's failure to object to other panel members who expressed views much like Warren's. [For example,] Sandra Jenkins, whom the State accepted (but who was then struck by the defense) testified that she thought "a harsher treatment is life imprisonment with no parole." *Id.*, at 542. Leta Girard, accepted by the State (but also struck by the defense) gave her opinion that "living sometimes is a worse—is worse to me than dying would be." *Id.*, at 624. The fact that Macaluso's reason also applied to these other panel members, most of them white, none of them struck, is evidence of pretext.

The suggestion of pretext is not, moreover, mitigated much by Macaluso's explanation that Warren was struck when the State had 10 peremptory challenges left and could afford to be liberal in using them. *Id.*, at 908. If that were the explanation for striking Warren and later accepting panel members who thought death would be too easy, the prosecutors should have struck Sandra Jenkins, whom they examined and accepted before Warren. . . . Yet the prosecutors accepted the white panel member Jenkins and struck the black venireman Warren.

Macaluso's explanation that the prosecutors grew more sparing with peremptory challenges as the jury selection wore on does, however, weaken any suggestion that the State's acceptance of [Troy] Woods, the one black juror, shows that race was not in play. Woods was the eighth juror, qualified in the fifth week of jury selection. Joint Lodging 125. When the State accepted him, 11 of its 15 peremptory strikes were gone, 7 of them used to strike black panel members. The juror questionnaires show that at least three members of the venire panel yet to be questioned on the stand were opposed to capital punishment, Janice Mackey, *id.*, at 79; Paul Bailey, *id.*, at 63; and Anna Keaton, *id.*, at 55. With at least three remaining panel members highly undesirable to the State, the prosecutors had to exercise prudent restraint in using strikes. This late-stage decision to accept a black panel member willing to impose a death sentence does not, therefore, neutralize the early-stage decision to challenge a comparable venireman, Warren. In fact, if the prosecutors were going to accept any black juror to obscure the otherwise consistent pattern of opposition to seating one, the time to do so was getting late. . . .

[T]he rule in *Batson* provides an opportunity to the prosecutor to give the reason for striking the juror, and it requires the judge to assess the plausibility of that reason in light of all evidence with a bearing on it. 476 U.S., at 96-97; Miller-El v. Cockrell, 537 U.S., at 339. It is true that peremptories are often the subjects of instinct, Batson v. Kentucky, 476 U.S., at 106 (Marshall, J., concurring), and it can sometimes be hard to say what the reason is. But when illegitimate grounds like race are in issue, a prosecutor simply has got to state his reasons as best he can and stand or fall on the plausibility of the reasons he gives. A *Batson* challenge does not call for a mere exercise in thinking up any rational basis. If the stated reason does not hold up, its pretextual significance does not fade because a trial judge, or an appeals court, can imagine a reason that might not have been shown up as false. The Court of Appeals's and the dissent's substitution of a reason for eliminating Warren does nothing to satisfy the prosecutors' burden of stating a racially neutral explanation for their own actions.

The whole of the *voir dire* testimony subject to consideration casts the prosecution's reasons for striking Warren in an implausible light. Comparing his strike with the treatment of panel members who expressed similar views supports a conclusion that race was significant in determining who was challenged and who was not.

B

The case for discrimination goes beyond these comparisons to include broader patterns of practice during the jury selection. The prosecution's shuffling of the venire panel, its enquiry into views on the death penalty, its questioning about minimum acceptable sentences: all indicate decisions probably based on race. Finally, the appearance of discrimination is confirmed by widely known evidence of the general policy of the Dallas County District Attorney's Office to exclude black venire members from juries at the time Miller-El's jury was selected.

The first clue to the prosecutors' intentions, distinct from the peremptory challenges themselves, is their resort during *voir dire* to a procedure known in Texas as the jury shuffle. In the State's criminal practice, either side may literally reshuffle the cards bearing panel members' names, thus rearranging the order in which members of a venire panel are seated and reached for questioning. Once the order is established, the panel members seated at the back are likely to escape *voir dire* altogether, for those not questioned by the end of the week are dismissed. . . .

In this case, the prosecution and then the defense shuffled the cards at the beginning of the first week of *voir dire;* the record does not reflect the changes in order. App. 113-114. At the beginning of the second week, when a number of black members were seated at the front of the panel, the prosecution shuffled. 2 Record 836-837. At the beginning of the third week, the first four panel members were black. The prosecution shuffled, and these black panel members ended up at the back. Then the defense shuffled, and the black panel members again appeared at the front. The prosecution requested another shuffle, but the trial court refused. App. 124-132. Finally, the defense shuffled at the beginning of the fourth and fifth weeks of *voir dire;* the record does not reflect the panel's racial composition before or after those shuffles. *Id.,* at 621-622; 9 Record 3585.

The State notes in its brief that there might be racially neutral reasons for shuffling the jury, and we suppose there might be. But no racially neutral reason has ever been offered in this case, and nothing stops the suspicion of discriminatory intent from rising to an inference.

The next body of evidence that the State was trying to avoid black jurors is the contrasting *voir dire* questions posed respectively to black and nonblack panel members, on two different subjects. First, there were the prosecutors' statements preceding questions about a potential juror's thoughts on capital punishment. Some of these prefatory statements were cast in general terms, but some followed the so-called graphic script, describing the method of execution in rhetorical and clinical detail. It is intended, Miller-El contends, to prompt some expression of hesitation to consider the death penalty and thus to elicit plausibly neutral grounds for a peremptory strike of a potential juror subjected to it, if not a strike for cause. If the graphic script is given to a higher proportion of blacks than whites, this is evidence that prosecutors more often wanted blacks off the jury, absent some neutral and extenuating explanation.

As we pointed out last time, for 94% of white venire panel members, prosecutors gave a bland description of the death penalty before asking about the individual's feelings on the subject. Miller-El v. Cockrell, 537 U.S., at 332. . . . Only 6% of white venire panelists, but 53% of those who were black, heard [the much more graphic] description of the death penalty before being asked their feelings about it. . . .

The State concedes that this disparate questioning did occur but argues that use of the graphic script turned not on a panelist's race but on expressed ambivalence about the death penalty in the preliminary questionnaire. Prosecutors were trying, the argument goes, to weed out noncommittal or uncertain jurors, not black jurors. And while some white venire members expressed opposition to the death penalty on their questionnaires, they were not read the graphic script because their feelings were already clear. The State says that giving the graphic script to these panel members would only have antagonized them. Brief for Respondent 27-32.

This argument, however, first advanced in dissent when the case was last here, Miller-El v. Cockrell, *supra*, at 364-368 (opinion of THOMAS, J.), and later adopted by the State and the Court of Appeals, simply does not fit the facts. Looking at the answers on the questionnaires, and at *voir dire* testimony expressly discussing answers on the questionnaires, we find that black venire members were more likely than nonblacks to receive the graphic script regardless of their expressions of certainty or ambivalence about the death penalty, and the State's chosen explanation for the graphic script fails in the cases of four out of the eight black panel members who received it. Two of them, Janice Mackey and Anna Keaton, clearly stated opposition to the death penalty but they received the graphic script, while the black panel members Wayman Kennedy and Jeannette Butler were unambiguously in favor but got the graphic description anyway. The State's explanation does even worse in the instances of the five nonblacks who received the graphic script, missing the mark four times out of five: Vivian Sztybel and Filemon Zablan received it, although each was unambiguously in favor of the death penalty, while Dominick Desinise and Clara Evans unambiguously opposed it but were given the graphic version. . . .

The State's attempt at a race-neutral rationalization thus simply fails to explain what the prosecutors did. But if we posit instead that the prosecutors' first object was to use the graphic script to make a case for excluding black panel members opposed to or ambivalent about the death penalty, there is a much tighter fit of fact and explanation. Of the 10 nonblacks whose questionnaires expressed ambivalence or opposition, only 30% received the graphic treatment. But of the seven blacks who expressed ambivalence or opposition, 86% heard the graphic script. As between the State's ambivalence explanation and Miller-El's racial one, race is much the better, and the reasonable inference is that race was the major consideration when the prosecution chose to follow the graphic script.

The same is true for another kind of disparate questioning, which might fairly be called trickery. The prosecutors asked members of the panel how low a sentence they would consider imposing for murder. Most potential jurors were first told that Texas law provided for a minimum term of five years, but some members of the panel were not, and if a panel member then insisted on a minimum above five years, the prosecutor would suppress his normal preference for tough jurors and claim cause to strike. Two Terms ago, we described how this disparate questioning was correlated with race:

> "Ninety-four percent of whites were informed of the statutory minimum sentence, compared [with] only twelve and a half percent of African-Americans. No explanation is proffered for the statistical disparity. . . . Indeed, while petitioner's appeal was pending before the Texas Court of Criminal Appeals, that court found a *Batson* violation where this precise line of disparate questioning on mandatory minimums was employed by one of the same prosecutors who tried the instant case. Chambers v. State, 784 S.W.2d 29, 31 (Tex. Crim. App. 1989)." Miller-El v. Cockrell, 537 U.S., at 345.

The State concedes that the manipulative minimum punishment questioning was used to create cause to strike, but now it offers the extenuation that prosecutors omitted the 5-year information not on the basis of race, but on stated opposition to the death penalty, or ambivalence about it, on the questionnaires and in the *voir dire* testimony. . . . But the State's rationale flatly fails to explain why most white panel members who expressed similar opposition or ambivalence were not subjected to it. . . . [O]nly 27% of nonblacks questioned on the subject who expressed these views were subjected to the trick question, as against 100% of black members. Once again, the implication of race in the prosecutors' choice of questioning cannot be explained away.

There is a final body of evidence that confirms this conclusion. We know that for decades leading up to the time this case was tried prosecutors in the Dallas County office had followed a specific policy of systematically excluding blacks from juries, as we explained the last time the case was here.

> " . . . [T]he defense presented evidence that the District Attorney's Office had adopted a formal policy to exclude minorities from jury service . . . .A manual entitled 'Jury Selection in a Criminal Case' [sometimes known as the Sparling Manual] was distributed to prosecutors. It contained an article authored by a former prosecutor (and later a judge) under the direction of his superiors in the District Attorney's Office, outlining the reasoning for excluding minorities from jury service. Although the manual was written

in 1968, it remained in circulation until 1976, if not later, and was available at least to one of the prosecutors in Miller-El's trial." Miller-El v. Cockrell, 537 U.S., at 334-335.

Prosecutors here "marked the race of each prospective juror on their juror cards." *Id.*, at 347.[38]

The Court of Appeals concluded that Miller-El failed to show by clear and convincing evidence that the state court's finding of no discrimination was wrong, whether his evidence was viewed collectively or separately. 361 F.3d at 862. We find this conclusion as unsupportable as the "dismissive and strained interpretation" of his evidence that we disapproved when we decided Miller-El was entitled to a certificate of appealability. See Miller-El v. Cockrell, *supra,* at 344. It is true, of course, that at some points the significance of Miller-El's evidence is open to judgment calls, but when this evidence on the issues raised is viewed cumulatively its direction is too powerful to conclude anything but discrimination.

In the course of drawing a jury to try a black defendant, 10 of the 11 qualified black venire panel members were peremptorily struck. At least two of them, Fields and Warren, were ostensibly acceptable to prosecutors seeking a death verdict, and Fields was ideal. The prosecutors' chosen race-neutral reasons for the strikes do not hold up and are so far at odds with the evidence that pretext is the fair conclusion, indicating the very discrimination the explanations were meant to deny.

The strikes that drew these incredible explanations occurred in a selection process replete with evidence that the prosecutors were selecting and rejecting potential jurors because of race. At least two of the jury shuffles conducted by the State make no sense except as efforts to delay consideration of black jury panelists to the end of the week, when they might not even be reached. The State has in fact never offered any other explanation. Nor has the State denied that disparate lines of questioning were pursued: 53% of black panelists but only 3% of nonblacks were questioned with a graphic script meant to induce qualms about applying the death penalty (and thus explain a strike), and 100% of blacks but only 27% of nonblacks were subjected to a trick question about the minimum acceptable penalty for murder, meant to induce a disqualifying answer. The State's attempts to explain the prosecutors' questioning of particular witnesses on nonracial grounds fit the evidence less well than the racially discriminatory hypothesis.

38. The State claimed at oral argument that prosecutors could have been tracking jurors' races to be sure of avoiding a *Batson* violation. Tr. of Oral Arg. 44. *Batson,* of course, was decided the month after Miller-El was tried.

If anything more is needed for an undeniable explanation of what was going on, history supplies it. The prosecutors took their cues from a 20- year old manual of tips on jury selection, as shown by their notes of the race of each potential juror. By the time a jury was chosen, the State had peremptorily challenged 12% of qualified nonblack panel members, but eliminated 91% of the black ones.

It blinks reality to deny that the State struck Fields and Warren, included in that 91%, because they were black. The strikes correlate with no fact as well as they correlate with race, and they occurred during a selection infected by shuffling and disparate questioning that race explains better than any race-neutral reason advanced by the State. The State's pretextual positions confirm Miller-El's claim, and the prosecutors' own notes proclaim that the Sparling Manual's emphasis on race was on their minds when they considered every potential juror.

The state court's conclusion that the prosecutors' strikes of Fields and Warren were not racially determined is shown up as wrong to a clear and convincing degree; the state court's conclusion was unreasonable as well as erroneous. The judgment of the Court of Appeals is reversed, and the case is remanded for entry of judgment for petitioner together with orders of appropriate relief.

JUSTICE BREYER, concurring.

In Batson v. Kentucky, 476 U.S. 79 (1986), the Court adopted a burden-shifting rule designed to ferret out the unconstitutional use of race in jury selection. In his separate opinion, Justice Thurgood Marshall predicted that the Court's rule would not achieve its goal. The only way to "end the racial discrimination that peremptories inject into the jury-selection process," he concluded, was to "eliminate peremptory challenges entirely." *Id.,* at 102-103 (concurring opinion). Today's case reinforces Justice Marshall's concerns.

I

To begin with, this case illustrates the practical problems of proof that Justice Marshall described. . . .

At *Batson*'s first step, litigants remain free to misuse peremptory challenges as long as the strikes fall *below* the prima facie threshold level. . . . At *Batson*'s second step, prosecutors need only tender a neutral reason, not a "persuasive, or even plausible" one. . . . And most importantly, at step three, *Batson* asks judges to engage in the awkward, sometime hopeless, task of second-guessing a prosecutor's instinctive judgment—the underlying basis for which may be invisible even to the prosecutor exercising the challenge. . . .

Given the inevitably clumsy fit between any objectively measurable standard and the subjective decision making at issue, I am not surprised to find studies and anecdotal reports suggesting that, despite *Batson*, the discriminatory use of peremptory challenges remains a problem. See, *e.g.*, Baldus, Woodworth, Zuckerman, Weiner, & Broffitt, The Use of Peremptory Challenges in Capital Murder Trials: A Legal and Empirical Analysis, 3 U. Pa. J. Const. L. 3, 52-53, 73, n. 197 (2001) (in 317 capital trials in Philadelphia between 1981 and 1997, prosecutors struck 51% of black jurors and 26% of nonblack jurors; defense counsel struck 26% of black jurors and 54% of nonblack jurors; and race-based uses of prosecutorial peremptories declined by only 2% after *Batson*); Rose, The Peremptory Challenge Accused of Race or Gender Discrimination? Some Data from One County, 23 Law and Human Behavior 695, 698-699 (1999) (in one North Carolina county, 71% of excused black jurors were removed by the prosecution; 81% of excused white jurors were removed by the defense); Tucker, In Moore's Trials, Excluded Jurors Fit Racial Pattern, Washington Post, Apr. 2, 2001, p. A1 (in a D. C. murder case spanning four trials, prosecutors excused 41 blacks or other minorities and 6 whites; defense counsel struck 29 whites and 13 black venire members); Mize, A Legal Discrimination; Juries Are Not Supposed to be Picked on the Basis of Race and Sex, But It Happens All the Time, Washington Post, Oct. 8, 2000, p. B8 (authored by judge on the D. C. Superior Court); see also Melilli, *Batson* in Practice: What We Have Learned About *Batson* and Peremptory Challenges, 71 Notre Dame L. Rev. 447, 462-464 (1996) (finding *Batson* challenges' success rates lower where peremptories were used to strike black, rather than white, potential jurors); Brand, The Supreme Court, Equal Protection and Jury Selection: Denying That Race Still Matters, 1994 Wis. L. Rev. 511, 583-589 (examining judicial decisions and concluding that few *Batson* challenges succeed); Note, Batson v. Kentucky and J. E. B. v. Alabama ex rel. T. B.: Is the Peremptory Challenge Still Preeminent?, 36 Boston College L. Rev. 161, 189, and n. 303 (1994) (same); Montoya, The Future of the Post-*Batson* Peremptory Challenge: Voir Dire by Questionnaire and the "Blind" Peremptory Challenge, 29 U. Mich. J. L. Reform 981, 1006, nn. 126-127, 1035 (1996) (reporting attorneys' views on the difficulty of proving *Batson* claims).

II

Practical problems of proof to the side, peremptory challenges seem increasingly anomalous in our judicial system. On the one hand, the

Court has widened and deepened *Batson*'s basic constitutional rule [by applying it to criminal defendants, private litigants, cases in which defendants and excluded jurors are of different races, and peremptory challenges based on gender].

On the other hand, the use of race- and gender-based stereotypes in the jury-selection process seems better organized and more systematized than ever before. See, e.g., Post, A Loaded Box of Stereotypes: Despite 'Batson,' Race, Gender Play Big Roles in Jury Selection., Nat. L. J., Apr. 25, 2005, pp. 1, 18 (discussing common reliance on race and gender in jury selection). For example, one jury-selection guide counsels attorneys to perform a "demographic analysis" that assigns numerical points to characteristics such as age, occupation, and marital status—in addition to race as well as gender. See V. Starr & A. McCormick, Jury Selection 193-200 (3d ed. 2001). Thus, in a hypothetical dispute between a white landlord and an African-American tenant, the authors suggest awarding two points to an African-American venire member while subtracting one point from her white counterpart. *Id.*, at 197-199.

For example, a bar journal article counsels lawyers to "rate" potential jurors "demographically (age, gender, marital status, etc.) and mark who would be under stereotypical circumstances [their] natural *enemies* and *allies.*" Drake, The Art of Litigating: Deselecting Jurors Like the Pros, 34 Md. Bar J. 18, 22 (Mar.-Apr. 2001) (emphasis in original).

For example, materials from a legal convention, while noting that "nationality" is less important than "once was thought," and emphasizing that "the answers a prospective juror gives to questions are much more valuable," still point out that "stereotypically" those of "Italian, French, and Spanish" origin "are thought to be pro-plaintiff as well as other minorities, such as Mexican and Jewish[;] persons of German, Scandinavian, Swedish, Finnish, Dutch, Nordic, British, Scottish, Oriental, and Russian origin are thought to be better for the defense"; African-Americans "have always been considered good for the plaintiff," and "more politically conservative minorities will be more likely to lean toward defendants." Blue, Mirroring, Proxemics, Nonverbal Communication and Other Psychological Tools, Advocacy Track—Psychology of Trial, Association of Trial Lawyers of America Annual Convention Reference Materials, 1 Ann. 2001 ATLA-CLE 153, available at WESTLAW, ATLA-CLE database (June 8, 2005). . . .

These examples reflect a professional effort to fulfill the lawyer's obligation to help his or her client. Cf. *J. E. B.*, *supra*, at 148-149 (O'CONNOR, J., concurring) (observing that jurors' race and gender may inform their perspective). Nevertheless, the outcome in terms of jury selection is the same as it would be were the motive less benign. And as long as that is so, the law's antidiscrimination command and a peremptory jury-selection system that permits or encourages the use of stereotypes work at cross-purposes.

Finally, a jury system without peremptories is no longer unthinkable. Members of the legal profession have begun serious consideration of that possibility. See, e.g., Allen v. Florida, 596 So. 2d 1083, 1088-1089 (Fla. App. 1992) (Hubbart, J., concurring). . . . And England, a common-law jurisdiction that has eliminated peremptory challenges, continues to administer fair trials based largely on random jury selection. See Criminal Justice Act, 1988, ch. 33, § 118(1), 22 Halsbury's Statutes 357 (4th ed. 2003 reissue) (U.K.); see also 2 Jury Service in Victoria, Final Report, ch. 5, p. 165 (Dec. 1997) (1993 study of English barristers showed majority support for system without peremptory challenges).

III

I recognize that peremptory challenges have a long historical pedigree. They may help to reassure a party of the fairness of the jury. But long ago, Blackstone recognized the peremptory challenge as an "arbitrary and capricious species of [a] challenge." 4 W. Blackstone, Commentaries on the Laws of England 346 (1769). . . .

. . . In light of the considerations I have mentioned, I believe it necessary to reconsider *Batson*'s test and the peremptory challenge system as a whole. With that qualification, I join the Court's opinion.

JUSTICE THOMAS, with whom CHIEF JUSTICE REHNQUIST and JUSTICE SCALIA join, dissenting.

. . . Miller-El's cumulative evidence does not come remotely close to clearly and convincingly establishing that the state court's factual finding was unreasonable. [This case involves] four types of evidence: (1) the alleged disparate treatment and (2) disparate questioning of black and white veniremen; (3) the prosecution's jury shuffles; and (4) historical discrimination by the D.A.'s Office in the selection of juries. Although each type of evidence "is open to judgment calls," *ante*, at—, the majority finds that a succession of unpersuasive arguments amounts to a compelling case. In the end, the majority's opinion is its own best refutation: It strains to demonstrate what should instead be patently obvious.

The majority devotes the bulk of its opinion to a side-by-side comparison of white panelists who were allowed to serve and two black panelists who were struck, Billy Jean Fields and Joe Warren. *Ante*, at 7-19. The majority argues that the prosecution's reasons for striking Fields and Warren apply equally to whites who were permitted to serve, and thus those reasons must have been pretextual. The *voir dire* transcript reveals that the majority is mistaken.

It is worth noting at the outset, however, that Miller-El's and the Court's claims have always been a moving target. Of the 20 black veniremen at Miller-El's trial, 9 were struck for cause or by the parties' agreement, and 1 served on the jury. Miller-El claimed at the *Batson* hearing that all 10 remaining black veniremen were dismissed on account of race. That number dropped to 7 on appeal, and then again to 6 during his federal habeas proceedings. . . .

The majority now focuses exclusively on Fields and Warren. But Warren was obviously equivocal about the death penalty. In the end, the majority's case reduces to a single venireman, Fields, and its reading of a 20-year-old *voir dire* transcript that is ambiguous at best. This is the antithesis of clear and convincing evidence.

From the outset of questioning, Warren did not specify when he would vote to impose the death penalty. When asked by prosecutor Paul Macaluso about his ability to impose the death penalty, Warren stated, "There are some cases where I would agree, you know, and there are others that I don't." 3 Record 1526. Macaluso then explained at length the types of crimes that qualified as capital murder under Texas law, and asked whether Warren would be able to impose the death penalty for those types of heinous crimes. *Id.*, at 1527-1530. Warren continued to hedge: "I would say it depends on the case and the circumstances involved at the time." *Id.*, at 1530. He offered no sense of the circumstances that would lead him to conclude that the death penalty was an appropriate punishment.

Macaluso then changed tack and asked whether Warren believed that the death penalty accomplished any social purpose. *Id.*, at 1531-1532. Once again, Warren proved impossible to pin down: "Yes and no. Sometimes I think it does and sometimes I think it don't. Sometimes you have mixed feelings about things like that." *Id.*, at 1532. Macaluso then focused on what the death penalty accomplished in those cases where Warren believed it useful. *Ibid.* Even then, Warren expressed no firm view:

"I don't know. It's really hard to say because I know sometimes you feel that it might help to deter crime and then you feel that the person is not really suffering. You're taking the suffering away from him. So it's like I said, sometimes you have mixed feelings about whether or not this is punishment or, you know, you're relieving personal punishment." *Ibid.*

While Warren's ambivalence was driven by his uncertainty that the death penalty was severe enough, that is beside the point. Throughout the examination, Warren gave no indication whether or when he would prefer the death penalty to other forms of punishment, specifically life imprisonment. 3 Record 1532-1533. To prosecutors seeking the death penalty, the reason for Warren's ambivalence was irrelevant. . . .

According to the majority, Macaluso testified that he struck Warren for his statement that the death penalty was "an easy way out," *ante*, at 14 (quoting App. 909), and not for his ambivalence about the death penalty, *ante*, at 17. This grossly mischaracterizes the record. Macaluso specifically testified at the *Batson* hearing that he was troubled by the "*inconsistency*" of Warren's responses. App. 909 (emphasis added). Macaluso was speaking of Warren's ambivalence about the death penalty, a reason wholly unrelated to race. This was Macaluso's "stated reason," and Macaluso ought to "stand or fall on the plausibility" of this reason—not one concocted by the majority. *Ante*, at 18.

The majority points to four other panel members—Kevin Duke, Troy Woods, Sandra Jenkins, and Leta Girard—who supposedly expressed views much like Warren's, but who were not struck by the State. According to the majority, this is evidence of pretext. But the majority's premise is faulty. None of these veniremen was as difficult to pin down on the death penalty as Warren. For instance, Duke supported the death penalty. App. 373 ("I've always believed in having the death penalty. I think it serves a purpose"); *ibid.* ("I mean, it's a sad thing to see, to have to kill someone, but they shouldn't have done the things that they did. Sometimes they deserve to be killed"); *id.*, at 394 ("If I feel that I can answer all three of these [special-issue] questions yes and I feel that he's done a crime worthy of the death penalty, yes, I will give the death penalty"). By contrast, Warren never expressed a firm view one way or the other. . . .

Nevertheless, even assuming that any of these veniremen expressed views similar to Warren's, Duke, Woods, and Girard were questioned much later in the jury selection process, when the State had fewer peremptories to spare. Only Sandra Jenkins was questioned early in the *voir dire* process, and thus only Jenkins was even arguably similarly situated to Warren. However, Jenkins and Warren were different in important respects. Jenkins expressed no doubt whatsoever about the death penalty. She testified that she had researched the death penalty in high school, and she said in response to questioning by both parties that she strongly believed in the death penalty's value as a deterrent to crime. 3 Record 1074-1075, 1103-1104. This alone explains why the State accepted Jenkins as a juror, while Miller-El struck her. In addition, Jenkins did not have a relative who had been convicted of a crime, but Warren did. At the *Batson* hearing, Macaluso testified that he struck Warren both for Warren's inconsistent responses regarding the death penalty and for his brother's conviction.

The majority thinks it can prove pretext by pointing to white veniremen who match only one of the State's proffered reasons for striking Warren. This defies logic. "'Similarly situated' does not mean matching any one of several reasons the prosecution gave for striking a potential juror—it means matching *all* of them." *Miller-El I*, 537 U.S., at 362-363 (THOMAS, J., dissenting). Given limited peremptories, prosecutors often must focus on the potential jurors most likely to disfavor their case. By ignoring the totality of reasons that a prosecutor strikes any particular venireman, it is the majority that treats potential jurors as "products of a set of cookie cutters"—as if potential jurors who share only some among many traits must be treated the same to avoid a *Batson* violation. Of course jurors must not be "identical in all respects" to gauge pretext, but to isolate race as a variable, the jurors must be comparable in all respects that the prosecutor proffers as important. This does not mean "that a defendant cannot win a *Batson* claim unless there is an exactly identical white juror." It means that a defendant cannot support a *Batson* claim by comparing veniremen of different races unless the veniremen are truly similar. . . .

The second black venireman on whom the majority relies is Billy Jean Fields. Fields expressed support for the death penalty, App. 174-175, but Fields also expressed views that called into question his ability to impose the death penalty. Fields was a deeply religious man, *id.*, at 173-174, 192-194, and prosecutors feared that his religious convictions might make him reluctant to impose the death penalty. Those fears were confirmed by Fields' view that all people could be rehabilitated if introduced to God, a fear that had special force considering the special-issue questions necessary to impose the death penalty in Texas. One of those questions asked whether there was a probability that the defendant would engage in future violence that threatened society. When they reached this question, Macaluso and Fields had the following exchange:

> "[*MACALUSO:*] What does that word probability mean to you in that connotation?
>
> "[*FIELDS:*] Well, it means is there a possibility that [a defendant] will continue to lead this type of life, will he be rehabilitated or does he intend to make this a life-long ambition.

"[*MACALUSO:*] Let me ask you, Mr. Fields, do you feel as though some people simply cannot be rehabilitated?

"[FIELDS:] No.

"[*MACALUSO:*] You think everyone can be rehabilitated?

"[*FIELDS:*] Yes." *Id.*, at 183-184.

Thus, Fields indicated that the possibility of rehabilitation was ever-present and relevant to whether a defendant might commit future acts of violence. In light of that view, it is understandable that prosecutors doubted whether he could vote to impose the death penalty.

Fields did testify that he could impose the death penalty, even on a defendant who could be rehabilitated. *Id.*, at 185. For the majority, this shows that the State's reason was pretextual. But of course Fields said that he could fairly consider the death penalty—if he had answered otherwise, he would have been challengeable *for cause*. The point is that Fields' earlier answers cast significant doubt on whether he could impose the death penalty. The very purpose of peremptory strikes is to allow parties to remove potential jurors whom they suspect, but cannot prove, may exhibit a particular bias. See *Swain*, 380 U.S., at 220, 202; J. E. B. v. Alabama ex rel. T. B., 511 U.S. 127, 148 (1994) (O'CONNOR, J., concurring). Based on Fields' *voir dire* testimony, it was perfectly reasonable for prosecutors to suspect that Fields might be swayed by a penitent defendant's testimony. The prosecutors may have been worried for nothing about Fields' religious sentiments, but that does not mean they were instead worried about Fields' race. . . .

Miller-El's claims of disparate questioning [involving use of the so-called "graphic script"] also do not fit the facts. . . . The State questioned panelists differently when their questionnaire responses indicated ambivalence about the death penalty. Any racial disparity in questioning resulted from the reality that more nonblack veniremen favored the death penalty and were willing to impose it.

Miller-El also alleges that the State employed two different scripts on the basis of race when asking questions about imposition of the minimum sentence. This disparate-questioning argument is even more flawed than the last one. The evidence confirms that, as the State argues, prosecutors used different questioning on minimum sentences to create cause to strike veniremen who were ambivalent about or opposed to the death penalty. . . .

Miller-El's argument that prosecutors shuffled the jury to remove blacks is pure speculation. At the *Batson* hearing, Miller-El did not raise, nor was there any discussion of, the topic of jury shuffling as a racial tactic. The record shows only that the State shuffled the jury during the first three weeks of jury selection, while Miller-El shuffled the jury during each of the five weeks. This evidence no more proves that prosecutors sought to eliminate blacks from the jury, than it proves that Miller-El sought to eliminate whites even more often. *Miller-El I*, 537 U.S., at 360 (THOMAS, J., dissenting).

Miller-El notes that the State twice shuffled the jury (in the second and third weeks) when a number of blacks were seated at the front of the panel. According to the majority, this gives rise to an "inference" that prosecutors were discriminating. But Miller-El should not be asking this Court to draw "inferences"; he should be asking it to examine clear and convincing proof. And the inference is not even a strong one. We do not know if the nonblacks near the front shared characteristics with the blacks near the front, providing race-neutral reasons for the shuffles. We also do not know the racial composition of the panel during the first week when the State shuffled, or during the fourth and fifth weeks when it did not.

More important, any number of characteristics other than race could have been apparent to prosecutors from a visual inspection of the jury panel. Granted, we do not know whether prosecutors relied on racially neutral reasons, but that is because Miller-El never asked at the *Batson* hearing. It is Miller-El's burden to prove racial discrimination, and the jury-shuffle evidence itself does not provide such proof.

The majority's speculation would not be complete, however, without its discussion (block-quoted from *Miller-El I*) of the history of discrimination in the D.A.'s Office. This is nothing more than guilt by association that is unsupported by the record. Some of the witnesses at the *Swain* hearing did testify that individual prosecutors had discriminated. However, no one testified that the prosecutors in Miller-El's trial—Norman Kinne, Paul Macaluso, and Jim Nelson—had ever been among those to engage in racially discriminatory jury selection.

The majority then tars prosecutors with a manual entitled Jury Selection in a Criminal Case (hereinafter Manual or Sparling Manual), authored by John Sparling, a former Dallas County prosecutor. There is no evidence, however, that Kinne, Macaluso, or Nelson had ever read the Manual—which was written in 1968, almost two decades before Miller- El's trial. The reason there is no evidence on the question is that Miller-El never asked. During the entire *Batson* hearing, there is no mention of the Sparling Manual. Miller-El never questioned Macaluso about it, and he never questioned Kinne or Nelson at all. The majority simply assumes that all Dallas County prosecutors were racist and remained that way through the mid-1980's.

Nor does the majority rely on the Manual for anything more than show. The Manual contains a single, admittedly stereotypical line on race: "Minority races almost always empathize with the Defendant." App. 102. Yet the Manual also tells prosecutors not to select "anyone who had a close friend or relative that was prosecuted by the State." *Id.*, at 112. That was true of both Warren and Fields, and yet the majority cavalierly dismisses as "makeweight" the State's justification that Warren and Fields were struck because they were related to individuals convicted of crimes. . . .

Finally, the majority notes that prosecutors "'marked the race of each prospective juror on their juror cards.'" *Ante*, at 31 (quoting *Miller-El I*, *supra*, at 347). This suffers from the same problems as Miller-El's other evidence. Prosecutors did mark the juror cards with the jurors' race, sex, and juror number. We have no idea—and even the majority cannot bring itself to speculate—whether this was done merely for identification purposes or for some more nefarious reason. The reason we have no idea is that the juror cards were never introduced before the state courts, and thus prosecutors were never questioned about their use of them.

* * *

. . . Miller-El has not established, much less established by clear and convincing evidence, that prosecutors racially discriminated in the selection of his jury—and he certainly has not done so on the basis of the evidence presented to the Texas courts. On the basis of facts and law, rather than sentiments, Miller-El does not merit the writ. I respectfully dissent.

What message can be drawn from the *Miller-El* saga? Is the Supreme Court trying to signal to the lower courts that *Batson* review, especially at stages two and three, should be conducted more aggressively than perhaps *Hernandez* and *Purkett* suggested? The outcome of *Miller-El* would seem to so indicate.

But what, exactly, is the nature of *Batson* review, as contemplated by the Court? One of the most striking aspects of *Miller-El* is the extent to which both the majority and the dissent become caught up in lengthy and complicated arguments over the myriad particular facts of the case. (Indeed, in its original form, *Miller-El* is far more lengthy and complicated than the version that appears above; radical editing was necessary in order to fit the case into the casebook.) And it is far from clear that, on balance, the majority has the better of the factual argument.

Why spend so much time and energy arguing about the meaning of specific words used by each prospective juror during voir dire? Or about subtle comparisons of one juror's views with another's? Or about the nuances of the prosecutor's explanations for challenged peremptory strikes? Can these fact-based arguments ever really settle the question whether the prosecutor's strikes were motivated by discrimination?

From an epistemological point of view, the problem is that such particular facts acquire meaning only when viewed in the context of patterns of behavior. And such patterns emerge only from analyzing behavior in the aggregate. To put it bluntly, without the evidence provided by the raw numbers in *Miller-El* (11 qualified black venire members, 10 of whom were eliminated by prosecution peremptory challenges)—together with the racially disparate use of different questioning "scripts," *and* the apparently longstanding prosecutorial abuse of the bizarre Texas "jury-shuffling" procedure, *and* the long history of racial discrimination by Dallas County prosecutors—would the peremptory strikes of Fields and Warren have been enough to prove discrimination in the case? The answer is almost certainly no (especially in light of the fact that, with even slightly more plausible race-neutral explanations, the prosecutors might well have prevailed *despite* such evidence).

Which leads us (and the Court) back to the basic issue: How does one prove discrimination in a particular case? *Batson* was designed to free defendants (and, after *McCollum*, prosecutors as well) from the necessity of conducting sophisticated statistical studies to identify patterns of discriminatory behavior. The *Batson* Court apparently believed that discrimination could be proved simply by examining the facts of a particular case. *Miller-El* (together with its predecessors, *Hernandez* and *Purkett*) demonstrates, however, that such fact-based inquiry is destined to be meaningless without context—the very kind of context provided by statistical studies. Absent the statistical studies, the Court is forced to rely on "statistics-lite" (some raw numbers, a little history) as a weak substitute.

Two recent post-*Miller-El* decisions reveal the kind of judicial confusion that can result whenever such "statistics-lite" are absent, or when context is similarly lacking. In Rice v. Collins, 546 U.S. 333 (2006), a unanimous Court overturned the Ninth Circuit's decision to find a *Batson* violation on habeas review. The Ninth Circuit's ruling was based on its rejection of the race-neutral reasons offered by the prosecutor for striking a particular prospective juror. Those reasons (which had been accepted by all previous state and federal courts to review the case) included that the prospective juror was young, single, lacked ties to the community, and had "rolled her eyes" in response to a *voir dire* question. The Court explained: "The panel majority's attempt to use a set of debatable inferences to set aside the conclusion reached by the state court does not satisfy [the] requirements for granting a writ of habeas corpus." *Id.*, at 342. In a separate concurrence, Justice Breyer, joined by Justice Souter, reiterated his view (first expressed in *Miller-El II*) that *Batson* itself might need to be revisited, and peremptory challenges might need to be abolished, because of the "unresolvable tension between, on the one hand, what Blackstone called an inherently 'arbitrary and capricious' peremptory challenge system, . . . and, on the other hand, the Constitution's nondiscrimination command." *Id.*, at 344 (Breyer, J., concurring).

The second case was Snyder v. Louisiana, 552 U.S. 472 (2008). There, the defendant complained about the peremptory strike of two black prospective jurors, Mr. Brooks and Ms. Scott. The Court noted that *Miller-El* "made it clear that in considering a *Batson* objection, or in reviewing a ruling claimed to be *Batson* error, all of the circumstances that bear upon the issue of racial animosity must be consulted. . . . Here, as just one example, if there were persisting doubts as to the outcome, a court would be required to consider the strike of Ms. Scott for the bearing it might have upon the strike of Mr. Brooks." But the Court ultimately ruled (by 7-2, with Justices Scalia and Thomas dissenting) that the strike of Mr. Brooks failed on its own, because it was based on an asserted rationale (the prosecutor's claim that Mr. Brooks was a student-teacher who might be "nervous" about the impact of a lengthy jury trial on his teaching job) that could equally have applied to numerous white prospective jurors who were not struck. The Court acknowledged that the trial judge, who had rejected the *Batson* challenge, usually would be in the best position to evaluate the credibility of the rationale proffered by the prosecutor, but explained that in the instant case, the trial judge made no findings on the record about Mr. Brooks's demeanor. Thus, the Court reversed Snyder's conviction.

In the end, can the *Batson/Miller-El* approach — well-intentioned though it may be — ever produce a truly satisfying conclusion about the existence (or non-existence) of discrimination in a particular case?

C. Influences upon the Jury

1. Publicity

Starting at page 1354, replace the main case of Mu'Min v. Virginia, and Notes 1 and 2 following Mu'Min, with the following new main case and notes:

SKILLING v. UNITED STATES

Certiorari to the United States Court of Appeals for the Fifth Circuit

__ S.Ct. __ (2010)

JUSTICE GINSBURG delivered the opinion of the Court.

In 2001, Enron Corporation, then the seventh highest-revenue-grossing company in America, crashed into bankruptcy. We consider in this opinion two questions arising from the prosecution of Jeffrey Skilling, a longtime Enron executive, for crimes committed before the corporation's collapse. First, did pretrial publicity and community prejudice prevent Skilling from obtaining a fair trial? Second, did the jury improperly convict Skilling of conspiracy to commit "honest-services" wire fraud, 18 U.S.C. § § 371, 1343, 1346?

Answering no to both questions, the Fifth Circuit affirmed Skilling's convictions. We conclude, in common with the Court of Appeals, that Skilling's fair-trial argument fails; Skilling, we hold, did not establish that a presumption of juror prejudice arose or that actual bias infected the jury that tried him. But we disagree with the Fifth Circuit's honest-services ruling. . . . We therefore affirm in part and vacate in part.

I

Founded in 1985, Enron Corporation grew from its headquarters in Houston, Texas, into one of the world's leading energy companies. Skilling launched his career there in 1990 when Kenneth Lay, the company's founder, hired him to head an Enron subsidiary. Skilling steadily rose through the corporation's ranks, serving as president and chief operating officer, and then, beginning in February 2001, as chief executive officer. Six months later, on August 14, 2001, Skilling resigned from Enron.

Less than four months after Skilling's departure, Enron spiraled into bankruptcy. The company's stock, which had traded at $90 per share in August 2000, plummeted to pennies per share in late 2001. Attempting to comprehend what caused the corporation's collapse, the U.S. Department of Justice formed an Enron Task Force, comprising prosecutors and FBI agents from around the Nation. The Government's investigation uncovered an elaborate conspiracy to prop up Enron's short-run stock prices by overstating the company's financial well-being. In the years following Enron's bankruptcy, the Government prosecuted dozens of Enron employees who participated in the scheme. In time, the Government worked its way up the corporation's chain of command: On July 7, 2004, a grand jury indicted Skilling, Lay, and Richard Causey, Enron's former chief accounting officer.

These three defendants, the indictment alleged,

> "engaged in a wide-ranging scheme to deceive the investing public, including Enron's shareholders, . . . about the true performance of Enron's businesses by: (a) manipulating Enron's publicly reported financial results;

> and (b) making public statements and representations about Enron's financial performance and results that were false and misleading."

Skilling and his co-conspirators, the indictment continued, "enriched themselves as a result of the scheme through salary, bonuses, grants of stock and stock options, other profits, and prestige."

In November 2004, Skilling moved to transfer the trial to another venue; he contended that hostility toward him in Houston, coupled with extensive pretrial publicity, had poisoned potential jurors. To support this assertion, Skilling, aided by media experts, submitted hundreds of news reports detailing Enron's downfall; he also presented affidavits from the experts he engaged portraying community attitudes in Houston in comparison to other potential venues.

The U.S. District Court for the Southern District of Texas, in accord with rulings in two earlier instituted Enron-related prosecutions, denied the venue-transfer motion. Despite "isolated incidents of intemperate commentary," the court observed, media coverage "ha[d] [mostly] been objective and unemotional," and the facts of the case were "neither heinous nor sensational." Moreover, "courts ha[d] commonly" favored "effective voir dire . . . to ferret out any [juror] bias." *Id.*, at 18a. Pretrial publicity about the case, the court concluded, did not warrant a presumption that Skilling would be unable to obtain a fair trial in Houston.

In the months leading up to the trial, the District Court solicited from the parties questions the court might use to screen prospective jurors. Unable to agree on a questionnaire's format and content, Skilling and the Government submitted dueling documents. On venire members' sources of Enron-related news, for example, the Government proposed that they tick boxes from a checklist of generic labels such as "[t]elevision," "[n]ewspaper," and "[r]adio"; Skilling proposed more probing questions asking venire members to list the specific names of their media sources and to report on "what st[ood] out in [their] mind[s]" of "all the things [they] ha[d] seen, heard or read about Enron."

The District Court rejected the Government's sparer inquiries in favor of Skilling's submission. Skilling's questions "[we]re more helpful," the court said, "because [they] [we]re generally . . . open-ended and w[ould] allow the potential jurors to give us more meaningful information." The court converted Skilling's submission, with slight modifications, into a 77-question, 14-page document that asked prospective jurors about, *inter alia,* their sources of news and exposure to Enron-related publicity, beliefs concerning Enron and what caused its collapse, opinions regarding the defendants and their possible guilt or innocence, and relationships to the company and to anyone affected by its demise.

In November 2005, the District Court mailed the questionnaire to 400 prospective jurors and received responses from nearly all the addressees. The court granted hardship exemptions to approximately 90 individuals, and the parties, with the court's approval, further winnowed the pool by excusing another 119 for cause, hardship, or physical disability. The parties agreed to exclude, in particular, "each and every" prospective juror who said that a preexisting opinion about Enron or the defendants would prevent her from impartially considering the evidence at trial.

On December 28, 2005, three weeks before the date scheduled for the commencement of trial, Causey pleaded guilty. Skilling's attorneys immediately requested a continuance, and the District Court agreed to delay the proceedings until the end of January 2006. In the interim, Skilling renewed his change-of-venue motion, arguing that the juror questionnaires revealed pervasive bias and that news accounts of Causey's guilty plea further tainted the jury pool. If Houston remained the trial venue, Skilling urged that "jurors need to be questioned individually by both the Court *and* counsel" concerning their opinions of Enron and "publicity issues."

The District Court again declined to move the trial. Skilling, the court concluded, still had not "establish[ed] that pretrial publicity and/or community prejudice raise[d] a presumption of inherent jury prejudice." The questionnaires and *voir dire,* the court observed, provided safeguards adequate to ensure an impartial jury.

Denying Skilling's request for attorney-led *voir dire,* the court said that in 17 years on the bench:

> "I've found . . . I get more forthcoming responses from potential jurors than the lawyers on either side. I don't know whether people are suspicious of lawyers — but I think if I ask a person a question, I will get a candid response much easier than if a lawyer asks the question."

But the court promised to give counsel an opportunity to ask follow-up questions, and it agreed that venire members should be examined individually about pretrial publicity. The court also allotted the defendants jointly 14 peremptory challenges, 2 more than the standard number prescribed by Federal Rule of Criminal Procedure 24(b)(2) and (c)(4)(B).

Voir dire began on January 30, 2006. The District Court first emphasized to the venire the importance of impartiality and explained the presumption of innocence and the Government's burden of proof. The trial, the court next instructed, was not a forum "to seek vengeance against Enron's former officers," or to "provide remedies for" its victims.

"The bottom line," the court stressed, "is that we want . . . jurors who . . . will faithfully, conscientiously and impartially serve if selected." In response to the court's query whether any prospective juror questioned her ability to adhere to these instructions, two individuals indicated that they could not be fair; they were therefore excused for cause.

After questioning the venire as a group, the District Court brought prospective jurors one by one to the bench for individual examination. Although the questions varied, the process generally tracked the following format: The court asked about exposure to Enron-related news and the content of any stories that stood out in the prospective juror's mind. Next, the court homed in on questionnaire answers that raised a red flag signaling possible bias. The court then permitted each side to pose follow-up questions. Finally, after the venire member stepped away, the court entertained and ruled on challenges for cause. In all, the court granted one of the Government's for cause challenges and denied four; it granted three of the defendants' challenges and denied six. The parties agreed to excuse three additional jurors for cause and one for hardship.

By the end of the day, the court had qualified 38 prospective jurors, a number sufficient, allowing for peremptory challenges, to empanel 12 jurors and 4 alternates. Before the jury was sworn in, Skilling objected to the seating of six jurors. He did not contend that they were in fact biased; instead, he urged that he would have used peremptories to exclude them had he not exhausted his supply by striking several venire members after the court refused to excuse them for cause. The court overruled this objection.

. . . .

Following a 4-month trial and nearly five days of deliberation, the jury found Skilling guilty of 19 counts, including the honest-services-fraud conspiracy charge, and not guilty of 9 insider-trading counts. The District Court sentenced Skilling to 292 months' imprisonment, 3 years' supervised release, and $45 million in restitution.

On appeal, Skilling raised a host of challenges to his convictions, including the fair-trial and honest-services arguments he presses here. Regarding the former, the Fifth Circuit initially determined that the volume and negative tone of media coverage generated by Enron's collapse created a presumption of juror prejudice. 554 F.3d 529, 559 (2009). The court also noted potential prejudice stemming from Causey's guilty plea and from the large number of victims in Houston—from the "[t]housands of Enron employees . . . [who] lost their jobs, and . . . saw their 401(k) accounts wiped out," to Houstonians who suffered spillover economic effects.

The Court of Appeals stated, however, that "the presumption [of prejudice] is rebuttable," and it therefore examined the *voir dire* to determine whether "the District Court empanelled an impartial jury." The *voir dire* was, in the Fifth Circuit's view, "proper and thorough." Moreover, the court noted, Skilling had challenged only one seated juror—Juror 11—for cause. Although Juror 11 made some troubling comments about corporate greed, the District Court "observed [his] demeanor, listened to his answers, and believed he would make the government prove its case." In sum, the Fifth Circuit found that the Government had overcome the presumption of prejudice and that Skilling had not "show[n] that any juror who actually sat was prejudiced against him."

Arguing that the Fifth Circuit erred in its consideration of these claims, Skilling sought relief from this Court. We granted certiorari, 558 U.S. __ (2009).

II

Pointing to "the community passion aroused by Enron's collapse and the vitriolic media treatment" aimed at him, Skilling argues that his trial "never should have proceeded in Houston." And even if it had been possible to select impartial jurors in Houston, "[t]he truncated voir dire . . . did almost nothing to weed out prejudices," he contends, so " [f]ar from rebutting the presumption of prejudice, the record below affirmatively confirmed it." Skilling's fair-trial claim thus raises two distinct questions. First, did the District Court err by failing to move the trial to a different venue based on a presumption of prejudice? Second, did actual prejudice contaminate Skilling's jury?

A

1

The Sixth Amendment secures to criminal defendants the right to trial by an impartial jury. By constitutional design, that trial occurs "in the State where the . . . Crimes . . . have been committed." Art. III, § 2, cl. 3. See also Amdt. 6 (right to trial by "jury of the State and district wherein the crime shall have been committed"). The Constitution's place-of-trial prescriptions, however, do not impede transfer of the proceeding to a different district at the defendant's request if extraordinary local prejudice will prevent a fair trial—a "basic requirement of due process," In re Murchison, 349 U.S. 133, 136 (1955).[11]

2

"The theory of our [trial] system is that the conclusions to be reached in a case will be induced only by evidence and argument in open court, and not by any outside influence, whether of private talk or public print." Patterson v. Colorado ex rel. Attorney General of Colo., 205 U.S. 454, 462 (1907) (opinion for the Court by Holmes, J.). When does the publicity attending conduct charged as criminal dim prospects that the trier can judge a case, as due process requires, impartially, unswayed by outside influence? Because most cases of consequence garner at least some pretrial publicity, courts have considered this question in diverse settings. We begin our discussion by addressing the presumption of prejudice from which the Fifth Circuit's analysis in Skilling's case proceeded. The foundation precedent is Rideau v. Louisiana, 373 U.S. 723 (1963).

Wilbert Rideau robbed a bank in a small Louisiana town, kidnaped three bank employees, and killed one of them. Police interrogated Rideau in jail without counsel present and obtained his confession. Without informing Rideau, no less seeking his consent, the police filmed the interrogation. On three separate occasions shortly before the trial, a local television station broadcast the film to audiences ranging from 24,000 to 53,000 individuals. Rideau moved for a change of venue, arguing that he could not receive a fair trial in the parish where the crime occurred, which had a population of approximately 150,000 people. The trial court denied the motion, and a jury eventually convicted Rideau. The Supreme Court of Louisiana upheld the conviction.

We reversed. "What the people [in the community] saw on their television sets," we observed, "was Rideau, in jail, flanked by the sheriff and two state troopers, admitting in detail the commission of the robbery, kidnapping, and murder." "[T]o the tens of thousands of people who saw and heard it," we explained, the interrogation "in a very real sense *was*

11. Venue transfer in federal court is governed by Federal Rule of Criminal Procedure 21, which instructs that a "court must transfer the proceeding . . . to another district if the court is satisfied that so great a prejudice against the defendant exists in the transferring district that the defendant cannot obtain a fair and impartial trial there." . . . Skilling does not argue, distinct from his due process challenge, that the District Court abused its discretion under Rule 21 by declining to move his trial. We therefore review the District Court's venue-transfer decision only for compliance with the Constitution

Rideau's trial—at which he pleaded guilty." We therefore "d[id] not hesitate to hold, without pausing to examine a particularized transcript of the *voir dire,*" that "[t]he kangaroo court proceedings" trailing the televised confession violated due process.

We followed *Rideau*'s lead in two later cases in which media coverage manifestly tainted a criminal prosecution. In Estes v. Texas, 381 U.S. 532, 538 (1965), extensive publicity before trial swelled into excessive exposure during preliminary court proceedings as reporters and television crews overran the courtroom and "bombard[ed] . . . the community with the sights and sounds of" the pretrial hearing. The media's overzealous reporting efforts, we observed, "led to considerable disruption" and denied the "judicial serenity and calm to which [Billie Sol Estes] was entitled."

Similarly, in Sheppard v. Maxwell, 384 U.S. 333 (1966), news reporters extensively covered the story of Sam Sheppard, who was accused of bludgeoning his pregnant wife to death. "[B]edlam reigned at the courthouse during the trial and newsmen took over practically the entire courtroom," thrusting jurors "into the role of celebrities." Pretrial media coverage, which we characterized as "months [of] virulent publicity about Sheppard and the murder," did not alone deny due process, we noted. But Sheppard's case involved more than heated reporting pretrial: We upset the murder conviction because a "carnival atmosphere" pervaded the trial.

In each of these cases, we overturned a "conviction obtained in a trial atmosphere that [was] utterly corrupted by press coverage"; our decisions, however, "cannot be made to stand for the proposition that juror exposure to . . . news accounts of the crime . . . alone presumptively deprives the defendant of due process." Murphy v. Florida, 421 U.S. 794, 798-799 (1975). See also, *e.g.*, Patton v. Yount, 467 U.S. 1025 (1984).[13] Prominence does not necessarily produce prejudice, and juror *impartiality,* we have reiterated, does not require *ignorance*. Irvin v. Dowd, 366 U.S. 717, 722 (1961) (Jurors are not required to be "totally ignorant of the facts and issues involved"; "scarcely any of those best qualified to

13. In *Yount,* the media reported on Jon Yount's confession to a brutal murder and his prior conviction for the crime, which had been reversed due to a violation of Miranda v. Arizona, 384 U.S. 436 (1966). During *voir dire,* 77% of prospective jurors acknowledged they would carry an opinion into the jury box, and 8 of the 14 seated jurors and alternates admitted they had formed an opinion as to Yount's guilt. Nevertheless, we rejected Yount's presumption-of-prejudice claim. The adverse publicity and community outrage, we noted, were at their height prior to Yount's first trial, four years before the second prosecution; time had helped "sooth[e] and eras[e]" community prejudice.

serve as jurors will not have formed some impression or opinion as to the merits of the case. A presumption of prejudice, our decisions indicate, attends only the extreme case.

3

Relying on *Rideau, Estes,* and *Sheppard,* Skilling asserts that we need not pause to examine the screening questionnaires or the *voir dire* before declaring his jury's verdict void. We are not persuaded. Important differences separate Skilling's prosecution from those in which we have presumed juror prejudice.[14]

First, we have emphasized in prior decisions the size and characteristics of the community in which the crime occurred. In *Rideau,* for example, we noted that the murder was committed in a parish of only 150,000 residents. Houston, in contrast, is the fourth most populous city in the Nation: At the time of Skilling's trial, more than 4.5 million individuals eligible for jury duty resided in the Houston area. Given this large, diverse pool of potential jurors, the suggestion that 12 impartial individuals could not be empaneled is hard to sustain. See Mu'Min v. Virginia, 500 U.S. 415, 429 (1991) (potential for prejudice mitigated by the size of the "metropolitan Washington [D.C.] statistical area, which has a population of over 3 million, and in which, unfortunately, hundreds of murders are committed each year").

Second, although news stories about Skilling were not kind, they contained no confession or other blatantly prejudicial information of the type readers or viewers could not reasonably be expected to shut from sight. Rideau's dramatically staged admission of guilt, for instance, was likely imprinted indelibly in the mind of anyone who watched it. Pretrial publicity about Skilling was less memorable and prejudicial. No evidence of the smoking-gun variety invited prejudgment of his culpability. See United States v. Chagra, 669 F.2d 241, 251-252, n.11 (C.A.5 1982) ("A jury may have difficulty in disbelieving or forgetting a defendant's opinion of his own guilt but have no difficulty in rejecting the opinions of others because they may not be well-founded.").

Third, unlike cases in which trial swiftly followed a widely reported crime, over four years elapsed between Enron's bankruptcy and Skilling's trial. Although reporters covered Enron-related news throughout this

14. Skilling's reliance on *Estes* and *Sheppard* is particularly misplaced; those cases involved media interference with courtroom proceedings *during* trial. Skilling does not assert that news coverage reached and influenced his jury after it was empaneled

period, the decibel level of media attention diminished somewhat in the years following Enron's collapse.

Finally, and of prime significance, Skilling's jury acquitted him of nine insider-trading counts. Similarly, earlier instituted Enron-related prosecutions yielded no overwhelming victory for the Government. In *Rideau, Estes,* and *Sheppard,* in marked contrast, the jury's verdict did not undermine in any way the supposition of juror bias. It would be odd for an appellate court to presume prejudice in a case in which jurors' actions run counter to that presumption.

4

Skilling's trial, in short, shares little in common with those in which we approved a presumption of juror prejudice. The Fifth Circuit reached the opposite conclusion based primarily on the magnitude and negative tone of media attention directed at Enron. But "pretrial publicity—even pervasive, adverse publicity—does not inevitably lead to an unfair trial." Nebraska Press Assn. v. Stuart, 427 U.S. 539, 554 (1976). In this case, as just noted, news stories about Enron did not present the kind of vivid, unforgettable information we have recognized as particularly likely to produce prejudice, and Houston's size and diversity diluted the media's impact.

Nor did Enron's "sheer number of victims" trigger a presumption of prejudice. Although the widespread community impact necessitated careful identification and inspection of prospective jurors' connections to Enron, the extensive screening questionnaire and follow-up *voir dire* were well suited to that task. And hindsight shows the efficacy of these devices; as we discuss *infra,* at 24, jurors' links to Enron were either nonexistent or attenuated.

Finally, although Causey's "well-publicized decision to plead guilty" shortly before trial created a danger of juror prejudice, the District Court took appropriate steps to reduce that risk. The court delayed the proceedings by two weeks, lessening the immediacy of that development. And during *voir dire,* the court asked about prospective jurors' exposure to recent publicity, including news regarding Causey. Only two venire members recalled the plea; neither mentioned Causey by name, and neither ultimately served on Skilling's jury. Although publicity about a codefendant's guilty plea calls for inquiry to guard against actual prejudice, it does not ordinarily—and, we are satisfied, it did not here—warrant an automatic presumption of prejudice.

Persuaded that no presumption arose,[18] we conclude that the District Court, in declining to order a venue change, did not exceed constitutional limitations.

B

We next consider whether actual prejudice infected Skilling's jury. *Voir dire,* Skilling asserts, did not adequately detect and defuse juror bias. "[T]he record . . . affirmatively confirm[s]" prejudice, he maintains, because several seated jurors "prejudged his guilt." We disagree with Skilling's characterization of the *voir dire* and the jurors selected through it.

1

No hard-and-fast formula dictates the necessary depth or breadth of *voir dire*. See United States v. Wood, 299 U.S. 123, 145-146 (1936) ("Impartiality is not a technical conception. It is a state of mind. For the ascertainment of this mental attitude of appropriate indifference, the Constitution lays down no particular tests and procedure is not chained to any ancient and artificial formula."). Jury selection, we have repeatedly emphasized, is "particularly within the province of the trial judge."

When pretrial publicity is at issue, "primary reliance on the judgment of the trial court makes [especially] good sense" because the judge "sits in the locale where the publicity is said to have had its effect" and may base her evaluation on her "own perception of the depth and extent of news stories that might influence a juror." *Mu'Min,* 500 U.S., at 427.

Reviewing courts are properly resistant to second-guessing the trial judge's estimation of a juror's impartiality, for that judge's appraisal is ordinarily influenced by a host of factors impossible to capture fully in the record—among them, the prospective juror's inflection, sincerity, demeanor, candor, body language, and apprehension of duty. In contrast to the cold transcript received by the appellate court, the in-the-moment *voir dire* affords the trial court a more intimate and immediate basis for assessing a venire member's fitness for jury service.

18. The parties disagree about whether a presumption of prejudice can be rebutted, and, if it can, what standard of proof governs that issue. Because we hold that no presumption arose, we need not, and do not, reach these questions.

2

Skilling deems the *voir dire* insufficient because, he argues, jury selection lasted "just five hours," "[m]ost of the court's questions were conclusory[,] high-level, and failed adequately to probe jurors' true feelings," and the court "consistently took prospective jurors at their word once they claimed they could be fair, no matter what other indications of bias were present." Our review of the record, however, yields a different appraisal.[21]

As noted, the District Court initially screened venire members by eliciting their responses to a comprehensive questionnaire drafted in large part by Skilling. That survey helped to identify prospective jurors excusable for cause and served as a springboard for further questions put to remaining members of the array. *Voir dire* thus was, in the court's words, the "culmination of a lengthy process."

The District Court conducted *voir dire,* moreover, aware of the greater-than-normal need, due to pretrial publicity, to ensure against jury bias. At Skilling's urging, the court examined each prospective juror individually, thus preventing the spread of any prejudicial information to other venire members. To encourage candor, the court repeatedly admonished that there were "no right and wrong answers to th[e] questions." The court denied Skilling's request for attorney-led *voir dire* because, in its experience, potential jurors were "more forthcoming" when the court, rather than counsel, asked the question. The parties, however, were accorded an opportunity to ask follow-up questions of every prospective juror brought to the bench for colloquy. Skilling's counsel declined to ask anything of more than half of the venire members questioned individually, including eight eventually selected for the jury, because, he explained, "the Court and other counsel have covered" everything he wanted to know.

Inspection of the questionnaires and *voir dire* of the individuals who actually served as jurors satisfies us that, notwithstanding the flaws Skilling lists, the selection process successfully secured jurors who were

21. In addition to focusing on the adequacy of *voir dire,* our decisions have also "take[n] into account . . . other measures [that] were used to mitigate the adverse effects of publicity." Nebraska Press Assn. v. Stuart, 427 U.S. 539, 565 (1976). We have noted, for example, the prophylactic effect of "emphatic and clear instructions on the sworn duty of each juror to decide the issues only on evidence presented in open court." *Id.,* at 564. Here, the District Court's instructions were unequivocal. . . . Peremptory challenges, too, "provid[e] protection against [prejudice]," United States ex rel. Darcy v. Handy, 351 U.S. 454, 462 (1956); the District Court, as earlier noted, exercised its discretion to grant the defendants two extra peremptories.

largely untouched by Enron's collapse.[24] Eleven of the seated jurors and alternates reported no connection at all to Enron, while all other jurors reported at most an insubstantial link. As for pretrial publicity, 14 jurors and alternates specifically stated that they had paid scant attention to Enron-related news. The remaining two jurors indicated that nothing in the news influenced their opinions about Skilling.

The questionnaires confirmed that, whatever community prejudice existed in Houston generally, Skilling's jurors were not under its sway. Although many expressed sympathy for victims of Enron's bankruptcy and speculated that greed contributed to the corporation's collapse, these sentiments did not translate into animus toward Skilling. When asked whether they "ha[d] an opinion about . . . Jeffrey Skilling," none of the seated jurors and alternates checked the "yes" box. And in response to the question whether "any opinion [they] may have formed regarding Enron or [Skilling] [would] prevent" their impartial consideration of the evidence at trial, every juror—despite options to mark "yes" or "unsure"—instead checked "no."

The District Court, Skilling asserts, should not have "accept[ed] *at face value* jurors' promises of fairness." In Irvin v. Dowd, 366 U.S., at 727-728, Skilling points out, we found actual prejudice despite jurors' assurances that they could be impartial. JUSTICE SOTOMAYOR, in turn, repeatedly relies on *Irvin,* which she regards as closely analogous to this case. We disagree with that characterization of *Irvin*.

The facts of *Irvin* are worlds apart from those presented here. Leslie Irvin stood accused of a brutal murder and robbery spree in a small rural community. In the months before Irvin's trial, "a barrage" of publicity was "unleashed against him," including reports of his confessions to the slayings and robberies. This Court's description of the media coverage in *Irvin* reveals why the dissent's "best case" is not an apt comparison:

> "[S]tories revealed the details of [Irvin's] background, including a reference to crimes committed when a juvenile, his convictions for arson almost 20 years previously, for burglary and by a court-martial on AWOL charges during the war. He was accused of being a parole violator. The headlines announced his police line-up identification, that he faced a lie detector test, had been placed at the scene of the crime and that the six murders were solved but [he] refused to confess. Finally, they announced [Irvin's]

24. In considering whether Skilling was tried before an impartial jury, the dissent relies extensively on venire members *not* selected for that jury. Statements by nonjurors do not themselves call into question the adequacy of the jury-selection process; elimination of these venire members is indeed one indicator that the process fulfilled its function.

> confession to the six murders and the fact of his indictment for four of them in Indiana. They reported [Irvin's] offer to plead guilty if promised a 99-year sentence, but also the determination, on the other hand, of the prosecutor to secure the death penalty, and that [Irvin] had confessed to 24 burglaries (the *modus operandi* of these robberies was compared to that of the murders and the similarity noted). One story dramatically relayed the promise of a sheriff to devote his life to securing [Irvin's] execution . . . . Another characterized [Irvin] as remorseless and without conscience but also as having been found sane by a court-appointed panel of doctors. In many of the stories [Irvin] was described as the 'confessed slayer of six,' a parole violator and fraudulent-check artist. [Irvin's] court-appointed counsel was quoted as having received 'much criticism over being Irvin's counsel' and it was pointed out, by way of excusing the attorney, that he would be subject to disbarment should he refuse to represent Irvin. On the day before the trial the newspapers carried the story that Irvin had orally admitted [to] the murder of [one victim] as well as 'the robbery-murder of [a second individual]; the murder of [a third individual], and the slaughter of three members of [a different family].'" *Id.,* at 725-726.
>
> "[N]ewspapers in which the[se] stories appeared were delivered regularly to 95% of the dwellings in" the county where the trial occurred, which had a population of only 30,000; "radio and TV stations, which likewise blanketed that county, also carried extensive newscasts covering the same incidents." *Id.,* at 725.

Reviewing Irvin's fair-trial claim, this Court noted that "the pattern of deep and bitter prejudice" in the community "was clearly reflected in the sum total of the *voir dire* ": "370 prospective jurors or almost 90% of those examined on the point . . . entertained some opinion as to guilt," and "[8] out of the 12 [jurors] thought [Irvin] was guilty." Although these jurors declared they could be impartial, we held that, "[w]ith his life at stake, it is not requiring too much that [Irvin] be tried in an atmosphere undisturbed by so huge a wave of public passion and by a jury other than one in which two-thirds of the members admit, before hearing any testimony, to possessing a belief in his guilt."

In this case, as noted, news stories about Enron contained nothing resembling the horrifying information rife in reports about Irvin's rampage of robberies and murders. Of key importance, Houston shares little in common with the rural community in which Irvin's trial proceeded, and circulation figures for Houston media sources were far lower than the 95% saturation level recorded in *Irvin,* see App. to Brief for United States 15a ("The *Houston Chronicle* . . . reaches less than one-third of occupied households in Houston."). Skilling's seated jurors, moreover, exhibited nothing like the display of bias shown in *Irvin*. In light of these large differences, the District Court had far less reason than did the trial court in *Irvin* to discredit jurors' promises of fairness.

The District Court, moreover, did not simply take venire members who proclaimed their impartiality at their word. As noted, all of Skilling's jurors had already affirmed on their questionnaires that they would have no trouble basing a verdict only on the evidence at trial. Nevertheless, the court followed up with each individually to uncover concealed bias. This face-to-face opportunity to gauge demeanor and credibility, coupled with information from the questionnaires regarding jurors' backgrounds, opinions, and sources of news, gave the court a sturdy foundation to assess fitness for jury service. The jury's not-guilty verdict on nine insider-trading counts after nearly five days of deliberation, meanwhile, suggests the court's assessments were accurate. Skilling, we conclude, failed to show that his *voir dire* fell short of constitutional requirements.

3

Skilling also singles out several jurors in particular and contends they were openly biased. See United States v. Martinez-Salazar, 528 U.S. 304, 316 (2000) ("[T]he seating of any juror who should have been dismissed for cause . . . require[s] reversal."). In reviewing claims of this type, the deference due to district courts is at its pinnacle: "A trial court's findings of juror impartiality may be overturned only for manifest error." *Mu'Min,* 500 U.S., at 428. Skilling, moreover, unsuccessfully challenged only one of the seated jurors for cause, "strong evidence that he was convinced the [other] jurors were not biased and had not formed any opinions as to his guilt." Beck v. Washington, 369 U.S. 541, 557-558 (1962).

Skilling contends that Juror 11—the only seated juror he challenged for cause—"expressed the most obvious bias." Juror 11 stated that "greed on Enron's part" triggered the company's bankruptcy and that corporate executives, driven by avarice, "walk a line that stretches sometimes the legality of something." But, as the Fifth Circuit accurately summarized, Juror 11

> "had 'no idea' whether Skilling had 'crossed that line,' and he 'didn't say that' every CEO is probably a crook. He also asserted that he could be fair and require the government to prove its case, that he did not believe everything he read in the paper, that he did not 'get into the details' of the Enron coverage, that he did not watch television, and that Enron was 'old news.'"

Despite his criticism of greed, Juror 11 remarked that Skilling "earned [his] salar[y]," and said he would have "no problem" telling his co-worker, who had lost 401(k) funds due to Enron's collapse, that the jury voted to acquit, if that scenario came to pass. The District Court, noting that it had "looked [Juror 11] in the eye and . . . heard all his [answers]," found his assertions of impartiality credible. We agree with the Court of Appeals that "[t]he express finding that Juror 11 was fair is not reversible error."[33]

Skilling also objected at trial to the seating of six specific jurors whom, he said, he would have excluded had he not already exhausted his peremptory challenges. . . .

[For example, Skilling points to] Juror 63, who, Skilling points out, wrote on her questionnaire "that [Skilling] 'probably knew [he] w[as] breaking the law.'" During *voir dire,* however, Juror 63 insisted that she did not "really have an opinion [about Skilling's guilt] either way"; she did not "know what [she] was thinking" when she completed the questionnaire, but she "absolutely" presumed Skilling innocent and confirmed her understanding that the Government would "have to prove" his guilt, *id.* In response to follow-up questions from Skilling's counsel, she again stated she would not presume that Skilling violated any laws and could "[a]bsolutely" give her word that she could be fair. "Jurors," we have recognized, "cannot be expected invariably to express themselves carefully or even consistently." *Yount,* 467 U.S., at 1039. From where we sit, we cannot conclude that Juror 63 was biased.

The [ ] remaining jurors Skilling said he would have excluded with extra peremptory strikes exhibited no sign of prejudice we can discern. . . .

In sum, Skilling failed to establish that a presumption of prejudice arose or that actual bias infected the jury that tried him. Jurors, the trial court correctly comprehended, need not enter the box with empty heads in order to determine the facts impartially. "It is sufficient if the juror[s] can lay aside [their] impression[s] or opinion[s] and render a verdict based on the evidence presented in court." *Irvin,* 366 U.S., at 723. Taking account of the full record, rather than incomplete exchanges selectively culled from it, we find no cause to upset the lower courts' judgment that Skilling's jury met that measure.

* * *

For the foregoing reasons, we affirm the Fifth Circuit's ruling on Skilling's fair-trial argument, vacate its ruling on his conspiracy conviction, and remand the case for proceedings consistent with this opinion.

It is so ordered.

33. Skilling's trial counsel and jury consultants apparently did not regard Juror 11 as so "obvious[ly] bias[ed]," as to warrant exercise of a peremptory challenge.

[The opinions of JUSTICE SCALIA, concurring in the Court's opinion on the pretrial publicity issue, and JUSTICE ALITO, concurring in part and concurring in the judgment, are omitted.]

JUSTICE SOTOMAYOR, with whom JUSTICE STEVENS and JUSTICE BREYER join, concurring in part and dissenting in part.

Under our relevant precedents, the more intense the public's antipathy toward a defendant, the more careful a court must be to prevent that sentiment from tainting the jury. In this case, passions ran extremely high. The sudden collapse of Enron directly affected thousands of people in the Houston area and shocked the entire community. The accompanying barrage of local media coverage was massive in volume and often caustic in tone. As Enron's one-time CEO, Skilling was at the center of the storm. Even if these extraordinary circumstances did not constitutionally compel a change of venue, they required the District Court to conduct a thorough *voir dire* in which prospective jurors' attitudes about the case were closely scrutinized. The District Court's inquiry lacked the necessary thoroughness and left serious doubts about whether the jury empaneled to decide Skilling's case was capable of rendering an impartial decision based solely on the evidence presented in the courtroom. Accordingly, I would grant Skilling relief on his fair-trial claim.

I

The majority understates the breadth and depth of community hostility toward Skilling and overlooks significant deficiencies in the District Court's jury selection process. The failure of Enron wounded Houston deeply. Virtually overnight, what had been the city's "largest, most visible, and most prosperous company," its "foremost social and charitable force," and "a source of civic pride" was reduced to a "shattered shell." Thousands of the company's employees lost their jobs and saw their retirement savings vanish. As the effects rippled through the local economy, thousands of additional jobs disappeared, businesses shuttered, and community groups that once benefited from Enron's largesse felt the loss of millions of dollars in contributions. Enron's community ties were so extensive that the entire local U.S. Attorney's Office was forced to recuse itself from the Government's investigation into the company's fall.

With Enron's demise affecting the lives of so many Houstonians, local media coverage of the story saturated the community. According to a defense media expert, the Houston Chronicle — the area's leading newspaper — assigned as many as 12 reporters to work on the Enron story full time. The paper mentioned Enron in more than 4,000 articles during the

3-year period following the company's December 2001 bankruptcy filing. Hundreds of these articles discussed Skilling by name. Skilling's expert, a professional journalist and academic with 30 years' experience, could not "recall another instance where a local paper dedicated as many resources to a single topic over such an extended period of time as the Houston Chronicle . . . dedicated to Enron." Local television news coverage was similarly pervasive and, in terms of "editorial theme," "largely followed the Chronicle's lead." Between May 2002 and October 2004, local stations aired an estimated 19,000 news segments involving Enron, more than 1600 of which mentioned Skilling.

While many of the stories were straightforward news items, many others conveyed and amplified the community's outrage at the top executives perceived to be responsible for the company's bankruptcy. A Chronicle report on Skilling's 2002 testimony before Congress is typical of the coverage. It began, "Across Houston, Enron employees watched former chief executive Jeffrey Skilling's congressional testimony on television, turning incredulous, angry and then sarcastic by turns, as a man they knew as savvy and detail-oriented pleaded memory failure and ignorance about critical financial transactions at the now-collapsed energy giant." "'He is lying; he knew everything,' said [an employee], who said she had seen Skilling frequently over her 18 years with the firm, where Skilling was known for his intimate grasp of the inner doings at the company. 'I am getting sicker by the minute.'"

Articles deriding Enron's senior executives were juxtaposed with pieces expressing sympathy toward and solidarity with the company's many victims. Skilling's media expert counted nearly a hundred victim-related stories in the Chronicle, including a "multi-page layout entitled 'The Faces of Enron,'" which poignantly described the gut-wrenching experiences of former employees who lost vast sums of money, faced eviction from their homes, could not afford Christmas gifts for their children, and felt "scared," "hurt," "humiliat[ed]," "helpless," and "betrayed."

When a federal grand jury indicted Skilling, Lay, and Richard Causey — Enron's former chief accounting officer — in 2004 on charges of conspiracy to defraud, securities fraud, and other crimes, the media placed them directly in its crosshairs. In the words of one article, "there was one thing those whose lives were touched by the once-exalted company all seemed to agree upon: The indictment of former Enron CEO Jeff Skilling was overdue." Scoffing at Skilling's attempts to paint himself as "a 'victim' of his subordinates," the Chronicle derided "the doofus defense" that Lay and Skilling were expected to offer.

Citing the widely felt sense of victimhood among Houstonians and the voluminous adverse publicity, Skilling moved in November 2004 for a change of venue. The District Court denied the motion, characterizing the media coverage as largely "objective and unemotional." *Voir dire*, it concluded, would provide an effective means to "ferret out any bias" in the jury pool.

To that end, the District Court began the jury selection process by mailing screening questionnaires to 400 prospective jurors in November 2005. The completed questionnaires of the 283 respondents not excused for hardship dramatically illustrated the widespread impact of Enron's collapse on the Houston community and confirmed the intense animosity of Houstonians toward Skilling and his codefendants. More than one-third of the prospective jurors indicated that they or persons they knew had lost money or jobs as a result of the Enron bankruptcy. Two-thirds of the jurors expressed views about Enron or the defendants that suggested a potential predisposition to convict. In many instances, they did not mince words, describing Skilling as "smug," "arrogant," "brash," "conceited," "greedy," "deceitful," "totally unethical and criminal," "a crook," "the biggest liar on the face of the earth," and "guilty as sin" (capitalization omitted). Only about 5 percent of the prospective jurors did not read the Houston Chronicle, had not otherwise "heard or read about any of the Enron cases," were not connected to Enron victims, and gave no answers suggesting possible antipathy toward the defendants. The parties jointly stipulated to the dismissal of 119 members of the jury pool for cause, hardship, or disability, but numerous individuals who had made harsh comments about Skilling remained.[6]

6. See, *e.g.*, Juror 29 (Skilling is "[n]ot an honest man"); Juror 104 (Skilling "knows more than he's admitting"); Juror 211 ("I believe he was involved in wrong doings"); Juror 219 ("So many people lost their life savings because of the dishonesty of some members of the executive team"; Skilling was "[t]oo aggressive w[ith] accounting"); Juror 234 ("With his level of control and power, hard to believe that he was unaware and not responsible in some way"); Juror 240 (Skilling "[s]eems to be very much involved in criminal goings on"); Juror 255 ("[T]housands of people were taken advantage of by executives at Enron"; Skilling is "arrogant"; "Skilling was Andrew Fastow's immediate superior. Fastow has plead[ed] guilty to felony charges. I believe Skilling was aware of Fastow's illegal behavior"); Juror 263 ("Nice try resigning 6 months before the collaps[e], but again, he had to know what was going on"); Juror 272 (Skilling " [k]new he was getting out before the [d]am [b]roke"); Juror 292 (Skilling "[b]ailed out when he knew Enron was going down"); Juror 315 ("[H]ow could they not know and they seem to be lying about some things"); Juror 328 ("They should be held responsible as officers of this company for what happened"); Juror 350 ("I believe he greatly misused his power and affected hundreds of lives as a result"; "I believe they are all guilty. Their 'doings' affected not only those employed by Enron but many others as well"); Juror 360 ("I seem to remember him trying to claim to have mental or emotional issues that would remove him from any guilt. I think that is deceitful. It seems as though he is a big player in the downfall"); Juror 378 ("I believe he knew, and certainly should have known as the CEO, that illegal and improper [activities] were rampant in Enron"; "I believe all of them were instrumental, and were co-conspirators, in the massive fraud perpetrated at Enron").

On December 28, 2005, shortly after the questionnaires had been returned, Causey pleaded guilty. The plea was covered in lead newspaper and television stories. A front-page headline in the Chronicle proclaimed that "Causey's plea wreaks havoc for Lay, Skilling." A Chronicle editorial opined that "Causey's admission of securities fraud. . . . makes less plausible Lay's claim that most of the guilty pleas were the result of prosecutorial pressure rather than actual wrongdoing."

II

The Court of Appeals incorporated the concept of presumptive prejudice into a burden-shifting framework: Once the defendant musters sufficient evidence of community hostility, the onus shifts to the Government to prove the impartiality of the jury. The majority similarly envisions a fixed point at which public passions become so intense that prejudice to a defendant's fair-trial rights must be presumed.

This Court has never treated the notion of presumptive prejudice so formalistically. Our decisions instead merely convey the commonsense understanding that as the tide of public enmity rises, so too does the danger that the prejudices of the community will infiltrate the jury. The underlying question has always been this: Do we have confidence that the jury's verdict was "induced only by evidence and argument in open court, and not by any outside influence, whether of private talk or public print"? Patterson v. Colorado ex rel. Attorney General of Colo., 205 U.S. 454, 462 (1907).

At one end of the spectrum, this Court has, on rare occasion, confronted such inherently prejudicial circumstances that it has reversed a defendant's conviction "without pausing to examine . . . the *voir dire* examination of the members of the jury." Rideau v. Louisiana, 373 U.S. 723, 727 (1963). In *Rideau,* repeated television broadcasts of the defendant's confession to murder, robbery, and kidnaping so thoroughly poisoned local sentiment as to raise doubts that even the most careful *voir dire* could have secured an impartial jury. A change of venue, the Court determined, was thus the only way to assure a fair trial.

Irvin offers an example of a case in which the trial court's *voir dire* did not suffice to counter the "wave of public passion" that had swept the community prior to the defendant's trial. The local news media had "extensively covered" the crimes (a murder spree), "arous[ing] great excitement and indignation." Following Irvin's arrest, the press "blanketed" the community with "a barrage of newspaper headlines, articles, cartoons and pictures" communicating numerous unfavorable details about Irvin, including that he had purportedly confessed. Nearly 90 percent of the 430 prospective jurors examined during the trial court's *voir dire* "entertained some opinion as to guilt—ranging in intensity from mere suspicion to absolute certainty." Of the 12 jurors seated, 8 "thought petitioner was guilty," although "each indicated that notwithstanding his opinion he could render an impartial verdict."

Despite the seated jurors' assurances of impartiality, this Court invalidated Irvin's conviction for want of due process. "It is not required," this Court declared, "that the jurors be totally ignorant of the facts and issues involved. . . . It is sufficient if the juror can lay aside his impression or opinion and render a verdict based on the evidence presented in court." The Court emphasized, however, that a juror's word on this matter is not decisive, particularly when "the build-up of prejudice [in the community] is clear and convincing."

III

It is necessary to determine how this case compares to our existing fair-trial precedents. Were the circumstances so inherently prejudicial that, as in *Rideau,* even the most scrupulous *voir dire* would have been "but a hollow formality" incapable of reliably producing an impartial jury? If the circumstances were not of this character, did the District Court conduct a jury selection process sufficiently adapted to the level of pretrial publicity and community animus to ensure the seating of jurors capable of presuming innocence and shutting out extrajudicial influences?

A

Though the question is close, I agree with the Court that the prospect of seating an unbiased jury in Houston was not so remote as to compel the conclusion that the District Court acted unconstitutionally in denying Skilling's motion to change venue. Three considerations lead me to this conclusion. First, as the Court observes, the size and diversity of the Houston community make it probable that the jury pool contained a nontrivial number of persons who were unaffected by Enron's collapse, neutral in their outlook, and unlikely to be swept up in the public furor. Second, media coverage of the case, while ubiquitous and often inflammatory, did not, as the Court points out, contain a confession by Skilling or similar "smoking-gun" evidence of specific criminal acts. For many prospective jurors, the guilty plea of codefendant and alleged co-conspirator

Causey, along with the pleas and convictions of other Enron executives, no doubt suggested guilt by association. But reasonable minds exposed to such information would not necessarily have formed an indelible impression that Skilling himself was guilty as charged. Third, there is no suggestion that the courtroom in this case became, as in *Estes* and *Sheppard,* a "carnival" in which the "calmness and solemnity" of the proceedings was compromised. It is thus appropriate to examine the *voir dire* and determine whether it instills confidence in the impartiality of the jury actually selected.

B

In conducting this analysis, I am mindful of the "wide discretion" owed to trial courts when it comes to jury-related issues. Trial courts are uniquely positioned to assess public sentiment and the credibility of prospective jurors. Proximity to events, however, is not always a virtue. Persons in the midst of a tumult often lack a panoramic view. In particular, reviewing courts are well qualified to inquire into whether a trial court implemented procedures adequate to keep community prejudices from infecting the jury. If the jury selection process does not befit the circumstances of the case, the trial court's rulings on impartiality are necessarily called into doubt.

1

As the Court of Appeals apprehended, the District Court gave short shrift to the mountainous evidence of public hostility. For Houstonians, Enron's collapse was an event of once-in-a-generation proportions. Not only was the volume of media coverage "immense" and frequently intemperate, but "the sheer number of victims" created a climate in which animosity toward Skilling ran deep and the desire for conviction was widely shared.

The level of public animus toward Skilling dwarfed that present in cases such as *Murphy* and *Mu'Min*. . . . The much closer analogy is thus to *Irvin,* which similarly featured a "barrage" of media coverage and a "huge . . . wave of public passion," although even that case did not, as here, involve direct harm to entire segments of the community.

Attempting to distinguish *Irvin,* the majority suggests that Skilling's economic offenses were less incendiary than Irvin's violent crime spree and that "news stories about Enron contained nothing resembling the horrifying information rife in reports about Irvin's rampage of robberies and murders." Along similar lines, the District Court described "the facts of this case [as] neither heinous nor sensational." The majority also points to the four years that passed between Enron's declaration of bankruptcy and the start of Skilling's trial, asserting that "the decibel level of media attention diminished somewhat" over this time. Neither of these arguments is persuasive.

First, while violent crimes may well provoke widespread community outrage more readily than crimes involving monetary loss, economic crimes are certainly capable of rousing public passions, particularly when thousands of unsuspecting people are robbed of their livelihoods and retirement savings. Indeed, the record in this case is replete with examples of visceral outrage toward Skilling and other Enron executives. Houstonians compared Skilling to, among other things, a rapist, an axe murderer, and an Al Qaeda terrorist. . . . The bad blood was so strong that Skilling and other top executives hired private security to protect themselves from persons inclined to take the law into their own hands.

Second, the passage of time did little to soften community sentiment. Contrary to the Court's suggestion, this case in no way resembles *Yount,* where, by the time of the defendant's retrial, "prejudicial publicity [had] greatly diminished" and community animus had significantly waned. The Enron story was a continuing saga, and "publicity remained intense throughout." Not only did Enron's downfall generate wall-to-wall news coverage, but so too did a succession of subsequent Enron-related events. Of particular note is the highly publicized guilty plea of codefendant Causey just weeks before Skilling's trial. If anything, the time that elapsed between the bankruptcy and the trial made the task of seating an unbiased jury more difficult, not less.

2

Given the extent of the antipathy evident both in the community at large and in the responses to the written questionnaire, it was critical for the District Court to take "strong measures" to ensure the selection of "an impartial jury free from outside influences." *Sheppard,* 384 U.S., at 362. As this Court has recognized, "[i]n a community where most veniremen will admit to a disqualifying prejudice, the reliability of the others' protestations may be drawn into question." *Murphy,* 421 U.S., at 803. Perhaps because it had underestimated the public's antipathy toward Skilling, the District Court's 5-hour *voir dire* was manifestly insufficient to identify and remove biased jurors.

As an initial matter, important lines of inquiry were not pursued at all. The majority accepts, for instance, that "publicity about a codefendant's guilty plea calls for inquiry to guard against actual prejudice." Implying that the District Court undertook this inquiry, the majority states that "[o]nly two venire members recalled [Causey's] plea." In fact, the court asked very few prospective jurors any questions directed to their knowledge of or feelings about that event. Considering how much news the plea generated, many more than two venire members were likely aware of it. The lack of questioning, however, makes the prejudicial impact of the plea on those jurors impossible to assess.

The topics that the District Court did cover were addressed in cursory fashion. Most prospective jurors were asked just a few yes/no questions about their general exposure to media coverage and a handful of additional questions concerning any responses to the written questionnaire that suggested bias. In many instances, their answers were unenlightening. Yet the court rarely sought to draw them out with open-ended questions about their impressions of Enron or Skilling and showed limited patience for counsel's followup efforts.

These deficiencies in the form and content of the *voir dire* questions contributed to a deeper problem: The District Court failed to make a sufficiently critical assessment of prospective jurors' assurances of impartiality. Although the Court insists otherwise, the *voir dire* transcript indicates that the District Court essentially took jurors at their word when they promised to be fair. Indeed, the court declined to dismiss for cause any prospective juror who ultimately gave a clear assurance of impartiality, no matter how much equivocation preceded it.

Worse still, the District Court on a number of occasions accepted declarations of impartiality that were equivocal on their face. Prospective jurors who "hope [d]" they could presume innocence and did "not necessarily" think Skilling was guilty were permitted to remain in the pool. Juror 61, for instance, wrote of Lay on her questionnaire, "Shame on him." Asked by the court about this, she stated that, "innocent or guilty, he was at the helm" and "should have known what was going on at the company." The court then asked, "can you presume, as you start this trial, that Mr. Lay is innocent?" She responded, "I hope so, but you know. I don't know. I can't honestly answer that one way or the other." Eventually, however, Juror 61 answered "Yes" when the court asked if she would be able to acquit if she had "a reasonable doubt that the defendants are guilty." Challenging her for cause, defense counsel insisted that they had not received "a clear and unequivocal answer" about her ability to be fair. The court denied the challenge, stating, "You know, she tried."

3

The majority suggests that the jury's decision to acquit Skilling on nine relatively minor insider trading charges confirms its impartiality. This argument, however, mistakes partiality with bad faith or blind vindictiveness. Jurors who act in good faith and sincerely believe in their own fairness may nevertheless harbor disqualifying prejudices. Such jurors may well acquit where evidence is wholly lacking, while subconsciously resolving closer calls against the defendant rather than giving him the benefit of the doubt.

* * *

In sum, I cannot accept the majority's conclusion that *voir dire* gave the District Court "a sturdy foundation to assess fitness for jury service." Taken together, the District Court's failure to cover certain vital subjects, its superficial coverage of other topics, and its uncritical acceptance of assurances of impartiality leave me doubtful that Skilling's jury was indeed free from the deep-seated animosity that pervaded the community at large. "[R]egardless of the heinousness of the crime charged, the apparent guilt of the offender[,] or the station in life which he occupies," our system of justice demands trials that are fair in both appearance and fact. *Irvin,* 366 U.S., at 722. Because I do not believe Skilling's trial met this standard, I would grant him relief.

NOTES AND QUESTIONS

1. Who has the better of the argument in *Skilling*, the majority or the dissent? Both sides recognize that the collapse of Enron had dramatic and far reaching effects in Houston, and that the financial pain and accompanying anger caused by the event were deeply felt. In such a case, how realistic is it to think that a jury will be able to close its ears and consider only the evidence presented in court? Part of the majority's reasoning was that the *Skilling* publicity was not like cases such as *Rideau* and *Sheppard v. Maxwell,* cases from an earlier age that involved violent crimes. But even acknowledging the differences in circumstances, isn't it fair to say that in modern times it is *easier* to be exposed to prejudicial pretrial publicity than it was when radio, television, and newspapers were the only credible sources of information?

More generally, why are courts so reluctant to grant a change of venue in high-profile cases? The convenience of the testifying witnesses and the need to transport potentially huge amounts of documents and physical evidence is part of the explanation, but is administrative efficiency a sufficient answer? If you were a federal prosecutor arguing against Skilling's motion to transfer, what interests might you identify as to why the case should stay in Houston?

2. On the other hand, isn't the majority correct that prejudicial pretrial publicity claims are inherently fact-intensive questions, and that deference to the trial judge should be at its peak? Can the dissent realistically conclude, based on its reading of a paper record, that despite the district judge's factual findings based on his observations, the jurors were not credible in their claims of being able to put their prior knowledge and impressions about the case aside while deliberating?

3. How should the problem of prejudicial pretrial publicity be remedied? Two psychology professors have evaluated the available options, based on the results of numerous empirical studies. See Christina Studebaker & Steven Penrod, Pretrial Publicity: The Media, the Law, and Common Sense, 3 Psychol. Pub. Pol'y. & L. 428 (1997). These options include (1) granting a continuance, in the hope that publicity will dissipate over time; (2) conducting extended voir dire to weed out prospective jurors who may have been influenced by publicity; (3) admonishing the jury not to be influenced by publicity; (4) encouraging the presentation of evidence, at trial, to counteract any impressions created by publicity; (5) relying on the jury's deliberations to overcome the effects of publicity; (6) changing the venire, i.e., bringing in jurors from another jurisdiction where there is less publicity; and (7) changing the venue, i.e., holding the trial in another jurisdiction.

Some of the more important research findings collected by Studebaker and Penrod include the following: With respect to voir dire, "jurors who claimed that they could disregard the pretrial publicity simply did not—despite their apparent belief that they could." *Id.* at 441. With respect to judicial admonitions, "[t]he pre-trial publicity instruction did not reduce the biasing effect of exposure to either the 'factual' or 'emotional' pretrial publicity." *Id.* at 443. With respect to jury deliberations, "existing research on deliberation effects in the pretrial publicity arena is more supportive of the accentuation theory—jury deliberation appears to strengthen, not reduce, bias." *Id.* at 444. Studebaker and Penrod conclude that these three particular methods (voir dire, judicial admonitions, and jury deliberations) are especially unlikely to succeed because they "are based on removing bias after it has been developed"—indeed, they "require jurors to disregard pretrial publicity immediately after attention has been brought to it." *Id.* at 445. More promising are the approaches that seek "to select jurors who were never biased to begin with," such as change of venire or change of venue. *Id.*

D. *The Defendant's Rights to Be Present, to Testify, to Obtain Evidence, to Confront His Accusers, and to Present a Defense at Trial*

Insert the following sentence at the end of the first paragraph of Note 3 on page 1391:

See also Carey v. Musladin, 549 U.S. 70 (2006), where the Court found no error warranting federal habeas corpus relief when a state court allowed members of a murder victim's family to wear buttons, while seated in the front row of the courtroom during the defendant's murder trial, displaying the victim's image.

Insert the following note after Note 5 on page 1392:

6. On the right to present evidence at trial on one's own behalf: In Holmes v. South Carolina, 547 U.S. 319 (2006), the defendant was precluded from introducing evidence that another man possibly had committed the crime with which he was charged. The exclusion was based on an odd South Carolina rule stating that evidence of third-party guilt is admissible only if it raises a "reasonable inference" of the defendant's innocence. The South Carolina Supreme Court held that such an inference could not be raised in the instant case because the prosecution's evidence of Holmes's guilt was strong; the court therefore did not even consider the probative value of Holmes's proffered third-party-guilt evidence in making its admissibility decision. The U.S. Supreme Court unanimously reversed. In an opinion by Justice Alito, the Court held that the South Carolina rule was "arbitrary" and "does not rationally serve the end" of excluding non-probative evidence. Therefore, the rule denied Holmes his right to "a meaningful opportunity to present a complete defense." *Id.,* at 331.

Insert the following main case and notes before Note 3 on page 1401:

Crawford, although subsequently held *not* to apply retroactively to convicted defendants whose criminal cases were already final, see Whorton v. Bockting, 549 U.S. 406 (2006), nevertheless impacted the world of criminal trials like a bombshell, not least because of the singular lack of guidance provided by Justice Scalia about the meaning of the crucial term, "testimony." Does the following case help?

DAVIS v. WASHINGTON

Certiorari to the Supreme Court of Washington
547 U.S. 813 (2006)

JUSTICE SCALIA delivered the opinion of the Court.

These cases require us to determine when statements made to law enforcement personnel during a 911 call or at a crime scene are "testimonial" and thus subject to the requirements of the Sixth Amendment's Confrontation Clause.

I

A

The relevant statements in Davis v. Washington, No. 05-5224, were made to a 911 emergency operator on February 1, 2001. When the operator answered the initial call, the connection terminated before anyone spoke. She reversed the call, and Michelle McCottry answered. In the ensuing conversation, the operator ascertained that McCottry was involved in a domestic disturbance with her former boyfriend Adrian Davis, the petitioner in this case:

"911 Operator: Hello.

"Complainant: Hello.

"911 Operator: What's going on?

"Complainant: He's here jumpin' on me again.

"911 Operator: Okay. Listen to me carefully. Are you in a house or an apartment?

"Complainant: I'm in a house.

"911 Operator: Are there any weapons?

"Complainant: No. He's usin' his fists.

"911 Operator: Okay. Has he been drinking?

"Complainant: No.

"911 Operator: Okay, sweetie. I've got help started. Stay on the line with me, okay?

"Complainant: I'm on the line.

"911 Operator: Listen to me carefully. Do you know his last name?

"Complainant: It's Davis.

"911 Operator: Davis? Okay, what's his first name?

"Complainant: Adran

"911 Operator: What is it?

"Complainant: Adrian.

"911 Operator: Adrian?

"Complainant: Yeah.

"911 Operator: Okay. What's his middle initial?

"Complainant: Martell. He's runnin' now."

App. in No. 05-5224, pp. 8-9.

As the conversation continued, the operator learned that Davis had "just run out the door" after hitting McCottry, and that he was leaving in a car with someone else. McCottry started talking, but the operator cut her off, saying, "Stop talking and answer my questions." She then gathered more information about Davis (including his birthday), and learned that Davis had told McCottry that his purpose in coming to the house was "to get his stuff," since McCottry was moving. McCottry described the context of the assault, after which the operator told her that the police were on their way. "They're gonna check the area for him first," the operator said, "and then they're gonna come talk to you." *Id.*, at 12-13.

The police arrived within four minutes of the 911 call and observed McCottry's shaken state, the "fresh injuries on her forearm and her face," and her "frantic efforts to gather her belongings and her children so that they could leave the residence." 154 Wn. 2d 291, 296, 111 P. 3d 844, 847 (2005) (en banc).

The State charged Davis with felony violation of a domestic no-contact order. "The State's only witnesses were the two police officers who responded to the 911 call. Both officers testified that McCottry exhibited injuries that appeared to be recent, but neither officer could testify as to the cause of the injuries." *Ibid.* McCottry presumably could have testified as to whether Davis was her assailant, but she did not appear. Over Davis's objection, based on the Confrontation Clause of the Sixth Amendment, the trial court admitted the recording of her exchange with the 911 operator, and the jury convicted him. The Washington Court of Appeals affirmed, 116 Wn. App. 81, 64 P. 3d 661 (2003). The Supreme Court of Washington, with one dissenting justice, also affirmed, concluding that the portion of the 911 conversation in which McCottry identified Davis was not testimonial, and that if other portions of the conversation were testimonial, admitting them was harmless beyond a reasonable doubt. 154 Wash. 2d, at 305, 111 P. 3d, at 851. We granted certiorari.

B

In Hammon v. Indiana, No. 05-5705, police responded late on the night of February 26, 2003, to a "reported domestic disturbance" at the home of Hershel and Amy Hammon. 829 N.E.2d 444, 446 (Ind. 2005). They found Amy alone on the front porch, appearing "'somewhat frightened,'" but she told them that "'nothing was the matter,'" *id.*, at 446, 447. She gave them permission to enter the house, where an officer saw "a gas heating unit in the corner of the living room" that had "flames coming out of the . . . partial glass front. There were pieces of glass on the ground in front of it and there was flame emitting from the front of the heating unit." App. in No. 05-5705, p. 16.

Hershel, meanwhile, was in the kitchen. He told the police "that he and his wife had 'been in an argument' but 'everything was fine now' and the argument 'never became physical.'" 829 N.E.2d, at 447. By this point Amy had come back inside. One of the officers remained with Hershel; the other went to the living room to talk with Amy, and "again asked [her] what had occurred." *Ibid.* Hershel made several attempts to participate in Amy's conversation with the police, but was rebuffed. The officer later testified that Hershel "became angry when I insisted that [he] stay separated from Mrs. Hammon so that we can investigate what had happened." After hearing Amy's account, the officer "had her fill out and sign a battery affidavit." Amy handwrote the following: "Broke our Furnace & shoved me down on the floor into the broken glass. Hit me in the chest and threw me down. Broke our lamps & phone. Tore up my van where I couldn't leave the house. Attacked my daughter." [App. in No. 05-5705,] at 2.

The State charged Hershel with domestic battery and with violating his probation. Amy was subpoenaed, but she did not appear at his subsequent bench trial. The State called the officer who had questioned Amy, and asked him to recount what Amy told him and to authenticate the affidavit. Hershel's counsel repeatedly objected to the admission of this evidence. At one point, after hearing the prosecutor defend the affidavit because it was made "under oath," defense counsel said, "That doesn't give us the opportunity to cross examine [the] person who allegedly drafted it. Makes me mad." Nonetheless, the trial court admitted the affidavit as a "present sense impression," and Amy's statements as "excited utterances" that "are expressly permitted in these kinds of cases even if the declarant is not available to testify." The officer thus testified that Amy

> "informed me that she and Hershel had been in an argument. That he became irrate [sic] over the fact of their daughter going to a boyfriend's house. The argument became . . . physical after being verbal and she

> informed me that Mr. Hammon, during the verbal part of the argument was breaking things in the living room and I believe she stated he broke the phone, broke the lamp, broke the front of the heater. When it became physical he threw her down into the glass of the heater . . . ..
>
> "She informed me Mr. Hammon had pushed her onto the ground, had shoved her head into the broken glass of the heater and that he had punched her in the chest twice I believe." *Id.,* at 17-18.

The trial judge found Hershel guilty on both charges, and the Indiana Court of Appeals affirmed in relevant part, 809 N.E.2d 945 (2004). The Indiana Supreme Court also affirmed, concluding that Amy's statement was admissible for state-law purposes as an excited utterance, 829 N.E. 2d, at 449; that "a 'testimonial' statement is one given or taken in significant part for purposes of preserving it for potential future use in legal proceedings," where "the motivations of the questioner and declarant are the central concerns," *id.*, at 456, 457; and that Amy's oral statement was not "testimonial" under these standards, *id.*, at 458. It also concluded that, although the affidavit was testimonial and thus wrongly admitted, it was harmless beyond a reasonable doubt, largely because the trial was to the bench. *Id.*, at 458-459. We granted certiorari.

II

The Confrontation Clause of the Sixth Amendment provides: "In all criminal prosecutions, the accused shall enjoy the right . . . to be confronted with the witnesses against him." In Crawford v. Washington, 541 U.S. 36, 53-54 (2004), we held that this provision bars "admission of testimonial statements of a witness who did not appear at trial unless he was unavailable to testify, and the defendant had had a prior opportunity for cross-examination." A critical portion of this holding, and the portion central to resolution of the two cases now before us, is the phrase "testimonial statements." Only statements of this sort cause the declarant to be a "witness" within the meaning of the Confrontation Clause. See *id.*, at 51. It is the testimonial character of the statement that separates it from other hearsay that, while subject to traditional limitations upon hearsay evidence, is not subject to the Confrontation Clause.

Our opinion in *Crawford* set forth "various formulations" of the core class of "'testimonial'" statements, *ibid.*, but found it unnecessary to endorse any of them, because "some statements qualify under any definition," *id.*, at 52. Among those, we said, were "statements taken by police officers in the course of interrogations," *ibid.;* see also *id.*, at 53. The questioning that generated the deponent's statement in *Crawford*—which was made and recorded while she was in police custody, after having been given *Miranda* warnings as a possible suspect herself—"qualifies under any conceivable definition" of an "'interrogation,'" 541 U.S., at 53, n. 4. We therefore did not define that term, except to say that "we use [it] . . . in its colloquial, rather than any technical legal, sense," and that "one can imagine various definitions . . ., and we need not select among them in this case." *Ibid.* The character of the statements in the present cases is not as clear, and these cases require us to determine more precisely which police interrogations produce testimony.

Without attempting to produce an exhaustive classification of all conceivable statements—or even all conceivable statements in response to police interrogation—as either testimonial or nontestimonial, it suffices to decide the present cases to hold as follows: Statements are nontestimonial when made in the course of police interrogation under circumstances objectively indicating that the primary purpose of the interrogation is to enable police assistance to meet an ongoing emergency. They are testimonial when the circumstances objectively indicate that there is no such ongoing emergency, and that the primary purpose of the interrogation is to establish or prove past events potentially relevant to later criminal prosecution.[1]

III

A

In *Crawford*, it sufficed for resolution of the case before us to determine that "even if the Sixth Amendment is not solely concerned with testimonial hearsay, that is its primary object, and interrogations by law enforcement officers fall squarely within that class." *Id.*, at 53. Moreover, as we have just described, the facts of that case spared us the need to define what we meant by "interrogations." The *Davis* case today does not permit us this luxury of indecision. The inquiries of a police operator

1. Our holding refers to interrogations because, as explained below, the statements in the cases presently before us are the products of interrogations—which in some circumstances tend to generate testimonial responses. This is not to imply, however, that statements made in the absence of any interrogation are necessarily nontestimonial. The Framers were no more willing to exempt from cross-examination volunteered testimony or answers to open-ended questions than they were to exempt answers to detailed interrogation. (Part of the evidence against Sir Walter Raleigh was a letter from Lord Cobham that was plainly not the result of sustained questioning. Raleigh's Case, 2 How. St. Tr. 1, 27 (1603).) And of course even when interrogation exists, it is in the final analysis the declarant's statements, not the interrogator's questions, that the Confrontation Clause requires us to evaluate.

in the course of a 911 call[2] are an interrogation in one sense, but not in a sense that "qualifies under any conceivable definition." We must decide, therefore, whether the Confrontation Clause applies only to testimonial hearsay; and, if so, whether the recording of a 911 call qualifies.

The answer to the first question was suggested in *Crawford,* even if not explicitly held:

> "The text of the Confrontation Clause reflects this focus [on testimonial hearsay]. It applies to 'witnesses' against the accused—in other words, those who 'bear testimony.' 1 N. Webster, An American Dictionary of the English Language (1828). 'Testimony,' in turn, is typically 'a solemn declaration or affirmation made for the purpose of establishing or proving some fact.' *Ibid.* An accuser who makes a formal statement to government officers bears testimony in a sense that a person who makes a casual remark to an acquaintance does not." 541 U.S., at 51.

A limitation so clearly reflected in the text of the constitutional provision must fairly be said to mark out not merely its "core," but its perimeter.

> [JUSTICE SCALIA next cited numerous early and modern cases to show that the Confrontation Clause has—with one exception, White v. Illinois, 502 U.S. 346 (1992), discussed and implicitly criticized in *Crawford*—been applied by the Court only in cases that "clearly involve testimony."—EDS.]

Most of the American cases applying the Confrontation Clause or its state constitutional or common-law counterparts involved testimonial statements of the most formal sort—sworn testimony in prior judicial proceedings or formal depositions under oath—which invites the argument that the scope of the Clause is limited to that very formal category. But the English cases that were the progenitors of the Confrontation Clause did not limit the exclusionary rule to prior court testimony and formal depositions, see *Crawford, supra,* at 52, and n. 3. In any event, we do not think it conceivable that the protections of the Confrontation Clause can readily be evaded by having a note-taking policeman *recite* the unsworn hearsay testimony of the declarant, instead of having the declarant sign a deposition. Indeed, if there is one point for which no case—English or early American, state or federal—can be cited, that is it.

2. If 911 operators are not themselves law enforcement officers, they may at least be agents of law enforcement when they conduct interrogations of 911 callers. For purposes of this opinion (and without deciding the point), we consider their acts to be acts of the police. As in Crawford v. Washington, 541 U.S. 36 (2004), therefore, our holding today makes it unnecessary to consider whether and when statements made to someone other than law enforcement personnel are "testimonial."

The question before us in *Davis*, then, is whether, objectively considered, the interrogation that took place in the course of the 911 call produced testimonial statements. When we said in *Crawford, supra*, at 53, that "interrogations by law enforcement officers fall squarely within [the] class" of testimonial hearsay, we had immediately in mind (for that was the case before us) interrogations solely directed at establishing the facts of a past crime, in order to identify (or provide evidence to convict) the perpetrator. The product of such interrogation, whether reduced to a writing signed by the declarant or embedded in the memory (and perhaps notes) of the interrogating officer, is testimonial. It is, in the terms of the 1828 American dictionary quoted in *Crawford*, "'[a] solemn declaration or affirmation made for the purpose of establishing or proving some fact.'" 541 U.S., at 51. (The solemnity of even an oral declaration of relevant past fact to an investigating officer is well enough established by the severe consequences that can attend a deliberate falsehood. See, e.g., United States v. Stewart, 433 F.3d 273, 288 (C.A.2 2006) (false statements made to federal investigators violate 18 U.S.C. § 1001); State v. Reed, 2005 WI 53, ¶30, 280 Wis. 2d 68, 695 N.W.2d 315, 323 (state criminal offense to "knowingly give false information to [an] officer with [the] intent to mislead the officer in the performance of his or her duty").) A 911 call, on the other hand, and at least the initial interrogation conducted in connection with a 911 call, is ordinarily not designed primarily to "establish or prove" some past fact, but to describe current circumstances requiring police assistance.

The difference between the interrogation in *Davis* and the one in *Crawford* is apparent on the face of things. In *Davis*, McCottry was speaking about events *as they were actually happening*, rather than "describing past events," Lilly v. Virginia, 527 U.S. 116, 137 (1999) (plurality opinion). Sylvia Crawford's interrogation, on the other hand, took place hours after the events she described had occurred. Moreover, any reasonable listener would recognize that McCottry (unlike Sylvia Crawford) was facing an ongoing emergency. Although one *might* call 911 to provide a narrative report of a crime absent any imminent danger, McCottry's call was plainly a call for help against bona fide physical threat. Third, the nature of what was asked and answered in *Davis*, again viewed objectively, was such that the elicited statements were necessary to be able to *resolve* the present emergency, rather than simply to learn (as in *Crawford*) what had happened in the past. That is true even of the operator's effort to establish the identity of the assailant, so that the dispatched officers might know whether they would be encountering a violent felon. See, e.g., Hiibel v. Sixth Judicial Dist. Court of Nev., Humboldt Cty., 542 U.S.

177, 186 (2004). And finally, the difference in the level of formality between the two interviews is striking. Crawford was responding calmly, at the station house, to a series of questions, with the officer-interrogator taping and making notes of her answers; McCottry's frantic answers were provided over the phone, in an environment that was not tranquil, or even (as far as any reasonable 911 operator could make out) safe.

We conclude from all this that the circumstances of McCottry's interrogation objectively indicate its primary purpose was to enable police assistance to meet an ongoing emergency. She simply was not acting as a *witness;* she was not *testifying*. What she said was not "a weaker substitute for live testimony" at trial, United States v. Inadi, 475 U.S. 387, 394 (1986), like Lord Cobham's statements in Raleigh's Case, 2 How. St. Tr. 1 (1603), or Jane Dingler's *ex parte* statements against her husband in King v. Dingler, 2 Leach 561, 168 Eng. Rep. 383 (1791), or Sylvia Crawford's statement in *Crawford*. In each of those cases, the *ex parte* actors and the evidentiary products of the *ex parte* communication aligned perfectly with their courtroom analogues. McCottry's emergency statement does not. No "witness" goes into court to proclaim an emergency and seek help.

Davis seeks to cast McCottry in the unlikely role of a witness by pointing to English cases. None of them involves statements made during an ongoing emergency. In King v. Brasier, 1 Leach 199, 168 Eng. Rep. 202 (1779), for example, a young rape victim, "immediately on her coming home, told all the circumstances of the injury" to her mother. *Id.*, at 200, 168 Eng. Rep., at 202. The case would be helpful to Davis if the relevant statement had been the girl's screams for aid as she was being chased by her assailant. But by the time the victim got home, her story was an account of past events.

This is not to say that a conversation which begins as an interrogation to determine the need for emergency assistance cannot, as the Indiana Supreme Court put it, "evolve into testimonial statements," 829 N.E. 2d, at 457, once that purpose has been achieved. In this case, for example, after the operator gained the information needed to address the exigency of the moment, the emergency appears to have ended (when Davis drove away from the premises). The operator then told McCottry to be quiet, and proceeded to pose a battery of questions. It could readily be maintained that, from that point on, McCottry's statements were testimonial, not unlike the "structured police questioning" that occurred in *Crawford*, 541 U.S., at 53, n. 4. This presents no great problem. Just as, for Fifth Amendment purposes, "police officers can and will distinguish almost instinctively between questions necessary to secure their own safety or the safety of the public and questions designed solely to elicit testimonial evidence from a suspect," New York v. Quarles, 467 U.S. 649, 658-659 (1984), trial courts will recognize the point at which, for Sixth Amendment purposes, statements in response to interrogations become testimonial. Through *in limine* procedure, they should redact or exclude the portions of any statement that have become testimonial, as they do, for example, with unduly prejudicial portions of otherwise admissible evidence. Davis's jury did not hear the *complete* 911 call, although it may well have heard some testimonial portions. We were asked to classify only McCottry's early statements identifying Davis as her assailant, and we agree with the Washington Supreme Court that they were not testimonial. That court also concluded that, even if later parts of the call were testimonial, their admission was harmless beyond a reasonable doubt. Davis does not challenge that holding, and we therefore assume it to be correct.

B

Determining the testimonial or nontestimonial character of the statements that were the product of the interrogation in *Hammon* is a much easier task, since they were not much different from the statements we found to be testimonial in *Crawford*. It is entirely clear from the circumstances that the interrogation was part of an investigation into possibly criminal past conduct—as, indeed, the testifying officer expressly acknowledged, App. in No. 05-5705, at 25, 32, 34. There was no emergency in progress; the interrogating officer testified that he had heard no arguments or crashing and saw no one throw or break anything. When the officers first arrived, Amy told them that things were fine, and there was no immediate threat to her person. When the officer questioned Amy for the second time, and elicited the challenged statements, he was not seeking to determine (as in *Davis*) "what is happening," but rather "what happened." Objectively viewed, the primary, if not indeed the sole, purpose of the interrogation was to investigate a possible crime—which is, of course, precisely what the officer *should* have done.

It is true that the *Crawford* interrogation was more formal. It followed a *Miranda* warning, was tape-recorded, and took place at the station house, see 541 U.S., at 53, n. 4. While these features certainly strengthened the statements' testimonial aspect—made it more objectively apparent, that is, that the purpose of the exercise was to nail down the truth about past criminal events—none was essential to the point. It was formal enough that Amy's interrogation was conducted in a separate room, away from her husband (who tried to intervene), with the officer receiving her replies for use in his "investigation." App. in No. 05-5705, at 34. What we called the "striking resemblance" of the *Crawford* statement to civil-law *ex parte* examinations, 541 U.S., at 52, is shared by Amy's statement here. Both declarants were actively separated from the defendant—officers forcibly prevented Hershel from participating in the interrogation. Both statements deliberately recounted, in response to police questioning, how potentially criminal past events began and progressed. And both took place some time after the events described were over. Such statements under official interrogation are an obvious substitute for live testimony, because they do precisely *what a witness does* on direct examination; they are inherently testimonial.[5]

Both Indiana and the United States as *amicus curiae* argue that this case should be resolved much like *Davis*. For the reasons we find the comparison to *Crawford* compelling, we find the comparison to *Davis* unpersuasive. The statements in *Davis* were taken when McCottry was alone, not only unprotected by police (as Amy Hammon was protected), but apparently in immediate danger from Davis. She was seeking aid, not telling a story about the past. McCottry's present-tense statements showed immediacy; Amy's narrative of past events was delivered at some remove in time from the danger she described. And after Amy answered the officer's questions, he had her execute an affidavit, in order, he testified, "to establish events that have occurred previously." App. in No. 05-5705, at 18.

Although we necessarily reject the Indiana Supreme Court's implication that virtually any "initial inquiries" at the crime scene will not be testimonial, see 829 N.E. 2d, at 453, 457, we do not hold the opposite—that *no* questions at the scene will yield nontestimonial answers. We have

5. The dissent criticizes our test for being "neither workable nor a targeted attempt to reach the abuses forbidden by the [Confrontation] Clause," post, at 9 (opinion of THOMAS, J.). As to the former: We have acknowledged that our holding is not an "exhaustive classification of all conceivable statements—or even all conceivable statements in response to police interrogation," *supra,* at 7, but rather a resolution of the cases before us and those like them. For those cases, the test is objective and quite "workable." . . .

As for the charge that our holding is not a "targeted attempt to reach the abuses forbidden by the [Confrontation] Clause," which the dissent describes as the depositions taken by Marian magistrates, characterized by a high degree of formality, see *post,* at 2-3: We do not dispute that formality is indeed essential to testimonial utterance. But we no longer have examining Marian magistrates; and we do have, as our 18th-century forebears did not, examining police officers, see L. Friedman, Crime and Punishment in American History 67-68 (1993)—who perform investigative and testimonial functions once performed by examining Marian magistrates, see J. Langbein, The Origins of Adversary Criminal Trial 41 (2003). It imports sufficient formality, in our view, that lies to such officers are criminal offenses. Restricting the Confrontation Clause to the precise forms against which it was originally directed is a recipe for its extinction. Cf. Kyllo v. United States, 533 U.S. 27 (2001).

already observed of domestic disputes that "officers called to investigate . . . need to know whom they are dealing with in order to assess the situation, the threat to their own safety, and possible danger to the potential victim." *Hübel,* 542 U.S., at 186. Such exigencies may *often* mean that "initial inquiries" produce nontestimonial statements. But in cases like this one, where Amy's statements were neither a cry for help nor the provision of information enabling officers immediately to end a threatening situation, the fact that they were given at an alleged crime scene and were "initial inquiries" is immaterial. Cf. *Crawford, supra,* at 52, n. 3.[6]

IV

Respondents in both cases, joined by a number of their *amici,* contend that the nature of the offenses charged in these two cases—domestic violence—requires greater flexibility in the use of testimonial evidence. This particular type of crime is notoriously susceptible to intimidation or coercion of the victim to ensure that she does not testify at trial. When this occurs, the Confrontation Clause gives the criminal a windfall. We may not, however, vitiate constitutional guarantees when they have the effect of allowing the guilty to go free. Cf. Kyllo v. United States, 533 U.S. 27 (2001) (suppressing evidence from an illegal search). But when defendants seek to undermine the judicial process by procuring or coercing silence from witnesses and victims, the Sixth Amendment does not require courts to acquiesce. While defendants have no duty to assist the State in proving their guilt, they *do* have the duty to refrain from acting in ways that destroy the integrity of the criminal-trial system. We reiterate what we said in *Crawford:* that "the rule of forfeiture by wrongdoing . . . extinguishes confrontation claims on essentially equitable grounds." 541 U.S., at 62 (citing *Reynolds,* 98 U.S., at 158-159). That is, one who obtains the absence of a witness by wrongdoing forfeits the constitutional right to confrontation.

We take no position on the standards necessary to demonstrate such forfeiture, but federal courts using Federal Rule of Evidence 804(b)(6), which codifies the forfeiture doctrine, have generally held the Government to the preponderance-of-the-evidence standard, see, e.g., United

6. Police investigations themselves are, of course, in no way impugned by our characterization of their fruits as testimonial. Investigations of past crimes prevent future harms and lead to necessary arrests. While prosecutors may hope that inculpatory "nontestimonial" evidence is gathered, this is essentially beyond police control. Their saying that an emergency exists cannot make it be so. The Confrontation Clause in no way governs police conduct, because it is the trial use of, not the investigatory *collection* of, *ex parte* testimonial statements which offends that provision. But neither can police conduct govern the Confrontation Clause; testimonial statements are what they are.

States v. Scott, 284 F.3d 758, 762 (C.A.7 2002). State courts tend to follow the same practice, see, e.g., Commonwealth v. Edwards, 444 Mass. 526, 542, 830 N.E.2d 158, 172 (2005). Moreover, if a hearing on forfeiture is required, *Edwards*, for instance, observed that "hearsay evidence, including the unavailable witness's out-of-court statements, may be considered." *Id.*, at 545, 830 N.E.2d, at 174. . . .

We have determined that, absent a finding of forfeiture by wrongdoing, the Sixth Amendment operates to exclude Amy Hammon's affidavit. The Indiana courts may (if they are asked) determine on remand whether such a claim of forfeiture is properly raised and, if so, whether it is meritorious.

* * *

We affirm the judgment of the Supreme Court of Washington in No. 05-5224. We reverse the judgment of the Supreme Court of Indiana in No. 05-5705, and remand the case to that Court for proceedings not inconsistent with this opinion.

JUSTICE THOMAS, concurring in the judgment in part and dissenting in part.

In Crawford v. Washington, 541 U.S. 36 (2004), we abandoned the general reliability inquiry we had long employed to judge the admissibility of hearsay evidence under the Confrontation Clause, describing that inquiry as "*inherently*, and therefore *permanently*, unpredictable." *Id.*, at 68, n. 10 (emphasis in original). Today, a mere two years after the Court decided *Crawford*, it adopts an equally unpredictable test, under which district courts are charged with divining the "primary purpose" of police interrogations. Besides being difficult for courts to apply, this test characterizes as "testimonial," and therefore inadmissible, evidence that bears little resemblance to what we have recognized as the evidence targeted by the Confrontation Clause. Because neither of the cases before the Court today would implicate the Confrontation Clause under an appropriately targeted standard, I concur only in the judgment in Davis v. Washington, No. 05-5224, and dissent from the Court's resolution of Hammon v. Indiana, No. 05-5705.

I

A

The Confrontation Clause provides that "in all criminal prosecutions, the accused shall enjoy the right . . . to be confronted with the witnesses against him . . . ." U.S. Const., Amdt. 6. We have recognized that the operative phrase in the Clause, "witnesses against him," could be interpreted narrowly, to reach only those witnesses who actually testify at trial, or more broadly, to reach many or all of those whose out-of-court statements are offered at trial. *Crawford, supra,* at 42-43; White v. Illinois, 502 U.S. 346, 359-363 (1992) (THOMAS, J., concurring in part and concurring in judgment). Because the narrowest interpretation of the Clause would conflict with both the history giving rise to the adoption of the Clause and this Court's precedent, we have rejected such a reading. See *Crawford, supra,* at 50-51; *White, supra,* at 360 (opinion of THOMAS, J.).

Rejection of the narrowest view of the Clause does not, however, require the broadest application of the Clause to exclude otherwise admissible hearsay evidence. The history surrounding the right to confrontation supports the conclusion that it was developed to target particular practices that occurred under the English bail and committal statutes passed during the reign of Queen Mary, namely, the "civil-law mode of criminal procedure, and particularly its use of *ex parte* examinations as evidence against the accused." *Crawford, supra,* at 43, 50; *White, supra,* at 361-362 (opinion of THOMAS, J.); Mattox v. United States, 156 U.S. 237, 242 (1895). "The predominant purpose of the [Marian committal] statute was to institute *systematic* questioning of the accused and the witnesses." J. Langbein, Prosecuting Crime in the Renaissance 23 (1974) (emphasis added). The statute required an oral examination of the suspect and the accusers, transcription within two days of the examinations, and physical transmission to the judges hearing the case. *Id.*, at 10, 23. These examinations came to be used as evidence in some cases, in lieu of a personal appearance by the witness. *Crawford, supra,* at 43-44; 9 W. Holdsworth, A History of English Law 223-229 (1926). Many statements that would be inadmissible as a matter of hearsay law bear little resemblance to these evidentiary practices, which the Framers proposed the Confrontation Clause to prevent. See, e.g., *Crawford, supra,* at 51 (contrasting "an off-hand, overheard remark" with the abuses targeted by the Confrontation Clause). Accordingly, it is unlikely that the Framers intended the word "witness" to be read so broadly as to include such statements. Cf. Dutton v. Evans, 400 U.S. 74, 94 (1970) (Harlan, J., concurring in result) (rejecting the "assumption that the core purpose of the Confrontation Clause of the Sixth Amendment is to prevent overly broad exceptions to the hearsay rule").

In *Crawford*, we recognized that this history could be squared with the language of the Clause, giving rise to a workable, and more accurate, interpretation of the Clause. "'Witnesses,'" we said, are those who "'bear testimony.'" 541 U.S., at 51 (quoting 1 N. Webster, An American Dictionary of the English Language (1828)). And "'testimony'" is "'[a] solemn declaration or affirmation made for the purpose of establishing or proving some fact.'" *Ibid.* (quoting Webster, *supra*). Admittedly, we did not set forth a detailed framework for addressing whether a statement is "testimonial" and thus subject to the Confrontation Clause. But the plain terms of the "testimony" definition we endorsed necessarily require some degree of solemnity before a statement can be deemed "testimonial."

This requirement of solemnity supports my view that the statements regulated by the Confrontation Clause must include "extrajudicial statements . . . contained in formalized testimonial materials, such as affidavits, depositions, prior testimony, or confessions." *White, supra*, at 365 (opinion of THOMAS, J.). Affidavits, depositions, and prior testimony are, by their very nature, taken through a formalized process. Likewise, confessions, when extracted by police in a formal manner, carry sufficient indicia of solemnity to constitute formalized statements and, accordingly, bear a "striking resemblance," *Crawford, supra*, at 52, to the examinations of the accused and accusers under the Marian statutes.[1] See generally Langbein, *supra*, at 21-34.

Although the Court concedes that the early American cases invoking the right to confrontation or the Confrontation Clause itself all "clearly involved testimony" as defined in *Crawford*, it fails to acknowledge that all of the cases it cites fall within the narrower category of formalized testimonial materials I have proposed.[2] Interactions between the police and an accused (or witnesses) resemble Marian proceedings—and these early cases—only when the interactions are somehow rendered "formal." In *Crawford*, for example, the interrogation was custodial, taken after warnings given pursuant to Miranda v. Arizona, 384 U.S. 436 (1966). 541 U.S., at 38. *Miranda* warnings, by their terms, inform a prospective defendant that "'anything he says can be used against him in a court of law.'" Dickerson v. United States, 530 U.S. 428, 435 (2000) (quoting *Miranda, supra*, at 479). This imports a solemnity to the process that is not present in a mere conversation between a witness or suspect and a police officer.[3]

1. Like the Court, I presume the acts of the 911 operator to be the acts of the police. Accordingly, I refer to both the operator in *Davis* and the officer in *Hammon*, and their counterparts in similar cases, collectively as "the police."

2. Our more recent cases, too, nearly all hold excludable under the Confrontation Clause materials that are plainly highly formal. . . .

3. The possibility that an oral declaration of past fact to a police officer, if false, could result in legal consequences to the speaker, may render honesty in casual conversations with police officers important. It does not, however, render those conversations solemn or formal in the ordinary meanings of those terms.

The Court all but concedes that no case can be cited for its conclusion that the Confrontation Clause also applies to informal police questioning under certain circumstances. Instead, the sole basis for the Court's conclusion is its apprehension that the Confrontation Clause will "readily be evaded" if it is only applicable to formalized testimonial materials. But the Court's proposed solution to the risk of evasion is needlessly overinclusive. Because the Confrontation Clause sought to regulate prosecutorial abuse occurring through use of *ex parte* statements as evidence against the accused, it also reaches the use of technically informal statements when used to evade the formalized process. That is, even if the interrogation itself is not formal, the production of evidence by the prosecution at trial would resemble the abuses targeted by the Confrontation Clause if the prosecution attempted to use out-of-court statements as a means of circumventing the literal right of confrontation, see Coy v. Iowa, 487 U.S. 1012 (1988). In such a case, the Confrontation Clause could fairly be applied to exclude the hearsay statements offered by the prosecution, preventing evasion without simultaneously excluding evidence offered by the prosecution in good faith.

The Court's standard is not only disconnected from history and unnecessary to prevent abuse; it also yields no predictable results to police officers and prosecutors attempting to comply with the law. Cf. *Crawford, supra*, at 68, n. 10 (criticizing unpredictability of the pre-*Crawford* test); *White*, 502 U.S., at 364-365 (THOMAS, J., concurring in part and concurring in judgment) (limiting the Confrontation Clause to the discrete category of materials historically abused would "greatly simplify" application of the Clause). In many, if not most, cases where police respond to a report of a crime, whether pursuant to a 911 call from the victim or otherwise, the purposes of an interrogation, viewed from the perspective of the police, are *both* to respond to the emergency situation *and* to gather evidence. See New York v. Quarles, 467 U.S. 649, 656 (1984) ("Undoubtedly most police officers [deciding whether to give *Miranda* warnings in a possible emergency situation] would act out of a host of different, instinctive, and largely unverifiable motives—their own safety, the safety of others, and perhaps as well the desire to obtain incriminating evidence from the suspect"). Assigning one of these two "largely unverifiable motives," primacy requires constructing a hierarchy of purpose that will rarely be present—and is not reliably discernible. It will inevitably be, quite simply, an exercise in fiction.

The Court's repeated invocation of the word "objective" to describe its test, however, suggests that the Court may not mean to reference purpose at all, but instead to inquire into the function served by the interrogation.

Certainly such a test would avoid the pitfalls that have led us repeatedly to reject tests dependent on the subjective intentions of police officers.[4] It would do so, however, at the cost of being even more disconnected from the prosecutorial abuses targeted by the Confrontation Clause. Additionally, it would shift the ability to control whether a violation occurred from the police and prosecutor to the judge, whose determination as to the "primary purpose" of a particular interrogation would be unpredictable and not necessarily tethered to the actual purpose for which the police performed the interrogation.

B

Neither the 911 call at issue in *Davis* nor the police questioning at issue in *Hammon* is testimonial under the appropriate framework. Neither the call nor the questioning is itself a formalized dialogue.[5] Nor do any circumstances surrounding the taking of the statements render those statements sufficiently formal to resemble the Marian examinations; the statements were neither Mirandized nor custodial, nor accompanied by any similar indicia of formality. Finally, there is no suggestion that the prosecution attempted to offer the women's hearsay evidence at trial in order to evade confrontation. See 829 N.E.2d 444, 447 (Ind. 2005) (prosecution subpoenaed Amy Hammon to testify, but she was not present); 154 Wn. 2d 291, 296, 111 P. 3d 844, 847 (2005) (en banc) (State was unable to locate Michelle McCottry at the time of trial). Accordingly, the statements at issue in both cases are nontestimonial and admissible under the Confrontation Clause.

The Court's determination that the evidence against Hammon must be excluded extends the Confrontation Clause far beyond the abuses it was intended to prevent. When combined with the Court's holding that the evidence against Davis is perfectly admissible, however, the Court's *Hammon* holding also reveals the difficulty of applying the Court's requirement that courts investigate the "primary purposes" of the investigation. The Court draws a line between the two cases based on its explanation that *Hammon* involves "no emergency in progress," but

4. See New York v. Quarles, 467 U.S. 649, 655-656, and n. 6 (1984) (subjective motivation of officer not relevant in considering whether the public safety exception to Miranda v. Arizona, 384 U.S. 436 (1966), is applicable); Rhode Island v. Innis, 446 U.S. 291, 301 (1980) (subjective intent of police officer to obtain incriminatory statement not relevant to whether an interrogation has occurred); Whren v. United States, 517 U.S. 806, 813 (1996) (refusing to evaluate Fourth Amendment reasonableness in light of the officers' actual motivations).

5. Although the police questioning in *Hammon* was ultimately reduced to an affidavit, all agree that the affidavit is inadmissible *per se* under our definition of the term "testimonial." Brief for Respondent in No. 05-5705, p. 46; Brief for United States as *Amicus Curiae* in No. 05-5705, p. 14.

instead, mere questioning as "part of an investigation into possibly criminal past conduct," and its explanation that *Davis* involves questioning for the "primary purpose" of "enabling police assistance to meet an ongoing emergency." But the fact that the officer in *Hammon* was investigating Mr. Hammon's past conduct does not foreclose the possibility that the primary purpose of his inquiry was to assess whether Mr. Hammon constituted a continuing danger to his wife, requiring further police presence or action. It is hardly remarkable that Hammon did not act abusively towards his wife in the presence of the officers, and his good judgment to refrain from criminal behavior in the presence of police sheds little, if any, light on whether his violence would have resumed had the police left without further questioning, transforming what the Court dismisses as "past conduct" back into an "ongoing emergency."[6] Nor does the mere fact that McCottry needed emergency aid shed light on whether the "primary purpose" of gathering, for example, the name of her assailant was to protect the police, to protect the victim, or to gather information for prosecution. In both of the cases before the Court, like many similar cases, pronouncement of the "primary" motive behind the interrogation calls for nothing more than a guess by courts.

II

Because the standard adopted by the Court today is neither workable nor a targeted attempt to reach the abuses forbidden by the Clause, I concur only in the judgment in Davis v. Washington, No. 05-5224, and respectfully dissent from the Court's resolution of Hammon v. Indiana, No. 05-5705.

NOTES AND QUESTIONS

1. Who's got the better of the argument here? Justice Scalia, whose definition of "testimony" seems to depend mostly on whether the statements at issue dealt with contemporaneous or past events? Or Justice Thomas, whose test would depend on the "formality" of the circumstances under which the statements were made? What, if anything, do

6. Some of the factors on which the Court relies to determine that the police questioning in *Hammon* was testimonial apply equally in *Davis*. For example, while Hammon was "actively separated from the [victim]" and thereby "prevented . . . from participating in the interrogation," Davis was apart from McCottry while she was questioned by the 911 operator and thus unable to participate in the questioning. Similarly, "the events described [by McCottry] were over" by the time she recounted them to the 911 operator. See 154 Wn. 2d 291, 295-296, 111 P.3d 844, 846-847 (2005) (en banc).

either of these competing approaches have to do with the underlying purpose of the Confrontation Clause, which is (presumably) to help ensure that trial testimony is adequately tested and, therefore, can be trusted as reasonably reliable? In particular, isn't it a little strange that, under both tests, most 911 calls (which are usually made under highly stressful, if not downright dangerous, circumstances that seem very likely to affect the witness's perceptions) will turn out to be non-problematic under the Confrontation Clause (and thus admissible without cross-examination, assuming all other requirements for admissibility are met)?

2. Why does Justice Scalia spend so much time discussing the behavior and purposes of the relevant government agents, when—as he himself clearly states, see fn. 1—it's the nature of the declarant's statements that matters to the application of the Confrontation Clause, and not the nature of the interrogator's questions? For example, if the 911 operator in *Davis* had asked no questions at all, but simply had listened quietly and patiently while Michelle McCottry blurted out her statements, would the result in the case have been any different? Wouldn't the Confrontation Clause have kicked in at exactly the same point, i.e., the moment when McCottry stated that "[h]e's runnin' now," thus indicating that the immediate emergency had passed? Why should the "primary purpose of the interrogation" matter at all, given that (to use Justice Scalia's own words, in fn. 6) "police conduct [cannot] govern the Confrontation Clause; testimonial statements are what they are'"?

2a. In *Davis*, the Court noted that a defendant can lose his Confrontation Clause protection through the equitable doctrine of "forfeiture by wrongdoing." Does the act of "wrongdoing" have to be for the purpose of preventing the witness from testifying? Or is any act of "wrongdoing" sufficient, as long as it has the effect of preventing the witness from testifying?

In Giles v. California, 128 U.S. 2678 (2008), the defendant was accused of murdering his wife, and the prosecution was allowed to use the "forfeiture by wrongdoing" exception to introduce prior unconfronted testimonial statements, made by the wife, accusing her husband of domestic violence. A fractured Court (in a lead opinion by Justice Scalia that garnered majority support for all but one section) held that the forfeiture exception applies "only when the defendant engaged in conduct *designed* to prevent the witness from testifying." Although this required reversal of the conviction, Scalia noted that on remand, an inquiry could be made into whether there might be evidence sufficient to show that the defendant did, indeed, murder his wife for the purpose of silencing her. Such evidence might include, for example, "[e]arlier abuse, or threats of abuse, intended to dissuade the victim from resorting to outside help," as well as "evidence of ongoing criminal proceedings at which the victim would have been expected to testify," all of which would be "highly relevant" to the key issue of whether the defendant's crime "expressed the intent to isolate the victim and to stop her from reporting abuse to the authorities or cooperating with a criminal prosecution." Justices Thomas and Alito joined the lead opinion, but wrote separately to express the view that, although not an issue properly before the Court, the contested statements might not even be "testimonial" in the first place (since they were not closely analogous to in-court witness statements). Justices Souter and Ginsburg joined all but one section of the lead opinion (a section that contained exceptionally strong rhetoric about the role of history and original intent in interpreting the Confrontation Clause, and correspondingly strong denigration of the dissenters' policy-oriented jurisprudence). Justices Breyer, Stevens, and Kennedy dissented, largely on the grounds that the Court's decision would allow domestic abusers to benefit from the violent results of their abuse.

2b. Near the end of his *Giles* lead opinion, in a portion joined by a majority of the Court, Justice Scalia penned the following interesting passage:

> The dissent closes by pointing out that a forfeiture rule which ignores *Crawford* would be particularly helpful to women in abusive relationships—or at least particularly helpful in punishing their abusers. Not as helpful as the dissent suggests, since only *testimonial* statements are excluded by the Confrontation Clause. Statements to friends and neighbors about abuse and intimidation, and statements to physicians in the course of receiving treatment would be excluded, if at all, only by hearsay rules. . . .

What does this mean? Recall that in *Davis*, Scalia's majority opinion cited—as an apparent example of "testimony"—the English case of King v. Brasier, 1 Leach 199, 168 Eng. Rep. 202 (1779), in which a young girl, immediately after being raped, reported the facts of the crime to her mother. If the *Brasier* case involved "testimony," because it was (in Scalia's words from *Davis*) "an account of past events," then how could "[s]tatements to friends and neighbors about abuse and intimidation" not also involve "testimony"? Aren't they all equally "account[s] of past events"? Is Scalia now going back on his position in *Davis*?

Does it help to note that, earlier in *Davis*, Scalia had stated, in a footnote, that "our holding today makes it unnecessary to consider whether and when statements made to someone other than law enforcement personnel are testimonial"? Perhaps the true meaning of "testimony" depends on *both* (1) the temporal dimension (i.e., whether the statement is given in "real time" or is made about "past events") *and* (2) the identity of the person or persons to whom the statement is made. We will have to wait and see.

3. In more general terms, doesn't the Court's fundamental approach to the Confrontation Clause in *Crawford* and *Davis* seem rather sterile? In particular, note Justice Scalia's back-of-the-hand dismissal of the concern that *Davis* will undermine the factual accuracy of criminal adjudication, especially in domestic violence cases: "When this occurs, the Confrontation Clause gives the criminal a windfall. We may not, however, vitiate constitutional guarantees when they have the effect of allowing the guilty to go free."

How can such a view be squared with, e.g., the Court's decision during the same Term in House v. Bell, 547 U.S. 518 (2006), see *infra* p. 279, a decision clearly motivated by the desire to improve factual accuracy in criminal cases (or, more specifically, to remedy factual *in*-accuracy)? Should constitutional criminal procedure rules be designed and applied with a primary focus on enhancing factual accuracy, or are some procedural rules an end in themselves—even when they may sometimes work *against* accuracy, as in *Crawford* and *Davis*?

It is undoubtedly true that procedural justice and factual accuracy often complement each other. But when these two values come into conflict, how should the Court choose between them? Does an absolutist statement like the one quoted in the preceding paragraph seem like the best way to resolve such a conflict? Do you think Justice Scalia really meant what he said?

4. Apparently Justice Scalia was quite serious. In an astonishing elevation of form over both substance and good sense, the same five-person majority, with Scalia writing the opinion, held in Melendez-Diaz v. Massachusetts, 129 S. Ct. 2527 (2009), that a certificate from a state laboratory after chemical testing certifying the contents and quantity of a seized substance was a "testimonial" statement, and thus within the rule in *Crawford* requiring the opportunity to cross-examine the maker of the statement.

To the majority, the "case involves little more than the application of our holding in *Crawford* . . . The Sixth Amendment does not permit the prosecution to prove its case via *ex parte* out-of-court affidavits . . . " In a biting and powerful dissent, however, Justice Kennedy pointed out that, regardless whether *Crawford* may stand for that proposition, the Sixth Amendment does not. It does not prohibit "*ex parte* affidavits"; it provides a right to confront the witnesses again you. The question is not what is "testimonial"; the question is who are the witnesses the Sixth Amendment refers to? As the dissent pointed out, there is virtually nothing in the constitutional language, history, precedent, or good sense justifying the majority's reworking of long-settled procedural and evidentiary rules that exempted such people as lab technicians from being called by the state in order to admit their lab results. The concern of the Sixth Amendment, according to the dissent, is the key factual witnesses against a defendant, with respect to whom face-to-face confrontation may make a difference. Face-to-face confrontation with lab technicians is highly unlikely to be of any benefit to the defense and will impose serious costs on the state. To be sure, errors are made by lab technicians, and it is not inconceivable that in a small number of cases cross-examining the lab technician may point out a problem. However, defendants now have the right under the compulsory process clause to subpoena whomever they like, including lab technicians, and examine them at trial.

Against the minimal benefits to factual accuracy of the Court's approach, consider the costs. As the dissent argued in passages to which the majority did not respond:

> The Court says that, before the results of a scientific test may be introduced into evidence, the defendant has the right to confront the "analyst." One must assume that this term, though it appears nowhere in the Confrontation Clause, nevertheless has some constitutional substance that now must be elaborated in future cases. There is no accepted definition of analyst, and there is no established precedent to define that term.
>
> Consider how many people play a role in a routine test for the presence of illegal drugs. One person prepares a sample of the drug, places it in a testing machine, and retrieves the machine's printout—often, a graph showing the frequencies of radiation absorbed by the sample or the masses of the sample's molecular fragments . . . A second person interprets the graph the machine prints out—perhaps by comparing that printout with published, standardized graphs of known drugs. Meanwhile, a third person—perhaps an independent contractor—has calibrated the machine and, having done so, has certified that the machine is in good working order. Finally, a fourth person—perhaps the laboratory's director—certifies that his subordinates followed established procedures.
>
> It is not at all evident which of these four persons is the analyst to be confronted under the rule the Court announces today. If all are witnesses who must appear for in-court confrontation, then the Court has, for all practical purposes, forbidden the use of scientific tests in criminal trials . . . . [R]equiring even one of these individuals to testify threatens to disrupt if not end many prosecutions where guilt is clear but a newly found formalism now holds sway.
>
> The Federal Government may face even graver difficulties than the States because its operations are so widespread. For example, the FBI laboratory at Quantico, Virginia, supports federal, state, and local investigations across the

country. Its 500 employees conduct over one million scientific tests each year. . . . The Court's decision means that before any of those million tests reaches a jury, at least one of the laboratory's analysts must board a plane, find his or her way to an unfamiliar courthouse, and sit there waiting to read aloud notes made months ago.

The Court purchases its meddling with the Confrontation Clause at a dear price, a price not measured in taxpayer dollars alone. Guilty defendants will go free, on the most technical grounds, as a direct result of today's decision, adding nothing to the truth-finding process. The analyst will not always make it to the courthouse in time. He or she may be ill; may be out of the country; may be unable to travel because of inclement weather; or may at that very moment be waiting outside some other courtroom for another defendant to exercise the right the Court invents today. If for any reason the analyst cannot make it to the courthouse in time, then, the Court holds, the jury cannot learn of the analyst's findings (unless, by some unlikely turn of events, the defendant previously cross-examined the analyst). The result, in many cases, will be that the prosecution cannot meet its burden of proof, and the guilty defendant goes free on a technicality that, because it results in an acquittal, cannot be reviewed on appeal.

5. To what, exactly, does this new rule apply? Suppose a lab technician is called to testify. Can he or she explain the chain of custody that led to the substance being brought to the lab for testing, or does every single person in the chain of custody have to be produced? If the latter, isn't that a bit ridiculous?

6. If the costs are as dear as the dissent in *Melendez-Diaz* seems to think, the results may not be quite what the dissent predicts but instead become the incentive for creative reengineering by the states and federal government. Recall that *Crawford* is satisfied with the right to confront and cross-examine at some point, and that point does not need to be at the trial on the merits. A pre-trial process involving notice to the defendant and the opportunity to cross-examine the relevant witnesses under oath suffices. Could a state thus satisfy *Melendez-Diaz* through largely pro forma pre-trial hearings, with notice to defendants, where lab technicians are sworn and made available for cross-examination? If the defendant appears in person or through counsel, the confrontation clause would be satisfied, and if the defendant does not appear, any such right would be waived. A state could likely conduct hundreds of such hearings in a few hours, and could thus preserve at relatively little cost the benefits of the previous way of doing business that the Court has now ruled unconstitutional. Do you think such possibilities support what the Court has done, or emphasize its curiousness?

7. What is the extension of the rule in *Crawford*? Consider the case of expert testimony. Typically, an expert can rely on inadmissible evidence

to form an opinion. Suppose an expert, offered by the state, relies on out-of-court statements about a defendant to draw an inference about the competence of the defendant at the time he committed a criminal act. Those statements may refer, for example, to the everyday functioning of the individual, and so on, and are only pertinent to competence if true. Can an expert testify on such a basis? Who is actually "testifying against the defendant" in such cases? Can the expert explain the basis of his opinion, or will each of the persons making a statement that the expert relied upon have to be called as a witness?

Take the matter one step further. Many forensic experts learn their discipline from books written by individuals who fully expect that the books will be used in the education of individuals who will testify in part on the basis of what they learn in those books. Indeed, most knowledge is transmitted through such forms of "testimony." When, say, a ballistics expert or a fingerprint expert who learned his field in part through the use of such books testifies, who is "testifying against the defendant"? The in-court expert is testifying in part on what the out-of-court expert asserted in the educational material relied upon, and in some ways is simply repeating the out-of-court statements that the author of the book fully expected would lead to in-court testimony. Does that violate *Crawford*? If not, why not?

If so, are we hovering over an abyss?

Add the following new subsection at the conclusion of subsection E., at page 1410, and re-letter subsection F., at page 1410, as subsection G.:

F. Criminal Trials and Factual Accuracy

To what extent should criminal trials (and, more generally, criminal justice—including the full range of pretrial proceedings, trials, direct appeals, and post-conviction proceedings) be designed to ensure, as much as humanly possible, factually accurate results? Should our choices about the structure and procedural rules of the criminal justice system be made mostly, or even exclusively, on the basis of whether those choices will further both the conviction of the guilty and the acquittal of the innocent (which are, after all, two sides of the very same coin)? Or are there other important values—such as autonomy, privacy, equality, fairness, respect for the individual—that deserve equal treatment?

In recent years, the Supreme Court has seemed increasingly ambivalent about where the primary emphasis should lie. On the one hand, the Court has manifested a growing discomfort about the number of criminal cases in which potentially innocent defendants have been found guilty of serious, and sometimes even capital, crimes. This concern about factual inaccuracy can clearly be seen in such decisions as Holmes v. South Carolina, 547 U.S. 319 (2006) (reversing a conviction because the defendant was precluded from introducing evidence at trial that pointed to a different suspect); Youngblood v. West Virginia, 547 U.S. 867 (2006) (reversing and remanding a potentially meritorious *Brady* claim to the state courts for further review); and especially House v. Bell, 547 U.S. 518 (2006).

In *House*, the Court (by 5-3, with Justice Alito not participating) reversed the Sixth Circuit, and allowed a Death-Row inmate's habeas corpus action to proceed despite the petitioner's failure to follow the applicable procedural rules in state court, because the Court found that the petitioner's newly discovered evidence of factual innocence (specifically, DNA test results) was strong enough that "it is more likely than not that no reasonable juror would have found petitioner guilty beyond a reasonable doubt" if the evidence had been available at trial. The Court's emphatic conclusion was based not only on the new DNA evidence itself, but also on the "evidentiary disarray" (which was described in great detail, and at great length, in Justice Breyer's majority opinion) surrounding the prosecution's forensic evidence at trial. Upon consideration of all of the evidence (including the new DNA evidence), the Court held that although the case was not one of "conclusive exoneration," it nevertheless qualified as one of those "rare case[s]" meriting habeas review despite the petitioner's procedural default.

On the other hand, the Court has also decided several recent cases in ways that seemingly ignored or downplayed the issue of factual accuracy in favor of something else. For example, in Davis v. Washington, 547 U.S. 813 (2006), the Court continued its development of a brand new Confrontation Clause approach that elevates the Framers' views about what kinds of evidence must be subjected to cross-examination (specifically, evidence resembling that which was introduced under certain English statutes passed during the reign of Queen Mary) over more functional considerations about whether, and to what extent, cross-examination might actually contribute to the reliability of evidence (and thus the factual accuracy of trials). Along somewhat similar lines, see Oregon v. Guzek, 546 U.S. 517 (2006) (holding that a capital defendant has no constitutional right to introduce evidence of his innocence at a capital sentencing hearing, once he has been found guilty at the trial stage of the case); United States v. Ruiz, 536 U.S. 622 (2002) (holding that prosecutors need not disclose to defendants, prior to accepting a guilty plea, evidence that would impeach prosecution in-formants or witnesses).

Is there a way to reconcile these apparent inconsistencies in approach? Is this a simple case of two different factions on the Court disagreeing about what matters most in criminal cases? Or does this confusing situation possibly reflect, instead, a gradual shift from the largely procedural emphasis of the Court during much of the 1960's and 1970's to a new substantive approach—perhaps motivated by the recent, highly publicized spate of DNA exonerations (especially in capital cases)? Will we see in the near future, perhaps, additional decisions by the Court along the lines of House v. Bell, opening up new avenues of opportunity for defendants with claims of factual innocence to challenge their convictions?

Any perception of a trend in this direction may have been dashed, at least temporarily, by the Court's ruling in District Attorney's Office for the Third Judicial District v. Osborne, 129 S. Ct. 2308 (2009). Osborne was convicted of kidnapping, sexual assault, and assault (but acquitted of attempted murder) in connection with a brutal 1993 attack on a prostitute, and was sentenced to 26 years in prison. Although Osborne's conviction and sentence were affirmed on appeal, and also in state and federal post-conviction review, he continued to profess his innocence. Osborne eventually filed a §1983 petition in federal court, seeking access to physical evidence in the state's possession so that he could have it tested by advanced DNA methods. His petition was premised on the argument that such access should be guaranteed by the Due Process Clause—in either the procedural sense, by analogy to the defendant's right to be notified of material exculpatory evidence under Brady v. Maryland, 373 U.S. 83 (1969), or in the substantive sense.

The Court, in a 5-4 decision, rejected both versions of the argument. According to the Court, claims of factual innocence made after conviction entitle the claimant to less stringent procedural protections than would attach to such claims made at trial, thus making *Brady* inapposite. "The State accordingly has more flexibility in deciding what procedures are needed in the context of postconviction relief. . . . Federal courts may upset a State's postconviction relief procedures only if they are fundamentally inadequate to vindicate the substantive rights provided. . . . We see nothing inadequate about the procedures Alaska has provided to vindicate its state right to postconviction relief in general, and nothing inadequate about how those procedures apply to those who seek access to DNA evidence." The Court also rejected Osborne's substantive due process argument, based on both the argument's "novelty" as well as the fact that it would embroil the Court in difficult policy choices (such as whether, and for how long, states should be required to preserve evidence for possible future testing). In the end, the Court concluded:

DNA evidence will undoubtedly lead to changes in the criminal justice system. It has done so already. The question is whether further change will primarily be made by legislative revision and judicial interpretation of the existing system, or whether the Federal Judiciary must leap ahead—revising (or even discarding) the system by creating a new constitutional right and taking over responsibility for refining it.

G. *Alternatives to the Traditional Criminal Trial — The Proposed Special Military Tribunal*

Substitute the following new paragraph for the first two full paragraphs on page 1417:

In Hamdan v. Rumsfeld, 548 U.S. 557 (2006), the Supreme Court held that certain aspects of the proposed special military tribunals—especially the fact that the evidence used to convict the defendant might never be revealed to him—violated both the Uniform Code of Military Justice (UCMJ) and the 1949 Geneva Conventions. The Court (in an opinion by Justice Stevens) found that the proposed deviations from the procedural rules applicable to normal U.S. military courts-martial were not sufficiently justified by any proven practical exigencies, as required by Article 36 of the UCMJ. The Court also concluded that the Geneva Conventions mandate that all persons detained during armed conflicts (including those who, like the al Qaeda detainees in question, are detained under circumstances that do not involve a declared war between nations) must be tried before "a regularly constituted court affording all the judicial guarantees . . . recognized as indispensable by civilized peoples." Common Article 3, 1949 Geneva Conventions. The Court held that the proposed special military tribunals cannot qualify as "regularly constituted court[s]," nor can their creation be sufficiently justified by any proven practical exigencies. Thus the special military tribunals, as proposed, violated the Geneva Conventions as well.

Congress responded to *Hamdan* by enacting the Military Commissions Act of 2006, Pub. L. No. 109-366, which was signed into law by President George W. Bush on October 17, 2006, and codified at Chapter 47A of Title 10 of the U.S. Code. The Act's purposes included creating "procedures governing the use of military commissions," and providing for "full and fair trials by military commissions." The Act, among other provisions, suspended habeas corpus for non-U.S. citizens accused of being "unlawful enemy combatants" (some commentators have questioned whether the suspension also might have been intended to apply to U.S. citizens facing the same accusation), thus removing such cases from the jurisdiction of the federal courts and leaving them to be adjudicated by military tribunals.

The military tribunals came under fire in the 2008 decision of Boumediene v. Bush, 128 S. Ct. 2229 (2008). There, the Court held that the military tribunals were not sufficiently compliant with the dictates of due process to serve as a constitutionally valid substitute for habeas corpus review of "enemy combatant" status. For more on the Boumediene case, see Chapter 15, *supra*.

PART FIVE

POSTTRIAL PROCEEDINGS

Chapter 13

Sentencing

A. Introduction to Sentencing

3. Substantive Limits on Sentencing — Eighth Amendment Proportionality

Insert the following notes and main case after Note 4 on page 1441:

5. In *Harmelin* and *Ewing*, the Court basically declined the invitation to engage in meaningful substantive review of noncapital prison sentences. This reluctance may have its roots in legitimacy concerns related to the Court's basic counter-majoritarian dilemma, which may be intensified in the particular legal and historical context of the Eighth Amendment. See Joseph L. Hoffmann, "The 'Cruel and Unusual Punishment' Clause: A Significant Limit on the Government's Power to Punish, or Mere Constitutional Rhetoric?," in The Bill of Rights in Modern America (Indiana University Press 1993; D. Bodenhamer & J. Ely, Jr., eds.). Or it may stem from the realization that the Court has few, if any, anchors to prevent substantive review of criminal sentences from devolving into standardless pronouncements of the Justices' own personal moral beliefs. Or it may reflect simply the Court's relative lack of experience, and thus lack of expertise, in such substantive review. See Ronald J. Allen & Ethan A. Hastert, "From *Winship* to *Apprendi* to *Booker* and *Fan-Fan*: Constitutional Command or Constitutional Blunder?," 58 Stanford Law Review 195-216 (2005).

In any event, it is impossible not to be struck by the stark contrast between the Court's cautious approach to Eighth Amendment substantive review of noncapital sentences, as seen in *Harmelin* and *Ewing*, and its much more aggressive approach to substantive review of capital sentences, as seen in the following recent case:

ROPER v. SIMMONS

Certiorari to the Supreme Court of Missouri
543 U.S. 551 (2005)

JUSTICE KENNEDY delivered the opinion of the Court.

This case requires us to address, for the second time in a decade and a half, whether it is permissible under the Eighth and Fourteenth Amendments to the Constitution of the United States to execute a juvenile offender who was older than 15 but younger than 18 when he committed a capital crime. In Stanford v. Kentucky, 492 U.S. 361 (1989), a divided Court rejected the proposition that the Constitution bars capital punishment for juvenile offenders in this age group. We reconsider the question.

I

[This section, detailing the brutal facts of the murder that was planned by Simmons, and that was committed by him and two younger accomplices, is omitted. —EDS.]

II

The Eighth Amendment provides: "Excessive bail shall not be required, nor excessive fines imposed, nor cruel and unusual punishments inflicted." The provision is applicable to the States through the Fourteenth Amendment. As the Court explained in Atkins [v. Virginia, 536 U.S. 304 (2002)], the Eighth Amendment guarantees individuals the right not to be subjected to excessive sanctions. The right flows from the basic '"precept of justice that punishment for crime should be graduated and proportioned to [the] offense."' 536 U.S., at 311 (quoting Weems v. United States, 217 U.S. 349, 367 (1910)). By protecting even those convicted of heinous crimes, the Eighth Amendment reaffirms the duty of the government to respect the dignity of all persons.

The prohibition against "cruel and unusual punishments," like other expansive language in the Constitution, must be interpreted according to its text, by considering history, tradition, and precedent, and with due regard for its purpose and function in the constitutional design. To implement this framework we have established the propriety and affirmed the necessity of referring to "the evolving standards of decency that mark the progress of a maturing society" to determine which punishments are so disproportionate as to be cruel and unusual. Trop v. Dulles, 356 U.S. 86, 100-101 (1958) (plurality opinion).

In Thompson v. Oklahoma, 487 U.S. 815 (1988), a plurality of the Court determined that our standards of decency do not permit the execution of any offender under the age of 16 at the time of the crime. The plurality opinion explained that no death penalty State that had given express consideration to a minimum age for the death penalty had set the age lower than 16. The plurality also observed that "[t]he conclusion that it would offend civilized standards of decency to execute a person who was less than 16 years old at the time of his or her offense is consistent with the views that have been expressed by respected professional organizations, by other nations that share our Anglo-American heritage, and by the leading members of the Western European community." The opinion further noted that juries imposed the death penalty on offenders under 16 with exceeding rarity; the last execution of an offender for a crime committed under the age of 16 had been carried out in 1948, 40 years prior.

Bringing its independent judgment to bear on the permissibility of the death penalty for a 15-year-old offender, the *Thompson* plurality stressed that "[t]he reasons why juveniles are not trusted with the privileges and responsibilities of an adult also explain why their irresponsible conduct is not as morally reprehensible as that of an adult." According to the plurality, the lesser culpability of offenders under 16 made the death penalty inappropriate as a form of retribution, while the low likelihood that offenders under 16 engaged in "the kind of cost-benefit analysis that attaches any weight to the possibility of execution" made the death penalty ineffective as a means of deterrence. With Justice O'CONNOR concurring in the judgment on narrower grounds, *id.*, at 848-859, the Court set aside the death sentence that had been imposed on the 15-year-old offender.

The next year, in Stanford v. Kentucky, 492 U.S. 361 (1989), the Court, over a dissenting opinion joined by four Justices, referred to contemporary standards of decency in this country and concluded the Eighth and Fourteenth Amendments did not proscribe the execution of juvenile offenders over 15 but under 18. The Court noted that 22 of the 37 death penalty States permitted the death penalty for 16-year-old offenders, and, among these 37 States, 25 permitted it for 17-year-old offenders. These numbers, in the Court's view, indicated there was no national consensus "sufficient to label a particular punishment cruel and unusual." A plurality of the Court also "emphatically reject[ed]" the suggestion that the Court should bring its own judgment to bear on the acceptability of the juvenile death penalty. *Id.*, at 377-378 (opinion of SCALIA, J., joined by REHNQUIST, C. J., and WHITE and KENNEDY, JJ.); see also *id.*, at 382 (O'CONNOR, J., concurring in part and concurring in judgment) (criticizing the plurality's refusal "to judge whether the "'nexus between the punishment imposed and the defendant's blameworthiness'" is proportional").

The same day the Court decided *Stanford*, it held that the Eighth Amendment did not mandate a categorical exemption from the death penalty for the mentally retarded. Penry v. Lynaugh, 492 U.S. 302 (1989). . . .

Three Terms ago the subject was reconsidered in *Atkins*. We held that standards of decency have evolved since *Penry* and now demonstrate that the execution of the mentally retarded is cruel and unusual punishment. The Court noted objective indicia of society's standards, as expressed in legislative enactments and state practice with respect to executions of the mentally retarded. When *Atkins* was decided only a minority of States permitted the practice, and even in those States it was rare. On the basis of these indicia the Court determined that executing mentally retarded offenders "has become truly unusual, and it is fair to say that a national consensus has developed against it." [536 U.S.,] at 316.

The inquiry into our society's evolving standards of decency did not end there. The *Atkins* Court neither repeated nor relied upon the statement in *Stanford* that the Court's independent judgment has no bearing on the acceptability of a particular punishment under the Eighth Amendment. Instead we returned to the rule, established in decisions predating *Stanford*, that "'the Constitution contemplates that in the end our own judgment will be brought to bear on the question of the acceptability of the death penalty under the Eighth Amendment."' 536 U.S., at 312. Mental retardation, the Court said, diminishes personal culpability even if the offender can distinguish right from wrong. The impairments of mentally retarded offenders make it less defensible to impose the death penalty as retribution for past crimes and less likely that the death penalty will have a real deterrent effect. Based on these considerations and on the finding of national consensus against executing the mentally retarded, the Court ruled that the death penalty constitutes an excessive sanction for the entire category of mentally retarded offenders. . . .

Just as the *Atkins* Court reconsidered the issue decided in *Penry*, we now reconsider the issue decided in *Stanford*. The beginning point is a review of objective indicia of consensus, as expressed in particular by the enactments of legislatures that have addressed the question. This data gives us essential instruction. We then must determine, in the exercise of our own independent judgment, whether the death penalty is a disproportionate punishment for juveniles.

III

A

The evidence of national consensus against the death penalty for juveniles is similar, and in some respects parallel, to the evidence *Atkins* held sufficient to demonstrate a national consensus against the death penalty for the mentally retarded. When *Atkins* was decided, 30 States prohibited the death penalty for the mentally retarded. This number comprised 12 that had abandoned the death penalty altogether, and 18 that maintained it but excluded the mentally retarded from its reach. By a similar calculation in this case, 30 States prohibit the juvenile death penalty, comprising 12 that have rejected the death penalty altogether and 18 that maintain it but, by express provision or judicial interpretation, exclude juveniles from its reach. *Atkins* emphasized that even in the 20 States without formal prohibition, the practice of executing the mentally retarded was infrequent. Since *Penry*, only five States had executed offenders known to have an IQ under 70. In the present case, too, even in the 20 States without a formal prohibition on executing juveniles, the practice is infrequent. Since *Stanford*, six States have executed prisoners for crimes committed as juveniles. In the past 10 years, only three have done so: Oklahoma, Texas, and Virginia. See V. Streib, The Juvenile Death Penalty Today: Death Sentences and Executions for Juvenile Crimes, January 1, 1973- December 31, 2004, No. 76, p 4 (2005), available at *http://www.law.onu.edu/faculty/streib/documents/JuvDeathDec2004.pdf* (last updated Jan. 31, 2005) (as visited Feb. 25, 2005, and available in the Clerk of Court's case file). . . .

. . . The number of States that have abandoned capital punishment for juvenile offenders since *Stanford* is smaller than the number of States that abandoned capital punishment for the mentally retarded after *Penry*; yet we think the same consistency of direction of change has been demonstrated. Since *Stanford*, no State that previously prohibited capital punishment for juveniles has reinstated it. This fact, coupled with the trend toward abolition of the juvenile death penalty, carries special force in light of the general popularity of anticrime legislation, *Atkins, supra*, at 315, and in light of the particular trend in recent years toward cracking down on juvenile crime in other respects, see H. Snyder & M. Sickmund, National Center for Juvenile Justice, Juvenile Offenders and Victims: 1999 National Report 89, 133 (Sept. 1999); Scott & Grisso, The Evolution of Adolescence: A Developmental Perspective on Juvenile Justice Reform, 88J. Crim. L. & C. 137, 148 (1997). Any difference between this case and *Atkins* with respect to the pace of abolition is thus counterbalanced by the consistent direction of the change.

The slower pace of abolition of the juvenile death penalty over the past 15 years, moreover, may have a simple explanation. When we heard *Penry*, only two death penalty States had already prohibited the execution of the mentally retarded. When we heard *Stanford*, by contrast, 12 death penalty States had already prohibited the execution of any juvenile under 18, and 15 had prohibited the execution of any juvenile under 17. If anything, this shows that the impropriety of executing juveniles between 16 and 18 years of age gained wide recognition earlier than the impropriety of executing the mentally retarded. . . .

Petitioner cannot show national consensus in favor of capital punishment for juveniles but still resists the conclusion that any consensus exists against it. Petitioner supports this position with, in particular, the observation that when the Senate ratified the International Covenant on Civil and Political Rights (ICCPR), Dec. 19, 1966, 999 U. N. T. S. 171 (entered into force Mar. 23, 1976), it did so subject to the President's proposed reservation regarding Article 6(5) of that treaty, which prohibits capital punishment for juveniles. Brief for Petitioner 27. This reservation at best provides only faint support for petitioner's argument. First, the reservation was passed in 1992; since then, five States have abandoned capital punishment for juveniles. Second, Congress considered the issue when enacting the Federal Death Penalty Act in 1994, and determined that the death penalty should not extend to juveniles. See 18 U.S.C. § 3591 [18 U. S.C.S. § 3591]. The reservation to Article 6(5) of the ICCPR provides minimal evidence that there is not now a national consensus against juvenile executions.

As in *Atkins*, the objective indicia of consensus in this case — the rejection of the juvenile death penalty in the majority of States; the infrequency of its use even where it remains on the books; and the consistency in the trend toward abolition of the practice — provide sufficient evidence that today our society views juveniles, in the words *Atkins* used respecting the mentally retarded, as "categorically less culpable than the average criminal." 536 U.S., at 316.

B

A majority of States have rejected the imposition of the death penalty on juvenile offenders under 18, and we now hold this is required by the Eighth Amendment.

Because the death penalty is the most severe punishment, the Eighth Amendment applies to it with special force. *Thompson*, 487 U.S., at 856 (O'Connor, J., concurring in judgment). Capital punishment must be limited to those offenders who commit "a narrow category of the most serious crimes" and whose extreme culpability makes them "the most deserving of execution." *Atkins, supra,* at 319. . . .

Three general differences between juveniles under 18 and adults demonstrate that juvenile offenders cannot with reliability be classified among the worst offenders. First, as any parent knows and as the scientific and sociological studies respondent and his *amici* cite tend to confirm, "[a] lack of maturity and an underdeveloped sense of responsibility are found in youth more often than in adults and are more understandable among the young. These qualities often result in impetuous and ill-considered actions and decisions." Johnson [v. Texas, 509 U.S. 350,] 367 [(1993)]. . . . It has been noted that "adolescents are overrepresented statistically in virtually every category of reckless behavior." Arnett, Reckless Behavior in Adolescence: A Developmental Perspective, 12 Developmental Review 339 (1992). In recognition of the comparative immaturity and irresponsibility of juveniles, almost every State prohibits those under 18 years of age from voting, serving on juries, or marrying without parental consent. . . .

The second area of difference is that juveniles are more vulnerable or susceptible to negative influences and outside pressures, including peer pressure. . . . This is explained in part by the prevailing circumstance that juveniles have less control, or less experience with control, over their own environment. See Steinberg & Scott, Less Guilty by Reason of Adolescence: Developmental Immaturity, Diminished Responsibility, and the Juvenile Death Penalty, 58 Am. Psychologist 1009, 1014 (2003) (hereinafter Steinberg & Scott) ("[A]s legal minors, [juveniles] lack the freedom that adults have to extricate themselves from a criminogenic setting").

The third broad difference is that the character of a juvenile is not as well formed as that of an adult. The personality traits of juveniles are more transitory, less fixed. See generally E. Erikson, Identity: Youth and Crisis (1968).

These differences render suspect any conclusion that a juvenile falls among the worst offenders. The susceptibility of juveniles to immature and irresponsible behavior means "their irresponsible conduct is not as morally reprehensible as that of an adult." *Thompson, supra,* at 835 (plurality opinion). Their own vulnerability and comparative lack of control over their immediate surroundings mean juveniles have a greater claim than adults to be forgiven for failing to escape negative influences in their whole environment. See *Stanford,* 492 U.S., at 395 (BRENNAN, J., dissenting). The reality that juveniles still struggle to define their identity means it is less supportable to conclude that even a heinous crime committed by a juvenile is evidence of irretrievably depraved character. From a moral standpoint it would be misguided to equate the failings of a minor with those of an adult, for a greater possibility exists that a minor's character deficiencies will be reformed. Indeed, "[t]he relevance of youth as a mitigating factor derives from the fact that the signature qualities of youth are transient; as individuals mature, the impetuousness and recklessness that may dominate in younger years can subside." *Johnson, supra,* at 368; see also Steinberg & Scott 1014 ("For most teens, [risky or antisocial] behaviors are fleeting; they cease with maturity as individual identity becomes settled. Only a relatively small proportion of adolescents who experiment in risky or illegal activities develop entrenched patterns of problem behavior that persist into adulthood").

In *Thompson,* a plurality of the Court recognized the import of these characteristics with respect to juveniles under 16, and relied on them to hold that the Eighth Amendment prohibited the imposition of the death penalty on juveniles below that age. We conclude the same reasoning applies to all juvenile offenders under 18.

Once the diminished culpability of juveniles is recognized, it is evident that the penological justifications for the death penalty apply to them with lesser force than to adults. We have held there are two distinct social purposes served by the death penalty: '"retribution and deterrence of capital crimes by prospective offenders."' *Atkins,* 536 U.S., at 319. . . . Whether viewed as an attempt to express the community's moral outrage or as an attempt to right the balance for the wrong to the victim, the case for retribution is not as strong with a minor as with an adult. Retribution is not proportional if the law's most severe penalty is imposed on one whose culpability or blameworthiness is diminished, to a substantial degree, by reason of youth and immaturity.

As for deterrence, it is unclear whether the death penalty has a significant or even measurable deterrent effect on juveniles, as counsel for the petitioner acknowledged at oral argument. Tr. of Oral Arg. 48. In general we leave to legislatures the assessment of the efficacy of various criminal penalty schemes, see Harmelin v. Michigan, 501 U.S. 957, 998-999 (1991) (KENNEDY, J., concurring in part and concurring in judgment). Here, however, the absence of evidence of deterrent effect is of special concern because the same characteristics that render juveniles less culpable than adults suggest as well that juveniles will be less susceptible to deterrence. . . . To the extent the juvenile death penalty might have residual deterrent effect, it is worth noting that the punishment of life imprisonment without the possibility of parole is itself a severe sanction, in particular for a young person.

In concluding that neither retribution nor deterrence provides adequate justification for imposing the death penalty on juvenile offenders, we cannot deny or overlook the brutal crimes too many juvenile offenders have committed. Certainly it can be argued, although we by no means concede the point, that a rare case might arise in which a juvenile offender has sufficient psychological maturity, and at the same time demonstrates sufficient depravity, to merit a sentence of death. Indeed, this possibility is the linchpin of one contention pressed by petitioner and his *amici*. They assert that even assuming the truth of the observations we have made about juveniles' diminished culpability in general, jurors nonetheless should be allowed to consider mitigating arguments related to youth on a case-by-case basis, and in some cases to impose the death penalty if justified. A central feature of death penalty sentencing is a particular assessment of the circumstances of the crime and the characteristics of the offender. The system is designed to consider both aggravating and mitigating circumstances, including youth, in every case. Given this Court's own insistence on individualized consideration, petitioner maintains that it is both arbitrary and unnecessary to adopt a categorical rule barring imposition of the death penalty on any offender under 18 years of age.

We disagree. The differences between juvenile and adult offenders are too marked and well understood to risk allowing a youthful person to receive the death penalty despite insufficient culpability. An unacceptable likelihood exists that the brutality or cold-blooded nature of any particular crime would overpower mitigating arguments based on youth as a matter of course, even where the juvenile offender's objective immaturity, vulnerability, and lack of true depravity should require a sentence less severe than death. In some cases a defendant's youth may even be counted against him. In this very case, as we noted above, the prosecutor argued Simmons' youth was aggravating rather than mitigating. While this sort of overreaching could be corrected by a particular rule to ensure that the mitigating force of youth is not overlooked, that would not address our larger concerns.

It is difficult even for expert psychologists to differentiate between the juvenile offender whose crime reflects unfortunate yet transient immaturity, and the rare juvenile offender whose crime reflects irreparable corruption. See Steinberg & Scott 1014-1016. As we understand it, this difficulty underlies the rule forbidding psychiatrists from diagnosing any patient under 18 as having antisocial personality disorder, a disorder also referred to as psychopathy or sociopathy, and which is characterized by callousness, cynicism, and contempt for the feelings, rights, and suffering of others. American Psychiatric Association, Diagnostic and Statistical Manual of Mental Disorders 701-706 (4th ed. text rev. 2000); see also Steinberg & Scott 1015. If trained psychiatrists with the advantage of clinical testing and observation refrain, despite diagnostic expertise, from assessing any juvenile under 18 as having antisocial personality disorder, we conclude that States should refrain from asking jurors to issue a far graver condemnation—that a juvenile offender merits the death penalty. When a juvenile offender commits a heinous crime, the State can exact forfeiture of some of the most basic liberties, but the State cannot extinguish his life and his potential to attain a mature understanding of his own humanity.

Drawing the line at 18 years of age is subject, of course, to the objections always raised against categorical rules. The qualities that distinguish juveniles from adults do not disappear when an individual turns 18. By the same token, some under 18 have already attained a level of maturity some adults will never reach. For the reasons we have discussed, however, a line must be drawn. The plurality opinion in *Thompson* drew the line at 16. In the intervening years the *Thompson* plurality's conclusion that offenders under 16 may not be executed has not been challenged. The logic of *Thompson* extends to those who are under 18. The age of 18 is the point where society draws the line for many purposes between childhood and adulthood. It is, we conclude, the age at which the line for death eligibility ought to rest.

These considerations mean Stanford v. Kentucky should be deemed no longer controlling on this issue. To the extent *Stanford* was based on review of the objective indicia of consensus that obtained in 1989, it suffices to note that those indicia have changed. It should be observed, furthermore, that the *Stanford* Court should have considered those States that had abandoned the death penalty altogether as part of the consensus against the juvenile death penalty; a State's decision to bar the death penalty altogether of necessity demonstrates a judgment that the death penalty is inappropriate for all offenders, including juveniles. Last, to the extent *Stanford* was based on a rejection of the idea that this Court is required to bring its independent judgment to bear on the proportionality of the death penalty for a particular class of crimes or offenders, it suffices to note that this rejection was inconsistent with prior Eighth Amendment decisions. It is also inconsistent with the premises of our recent decision in *Atkins*. 536 U.S., at 312-313.

In holding that the death penalty cannot be imposed upon juvenile offenders, we take into account the circumstance that some States have relied on *Stanford* in seeking the death penalty against juvenile offenders.

This consideration, however, does not outweigh our conclusion that *Stanford* should no longer control in those few pending cases or in those yet to arise.

IV

Our determination that the death penalty is disproportionate punishment for offenders under 18 finds confirmation in the stark reality that the United States is the only country in the world that continues to give official sanction to the juvenile death penalty. This reality does not become controlling, for the task of interpreting the Eighth Amendment remains our responsibility. Yet at least from the time of the Court's decision in *Trop*, the Court has referred to the laws of other countries and to international authorities as instructive for its interpretation of the Eighth Amendment's prohibition of "cruel and unusual punishments."

As respondent and a number of *amici* emphasize, Article 37 of the United Nations Convention on the Rights of the Child, which every country in the world has ratified save for the United States and Somalia, contains an express prohibition on capital punishment for crimes committed by juveniles under 18. United Nations Convention on the Rights of the Child, Art. 37, Nov. 20, 1989, 1577 U. N. T. S. 3, 28 I. L. M. 1448, 1468-1470 (entered into force Sept. 2, 1990); Brief for Respondent 48; Brief for European Union et al. as *Amici Curiae* 12-13; Brief for President James Earl Carter, Jr., et al. as *Amici Curiae* 9; Brief for Former U.S. Diplomats Morton Abramowitz et al. as *Amici Curiae* 7; Brief for Human Rights Committee of the Bar of England and Wales et al. as *Amici Curiae* 13-14. No ratifying country has entered a reservation to the provision prohibiting the execution of juvenile offenders. Parallel prohibitions are contained in other significant international covenants.

Respondent and his *amici* have submitted, and petitioner does not contest, that only seven countries other than the United States have executed juvenile offenders since 1990: Iran, Pakistan, Saudi Arabia, Yemen, Nigeria, the Democratic Republic of Congo, and China. Since then each of these countries has either abolished capital punishment for juveniles or made public disavowal of the practice. Brief for Respondent 49- 50. In sum, it is fair to say that the United States now stands alone in a world that has turned its face against the juvenile death penalty.

Though the international covenants prohibiting the juvenile death penalty are of more recent date, it is instructive to note that the United Kingdom abolished the juvenile death penalty before these covenants came into being. The United Kingdom's experience bears particular relevance here in light of the historic ties between our countries and in light of the Eighth Amendment's own origins. The Amendment was modeled on a parallel provision in the English Declaration of Rights of 1689, which provided: "[E]xcessive Bail ought not to be required nor excessive Fines imposed; nor cruel and unusual Punishments inflicted." 1 W. & M., ch. 2, § 10, in 3 Eng. Stat. at Large 441 (1770). As of now, the United Kingdom has abolished the death penalty in its entirety; but, decades before it took this step, it recognized the disproportionate nature of the juvenile death penalty; and it abolished that penalty as a separate matter. . . .

It is proper that we acknowledge the overwhelming weight of international opinion against the juvenile death penalty, resting in large part on the understanding that the instability and emotional imbalance of young people may often be a factor in the crime. See Brief for Human Rights Committee of the Bar of England and Wales et al. as *Amici Curiae* 10-11. The opinion of the world community, while not controlling our outcome, does provide respected and significant confirmation for our own conclusions.

Over time, from one generation to the next, the Constitution has come to earn the high respect and even, as Madison dared to hope, the veneration of the American people. See The Federalist No. 49, p. 314 (C. Rossiter ed. 1961). The document sets forth, and rests upon, innovative principles original to the American experience, such as federalism; a proven balance in political mechanisms through separation of powers; specific guarantees for the accused in criminal cases; and broad provisions to secure individual freedom and preserve human dignity. These doctrines and guarantees are central to the American experience and remain essential to our present-day self-definition and national identity. Not the least of the reasons we honor the Constitution, then, is because we know it to be our own. It does not lessen our fidelity to the Constitution or our pride in its origins to acknowledge that the express affirmation of certain fundamental rights by other nations and peoples simply underscores the centrality of those same rights within our own heritage of freedom.

* * *

The Eighth and Fourteenth Amendments forbid imposition of the death penalty on offenders who were under the age of 18 when their crimes were committed. The judgment of the Missouri Supreme Court setting aside the sentence of death imposed upon Christopher Simmons is affirmed.

JUSTICE STEVENS, with whom JUSTICE GINSBURG joins, concurring.

Perhaps even more important than our specific holding today is our reaffirmation of the basic principle that informs the Court's interpretation of the Eighth Amendment. If the meaning of that Amendment had been frozen when it was originally drafted, it would impose no impediment to the execution of 7-year-old children today. See Stanford v. Kentucky, 492 U.S. 361, 368 (1989) (describing the common law at the time of the Amendment's adoption). The evolving standards of decency that have driven our construction of this critically important part of the Bill of Rights foreclose any such reading of the Amendment. In the best tradition of the common law, the pace of that evolution is a matter for continuing debate; but that our understanding of the Constitution does change from time to time has been settled since John Marshall breathed life into its text. If great lawyers of his day—Alexander Hamilton, for example—were sitting with us today, I would expect them to join Justice Kennedy's opinion for the Court. In all events, I do so without hesitation.

JUSTICE O'CONNOR, dissenting.

The Court's decision today establishes a categorical rule forbidding the execution of any offender for any crime committed before his 18th birthday, no matter how deliberate, wanton, or cruel the offense. Neither the objective evidence of contemporary societal values, nor the Court's moral proportionality analysis, nor the two in tandem suffice to justify this ruling.

Although the Court finds support for its decision in the fact that a majority of the States now disallow capital punishment of 17-year-old offenders, it refrains from asserting that its holding is compelled by a genuine national consensus. Indeed, the evidence before us fails to demonstrate conclusively that any such consensus has emerged in the brief period since we upheld the constitutionality of this practice in Stanford v. Kentucky, 492 U.S. 361 (1989).

Instead, the rule decreed by the Court rests, ultimately, on its independent moral judgment that death is a disproportionately severe punishment for any 17-year-old offender. I do not subscribe to this judgment. . . .

It is beyond cavil that juveniles as a class are generally less mature, less responsible, and less fully formed than adults, and that these differences bear on juveniles' comparative moral culpability. But even accepting this premise, the Court's proportionality argument fails to support its categorical rule.

First, the Court adduces no evidence whatsoever in support of its sweeping conclusion . . . that it is only in "rare" cases, if ever, that 17-year-old murderers are sufficiently mature and act with sufficient depravity to warrant the death penalty. The fact that juveniles are generally *less* culpable for their misconduct than adults does not necessarily mean that a 17-year-old murderer cannot be *sufficiently* culpable to merit the death penalty. . . . Similarly, the fact that the availability of the death penalty may be *less* likely to deter a juvenile from committing a capital crime does not imply that this threat cannot *effectively* deter some 17-year-olds from such an act. Surely there is an age below which no offender, no matter what his crime, can be deemed to have the cognitive or emotional maturity necessary to warrant the death penalty. But at least at the margins between adolescence and adulthood . . . the relevant differences between "adults" and "juveniles" appear to be a matter of degree, rather than of kind. . . .

The Court's proportionality argument suffers from a second and closely related defect: It fails to establish that the differences in maturity between 17-year-olds and young "adults" are both universal enough and significant enough to justify a bright-line prophylactic rule against capital punishment of the former. The Court's analysis is premised on differences *in the aggregate* between juveniles and adults, which frequently do not hold true when comparing individuals. Although it may be that many 17-year-old murderers lack sufficient maturity to deserve the death penalty, some juvenile murderers may be quite mature. Chronological age is not an unfailing measure of psychological development, and common experience suggests that many 17-year-olds are more mature than the average young "adult." In short, the class of offenders exempted from capital punishment by today's decision is too broad and too diverse to warrant a categorical prohibition. Indeed, the age-based line drawn by the Court is indefensibly arbitrary—it quite likely will protect a number of offenders who are mature enough to deserve the death penalty and may well leave vulnerable many who are not.

For purposes of proportionality analysis, 17-year-olds as a class are qualitatively and materially different from the mentally retarded. "Mentally retarded" offenders, as we understood that category in *Atkins*, are *defined* by precisely the characteristics which render death an excessive punishment. A mentally retarded person is, "by definition," one whose cognitive and behavioral capacities have been proven to fall below a certain minimum. . . . Accordingly, for purposes of our decision in *Atkins*, the mentally retarded are not merely *less* blameworthy for their misconduct or *less* likely to be deterred by the death penalty than others.

Rather, a mentally retarded offender is one whose demonstrated impairments make it so highly unlikely that he is culpable enough to deserve the death penalty or that he could have been deterred by the threat of death, that execution is not a defensible punishment. There is no such inherent or accurate fit between an offender's chronological age and the personal limitations which the Court believes make capital punishment excessive for 17- year-old murderers. . . .

The proportionality issues raised by the Court clearly implicate Eighth Amendment concerns. But these concerns may properly be addressed not by means of an arbitrary, categorical age-based rule, but rather through individualized sentencing in which juries are required to give appropriate mitigating weight to the defendant's immaturity, his susceptibility to outside pressures, his cognizance of the consequences of his actions, and so forth. In that way the constitutional response can be tailored to the specific problem it is meant to remedy. . . .

Because I do not believe that a genuine *national* consensus against the juvenile death penalty has yet developed, and because I do not believe the Court's moral proportionality argument justifies a categorical, age-based constitutional rule, I can assign no . . . *confirmatory* role to the international consensus described by the Court. In short, the evidence of an international consensus does not alter my determination that the Eighth Amendment does not, at this time, forbid capital punishment of 17-year-old murderers in all cases.

Nevertheless, I disagree with Justice Scalia's contention that foreign and international law have no place in our Eighth Amendment jurisprudence. Over the course of nearly half a century, the Court has consistently referred to foreign and international law as relevant to its assessment of evolving standards of decency. This inquiry reflects the special character of the Eighth Amendment, which, as the Court has long held, draws its meaning directly from the maturing values of civilized society. Obviously, American law is distinctive in many respects, not least where the specific provisions of our Constitution and the history of its exposition so dictate. But this Nation's evolving understanding of human dignity certainly is neither wholly isolated from, nor inherently at odds with, the values prevailing in other countries. On the contrary, we should not be surprised to find congruence between domestic and international values, especially where the international community has reached clear agreement—expressed in international law or in the domestic laws of individual countries—that a particular form of punishment is inconsistent with fundamental human rights. At least, the existence of an international consensus of this nature can serve to confirm the reasonableness of a consonant and genuine American consensus. The instant case presents no such domestic consensus, however, and the recent emergence of an otherwise global consensus does not alter that basic fact.

* * *

In determining whether the Eighth Amendment permits capital punishment of a particular offense or class of offenders, we must look to whether such punishment is consistent with contemporary standards of decency. We are obligated to weigh both the objective evidence of societal values and our own judgment as to whether death is an excessive sanction in the context at hand. In the instant case, the objective evidence is inconclusive; standing alone, it does not demonstrate that our society has repudiated capital punishment of 17-year-old offenders in all cases. Rather, the actions of the Nation's legislatures suggest that, although a clear and durable national consensus against this practice may in time emerge, that day has yet to arrive. By acting so soon after our decision in *Stanford*, the Court both pre-empts the democratic debate through which genuine consensus might develop and simultaneously runs a considerable risk of inviting lower court reassessments of our Eighth Amendment precedents. . . .

Reasonable minds can differ as to the minimum age at which commission of a serious crime should expose the defendant to the death penalty, if at all. Many jurisdictions have abolished capital punishment altogether, while many others have determined that even the most heinous crime, if committed before the age of 18, should not be punishable by death. Indeed, were my office that of a legislator, rather than a judge, then I, too, would be inclined to support legislation setting a minimum age of 18 in this context. But a significant number of States, including Missouri, have decided to make the death penalty potentially available for 17- year-old capital murderers such as respondent. Without a clearer showing that a genuine national consensus forbids the execution of such offenders, this Court should not substitute its own "inevitably subjective judgment" on how best to resolve this difficult moral question for the judgments of the Nation's democratically elected legislatures. I respectfully dissent.

JUSTICE SCALIA, with whom CHIEF JUSTICE REHNQUIST and JUSTICE THOMAS join, dissenting.

In urging approval of a constitution that gave life-tenured judges the power to nullify laws enacted by the people's representatives, Alexander Hamilton assured the citizens of New York that there was little risk in this, since "[t]he judiciary . . . ha[s] neither FORCE nor WILL but merely judgment." The Federalist No. 78, p. 465 (C. Rossiter ed. 1961). But

Hamilton had in mind a traditional judiciary, "bound down by strict rules and precedents which serve to define and point out their duty in every particular case that comes before them." *Id.*, at 471. Bound down, indeed. What a mockery today's opinion makes of Hamilton's expectation, announcing the Court's conclusion that the meaning of our Constitution has changed over the past 15 years—not, mind you, that this Court's decision 15 years ago was *wrong*, but that the Constitution *has changed.* The Court reaches this implausible result by purporting to advert, not to the original meaning of the Eighth Amendment, but to "the evolving standards of decency" of our national society. It then finds, on the flimsiest of grounds, that a national consensus which could not be perceived in our people's laws barely 15 years ago now solidly exists. Worse still, the Court says in so many words that what our people's laws say about the issue does not, in the last analysis, matter. The Court thus proclaims itself sole arbiter of our Nation's moral standards—and in the course of discharging that awesome responsibility purports to take guidance from the views of foreign courts and legislatures. Because I do not believe that the meaning of our Eighth Amendment, any more than the meaning of other provisions of our Constitution, should be determined by the subjective views of five Members of this Court and like-minded foreigners, I dissent.

I

In determining that capital punishment of offenders who committed murder before age 18 is "cruel and unusual" under the Eighth Amendment, the Court first considers, in accordance with our modern (though in my view mistaken) jurisprudence, whether there is a "national consensus" that laws allowing such executions contravene our modern "standards of decency." . . . As in Atkins v. Virginia, 536 U.S. 304, 312 (2002), the Court dutifully recites this test and claims halfheartedly that a national consensus has emerged since our decision in *Stanford*, because 18 States—or 47% of States that permit capital punishment—now have legislation prohibiting the execution of offenders under 18, and because all of four States have adopted such legislation since *Stanford.*

Words have no meaning if the views of less than 50% of death penalty States can constitute a national consensus. Our previous cases have required overwhelming opposition to a challenged practice, generally over a long period of time. . . .

In an attempt to keep afloat its implausible assertion of national consensus, the Court throws overboard a proposition well established in our Eighth Amendment jurisprudence. . . . *None* of our cases dealing with an alleged constitutional limitation upon the death penalty has counted, as States supporting a consensus in favor of that limitation, States that have eliminated the death penalty entirely. And with good reason. Consulting States that bar the death penalty concerning the necessity of making an exception to the penalty for offenders under 18 is rather like including old-order Amishmen in a consumer-preference poll on the electric car. Of *course* they don't like it, but that sheds no light whatever on the point at issue. That 12 States favor *no* executions says something about consensus against the death penalty, but nothing—absolutely nothing—about consensus that offenders under 18 deserve special immunity from such a penalty. . . . What might be relevant, perhaps, is how many of those States permit 16- and 17-year-old offenders to be treated as adults with respect to noncapital offenses. (They all do; indeed, some even *require* that juveniles as young as 14 be tried as adults if they are charged with murder.) The attempt by the Court to turn its remarkable minority consensus into a faux majority by counting Amishmen is an act of nomological desperation.

Recognizing that its national-consensus argument was weak compared with our earlier cases, the *Atkins* Court found additional support in the fact that 16 States had prohibited execution of mentally retarded individuals since Penry v. Lynaugh, 492 U.S. 302 (1989). . . . Now, the Court says a legislative change in four States is "significant" enough to trigger a constitutional prohibition. It is amazing to think that this subtle shift in numbers can take the issue entirely off the table for legislative debate.

I also doubt whether many of the legislators who voted to change the laws in those four States would have done so if they had known their decision would (by the pronouncement of this Court) be rendered irreversible. After all, legislative support for capital punishment, in any form, has surged and ebbed throughout our Nation's history. . . .

Relying on such narrow margins is especially inappropriate in light of the fact that a number of legislatures and voters have expressly affirmed their support for capital punishment of 16- and 17-year-old offenders since *Stanford.* Though the Court is correct that no State has lowered its death penalty age, both the Missouri and Virginia Legislatures—which, at the time of *Stanford,* had no minimum age requirement—expressly established 16 as the minimum. Mo. Rev. Stat. § 565.020.2 (2000); Va. Code Ann. § 18.2–10(a) (Lexis 2004). The people of Arizona and Florida have done the same by ballot initiative. Thus, even States that have not executed an under-18 offender in recent years unquestionably favor the possibility of capital punishment in some circumstances. . . .

II

Of course, the real force driving today's decision is not the actions of four state legislatures, but the Court's "own judgment" that murderers younger than 18 can never be as morally culpable as older counterparts. The Court claims that this usurpation of the role of moral arbiter is simply a "retur[n] to the rul[e] established in decisions predating *Stanford*." That supposed rule . . . was repudiated in *Stanford* for the very good reason that it has no foundation in law or logic. If the Eighth Amendment set forth an ordinary rule of law, it would indeed be the role of this Court to say what the law is. But the Court having pronounced that the Eighth Amendment is an ever-changing reflection of "the evolving standards of decency" of our society, it makes no sense for the Justices then to *prescribe* those standards rather than discern them from the practices of our people. On the evolving-standards hypothesis, the only legitimate function of this Court is to identify a moral consensus of the American people. By what conceivable warrant can nine lawyers presume to be the authoritative conscience of the Nation?[8]

. . . Today's opinion provides a perfect example of why judges are ill equipped to make the type of legislative judgments the Court insists on making here. To support its opinion that States should be prohibited from imposing the death penalty on anyone who committed murder before age 18, the Court looks to scientific and sociological studies, picking and choosing those that support its position. It never explains why those particular studies are methodologically sound; none was ever entered into evidence or tested in an adversarial proceeding. . . .

That "almost every State prohibits those under 18 years of age from voting, serving on juries, or marrying without parental consent," is patently irrelevant. . . . As we explained in *Stanford*, 492 U.S., at 374, it is "absurd to think that one must be mature enough to drive carefully, to drink responsibly, or to vote intelligently, in order to be mature enough to understand that murdering another human being is profoundly wrong, and to conform one's conduct to that most minimal of all civilized standards." Serving on a jury or entering into marriage also involve decisions far more sophisticated than the simple decision not to take another's life.

8. Justice O'CONNOR agrees with our analysis that no national consensus exists here. She is nonetheless prepared (like the majority) to override the judgment of America's legislatures if it contradicts her own assessment of "moral proportionality." She dissents here only because it does not. The votes in today's case demonstrate that the offending of selected lawyers' moral sentiments is not a predictable basis for law—much less a democratic one.

... In other contexts where individualized consideration is provided, we have recognized that at least some minors will be mature enough to make difficult decisions that involve moral considerations. For instance, we have struck down abortion statutes that do not allow minors deemed mature by courts to bypass parental notification provisions. See, e.g., Bellotti v. Baird, 443 U.S. 622, 643-644 (1979) (opinion of Powell, J.); Planned Parenthood of Central Mo. v. Danforth, 428 U.S. 52, 74-75 (1976). It is hard to see why this context should be any different. Whether to obtain an abortion is surely a much more complex decision for a young person than whether to kill an innocent person in cold blood.

The Court concludes, however, that juries cannot be trusted with the delicate task of weighing a defendant's youth along with the other mitigating and aggravating factors of his crime. This startling conclusion undermines the very foundations of our capital sentencing system. . . . The Court says that juries will be unable to appreciate the significance of a defendant's youth when faced with details of a brutal crime. This assertion is based on no evidence; to the contrary, the Court itself acknowledges that the execution of under-18 offenders is "infrequent" even in the States "without a formal prohibition on executing juveniles," suggesting that juries take seriously their responsibility to weigh youth as a mitigating factor.

Nor does the Court suggest a stopping point for its reasoning. If juries cannot make appropriate determinations in cases involving murderers under 18, in what other kinds of cases will the Court find jurors deficient? We have already held that no jury may consider whether a mentally deficient defendant can receive the death penalty, irrespective of his crime. See *Atkins*, 536 U.S., at 321. Why not take other mitigating factors, such as considerations of childhood abuse or poverty, away from juries as well? Surely jurors "overpower[ed]" by "the brutality or cold-blooded nature" of a crime, could not adequately weigh these mitigating factors either.

III

Though the views of our own citizens are essentially irrelevant to the Court's decision today, the views of other countries and the so-called international community take center stage.

... [T]he basic premise of the Court's argument — that American law should conform to the laws of the rest of the world — ought to be rejected out of hand. In fact the Court itself does not believe it. In many significant respects the laws of most other countries differ from our law — including not only such explicit provisions of our Constitution as the right to jury trial and grand jury indictment, but even many interpretations of the Constitution prescribed by this Court itself. The Court-pronounced exclusionary rule, for example, is distinctively American. When we adopted that rule in Mapp v. Ohio, 367 U.S. 643, 655 (1961), it was "unique to American Jurisprudence." Bivens v. Six Unknown Fed. Narcotics Agents, 403 U.S. 388, 415 (1971) (BURGER, C. J., dissenting). Since then a categorical exclusionary rule has been "universally rejected" by other countries, including those with rules prohibiting illegal searches and police misconduct, despite the fact that none of these countries "appears to have any alternative form of discipline for police that is effective in preventing search violations." Bradley, *Mapp* Goes Abroad, 52 Case W. Res. L. Rev. 375, 399-400 (2001). . . .

The Court has been oblivious to the views of other countries when deciding how to interpret our Constitution's requirement that "Congress shall make no law respecting an establishment of religion. . . . " Amdt. 1. Most other countries—including those committed to religious neutrality—do not insist on the degree of separation between church and state that this Court requires. . . .

And let us not forget the Court's abortion jurisprudence, which makes us one of only six countries that allow abortion on demand until the point of viability. See Larsen, Importing Constitutional Norms from a "Wider Civilization": *Lawrence* and the Rehnquist Court's Use of Foreign and International Law in Domestic Constitutional Interpretation, 65 Ohio St. L. J. 1283, 1320 (2004); Center for Reproductive Rights, The World's Abortion Laws (June 2004), *http://www.reproductiverights.org/pub_fac_abortion_laws.html*. Though the Government and *amici* in cases following Roe v. Wade, 410 U.S. 113 (1973), urged the Court to follow the international community's lead, these arguments fell on deaf ears. . . .

The Court's special reliance on the laws of the United Kingdom is perhaps the most indefensible part of its opinion. It is of course true that we share a common history with the United Kingdom, and that we often consult English sources when asked to discern the meaning of a constitutional text written against the backdrop of 18th-century English law and legal thought. If we applied that approach today, our task would be an easy one. As we explained in Harmelin v. Michigan, 501 U.S. 957, 973-974 (1991), the "Cruell and Unusuall Punishments" provision of the English Declaration of Rights was originally meant to describe those punishments "'out of [the Judges'] Power'"—that is, those punishments that were not authorized by common law or statute, but that were nonetheless administered by the Crown or the Crown's judges. Under that reasoning, the death penalty for under-18 offenders would easily survive this challenge. The Court has, however—I think wrongly—long rejected a purely originalist approach to our Eighth Amendment, and that is certainly not the approach the Court takes today. Instead, the Court undertakes the majestic task of determining (and thereby prescribing) *our* Nation's *current* standards of decency. It is beyond comprehension why we should look, for that purpose, to a country that has developed, in the centuries since the Revolutionary War—and with increasing speed since the United Kingdom's recent submission to the jurisprudence of European courts dominated by continental jurists—a legal, political, and social culture quite different from our own. If we took the Court's directive seriously, we would also consider relaxing our double jeopardy prohibition, since the British Law Commission recently published a report that would significantly extend the rights of the prosecution to appeal cases where an acquittal was the result of a judge's ruling that was legally incorrect. See Law Commission, Double Jeopardy and Prosecution Appeals, LAW COM No. 267, Cm 5048, p. 6, P 1.19 (Mar. 2001); J. Spencer, The English System in European Criminal Procedures 142, 204, and n. 239 (M. Delmas-Marty & J. Spencer eds. 2002). We would also curtail our right to jury trial in criminal cases since, despite the jury system's deep roots in our shared common law, England now permits all but the most serious offenders to be tried by magistrates without a jury. See D. Feldman, England and Wales, in Criminal Procedure: A Worldwide Study 91, 114-115 (C. Bradley ed. 1999).

The Court should either profess its willingness to reconsider all these matters in light of the views of foreigners, or else it should cease putting forth foreigners' views as part of the *reasoned basis* of its decisions. To invoke alien law when it agrees with one's own thinking, and ignore it otherwise, is not reasoned decisionmaking, but sophistry.

. . . I do not believe that approval by "other nations and peoples" should buttress our commitment to American principles any more than (what should logically follow) disapproval by "other nations and peoples" should weaken that commitment. More importantly, however, the Court's statement flatly misdescribes what is going on here. Foreign sources are cited today, *not* to underscore our "fidelity" to the Constitution, our "pride in its origins," and "our own [American] heritage." To the contrary, they are cited *to set aside* the centuries-old American practice—a practice still engaged in by a large majority of the relevant States—of letting a jury of 12 citizens decide whether, in the particular case, youth should be the basis for withholding the death penalty. What these foreign sources "affirm," rather than repudiate, is the Justices' own notion of how the world ought to be, and their diktat that it shall be so henceforth in America. The Court's parting attempt to downplay the significance of its extensive discussion of foreign law is unconvincing. "Acknowledgment" of foreign approval has no place in the legal opinion of this Court *unless it is part of the basis for the Court's judgment*—which is surely what it parades as today.

IV

To add insult to injury, the Court affirms the Missouri Supreme Court without even admonishing that court for its flagrant disregard of our precedent in *Stanford.* Until today, we have always held that "it is this Court's prerogative alone to overrule one of its precedents." State Oil Co. v. Khan, 522 U.S. 3, 20 (1997). That has been true even where "'changes in judicial doctrine' ha[ve] significantly undermined" our prior holding, United States v. Hatter, 532 U.S. 557, 567 (2001), and even where our prior holding "appears to rest on reasons rejected in some other line of decisions," Rodriguez de Quijas v. Shearson/American Express, Inc., 490 U.S. 477, 484 (1989). Today, however, the Court silently approves a state-court decision that blatantly rejected controlling precedent.

One must admit that the Missouri Supreme Court's action, and this Court's indulgent reaction, are, in a way, understandable. In a system based upon constitutional and statutory text democratically adopted, the concept of "law" ordinarily signifies that particular words have a fixed meaning. Such law does not change, and this Court's pronouncement of it therefore remains authoritative until (confessing our prior error) we overrule. The Court has purported to make of the Eighth Amendment, however, a mirror of the passing and changing sentiment of American society regarding penology. The lower courts can look into that mirror as well as we can; and what we saw 15 years ago bears no necessary relationship to what they see today. Since they are not looking at the same text, but at a different scene, why should our earlier decision control their judgment?

However sound philosophically, this is no way to run a legal system. We must disregard the new reality that, to the extent our Eighth Amendment decisions constitute something more than a show of hands on the current Justices' current personal views about penology, they purport to be nothing more than a snapshot of American public opinion at a particular point in time (with the timeframes now shortened to a mere 15 years). We must treat these decisions just as though they represented *real* law, *real* prescriptions democratically adopted by the American people, as conclusively (rather than sequentially) construed by this Court. Allowing lower courts to reinterpret the Eighth Amendment whenever they decide enough time has passed for a new snapshot leaves this Court's decisions without any force—especially since the "evolution" of our Eighth Amendment is no longer determined by objective criteria. To allow lower courts to behave as we do, "updating" the Eighth Amendment as needed, destroys stability and makes our case law an unreliable basis for the designing of laws by citizens and their representatives, and for action by public officials. The result will be to crown arbitrariness with chaos.

NOTES AND QUESTIONS

1. Other than the recognized fact that "death is different," see Gregg v. Georgia, 428 U.S. 153, 188 (1976), is there any way to explain the dramatic divergence, in both result and Eighth Amendment methodology, between *Harmelin* and *Ewing*, on the one hand, and *Simmons*, on the other? Even if "death is different," is that a satisfactory explanation for the divergence? Why is a marginal "national consensus" of either 30 states (per Justice Kennedy) or 18 states (per Justice Scalia) sufficient to establish a categorical Eighth Amendment rule in *Simmons*, whereas a consensus of 49 states was held insufficient in both *Harmelin* and *Ewing*? (Recall that, in both of those cases, the relevant states stood alone in the harshness of the prison sentences they imposed.) Why are the views of the United Kingdom and the European Union relevant to the Eighth Amendment issue in *Simmons*, but not even mentioned in *Harmelin* and *Ewing*? Isn't there a consistency problem with the Court's view that 17-year-olds, as a class, are insufficiently "mature" and "responsible" to commit crimes that might justify capital punishment, but sufficiently "mature" and "responsible" to exercise the right to an abortion without parental consent?

Might the result in *Simmons* simply reflect the Court's seemingly growing concern with the morality of capital punishment itself? If so, then wouldn't it be better for the Court to 'fess up and address the problem in a more direct and honest manner?

2. Do the above questions, and apparent inconsistencies, provide further evidence in support of Justice Scalia's claim that the Court should (as it seemed to do in *Harmelin* and *Ewing*) get out of the business of Eighth Amendment proportionality review entirely? Is this one of those areas of constitutional adjudication—like substantive due process—in which the Court's decisions are destined, at least much of the time, to appear arbitrary and lawless? Or is there another possible approach

to proportionality review that would offer greater predictability and doctrinal stability?

3. In Kennedy v. Louisiana, 128 S. Ct. 2641 (2008), the Court, by 5-4, struck down the death penalty as a punishment for the rape of a child that does not result in the victim's death. The majority opinion acknowledged that, since 1995, 6 states (including Louisiana) had enacted legislation authorizing the death penalty for child rape, while 5 others were considering similar legislation, but found this trend insufficient to outweigh the fact that—at least as of now—44 states would not allow a defendant to be executed for such a crime. The Court also emphasized that the Eighth Amendment is measured by the "evolving standards of human decency," and expressed the view that "decency, in its essence, presumes respect for the individual and thus moderation or restraint in the application of capital punishment."

4. Just how "different" *is* death, anyway, in Eighth Amendment proportionality terms? The Court injected more than a little bit of uncertainty into the answer to this question in Graham v. Florida, 130 S.Ct. 2011 (2010). There, the Court held, per Justice Kennedy, that juveniles who are convicted of a non-homicide crime may not be sentenced to life in prison without possibility of parole, but instead must be provided with "some meaningful opportunity to obtain release based on demonstrated maturity and rehabilitation." *Id.*, at 2030. The decision was based on a categorical analysis of crime and punishment essentially identical to that employed in the capital cases of *Atkins*, *Roper*, and *Kennedy*, and drew heavily on similar "objective" indicia of an emerging "national consensus." The *Graham* Court, like the *Roper* Court, also engaged in a detailed and lengthy discussion of the reduced maturity and moral responsibility of juveniles, and cited extensively the views of other nations.

Justice Thomas, joined by Justices Scalia and Alito, sharply dissented:

> The question of what acts are "deserving" of what punishments is bound so tightly with questions of morality and social conditions as to make it, almost by definition, a question for legislative resolution. It is true that the Court previously has relied on the notion of proportionality in holding certain classes of offenses categorically exempt from capital punishment. But never before today has the Court relied on its own view of just deserts to impose a categorical limit on the imposition of a lesser punishment. Its willingness to cross that well-established boundary raises the question whether any democratic choice regarding appropriate punishment is safe from the Court's ever-expanding constitutional veto.

Id., at 2056.

C. *Do the Rules of Constitutional Criminal Procedure Apply to Sentencing?*

Insert the following notes after Note 5 at page 1721 (in the Addendum to the Casebook):

5a. So, what does "reasonableness" in appellate review really mean? Does it mean a presumption in favor of within-Guidelines sentences, and against outside-Guideline sentences? If so, doesn't that essentially recreate the constitutional problem the Court faced in *Blakely* and *Booker*? And if not, aren't we right back to the "bad old days" of unfettered sentencing discretion, which led to the Guidelines in the first place? The Court has begun to address these issues in a series of recent decisions.

GALL v. UNITED STATES

Certiorari to the United States Court of Appeals for the Eighth Circuit
552 U.S. 38 (2007)

JUSTICE STEVENS delivered the opinion of the Court.

In two cases argued on the same day last Term we considered the standard that courts of appeals should apply when reviewing the reasonableness of sentences imposed by district judges. The first, Rita v. United States, 551 U.S. 338 (2007), involved a sentence *within* the range recommended by the Federal Sentencing Guidelines; we held that when a district judge's discretionary decision in a particular case accords with the sentence the United States Sentencing Commission deems appropriate "in the mine run of cases," the court of appeals may presume that the sentence is reasonable. *Id.*, at ____, 127 S. Ct. 2456.

The second case, Claiborne v. United States, involved a sentence *below* the range recommended by the Guidelines, and raised the converse question whether a court of appeals may apply a "proportionality test," and require that a sentence that constitutes a substantial variance from the Guidelines be justified by extraordinary circumstances. We did not have the opportunity to answer this question because the case was mooted by Claiborne's untimely death. Claiborne v. United States, 549 U.S. 1016 (2007) *(per curiam)*. We granted certiorari in the case before us today in order to reach that question, left unanswered last Term. We now hold that, while the extent of the difference between a particular sentence and the recommended Guidelines range is surely relevant, courts of appeals must review all sentences—whether inside, just outside, or significantly outside the Guidelines range—under a deferential abuse-of-discretion standard. We also hold that the sentence imposed by the experienced District Judge in this case was reasonable.

I

In February or March 2000, petitioner Brian Gall, a second-year college student at the University of Iowa, was invited by Luke Rinderknecht to join an ongoing enterprise distributing a controlled substance popularly known as "ecstasy." Gall—who was then a user of ecstasy, cocaine, and marijuana—accepted the invitation. During the ensuing seven months, Gall delivered ecstasy pills, which he received from Rinderknecht, to other conspirators, who then sold them to consumers. He netted over $30,000.

A month or two after joining the conspiracy, Gall stopped using ecstasy. A few months after that, in September 2000, he advised Rinderknecht and other co-conspirators that he was withdrawing from the conspiracy. He has not sold illegal drugs of any kind since. He has, in the words of the District Court, "self-rehabilitated." App. 75. He graduated from the University of Iowa in 2002, and moved first to Arizona, where he obtained a job in the construction industry, and later to Colorado, where he earned $18 per hour as a master carpenter. He has not used any illegal drugs since graduating from college.

After Gall moved to Arizona, he was approached by federal law enforcement agents who questioned him about his involvement in the ecstasy distribution conspiracy. Gall admitted his limited participation in the distribution of ecstasy, and the agents took no further action at that time. On April 28, 2004—approximately a year and a half after this initial interview, and three and a half years after Gall withdrew from the conspiracy—an indictment was returned in the Southern District of Iowa charging him and seven other defendants with participating in a conspiracy to distribute ecstasy, cocaine, and marijuana, that began in or about May 1996 and continued through October 30, 2002. The Government has never questioned the truthfulness of any of Gall's earlier statements or contended that he played any role in, or had any knowledge of, other aspects of the conspiracy described in the indictment. When he received notice of the indictment, Gall moved back to Iowa and surrendered to the authorities. While free on his own recognizance,

Gall started his own business in the construction industry, primarily engaged in subcontracting for the installation of windows and doors. In his first year, his profits were over $2,000 per month.

Gall entered into a plea agreement with the Government, stipulating that he was "responsible for, but did not necessarily distribute himself, at least 2,500 grams of [ecstasy], or the equivalent of at least 87.5 kilograms of marijuana." *Id.*, at 25. In the agreement, the Government acknowledged that by "on or about September of 2000," Gall had communicated his intent to stop distributing ecstasy to Rinderknecht and other members of the conspiracy. *Ibid.* The agreement further provided that recent changes in the Guidelines that enhanced the recommended punishment for distributing ecstasy were not applicable to Gall because he had withdrawn from the conspiracy prior to the effective date of those changes.

In her presentence report, the probation officer concluded that Gall had no significant criminal history; that he was not an organizer, leader, or manager; and that his offense did not involve the use of any weapons. The report stated that Gall had truthfully provided the Government with all of the evidence he had concerning the alleged offenses, but that his evidence was not useful because he provided no new information to the agents. The report also described Gall's substantial use of drugs prior to his offense and the absence of any such use in recent years. The report recommended a sentencing range of 30 to 37 months of imprisonment.

The record of the sentencing hearing held on May 27, 2005, includes a "small flood" of letters from Gall's parents and other relatives, his fiance, neighbors, and representatives of firms doing business with him, uniformly praising his character and work ethic. . . . The [federal prosecutor] did not contest any of the evidence concerning Gall's law-abiding life during the preceding five years, but urged that "the Guidelines are appropriate and should be followed," and requested that the court impose a prison sentence within the Guidelines range. *Id.*, at 93. He mentioned that two of Gall's co-conspirators had been sentenced to 30 and 35 months, respectively, but upon further questioning by the District Court, he acknowledged that neither of them had voluntarily withdrawn from the conspiracy.

The District Judge sentenced Gall to probation for a term of 36 months. In addition to making a lengthy statement on the record, the judge filed a detailed sentencing memorandum explaining his decision, and provided the following statement of reasons in his written judgment:

> The Court determined that, considering all the factors under 18 U.S.C. 3553 (a), the Defendant's explicit withdrawal from the conspiracy almost four years

> before the filing of the Indictment, the Defendant's post-offense conduct, especially obtaining a college degree and the start of his own successful business, the support of family and friends, lack of criminal history, and his age at the time of the offense conduct, all warrant the sentence imposed, which was sufficient, but not greater than necessary to serve the purposes of sentencing. *Id.*, at 117.

At the end of both the sentencing hearing and the sentencing memorandum, the District Judge reminded Gall that probation, rather than "an act of leniency," is a "substantial restriction of freedom." *Id.*, at 99, 125. In the memorandum, he emphasized:

> [Gall] will have to comply with strict reporting conditions along with a three-year regime of alcohol and drug testing. He will not be able to change or make decisions about significant circumstances in his life, such as where to live or work, which are prized liberty interests, without first seeking authorization from his Probation Officer or, perhaps, even the Court. Of course, the Defendant always faces the harsh consequences that await if he violates the conditions of his probationary term. *Id.*, at 125.

Finally, the District Judge explained why he had concluded that the sentence of probation reflected the seriousness of Gall's offense and that no term of imprisonment was necessary:

> Any term of imprisonment in this case would be counter effective by depriving society of the contributions of the Defendant who, the Court has found, understands the consequences of his criminal conduct and is doing everything in his power to forge a new life. The Defendant's post-offense conduct indicates neither that he will return to criminal behavior nor that the Defendant is a danger to society. In fact, the Defendant's post-offense conduct was not motivated by a desire to please the Court or any other governmental agency, but was the pre-Indictment product of the Defendant's own desire to lead a better life." *Id.*, at 125-126.

II

The Court of Appeals reversed and remanded for resentencing. Relying on its earlier opinion in United States v. Claiborne, 439 F.3d 479 (8th Cir. 2006), it held that a sentence outside of the Guidelines range must be supported by a justification that ""is proportional to the extent of the difference between the advisory range and the sentence imposed."" 446 F.3d 884, 889 (8th Cir. 2006) (quoting *Claiborne*, 439 F.3d at 481, in turn quoting United States v. Johnson, 427 F.3d 423, 426-427 (7th Cir.

2005)). Characterizing the difference between a sentence of probation and the bottom of Gall's advisory Guidelines range of 30 months as "extraordinary" because it amounted to "a 100% downward variance," 446 F.3d at 889, the Court of Appeals held that such a variance must be—and here was not—supported by extraordinary circumstances.

Rather than making an attempt to quantify the value of the justifications provided by the District Judge, the Court of Appeals identified what it regarded as five separate errors in the District Judge's reasoning: (1) He gave "too much weight to Gall's withdrawal from the conspiracy"; (2) given that Gall was 21 at the time of his offense, the District Judge erroneously gave "significant weight" to studies showing impetuous behavior by persons under the age of 18; (3) he did not "properly weigh" the seriousness of Gall's offense; (4) he failed to consider whether a sentence of probation would result in "unwarranted" disparities; and (5) he placed "too much emphasis on Gall's post-offense rehabilitation." *Id.*, at 889-890. As we shall explain, we are not persuaded that these factors, whether viewed separately or in the aggregate, are sufficient to support the conclusion that the District Judge abused his discretion. As a preface to our discussion of these particulars, however, we shall explain why the Court of Appeals' rule requiring "proportional" justifications for departures from the Guidelines range is not consistent with our remedial opinion in United States v. Booker, 543 U.S. 220 (2005).

III

In *Booker* we invalidated both the statutory provision, 18 U.S.C. § 3553(b)(1) (2000 ed., Supp. IV), which made the Sentencing Guidelines mandatory, and § 3742(e) (2000 ed. and Supp. IV), which directed appellate courts to apply a *de novo* standard of review to departures from the Guidelines. As a result of our decision, the Guidelines are now advisory, and appellate review of sentencing decisions is limited to determining whether they are "reasonable." Our explanation of "reasonableness" review in the *Booker* opinion made it pellucidly clear that the familiar abuse-of-discretion standard of review now applies to appellate review of sentencing decisions. See 543 U.S., at 260-262; see also *Rita*, 551 U.S., at _____, 127 S. Ct. 2456, at 2470 (Stevens, J., concurring).

It is also clear that a district judge must give serious consideration to the extent of any departure from the Guidelines and must explain his conclusion that an unusually lenient or an unusually harsh sentence is appropriate in a particular case with sufficient justifications. For even though the Guidelines are advisory rather than mandatory, they are, as we pointed out in *Rita,* the product of careful study based on extensive empirical evidence derived from the review of thousands of individual sentencing decisions. *Id.*, at ____, 127 S. Ct. 2456.

In reviewing the reasonableness of a sentence outside the Guidelines range, appellate courts may therefore take the degree of variance into account and consider the extent of a deviation from the Guidelines. We reject, however, an appellate rule that requires "extraordinary" circumstances to justify a sentence outside the Guidelines range. We also reject the use of a rigid mathematical formula that uses the percentage of a departure as the standard for determining the strength of the justifications required for a specific sentence.

As an initial matter, the approaches we reject come too close to creating an impermissible presumption of unreasonableness for sentences outside the Guidelines range. See *id.*, 127 S. Ct. 2456 at 2467 ("The fact that we permit courts of appeals to adopt a presumption of reasonableness does not mean that courts may adopt a presumption of unreasonableness"). Even the Government has acknowledged that such a presumption would not be consistent with *Booker.* See Brief for United States in Rita v. United States, O. T. 2006, No. 06-5754, pp. 34-35.

The mathematical approach also suffers from infirmities of application. On one side of the equation, deviations from the Guidelines range will always appear more extreme—in percentage terms—when the range itself is low, and a sentence of probation will always be a 100% departure regardless of whether the Guidelines range is 1 month or 100 years. Moreover, quantifying the variance as a certain percentage of the maximum, minimum, or median prison sentence recommended by the Guidelines gives no weight to the "substantial restriction of freedom" involved in a term of supervised release or probation. App. 95.

We recognize that custodial sentences are qualitatively more severe than probationary sentences of equivalent terms. Offenders on probation are nonetheless subject to several standard conditions that substantially restrict their liberty. . . . Probationers may not leave the judicial district, move, or change jobs without notifying, and in some cases receiving permission from, their probation officer or the court. They must report regularly to their probation officer, permit unannounced visits to their homes, refrain from associating with any person convicted of a felony, and refrain from excessive drinking. USSG § 5B1.3. Most probationers are also subject to individual "special conditions" imposed by the court. Gall, for instance, may not patronize any establishment that derives more than 50% of its revenue from the sale of alcohol, and must submit to random drug tests as directed by his probation officer. App. 109.

On the other side of the equation, the mathematical approach assumes the existence of some ascertainable method of assigning percentages to various justifications. Does withdrawal from a conspiracy justify more or less than, say, a 30% reduction? Does it matter that the withdrawal occurred several years ago? Is it relevant that the withdrawal was motivated by a decision to discontinue the use of drugs and to lead a better life? What percentage, if any, should be assigned to evidence that a defendant poses no future threat to society, or to evidence that innocent third parties are dependent on him? The formula is a classic example of attempting to measure an inventory of apples by counting oranges.

Most importantly, both the exceptional circumstances requirement and the rigid mathematical formulation reflect a practice—common among courts that have adopted "proportional review"—of applying a heightened standard of review to sentences outside the Guidelines range. This is inconsistent with the rule that the abuse-of-discretion standard of review applies to appellate review of all sentencing decisions—whether inside or outside the Guidelines range.

As we explained in *Rita*, a district court should begin all sentencing proceedings by correctly calculating the applicable Guidelines range. See 551 U.S., at ____, 127 S. Ct. 2456 at 2480. As a matter of administration and to secure nationwide consistency, the Guidelines should be the starting point and the initial benchmark. The Guidelines are not the only consideration, however. Accordingly, after giving both parties an opportunity to argue for whatever sentence they deem appropriate, the district judge should then consider all of the § 3553(a) factors to determine whether they support the sentence requested by a party.[6] In so doing, he may not presume that the Guidelines range is reasonable. See *id.*, at ____, 127 S. Ct. 2456. He must make an individualized assessment based on the facts presented. If he decides that an outside-Guidelines sentence is warranted, he must consider the extent of the deviation and ensure that the justification is sufficiently compelling to support the degree of the variance. We find it uncontroversial that a major departure should be supported by a more significant justification than a minor one. After settling on the appropriate sentence, he must adequately explain the chosen sentence to allow for meaningful appellate review and to promote the perception of fair sentencing. *Id.*, at ____, 127 S. Ct. 2456.

Regardless of whether the sentence imposed is inside or outside the Guidelines range, the appellate court must review the sentence under an abuse-of-discretion standard. It must first ensure that the district court

6. . . . The fact that § 3553(a) explicitly directs sentencing courts to consider the Guidelines supports the premise that district courts must begin their analysis with the Guidelines and remain cognizant of them throughout the sentencing process.

committed no significant procedural error, such as failing to calculate (or improperly calculating) the Guidelines range, treating the Guidelines as mandatory, failing to consider the § 3553(a) factors, selecting a sentence based on clearly erroneous facts, or failing to adequately explain the chosen sentence—including an explanation for any deviation from the Guidelines range. Assuming that the district court's sentencing decision is procedurally sound, the appellate court should then consider the substantive reasonableness of the sentence imposed under an abuse-of-discretion standard. When conducting this review, the court will, of course, take into account the totality of the circumstances, including the extent of any variance from the Guidelines range. If the sentence is within the Guidelines range, the appellate court may, but is not required to, apply a presumption of reasonableness. *Id.*, at ____, 127 S. Ct. 2456. But if the sentence is outside the Guidelines range, the court may not apply a presumption of unreasonableness. It may consider the extent of the deviation, but must give due deference to the district court's decision that the § 3553(a) factors, on a whole, justify the extent of the variance. The fact that the appellate court might reasonably have concluded that a different sentence was appropriate is insufficient to justify reversal of the district court.

Practical considerations also underlie this legal principle. "The sentencing judge is in a superior position to find facts and judge their import under § 3553(a) in the individual case. The judge sees and hears the evidence, makes credibility determinations, has full knowledge of the facts and gains insights not conveyed by the record." Brief for Federal Public and Community Defenders et al. as Amici Curiae 16. "The sentencing judge has access to, and greater familiarity with, the individual case and the individual defendant before him than the Commission or the appeals court." *Rita,* 551 U.S., at ____, 127 S. Ct. 2456. Moreover, "district courts have an institutional advantage over appellate courts in making these sorts of determinations, especially as they see so many more Guidelines sentences than appellate courts do." Koon v. United States, 518 U.S. 81, 98 (1996).[7]

7. District judges sentence, on average, 117 defendants every year. Administrative Office of United States Courts, 2006 Federal Court Management Statistics 167. . . .

8. It is particularly revealing that when we adopted an abuse-of-discretion standard in *Koon,* we explicitly rejected the Government's argument that "*de novo* review of departure decisions is necessary 'to protect against unwarranted disparities arising from the differing sentencing approaches of individual district judges.'" 518 U.S., at 97 (quoting Brief for United States in O. T. 1995, No. 94-1664, p. 12). Even then we were satisfied that a more deferential abuse-of-discretion standard could successfully balance the need to "reduce unjustified disparities" across the Nation and "consider every convicted person as an individual." 518 U.S., at 113.

"It has been uniform and constant in the federal judicial tradition for the sentencing judge to consider every convicted person as an individual and every case as a unique study in the human failings that sometimes mitigate, sometimes magnify, the crime and the punishment to ensue." *Id.*, at 113.[8] The uniqueness of the individual case, however, does not change the deferential abuse-of-discretion standard of review that applies to all sentencing decisions. As we shall now explain, the opinion of the Court of Appeals in this case does not reflect the requisite deference and does not support the conclusion that the District Court abused its discretion.

IV

As an initial matter, we note that the District Judge committed no significant procedural error. He correctly calculated the applicable Guidelines range, allowed both parties to present arguments as to what they believed the appropriate sentence should be, considered all of the § 3553(a) factors, and thoroughly documented his reasoning. The Court of Appeals found that the District Judge erred in failing to give proper weight to the seriousness of the offense, as required by § 3553(a)(2)(A), and failing to consider whether a sentence of probation would create unwarranted disparities, as required by § 3553(a)(6). We disagree.

. . . The Court of Appeals concluded that "the district court did not properly weigh the seriousness of Gall's offense" because it "ignored the serious health risks ecstasy poses." 446 F.3d at 890. Contrary to the Court of Appeals' conclusion, the District Judge plainly did consider the seriousness of the offense. . . . It is true that the District Judge did not make specific reference to the (unquestionably significant) health risks posed by ecstasy, but the prosecutor did not raise ecstasy's effects at the sentencing hearing. Had the prosecutor raised the issue, specific discussion of the point might have been in order, but it was not incumbent on the District Judge to raise every conceivably relevant issue on his own initiative.

The Government's legitimate concern that a lenient sentence for a serious offense threatens to promote disrespect for the law is at least to some extent offset by the fact that seven of the eight defendants in this case have been sentenced to significant prison terms. Moreover, the unique facts of Gall's situation provide support for the District Judge's conclusion that, in Gall's case, "a sentence of imprisonment may work to promote not respect, but derision, of the law if the law is viewed as merely a means to dispense harsh punishment without taking into account the real conduct and circumstances involved in sentencing." *Id.*, at 126.

Section 3553(a)(6) requires judges to consider "the need to avoid unwarranted sentence disparities among defendants with similar records who have been found guilty of similar conduct." . . . [A]voidance of unwarranted disparities was clearly considered by the Sentencing Commission when setting the Guidelines ranges. Since the District Judge correctly calculated and carefully reviewed the Guidelines range, he necessarily gave significant weight and consideration to the need to avoid unwarranted disparities.

Moreover, . . . it seems that the judge gave specific attention to the issue of disparity when he inquired about the sentences already imposed by a different judge on two of Gall's codefendants. . . . [I]t is perfectly clear that the District Judge considered the need to avoid unwarranted disparities, but also considered the need to avoid unwarranted *similarities* among other co-conspirators who were not similarly situated. The District Judge regarded Gall's voluntary withdrawal as a reasonable basis for giving him a less severe sentence than the three codefendants . . . , who neither withdrew from the conspiracy nor rehabilitated themselves as Gall had done. We also note that neither the Court of Appeals nor the Government has called our attention to a comparable defendant who received a more severe sentence.

Since the District Court committed no procedural error, the only question for the Court of Appeals was whether the sentence was reasonable—*i.e.*, whether the District Judge abused his discretion in determining that the § 3553(a) factors supported a sentence of probation and justified a substantial deviation from the Guidelines range. As we shall now explain, the sentence was reasonable. The Court of Appeals' decision to the contrary was incorrect and failed to demonstrate the requisite deference to the District Judge's decision.

V

The Court of Appeals gave virtually no deference to the District Court's decision that the § 3553(a) factors justified a significant variance in this case. Although the Court of Appeals correctly stated that the appropriate standard of review was abuse of discretion, it engaged in an analysis that more closely resembled *de novo* review of the facts presented and determined that, in its view, the degree of variance was not warranted.

10. The Court of Appeals explained that under the current Guidelines, which treat ecstasy more harshly, Gall's base offense level would have been 32, eight levels higher than the base offense level imposed under the 1999 Guidelines.

The Court of Appeals thought that the District Court "gave too much weight to Gall's withdrawal from the conspiracy because the court failed to acknowledge the significant benefit Gall received from being subject to the 1999 Guidelines."[10] 446 F.3d at 889. This criticism is flawed in that it ignores the critical relevance of Gall's voluntary withdrawal, a circumstance that distinguished his conduct not only from that of all his codefendants, but from the vast majority of defendants convicted of conspiracy in federal court. The District Court quite reasonably attached great weight to the fact that Gall voluntarily withdrew from the conspiracy after deciding, on his own initiative, to change his life. This lends strong support to the District Court's conclusion that Gall is not going to return to criminal behavior and is not a danger to society. See 18 U.S.C. § § 3553(a)(2)(B), (C). Compared to a case where the offender's rehabilitation occurred after he was charged with a crime, the District Court here had greater justification for believing Gall's turnaround was genuine, as distinct from a transparent attempt to build a mitigation case.

The Court of Appeals thought the District Judge "gave significant weight to an improper factor" when he compared Gall's sale of ecstasy when he was a 21-year-old adult to the "impetuous and ill-considered" actions of persons under the age of 18. 446 F.3d at 890. The appellate court correctly observed that the studies cited by the District Judge do not explain how Gall's "specific behavior in the instant case was impetuous or ill-considered." *Ibid.*

In that portion of his sentencing memorandum, however, the judge was discussing the "character of the defendant," not the nature of his offense. App. 122. He noted that Gall's criminal history included a ticket for underage drinking when he was 18 years old and possession of marijuana that was contemporaneous with his offense in this case. In summary, the District Judge observed that all of Gall's criminal history "including the present offense, occurred when he was twenty-one-years old or younger" and appeared "to stem from his addictions to drugs and alcohol." Id., at 123. . . .

Given the dramatic contrast between Gall's behavior before he joined the conspiracy and his conduct after withdrawing, it was not unreasonable for the District Judge to view Gall's immaturity at the time of the offense as a mitigating factor, and his later behavior as a sign that he had matured and would not engage in such impetuous and ill-considered conduct in the future. Indeed, his consideration of that factor finds support in our cases. See, e.g., Johnson v. Texas, 509 U.S. 350, 367 (1993) (holding that a jury was free to consider a 19-year-old defendant's youth when determining whether there was a probability that he would continue to commit violent acts in the future and stating that "'youth is more than a chronological fact. It is a time and condition of life when a person may be most susceptible to influence and to psychological damage'" (quoting Eddings v. Oklahoma, 455 U.S. 104, 115 (1982))).

Finally, the Court of Appeals thought that, even if Gall's rehabilitation was dramatic and permanent, a sentence of probation for participation as a middleman in a conspiracy distributing 10,000 pills of ecstasy "lies outside the range of choice dictated by the facts of the case." 446 F.3d at 890. If the Guidelines were still mandatory, and assuming the facts did not justify a Guidelines-based downward departure, this would provide a sufficient basis for setting aside Gall's sentence because the Guidelines state that probation alone is not an appropriate sentence for comparable offenses. But the Guidelines are not mandatory, and thus the "range of choice dictated by the facts of the case" is significantly broadened. Moreover, the Guidelines are only one of the factors to consider when imposing sentence, and § 3553(a)(3) directs the judge to consider sentences other than imprisonment.

We also note that the Government did not argue below, and has not argued here, that a sentence of probation could never be imposed for a crime identical to Gall's. Indeed, it acknowledged that probation could be permissible if the record contained different—but in our view, no more compelling—mitigating evidence. Tr. of Oral Arg. 37-38 (stating that probation could be an appropriate sentence, given the exact same offense, if "there are compelling family circumstances where individuals will be very badly hurt in the defendant's family if no one is available to take care of them"). . . .

The Court of Appeals clearly disagreed with the District Judge's conclusion that consideration of the § 3553(a) factors justified a sentence of probation; it believed that the circumstances presented here were insufficient to sustain such a marked deviation from the Guidelines range. But it is not for the Court of Appeals to decide *de novo* whether the justification for a variance is sufficient or the sentence reasonable. On abuse-of-discretion review, the Court of Appeals should have given due deference to the District Court's reasoned and reasonable decision that the § 3553 (a) factors, on the whole, justified the sentence. Accordingly, the judgment of the Court of Appeals is reversed.

It is so ordered.

JUSTICE SCALIA, concurring.

I join the opinion of the Court.

In Rita v. United States, 551 U.S. 338 (2007), I wrote separately to state my view that any appellate review of sentences for substantive reasonableness will necessarily result in a sentencing scheme constitutionally indistinguishable from the mandatory Guidelines struck down in United States v. Booker, 543 U.S. 220 (2005). Whether a sentencing scheme uses mandatory Guidelines, a "proportionality test" for Guidelines variances, or a deferential abuse-of-discretion standard, there will be some sentences upheld only on the basis of additional judge-found facts.

Although I continue to believe that substantive-reasonableness review is inherently flawed, I give stare decisis effect to the statutory holding of *Rita*. The highly deferential standard adopted by the Court today will result in far fewer unconstitutional sentences than the proportionality standard employed by the Eighth Circuit. Moreover, as I noted in *Rita*, the Court has not foreclosed as-applied constitutional challenges to sentences. The door therefore remains open for a defendant to demonstrate that his sentence, whether inside or outside the advisory Guidelines range, would not have been upheld but for the existence of a fact found by the sentencing judge and not by the jury.

JUSTICE SOUTER, concurring.

I join the Court's opinion here, as I do in today's companion case of Kimbrough v. United States, 128 S. Ct. 558 (2007), which follow United States v. Booker, 543 U.S. 220 (2005), and Rita v. United States, 551 U.S. 338 (2007). My disagreements with holdings in those earlier cases are not the stuff of formally perpetual dissent, but I see their objectionable points hexing our judgments today, see id., at ____, 127 S. Ct. 2456, at 2484 (Souter, J., dissenting), and *Booker*, supra, at 272 (Stevens, J., dissenting in part). After *Booker's* remedial holding, I continue to think that the best resolution of the tension between substantial consistency throughout the system and the right of jury trial would be a new Act of Congress: reestablishing a statutory system of mandatory sentencing guidelines (though not identical to the original in all points of detail), but providing for jury findings of all facts necessary to set the upper range of sentencing discretion. See *Rita*, supra, at ____, 127 S. Ct. 2456.

JUSTICE THOMAS, dissenting.

Consistent with my dissenting opinion in Kimbrough v. United States, 552 U.S. 85 (2007), I would affirm the judgment of the Court of Appeals because the District Court committed statutory error when it departed below the applicable Guidelines range.

JUSTICE ALITO, dissenting.

The fundamental question in this case is whether, under the remedial decision in United States v. Booker, 543 U.S. 220 (2005), a district court must give the policy decisions that are embodied in the Sentencing Guidelines at least some significant weight in making a sentencing decision. I would answer that question in the affirmative and would therefore affirm the decision of the Court of Appeals.

I

In *Booker,* . . . the lower federal courts were instructed that the Guidelines must be regarded as "effectively advisory," *Booker*, 543 U.S., at 245, and that individual sentencing decisions are subject to appellate review for "'reasonableness.'" *Id.,* at 262. The *Booker* remedial opinion did not explain exactly what it meant by a system of "advisory" guidelines or by "reasonableness" review, and the opinion is open to different interpretations.

It is possible to read the opinion to mean that district judges, after giving the Guidelines a polite nod, may then proceed essentially as if the Sentencing Reform Act had never been enacted. This is how two of the dissents interpreted the Court's opinion. . . .

While this is a possible understanding of the remedial opinion, a better reading is that sentencing judges must still give the Guidelines' policy decisions some significant weight and that the courts of appeals must still police compliance. . . . [Under such a reading], district courts are still required to give some deference to the policy decisions embodied in the Guidelines and . . . appellate review must monitor compliance. District courts must not only "consult" the Guidelines, they must "take them into account." *Id.*, at 264. In addition, the remedial majority [in *Booker* distanced itself] from Justice Scalia's position that, under an advisory Guidelines scheme, a district judge would have "discretion to sentence anywhere within the ranges authorized by statute" so long as the judge "stated that 'this court does not believe that the punishment set forth in the Guidelines is appropriate for this sort of offense.'" *Id.,* at 305 (opinion dissenting in part).

[I]n the remedial opinion, the Court expressed confidence that appellate review for reasonableness would help to avoid "'excessive sentencing disparities'" and "would tend to iron out sentencing differences." *Id.*, at 263. Indeed, a major theme of the remedial opinion, as well as our decision last Term in Rita v. United States, 551 U.S. 338 (2007), was that the post-*Booker* sentencing regime would still promote the Sentencing Reform Act's goal of reducing sentencing disparities. . . .

It is unrealistic to think this goal can be achieved over the long term if sentencing judges need only give lip service to the Guidelines. The other sentencing factors set out in § 3553(a) are so broad that they impose few real restraints on sentencing judges. See *id.,* at 305 (SCALIA, J., dissenting in part). Thus, if judges are obligated to do no more than consult the Guidelines before deciding upon the sentence that is, in their independent judgment, sufficient to serve the other § 3553(a) factors, federal sentencing will not "move . . . in Congress' preferred direction." *Id.,* at 264 (opinion of the Court). On the contrary, sentencing disparities will gradually increase. Appellate decisions affirming sentences that diverge from the Guidelines (such as the Court's decision today) will be influential, and the sentencing habits developed during the pre-*Booker* era will fade.

Finally, in reading the *Booker* remedial opinion, we should not forget the decision's constitutional underpinnings. *Booker* and its antecedents are based on the Sixth Amendment right to trial by jury. . . . It is telling that the rules set out in the Court's opinion in the present case have nothing to do with juries or factfinding and, indeed, that not one of the facts that bears on petitioner's sentence is disputed. What is at issue, instead, is the allocation of the authority to decide issues of substantive sentencing policy, an issue on which the Sixth Amendment says absolutely nothing. The yawning gap between the Sixth Amendment and the Court's opinion should be enough to show that the *Blakely-Booker* line of cases has gone astray. . . .

I recognize that the Court is committed to the *Blakely-Booker* line of cases, but we are not required to continue along a path that will take us further and further off course. Because the *Booker* remedial opinion may be read to require sentencing judges to give weight to the Guidelines, I would adopt that interpretation and thus minimize the gap between what the Sixth Amendment requires and what our cases have held.

II

[In this last section, which is omitted, Justice Alito found "no evidence that the District Court deferred to the Guidelines to any significant degree," but instead simply "determined what it thought was appropriate under the circumstances and sentenced petitioner accordingly." He noted that "abuse-of-discretion review is not toothless," and ultimately agreed with the Eighth Circuit that "the District Court did not properly exercise its discretion."–EDS.]

NOTES AND QUESTIONS

1. Does *Gall* resolve the conflict between Justice Breyer and Justice Scalia over the proper standard of review for Guideline cases? Or does it leave the issue still unsettled? Does the fact that both Breyer and Scalia joined the majority opinion help you to answer these questions?

2. In Kimbrough v. United States, 552 U.S. 85 (2007), the companion case to *Gall*, the Supreme Court upheld as "reasonable" a district judge's decision to deviate from the Guidelines based on the judge's disagreement with the wide sentencing disparity between crimes involving crack cocaine and powder cocaine. The Court, in a majority opinion by Justice Ginsburg, explained that "closer review may be in order when the sentencing judge varies from the Guidelines based solely on the judge's view that the Guidelines range 'fails properly to reflect § 3553(a) considerations' even in a mine-run case," but concluded that the instant case "presents no occasion for elaborative discussion of this matter," because the Guidelines for crack cocaine crimes "do not exemplify the Commission's exercise of its characteristic institutional role." Instead, those Guidelines, according to the Court, were more or less forced upon the Sentencing Commission by Congress's failure properly to address the crack/powder distinction in several statutes creating mandatory minimum sentences. Justice Scalia joined the majority opinion, but also added, in concurrence, that nothing in *Kimbrough* should be read as inconsistent with prior Court decisions holding that "the district court is free to make its own reasonable application of the § 3553(a) factors, and to reject (after due consideration) the advice of the Guidelines."

3. The effects of *Blakely* and *Booker* continue to reverberate through the federal and state criminal justice systems. Some jurisdictions have already decided to completely rewrite their sentencing laws in an attempt to conform to *Blakely/Booker*; others have taken the position (perhaps just wishful thinking?) that their sentencing schemes can be distinguished from those at issue in *Blakely* and *Booker*, and thus can be spared from the *Blakely/Booker* avalanche. See, e.g., Cunningham v. California, 549 U.S. 270 (2007), in which California's determinate sentencing law was struck down by 6-3 (with Justices Kennedy, Breyer, and Alito dissenting); the Court, in a majority opinion written by Justice Ginsburg, rejected California's claim that its sentencing law could survive *Blakely/Booker* because it did not specify the particular "aggravating" facts necessary for a trial judge to move a defendant up from the "middle term" sentence to the "upper term" sentence for the crime of conviction, but instead left such factual findings to the "broad discretion" of the trial judge. And still

other jurisdictions are taking a "wait and see" attitude, apparently waiting for the next shoe to drop from the Supreme Court. For a helpful summary account of the post-*Booker* landscape, see Joshua Dressler, Understanding Criminal Procedure (Volume 2: Adjudication) (Lexis-Nexis 2006), § 15.04 (pages 366-375); for a set of insightful scholarly contributions on the subject, see the aptly titled special issue, "The *Booker* Aftershock," Federal Sentencing Reporter, Volume 17, Number 4 (April 2005).

At least one important subsidiary question has been answered by the Court: *Blakely/Booker* errors *can* be held "harmless." In Washington v. Recuenco, 548 U.S. 212 (2006), the Court, in a 7-2 majority opinion written by Justice Thomas (with Justices Stevens and Ginsburg dissenting), rejected the defendant's argument that failure to submit a sentencing factor to a jury determination, under a "beyond reasonable doubt" standard, is the kind of "structural error" that automatically requires reversal in every case. The Court relied heavily on the case of Neder v. United States, 527 U.S. 1 (1999), which held that a trial court's erroneous failure to submit an element of a crime (in that case, the "materiality" of an alleged mail and wire fraud) to the jury could be subjected to "harmless error" review, because such an error "does not *necessarily* render a criminal trial fundamentally unfair or an unreliable vehicle for determining guilt or innocence." *Id.*, at 9. The Court in *Recuenco* concluded that *Blakely/Booker* errors are "indistinguishable" from the kind of error involved in *Neder*, and thus require the same result with respect to "harmless error" analysis.

4. *Booker*, *Gall*, and *Kimbrough* might be viewed as calling into question the fundamental premises underlying *Apprendi* and *Blakely*, because they approved a remedial scheme that (at least in the view of Justice Scalia, the author of *Blakely* and thus the chief architect of the prevailing doctrine) is incompatible with those premises. But those cases did not directly challenge the *Apprendi/Blakely* doctrine itself. The first such direct challenge might be the case of Oregon v. Ice 129 S. Ct. 711 (2009). Under Oregon law, Ice—who was convicted of multiple crimes in a single trial—was subject to consecutive rather than concurrent sentences only if the trial judge made a factual finding that the crimes involved separate incidents, or if (in the same incident) the defendant manifested a "willingness to commit more than one criminal offense" or the crimes created a risk of "greater or qualitatively different loss, injury or harm to the victim." The judge made such findings in Ice's case, and Ice was given consecutive sentences that totaled 340 months in prison.

The Court held that Ice's consecutive sentencing did not violate *Apprendi* and *Blakely*. In a majority opinion by Justice Ginsburg, joined by Justices Stevens, Kennedy, Breyer, and Alito, the Court explained:

> This case concerns the scope of the Sixth Amendment's jury-trial guarantee, as construed in Apprendi v. New Jersey, 530 U.S. 466 (2000), and Blakely v. Washington, 542 U.S. 296 (2004). Those decisions are rooted in the historic jury function—determining whether the prosecution has proved each element of an offense beyond a reasonable doubt. They hold that it is within the jury's province to determine any fact (other than the existence of a prior conviction) that increases the maximum punishment authorized for a particular offense. Thus far, the Court has not extended the *Apprendi* and *Blakely* line of decisions beyond the offense-specific context that supplied the historic grounding for the decisions. The question here presented concerns a sentencing function in which the jury traditionally played no part: When a defendant has been tried and convicted of multiple offenses, each involving discrete sentencing prescriptions, does the Sixth Amendment mandate jury determination of any fact declared necessary to the imposition of consecutive, in lieu of concurrent, sentences?
>
> Our application of *Apprendi*'s rule must honor the "long-standing common-law practice" in which the rule is rooted. . . . The rule's animating principle is the preservation of the jury's historic role as a bulwark between the State and the accused at the trial for an alleged offense. See *Apprendi*, 530 U.S., at 477. Guided by that principle, our opinions make clear that the Sixth Amendment does not countenance legislative encroachment on the jury's traditional domain. See *id.*, at 497. We accordingly considered whether the finding of a particular fact was understood as within "the domain of the jury . . . by those who framed the Bill of Rights." Harris v. United States, 536 U.S. 545, 557 (2002) (plurality opinion). In undertaking this inquiry, we remain cognizant that administration of a discrete criminal justice system is among the basic sovereign prerogatives States retain. See, *e.g.*, Patterson v. New York, 432 U.S. 197, 201 (1977).
>
> These twin considerations–historical practice and respect for state sovereignty—counsel against extending *Apprendi*'s rule to the imposition of sentences for discrete crimes. The decision to impose sentences consecutively is not within the jury function that "extends down centuries into the common law." *Apprendi*, 530 U.S., at 477. Instead, specification of the regime for administering multiple sentences has long been considered the prerogative of state legislatures.
>
> Members of this Court have warned against "wooden, unyielding insistence on expanding the *Apprendi* doctrine far beyond its necessary boundaries." Cunningham [v. California], 549 U.S. [270], 295 (KENNEDY, J., dissenting). The jury-trial right is best honored through a "principled rationale" that applies the rule of the *Apprendi* cases "within the central sphere of their concern." 549 U.S., at 295. Our disposition today—upholding an Oregon statute that assigns to judges a decision that has not traditionally belonged to the jury—is faithful to that aim.

Justice Scalia, predictably, was not amused:

> [T]he Court attempts to distinguish Oregon's sentencing scheme by reasoning that the rule of *Apprendi* applies only to the length of a sentence for an individual crime and not to the total sentence for a defendant. I cannot understand why we would make such a strange exception to the treasured right of trial by jury. Neither the reasoning of the *Apprendi* line of cases, nor any distinctive history of the factfinding necessary to imposition of consecutive sentences, nor (of course) logic supports such an odd rule . . . .
>
> To support its distinction-without-a-difference, the Court puts forward the same (the *very* same) arguments regarding the history of sentencing that were rejected by *Apprendi.* Here, it is entirely irrelevant that common-law judges had discretion to impose either consecutive or concurrent sentences, just as there it was entirely irrelevant that common-law judges had discretion to impose greater or lesser sentences (within the prescribed statutory maximum) for individual convictions . . . . Our concern here is precisely the same as our concern in *Apprendi*: What happens when a State breaks from the common-law practice of discretionary sentences and permits the imposition of an elevated sentence only upon the showing of extraordinary facts? In such a system, the defendant "is *entitled* to" the lighter sentence "and by reason of the Sixth Amendment[,] the facts bearing upon that entitlement must be found by a jury." *Blakely*, 542 U.S., at 309 . . . .
>
> Today's opinion muddies the waters, and gives cause to doubt whether the Court is willing to stand by *Apprendi*'s interpretation of the Sixth Amendment's jury-trial guarantee.

Does *Ice* truly represent the beginning of the end for the *Apprendi/Blakely* doctrine? Or is it a one-off exception that will leave the core of the rule unscathed? Only time will tell.

Chapter 14

Double Jeopardy

A. "Twice Put in Jeopardy"

1. Acquittals

Insert the following material at the end of the last full paragraph on page 1497, just before the heading "Protecting Acquittals":

SMITH v. MASSACHUSETTS
Certiorari to the Appeals Court of Massachusetts
543 U.S. 462 (2005)

JUSTICE SCALIA delivered the opinion of the Court.

Midway through a jury trial, the judge acquitted petitioner of one of the three offenses charged. The question presented in this case is whether the Double Jeopardy Clause forbade the judge to reconsider that acquittal later in the trial.

I

Petitioner Melvin Smith was tried before a jury in the Superior Court of Suffolk County, Massachusetts, on charges relating to the shooting of his girlfriend's cousin. The indictments charged three counts: armed assault with intent to murder; assault and battery by means of a dangerous weapon; and unlawful possession of a firearm. The "firearm" element of the last offense requires proof that the weapon had a barrel "less than 16 inches" in length. See Mass. Gen. Laws Ann., ch. 140, § 121 (West 2002) (definition of "firearm"). The indictment in petitioner's case so charged. Petitioner's girlfriend was tried before the same jury as an accessory after the fact.

The victim testified at trial that petitioner had shot him with "a pistol," specifically "a revolver" that "appeared to be a .32 or a .38." The prosecution introduced no other evidence about the firearm.

At the conclusion of the prosecution's case, petitioner moved for a required finding of not guilty on the firearm count, see Mass. Rule Crim. Proc. 25(a) (2002), in part because the Commonwealth had not proved that the gun barrel was less than 16 inches. At sidebar, after hearing argument from the prosecutor, the trial judge granted the motion, reasoning that there was "not a scintilla of evidence" that petitioner had possessed a weapon with a barrel length of less than 16 inches. The trial court marked petitioner's motion with the handwritten endorsement "Filed and after hearing, Allowed," and the allowance of the motion was entered on the docket. The sidebar conference then concluded, and the prosecution rested.[1] The judge did not notify the jury of petitioner's acquittal on the firearm count.

The defense case then proceeded. Petitioner's codefendant presented one witness, and both defendants then rested. During the short recess before closing arguments, the prosecutor brought to the court's attention a Massachusetts precedent under which (he contended) the victim's testimony about the kind of gun sufficed to establish that the barrel was shorter than 16 inches. He requested that the court defer ruling on the sufficiency of the evidence until after the jury verdict. The judge agreed, announcing orally that she was "reversing" her previous ruling and allowing the firearm-possession count to go to the jury. Corresponding notations were made on the original of petitioner's motion and on the docket.

The jury convicted petitioner on all three counts, though it acquitted his codefendant of the accessory charge. Petitioner then submitted to a bench trial on an additional repeat-offender element of the firearm-possession charge; the judge found him guilty. Petitioner received a sentence of ten to twelve years' incarceration on the firearm-possession charge, concurrent with his sentence on the other counts.

Petitioner sought review in the Appeals Court of Massachusetts. That court affirmed, holding that the Double Jeopardy Clause was not implicated because the trial judge's correction of her ruling had not subjected petitioner to a second prosecution or proceeding. It also rejected petitioner's argument that the trial judge's initial ruling was final because Massachusetts Rule of Criminal Procedure 25(a) required the judge to decide petitioner's motion when it was made, without reserving decision;[2]

1. Although, before the judge ruled, the prosecutor had said that he would "be requesting to reopen and allow [the victim] to testify to" the barrel length, he made no motion to reopen before resting his case.

2. The Rule provides in pertinent part:

"The judge on motion of a defendant or on his own motion shall enter a finding of not guilty of the offense charged in an indictment or complaint or any part thereof after the evidence the court reasoned that the Rule does not preclude the judge from reconsidering. 58 Mass. App. 166, 170-171, 788 N.E.2d 977, 982-983 (2003).

The Supreme Judicial Court of Massachusetts denied further appellate review. We granted certiorari.

II

Although the common-law protection against double jeopardy historically applied only to charges on which a jury had rendered a verdict, we have long held that the Double Jeopardy Clause of the Fifth Amendment prohibits reexamination of a court-decreed acquittal to the same extent it prohibits reexamination of an acquittal by jury verdict. This is so whether the judge's ruling of acquittal comes in a bench trial or, as here, in a trial by jury. See Fong Foo v. United States, 369 U.S. 141, 143 (1962) (*per curiam*).

Our cases have made a single exception to the principle that acquittal by judge precludes reexamination of guilt no less than acquittal by jury: When a jury returns a verdict of guilty and a trial judge (or an appellate court) sets aside that verdict and enters a judgment of acquittal, the Double Jeopardy Clause does not preclude a prosecution appeal to reinstate the jury verdict of guilty. United States v. Wilson, 420 U.S. 332, 352-353 (1975). But if the prosecution has not yet obtained a conviction, further proceedings to secure one are impermissible: "[S]ubjecting the defendant to postacquittal factfinding proceedings going to guilt or innocence violates the Double Jeopardy Clause." Smalis v. Pennsylvania, 476 U.S. 140, 145 (1986).

When the judge in this case first granted petitioner's motion, there had been no jury verdict. Submission of the firearm count to the jury plainly subjected petitioner to further "factfinding proceedings going to guilt or innocence," prohibited by *Smalis* following an acquittal. The first question, then, is whether the judge's initial ruling on petitioner's motion was, in fact, a judgment of acquittal.

It certainly appeared to be. Massachusetts Rule of Criminal Procedure 25(a) directs the trial judge to enter a finding of not guilty "if the evidence is insufficient as a matter of law to sustain a conviction." An order entering such a finding thus meets the definition of acquittal that

---

on either side is closed if the evidence is insufficient as a matter of law to sustain a conviction on the charge. *If a defendant's motion for a required finding of not guilty is made at the close of the Commonwealth's evidence, it shall be ruled upon at that time.*" Mass. Rule Crim. Proc. 25(a) (2002) (emphasis added).

our double-jeopardy cases have consistently used: it "actually represents a resolution, correct or not, of some or all of the factual elements of the offense charged." [United States v. Martin Linen Supply Co., 430 U.S. 564, 571 (1977).]

The Commonwealth contends that the grant of a motion for a required finding of not guilty in a jury trial is a purely legal determination, the factfinding function being reserved to the jury. Thus, the Commonwealth reasons, jeopardy did not terminate midtrial on any of the three counts, since neither judge nor jury had rendered a factual determination that would bring jeopardy to an end. We rejected identical reasoning in *Martin Linen, supra*, holding that jeopardy ends when, following discharge of a hung jury, a judge grants a motion for judgment of acquittal under Federal Rule of Criminal Procedure 29. Rule 29 created the judge-ordered "judgment of acquittal" in place of the directed verdict, which was at least fictionally returned by the jury at the judge's direction, rather than coming from the judge alone. But, we said in *Martin Linen,* change in nomenclature and removal of the jury's theoretical role make no difference; the Rule 29 judgment of acquittal is a substantive determination that the prosecution has failed to carry its burden. Thus, even when the jury is the *primary* factfinder, the trial judge still resolves elements of the offense in granting a Rule 29 motion in the absence of a jury verdict. See *Martin Linen, supra*, at 571-575.

The same is true here. . . . Massachusetts' characterization of the required finding of not guilty as a legal rather than factual determination is, "as a matter of double jeopardy law, . . . not binding on us," *Smalis, supra*, at 144, n.5; what matters is that, as the Massachusetts rules authorize, the judge "evaluated the [Commonwealth's] evidence and determined that it was legally insufficient to sustain a conviction." *Martin Linen, supra*, at 572.

III

Having concluded that the judge acquitted petitioner of the firearm-possession charge,[3] we must turn to the more difficult question whether the Double Jeopardy Clause permitted her to reconsider that acquittal once petitioner and his codefendant had rested their cases.

3. It is of no moment that jeopardy continued on the two assault charges, for which the jury remained empaneled. Double-jeopardy analysis focuses on the individual "offence" charged, and our cases establish that jeopardy may terminate on some counts even as it continues on others. See, e.g., Price v. Georgia, 398 U.S. 323, 329 (1970).

It is important to note, at the outset, that the facts of this case gave petitioner no reason to doubt the finality of the state court's ruling. The prosecutor did not make or reserve a motion for reconsideration, or seek a continuance that would allow him to provide the court with favorable authority. Rather, the sidebar conference concluded, the court asked the prosecutor if he had "any further evidence," and he replied, "No. At this point, the Commonwealth rests their case." Nor did the court's ruling appear on its face to be tentative. The trial court was not permitted by Massachusetts procedure to defer ruling on petitioner's motion, Mass. Rule Crim. Proc. 25(a), or to require the defendants to go forward with their cases while the prosecution reserved the right to present more evidence, Commonwealth v. Cote, 15 Mass. App. 229, 242, 444 N.E.2d 1282, 1290-1291 (1983). And when the prosecutor suggested that he be given a chance to reopen his case before the defendants proceeded, the court rejected the suggestion because it was time to rule on petitioner's motion.

Was this apparently final ruling in fact final? We think . . . that as a general matter state law may prescribe that a judge's midtrial determination of the sufficiency of the State's proof can be reconsidered. Cf. Pennsylvania v. Goldhammer, 474 U.S. 28, 30 (1985) (per curiam) (state law regarding appealability may affect defendant's expectation that a sentence is final for double-jeopardy purposes). We can find no instance in which a State has done this by statute or rule, but some state courts have held, as a matter of common law or in the exercise of their supervisory power, that a court-directed judgment of acquittal is not effective until it is signed and entered in the docket, Harden v. State, 160 Ga. App. 514, 515, 287S. E. 2d 329, 331 (1981), until a formal order is issued, State v. Collins, 112 Wn.2d 303, 308-309, 771 P.2d 350, 353 (1989), or until the motion hearing is concluded, Watson v. State, 410 So. 2d 207, 209 (Fla. App. 1982).

At the time of petitioner's trial, however, Massachusetts had not adopted any such rule of nonfinality. Its Rules of Criminal Procedure provided that only clerical errors in a judgment or order, or errors "arising from oversight or omission," were subject to correction at any time. Mass. Rule Crim. Proc. 42 (2002). Massachusetts cites a few Commonwealth cases supporting the general proposition that interlocutory rulings (rulings on pretrial motions, evidentiary rulings, and the like) are subject to reconsideration. But it is far from obvious that this principle extends to entry of a required finding of not guilty under Rule 25 (or to its common-law predecessor, the directed verdict)—which on its face, at least, purports not to be interlocutory but to end the case. We think much more was required here.

It may suffice for an appellate court to announce the state-law rule that midtrial acquittals are tentative in a case where reconsideration of the acquittal occurred at a stage in the trial where the defendant's justifiable ignorance of the rule could not possibly have caused him prejudice. But when, as here, the trial has proceeded to the defendant's presentation of his case, the possibility of prejudice arises. The seeming dismissal may induce a defendant to present a defense to the undismissed charges when he would be better advised to stand silent. Many jurisdictions still follow the traditional rule that after trial or on appeal, sufficiency-of-the-evidence challenges are reviewed on the basis of the *entire* trial record, even if the defendant moved for acquittal when the prosecution rested and the court erroneously denied that motion. In these jurisdictions, the defendant who puts on a case runs "the risk that . . . he will bolster the Government case enough for it to support a verdict of guilty." McGautha v. California, 402 U.S. 183, 215 (1971). The defendant's evidence "may lay the foundation for otherwise inadmissible evidence in the Government's initial presentation or provide corroboration for essential elements of the Government's case." United States v. Calderon, 348 U.S. 160, 164, n.1 (1954). In all jurisdictions, moreover, false assurance of acquittal on one count may induce the defendant to present defenses to the remaining counts that are inadvisable—for example, a defense that entails admission of guilt on the acquitted count.

The Double Jeopardy Clause's guarantee cannot be allowed to become a potential snare for those who reasonably rely upon it. If, after a facially unqualified midtrial dismissal of one count, the trial has proceeded to the defendant's introduction of evidence, the acquittal must be treated as final, unless the availability of reconsideration has been plainly established by pre-existing rule or case authority expressly applicable to midtrial rulings on the sufficiency of the evidence. That requirement was not met here. The Commonwealth has failed to show that under state procedure as it existed at the time of petitioner's trial, the trial court's ruling on the motion for a required finding of not guilty was automatically, or even presumptively, nonfinal. At most it has shown that the ruling was wrong because the Commonwealth's evidence was, as a matter of law, sufficient. . . . But any contention that the Double Jeopardy Clause must itself (even absent provision by the State) leave open a way of correcting legal errors is at odds with the well established rule that the bar will attach to a pre-verdict acquittal that is patently wrong in law. See, e.g., *Smalis,* 476 U.S., at 144, n. 7; *Sanabria,* 437 U.S., at 68-69, 75, 78; *Martin Linen,* 430 U.S., at 571; *Fong Foo,* 369 U.S., at 143.[7]

Massachusetts argues that if the Double Jeopardy Clause does not allow for reconsideration, every erroneous grant of a directed-verdict motion will be unremediable, even one attributable to mistaken expression that is promptly corrected. We think not. Double-jeopardy principles have never been thought to bar the immediate repair of a genuine error in the announcement of an acquittal, even one rendered by a jury. See M. Friedland, Double Jeopardy 61 (1969); King v. Parkin, 1 Mood. 45, 46- 47, 168 Eng. Rep. 1179, 1180 (1824). And of course States can protect themselves still further against the "occasional errors" of law that the dissent thinks "inevitabl[e]" in the course of trial, by rendering midtrial acquittals nonfinal. (Massachusetts, as we have observed, has specifically provided for the correction of mistaken utterances or scrivener's errors, but not for the reconsideration of legal conclusions. See Mass. Rule Crim. Proc. 42 (2002).)

Prosecutors are not without protection against ill-considered acquittal rulings. States can and do craft procedural rules that allow trial judges "the maximum opportunity to consider with care a pending acquittal motion," *Martin Linen, supra,* at 574, including the option of deferring consideration until after the verdict. See, e.g., D.C. Super. Ct. Crim. Proc. Rule 29(b) (2003); N.Y. Crim. Proc. Law Ann. § 290.10(1)(b) (West 2002); W. Va. Rule Crim. Proc. 29(b) (2004). . . . Moreover, a prosecutor can seek to persuade the court to correct its legal error before it rules, or at least before the proceedings move forward. Indeed, the prosecutor in this case convinced the judge to reconsider her acquittal ruling on the basis of legal authority he had obtained during a 15-minute recess before closing arguments. See App. 71-72, 74. Had he sought a short continuance at the time of the acquittal motion, the matter could have been resolved satisfactorily before petitioner went forward with his case.

7. The dissent goes to great lengths to establish that there was no prejudice here, since the acquittal was legally wrong and the defendant was deprived of no available defense. But the Double Jeopardy Clause has never required prejudice beyond the very exposure to a second jeopardy. To put it differently: requiring someone to defend against a charge of which he has already been acquitted is prejudice per se for purposes of the Double Jeopardy Clause — even when the acquittal was erroneous because the evidence was sufficient. See, e.g., Sanabria v. United States, 437 U.S. 54, 77-78 (1978). Of course it is not even clear that the dissent's due-process analysis would acknowledge prejudice when a midtrial acquittal was correct when rendered, so long as evidence sufficient to sustain the charge was eventually introduced (after the acquittal and during the defendant's case). Our double-jeopardy cases make clear that an acquittal bars the prosecution from seeking "another opportunity to supply evidence which it failed to muster" before jeopardy terminated. Burks v. United States, 437 U.S. 1, 11 (1978).

The judgment of the Appeals Court of Massachusetts is reversed, and the case is remanded for further proceedings not inconsistent with this opinion.

JUSTICE GINSBURG, with whom CHIEF JUSTICE REHNQUIST, JUSTICE KENNEDY, and JUSTICE BREYER join, dissenting.

Does the Double Jeopardy Clause bar the States from allowing trial judges to reconsider a midtrial grant of a motion to acquit on one or more but fewer than all counts of an indictment? The Court unanimously answers "No." See *ante*, at 470 ("[A]s a general matter state law may prescribe that a judge's midtrial determination of the sufficiency of the State's proof can be reconsidered."). A State may provide for such reconsideration, the Court also recognizes, by legislation or by judicial rule, common-law decision, or exercise of supervisory power. According to the Appeals Court of Massachusetts, the State has so provided through its decisional law. See Commonwealth v. Haskell, 438 Mass. 790, 792, 784 N.E.2d 625, 628 (2003) ("A judge's power to reconsider his own decisions during the pendency of a case is firmly rooted in the common law. . . . "). The view held by the Massachusetts court on this issue is hardly novel. See, e.g., United States v. LoRusso, 695 F.2d 45, 53 (C.A.2 1982) ("A district court has the inherent power to reconsider and modify its interlocutory orders prior to the entry of judgment. . . . ").

Nevertheless, the trial court here was locked into its on-the-spot error, the Court maintains, because "the availability of reconsideration [had not] been plainly established by pre-existing rule or case authority expressly applicable to midtrial rulings on the sufficiency of the evidence." Otherwise, according to the Court, "[t]he Double Jeopardy Clause's guarantee [would] become a potential snare for those who reasonably rely upon it." *Ibid.*

I agree that, as a trial unfolds, a defendant must be accorded a timely, fully informed opportunity to meet the State's charges. I would so hold as a matter not of double jeopardy, but of due process. On the facts presented here, however, as the Massachusetts Appeals Court observed, see 58 Mass. App., at 171, 788 N. E. 2d, at 983, defendant-petitioner Smith suffered no prejudice fairly attributable to the trial court's error.

The trial judge in Smith's case acted impatiently and made a mistake at the close of the State's case. Cutting short the prosecutor's objections, she granted Smith's motion for a "required finding of not guilty" on one of the three charges contained in the indictment, unlawful possession of a firearm. She did so on the ground that the State had failed to prove an essential element of the crime, i.e., that the barrel of the gun Smith was charged with possessing was less than 16 inches. The ruling for Smith was endorsed on the motion and recorded on the docket, but it was not communicated to the jury.

The trial judge corrected her error the same day it was made. She did so in advance of closing arguments and her charge to the jury. The trial judge retracted her initial ruling and denied the motion for a required finding of not guilty because the prosecutor had called to her attention a decision of the Supreme Judicial Court of Massachusetts directly on point, Commonwealth v. Sperrazza, 372 Mass. 667, 363 N.E.2d 673 (1977). In that case, Massachusetts' highest court held that a jury may infer a barrel length of less than 16 inches from testimony that the weapon in question was a revolver or handgun. Id., at 670, 363 N. E. 2d, at 675. Here, there was such testimony. The victim in Smith's case had testified that the gun he saw in the defendant's hand was a ".32 or .38" caliber "pistol." The trial court's new ruling based on *Sperrazza* was entered on the docket, Smith did not move to reopen the case, and the jury convicted him on all charges.

Smith urges that our decision in Smalis v. Pennsylvania, 476 U.S. 140 (1986), controls this case. I disagree. In *Smalis,* the Court held that the Double Jeopardy Clause bars appellate review of a trial court's grant of a motion to acquit, because reversal would lead to a remand for further trial proceedings. *Id.*, at 146. An appeal, including an interlocutory appeal, moves a case from a court of first instance to an appellate forum, and necessarily signals that the trial court has ruled with finality on the appealed issue or issues. A trial court's reconsideration of its initial decision to grant a motion, on the other hand, occurs before the court of first instance has disassociated itself from the case or any issue in it. Trial courts have historically revisited midtrial rulings, . . . for the practical exigencies of trial mean that judges inevitably will commit occasional errors. In contrast, the government traditionally could pursue no appeal at any stage of a criminal case, however mistaken the trial court's pro-defense ruling. See United States v. Scott, 437 U.S. 82, 84-86 (1978) (discussing the evolution of the Government's right to appeal). This Court has long recognized the distinction between appeals and continuing proceedings before the initial tribunal prior to the rendition of a final adjudication. . . .

Nor is Massachusetts Rule of Criminal Procedure 25(a) dispositive here. That Rule states: "If a defendant's motion for a required finding of not guilty is made at the close of the Commonwealth's evidence, *it shall be ruled upon at that time*." (Emphasis added.) While Rule 25(a) plainly instructs an immediate ruling on the motion, it says nothing about reconsideration.

The Appeals Court of Massachusetts determined that Rule 25(a) did not place the incorrect midtrial ruling beyond the trial court's capacity to repair its error. Rule 25(a)'s demand for an immediate ruling rather than reservation of the question,[2] the Appeals Court said, "protects a defendant's right to insist that the Commonwealth present proof of every element of the crime with which he is charged before he decides whether to rest or to introduce proof." 58 Mass. App., at 171, 788 N. E. 2d, at 982-983.[3] That protection was accorded the defendant here, the court observed, for the State's evidence, presented before the "required finding of not guilty" motion was made and granted, in fact sufficed to prove every element of the firearm possession charge. See 58 Mass. App., at 171, 788 N. E. 2d, at 983. Rule 25(a) does not import more, the Appeals Court indicated. Because the jury remained seated with no break in the trial, and the defendant retained the opportunity to counter the State's case,[4] that court concluded, neither Rule 25(a) nor the Double Jeopardy Clause froze as final the erroneous midtrial ruling on the firearm possession charge. I would not pretend to comprehend Rule 25(a) or Massachusetts' decisional law regarding state practice better than the Massachusetts Appeals Court did.

In sum, Smith was subjected to a single, unbroken trial proceeding in which he was denied no opportunity to air his defense before presentation of the case to the jury. I would not deny prosecutors in such circumstances, based on a trial judge's temporary error, *one* full and fair opportunity to present the State's case.

NOTES AND QUESTIONS

1. Both Justice Scalia's majority opinion and Justice Ginsburg's dissent cite and discuss Smalis v. Pennsylvania, 476 U.S. 140 (1986). In *Smalis,*

2. Cf. Fed. Rule Crim. Proc. 29(b) (providing that a trial court may reserve decision on a defendant's challenge to the sufficiency of the evidence until after the jury has returned a verdict). Several States follow the federal model. See, e.g., Alaska Rule Crim. Proc. 29 (b) (2004); Del. Super. Ct. Rule Crim. Proc. 29(b) (2004); Iowa Rule Crim. Proc. 2.19(8)(b) (2004); N. Y. Crim. Proc. Law Ann. § 290.10(1) (West 2002); W. Va. Rule Crim. Proc. 29(b) (2004).

3. Counsel for petitioner suggested at oral argument that the protection is more theoretical than real, for "what [judges] do as . . . a matter of practice in Massachusetts is they simply deny [the motion]." Tr. of Oral Arg. 56 (also noting that the motion to acquit may be renewed at the close of defendant's case and after the jury has returned a verdict).

4. The Court hypothesizes that dismissal of one count might affect a defendant's course regarding the undismissed charges. The Appeals Court addressed that prospect concretely: Defendant Smith "has not suggested that the initial allowance of the motion affected his trial strategy with regard to the other charges." 58 Mass. App. 166, 171, 788 N.E.2d 977, 983 (2003). Further, there is not even the slightest suggestion that Smith's codefendant, who was acquitted by the jury, "alter[ed] [her case] in harmful ways."

the defendants were charged with homicide and reckless endangerment in connection with a fire of a building they owned. At the close of the government's case-in-chief, the defendants filed for a demurrer, on the ground that the evidence was insufficient to support a conviction. The trial judge (there was no jury—does that matter?) granted the demurrer. The government appealed, arguing that under Pennsylvania law the demurrer had the status of a procedural dismissal, not an acquittal. The Supreme Court held, unanimously, that the trial judge's ruling amounted to an acquittal and was final and unappealable; Justice White's opinion in *Smalis* emphasized that, had the appeal been allowed and had the government prevailed, further factfinding would have been required. Which side in *Smith* does *Smalis* help?

2. The trial judge in *Smith* dismissed the firearm charge, then reconsidered her ruling and reinstated that charge. According to the Supreme Court, that constituted double jeopardy—but only because Massachusetts law did not clearly authorize reconsideration of the trial judge's ruling. The idea is that Smith might have relied on that ruling to his detriment; apparently, the Double Jeopardy Clause protects that reliance interest. Why? The dissenters suggest that any reliance interest Smith might have is better seen as a problem for the Due Process Clause, not for double jeopardy. Are you persuaded? Does it matter where the relevant interest is located, as long as it receives constitutional protection?

The answer to that last question is yes. Reread note 7 in Justice Scalia's opinion. As he correctly notes, "the Double Jeopardy Clause has never required prejudice beyond the very exposure to a second jeopardy." Due process is different; prejudice standards are the norm there. So perhaps the disagreement between Justices Scalia and Ginsburg boils down to this question: Should someone in Smith's position be given relief only if he has suffered some prejudice—only if, say, he can point to some way in which he detrimentally relied on the trial judge's initial ruling? What is the best way to answer that question?

3. Why should federal double jeopardy claims turn on the clarity (or lack thereof) of state law? Doesn't Justice Ginsburg have a good point when she criticizes the majority for overturning Massachusetts courts on Massachusetts law? Aren't state courts the best judges of how clear (or not) their own states' laws are?

Suppose Massachusetts law clearly allowed for motions for reconsideration—as the dissent says it did but the majority says it didn't. Now suppose the trial judge in *Smith* had dismissed the firearm charge and said "this decision is final and irrevocable. I will not, under any circumstances, entertain a motion for reconsideration." Later in the trial, the prosecution moves to reconsider, points out the relevant state law, and the trial judge corrects her mistake. Does Smith have a valid double jeopardy claim now? Does *Fong Foo* bear on this question?

4. Consider another hypothetical. Suppose *Smith* were a bench trial, not a jury trial; suppose further that, at the trial's conclusion, the trial judge acquitted Smith, after which the prosecution immediately moved for reconsideration. Finally, suppose the trial judge granted the prosecutor's motion — the judge concluded that she had simply been wrong about the evidence on the length of the gun barrel — vacated her own judgment of acquittal, and entered a judgment of conviction. Assuming Massachusetts law authorized such a procedure — as clearly as is necessary — would Smith have a valid double jeopardy claim? Should he?

5. Think again about *Fong Foo*. The trial judge in that case ordered judgment for defendants based on a patently wrong view of the relevant procedural law: Contrary to what the trial judge apparently assumed, there was nothing wrong with the prosecutor conferring with his own witness during a recess. That erroneous judgment was final and unreviewable. In *Smith,* the trial judge made an error that one can plausibly characterize as substantive: She misunderstood the proper construction of the gun barrel length element in the firearm offense. *That* judgment was *not* deemed final. Does that sound right? Recall United States v. Scott, 437 U.S. 82 (1978), where the Court distinguished between (procedural) dismissals and (substantive) acquittals. Is *Smith* consistent with *Scott*?

Chapter 15

Appellate and Collateral Review

A. Appellate Review

5. Prejudice and Harmless Error

Insert the following material at the end of Note 4, page 1570:

In Washington v. Recuenco, 548 U.S. 212 (2006), the Court relied on *Neder* to hold that *Blakely/Booker* errors (involving the failure to submit to a jury, under a "beyond reasonable doubt" standard, the existence of certain sentencing factors that operate functionally as elements of a new, enhanced crime) are subject to "harmless error" review.

B. Collateral Review

2. The Nature and Purposes of Federal Habeas

Insert the following note after Note 4 on page 1606:

5. In Boumediene v. Bush, 553 U.S. 723 (2008), the Supreme Court, in a hotly contested 5-4 decision, ruled that aliens held as "enemy combatants" at Guantanamo Bay have the constitutional right, protected by the Suspension Clause, to file a habeas corpus petition in federal court challenging their status as an "enemy combatant" and thus their continued detention. The Court also held that the procedures set forth by Congress, in the Detainee Treatment Act of 2005 (DTA), for reviewing such challenges to alleged "enemy combatant" status before so-called Combatant Status Review Tribunals (CSRTs) are not an "adequate substitute" for a traditional habeas corpus action, and thus cannot suffice to satisfy the Suspension Clause. Although the Court did not purport to set

forth a comprehensive guide to compliance with the Suspension Clause, it did note that, at a minimum:

> [T]he privilege of habeas corpus entitles the prisoner to a meaningful opportunity to demonstrate that he is being held pursuant to "the erroneous application or interpretation" of relevant law. *St. Cyr*, 533 U.S. [289], at 302 [(2001)]. And the habeas court must have the power to order the conditional release of an individual unlawfully detained—though release need not be the exclusive remedy and is not the appropriate one in every case in which the writ is granted."

Because the CSRTs, as provided under the DTA, could not meet these minimum requirements, the Court concluded that the denial of access to habeas corpus would violate the Suspension Clause.

Although the situation of aliens held in executive detention at Guantanamo Bay is not entirely analogous to that of prisoners convicted of crimes in judicial proceedings, the *Boumediene* case is nonetheless significant in the context of a criminal procedure course, mostly because of what the Court says therein about the historical role and significance of the writ of habeas corpus, and about the meaning and scope of the Suspension Clause.

Selected Statutes and Rules

Federal Rules of Criminal Procedure

Rule 6. The Grand Jury

(a) Summoning a Grand Jury.

(1) In General. When the public interest so requires, the court must order that one or more grand juries be summoned. A grand jury must have 16 to 23 members, and the court must order that enough legally qualified persons be summoned to meet this requirement.

(2) Alternate Jurors. When a grand jury is selected, the court may also select alternate jurors. Alternate jurors must have the same qualifications and be selected in the same manner as any other juror. Alternate jurors replace jurors in the same sequence in which the alternates were selected. An alternate juror who replaces a juror is subject to the same challenges, takes the same oath, and has the same authority as the other jurors.

(b) Objection to the Grand Jury or to a Grand Juror.

(1) Challenges. Either the government or a defendant may challenge the grand jury on the ground that it was not lawfully drawn, summoned, or selected, and may challenge an individual juror on the ground that the juror is not legally qualified.

(2) Motion to Dismiss an Indictment. A party may move to dismiss the indictment based on an objection to the grand jury or on an individual juror's lack of legal qualification, unless the court has previously ruled on the same objection under Rule 6(b)(1). The motion to dismiss is governed by 28 U.S.C. § 1867(e). The court must not dismiss the indictment on the ground that a grand juror was not legally qualified if the record shows that at least 12 qualified jurors concurred in the indictment.

(c) Foreperson and Deputy Foreperson. The court will appoint one juror as the foreperson and another as the deputy foreperson. In the foreperson's absence, the deputy foreperson will act as the foreperson. The foreperson may administer oaths and affirmations and will sign all indictments. The foreperson—or another juror designated by the foreperson—will record the number of jurors concurring in every indictment and will file the record with the clerk, but the record may not be made public unless the court so orders.

(d) Who May Be Present.

(1) While the Grand Jury Is in Session. The following persons may be present while the grand jury is in session: attorneys for the government, the witness being questioned, interpreters when needed, and a court reporter or an operator of a recording device.

(2) During Deliberations and Voting. No person other than the jurors, and any interpreter needed to assist a hearing-impaired or speech-impaired juror, may be present while the grand jury is deliberating or voting.

(e) Recording and Disclosing the Proceedings.

(1) Recording the Proceedings. Except while the grand jury is deliberating or voting, all proceedings must be recorded by a court reporter or by a suitable recording device. But the validity of a prosecution is not affected by the unintentional failure to make a recording. Unless the court orders otherwise, an attorney for the government will retain control of the recording, the reporter's notes, and any transcript prepared from those notes.

(2) Secrecy.

(A) No obligation of secrecy may be imposed on any person except in accordance with Rule 6(e)(2)(B).

(B) Unless these rules provide otherwise, the following persons must not disclose a matter occurring before the grand jury:

(i) a grand juror;

(ii) an interpreter;

(iii) a court reporter;

(iv) an operator of a recording device;

(v) a person who transcribes recorded testimony;

(vi) an attorney for the government; or

(vii) a person to whom disclosure is made under Rule 6 (e)(3)(A)(ii) or (iii).

(3) Exceptions.

(A) Disclosure of a grand-jury matter—other than the grand jury's deliberations or any grand juror's vote—may be made to:

(i) an attorney for the government for use in performing that attorney's duty;

(ii) any government personnel—including those of a state, state subdivision, Indian tribe, or foreign government—that an attorney for the government considers necessary to assist in performing that attorney's duty to enforce federal criminal law; or

(iii) a person authorized by 18 U.S.C. § 3322.

(B) A person to whom information is disclosed under Rule 6 (e)(3)(A)(ii) may use that information only to assist an attorney for the government in performing that attorney's duty to enforce federal criminal law. An attorney for the government must promptly provide the court that impaneled the grand jury with the names of all persons to whom a disclosure has been made, and must certify that the attorney has advised those persons of their obligation of secrecy under this rule.

(C) An attorney for the government may disclose any grand-jury matter to another federal grand jury.

(D) An attorney for the government may disclose any grand-jury matter involving foreign intelligence, counterintelligence (as defined in 50 U.S.C. § 401a), or foreign intelligence information (as defined in Rule 6(e)(3)(D)(iii)) to any federal law enforcement, intelligence, protective, immigration, national defense, or national security official to assist the official receiving the information in the performance of that official's duties. An attorney for the government may also disclose any grand-jury matter involving, within the United States or elsewhere, a threat of attack or other grave hostile acts of a foreign power or its agent, a threat of domestic or international sabotage or terrorism, or clandestine intelligence gathering activities by an intelligence service or network of a foreign power or by its agent, to any appropriate federal, state, state subdivision, Indian tribal, or foreign government official, for the purpose of preventing or responding to such threat or activities.

(i) Any official who receives information under Rule 6(e)(3)(D) may use the information only as necessary in the conduct of that person's official duties subject to any limitations on the unauthorized disclosure of such information. Any state, state subdivision, Indian tribal, or foreign government official who receives information under Rule 6(e)(3)(D) may use the information only in a manner consistent with any guidelines issued by the Attorney General and the Director of National Intelligence.

(ii) Within a reasonable time after disclosure is made under Rule 6(e)(3)(D), an attorney for the government must file, under seal, a notice with the court in the district where the grand jury convened stating that such information was disclosed and the departments, agencies, or entities to which the disclosure was made.

(iii) As used in Rule 6(e)(3)(D), the term "foreign intelligence information" means:

(a) information, whether or not it concerns a United States person, that relates to the ability of the United States to protect against—

- actual or potential attack or other grave hostile acts of a foreign power or its agent;
- sabotage or international terrorism by a foreign power or its agent; or
- clandestine intelligence activities by an intelligence service or network of a foreign power or by its agent; or

(b) information, whether or not it concerns a United States person, with respect to a foreign power or foreign territory that relates to—

- the national defense or the security of the United States; or
- the conduct of the foreign affairs of the United States.

(E) The court may authorize disclosure—at a time, in a manner, and subject to any other conditions that it directs—of a grand-jury matter:

(i) preliminarily to or in connection with a judicial proceeding;

(ii) at the request of a defendant who shows that a ground may exist to dismiss the indictment because of a matter that occurred before the grand jury;

(iii) at the request of the government, when sought by a foreign court or prosecutor for use in an official criminal investigation;

(iv) at the request of the government if it shows that the matter may disclose a violation of State, Indian tribal, or foreign criminal law, as long as the disclosure is to an appropriate state, state-subdivision, Indian tribal, or foreign government official for the purpose of enforcing that law; or

(v) at the request of the government if it shows that the matter may disclose a violation of military criminal law under the Uniform Code of Military Justice, as long as the disclosure is to an appropriate military official for the purpose of enforcing that law.

(F) A petition to disclose a grand-jury matter under Rule 6 (e)(3)(E)(i) must be filed in the district where the grand jury convened. Unless the hearing is ex parte—as it may be when the government is the petitioner—the petitioner must serve the petition on, and the court must afford a reasonable opportunity to appear and be heard to:

(i) an attorney for the government;

(ii) the parties to the judicial proceeding; and

(iii) any other person whom the court may designate.

(G) If the petition to disclose arises out of a judicial proceeding in another district, the petitioned court must transfer the petition to the other court unless the petitioned court can reasonably determine whether disclosure is proper. If the petitioned court decides to transfer, it must send to the transferee court the material sought to be disclosed, if feasible, and a written evaluation of the need for continued grand-jury secrecy. The transferee court must afford those persons identified in Rule 6(e)(3)(F) a reasonable opportunity to appear and be heard.

(4) Sealed Indictment. The magistrate judge to whom an indictment is returned may direct that the indictment be kept secret until the defendant is in custody or has been released pending trial. The clerk must then seal the indictment, and no person may disclose the indictment's existence except as necessary to issue or execute a warrant or summons.

(5) Closed Hearing. Subject to any right to an open hearing in a contempt proceeding, the court must close any hearing to the extent necessary to prevent disclosure of a matter occurring before a grand jury.

(6) Sealed Records. Records, orders, and subpoenas relating to grand-jury proceedings must be kept under seal to the extent and as long as necessary to prevent the unauthorized disclosure of a matter occurring before a grand jury.

(7) Contempt. A knowing violation of Rule 6, or of any guidelines jointly issued by the Attorney General and the Director of National Intelligence under Rule 6, may be punished as a contempt of court.

(f) Indictment and Return. A grand jury may indict only if at least 12 jurors concur. The grand jury—or its foreperson or deputy foreperson—must return the indictment to a magistrate judge in open court. If a complaint or information is pending against the defendant and 12 jurors do not concur in the indictment, the foreperson must promptly and in writing report the lack of concurrence to the magistrate judge.

(g) Discharging the Grand Jury. A grand jury must serve until the court discharges it, but it may serve more than 18 months only if the court, having determined that an extension is in the public interest, extends the grand jury's service. An extension may be granted for no more than 6 months, except as otherwise provided by statute.

(h) Excusing a Juror. At any time, for good cause, the court may excuse a juror either temporarily or permanently, and if permanently, the court may impanel an alternate juror in place of the excused juror.

(i) "Indian Tribe" Defined. "Indian tribe" means an Indian tribe recognized by the Secretary of the Interior on a list published in the Federal Register under 25 U.S.C. § 479a-1.

Rule 8. Joinder of Offenses or Defendants

(a) Joinder of Offenses. The indictment or information may charge a defendant in separate counts with two or more offenses if the offenses charged— whether felonies or misdemeanors or both—are of the same or similar character, or are based on the same act or transaction, or are connected with or constitute parts of a common scheme or plan.

(b) Joinder of Defendants. The indictment or information may charge two or more defendants if they are alleged to have participated in the same act or transaction, or in the same series of acts or transactions, constituting an offense or offenses. The defendants may be charged in one or more counts together or separately. All defendants need not be charged in each count.

Rule 11. Pleas

(a) Entering a Plea.

(1) In General. A defendant may plead not guilty, guilty, or (with the court's consent) nolo contendere.

(2) Conditional Plea. With the consent of the court and the government, a defendant may enter a conditional plea of guilty or nolo contendere, reserving in writing the right to have an appellate court review an adverse determination of a specified pretrial motion. A defendant who prevails on appeal may then withdraw the plea.

(3) Nolo Contendere Plea. Before accepting a plea of nolo contendere, the court must consider the parties' views and the public interest in the effective administration of justice.

(4) Failure to Enter a Plea. If a defendant refuses to enter a plea or if a defendant organization fails to appear, the court must enter a plea of not guilty.

(b) Considering and Accepting a Guilty or Nolo Contendere Plea.

(1) Advising and Questioning the Defendant. Before the court accepts a plea of guilty or nolo contendere, the defendant may be placed under oath and the court must address the defendant personally in open court. During this address, the court must inform the defendant of, and determine that the defendant understands, the following:

(A) the government's right, in a prosecution for perjury or false statement, to use against the defendant any statement that the defendant gives under oath;

(B) the right to plead not guilty, or having already so pleaded, to persist in that plea;

(C) the right to a jury trial;

(D) the right to be represented by counsel—and, if necessary, have the court appoint counsel—at trial and at every other stage of the proceeding;

(E) the right at trial to confront and cross-examine adverse witnesses, to be protected from compelled self-incrimination, to testify and present evidence, and to compel the attendance of witnesses;

(F) the defendant's waiver of these trial rights if the court accepts a plea of guilty or nolo contendere;

(G) the nature of each charge to which the defendant is pleading;

(H) any maximum possible penalty, including imprisonment, fine, and term of supervised release;

(I) any mandatory minimum penalty;

(J) any applicable forfeiture;

(K) the court's authority to order restitution;

(L) the court's obligation to impose a special assessment;

(M) the court's obligation to apply the Sentencing Guidelines, and the court's discretion to depart from those guidelines under some circumstances; and

(N) the terms of any plea-agreement provision waiving the right to appeal or to collaterally attack the sentence.

(2) Ensuring That a Plea Is Voluntary. Before accepting a plea of guilty or nolo contendere, the court must address the defendant personally in open court and determine that the plea is voluntary and did not result from force, threats, or promises (other than promises in a plea agreement).

(3) Determining the Factual Basis for a Plea. Before entering judgment on a guilty plea, the court must determine that there is a factual basis for the plea.

(c) Plea Agreement Procedure.

(1) In General. An attorney for the government and the defendant's attorney, or the defendant when proceeding pro se, may discuss and reach a plea agreement. The court must not participate in these discussions. If the defendant pleads guilty or nolo contendere to either a charged offense or a lesser or related offense, the plea agreement may specify that an attorney for the government will:

(A) not bring, or will move to dismiss, other charges;

(B) recommend, or agree not to oppose the defendant's request, that a particular sentence or sentencing range is appropriate or that a particular provision of the Sentencing Guidelines, or policy statement, or sentencing factor does or does not apply (such a recommendation or request does not bind the court); or

(C) agree that a specific sentence or sentencing range is the appropriate disposition of the case, or that a particular provision of the Sentencing Guidelines, policy statement, or sentencing factor does or does not apply (such a recommendation or request binds the court once the court accepts the plea agreement).

(2) Disclosing a Plea Agreement. The parties must disclose the plea agreement in open court when the plea is offered, unless the court for good cause allows the parties to disclose the plea agreement in camera.

(3) Judicial Consideration of a Plea Agreement.

(A) To the extent the plea agreement is of the type specified in Rule 11(c)(l)(A) or (C), the court may accept the agreement, reject it, or defer a decision until the court has reviewed the presentence report.

(B) To the extent the plea agreement is of the type specified in Rule 11(c)(l)(B), the court must advise the defendant that the defendant has no right to withdraw the plea if the court does not follow the recommendation or request.

(4) Accepting a Plea Agreement. If the court accepts the plea agreement, it must inform the defendant that to the extent the plea agreement is of the type specified in Rule 11(c)(1)(A) or (C), the agreed disposition will be included in the judgment.

(5) Rejecting a Plea Agreement. If the court rejects a plea agreement containing provisions of the type specified in Rule 11 (c)(1)(A) or (C), the court must do the following on the record and in open court (or, for good cause, in camera):

(A) inform the parties that the court rejects the plea agreement;

(B) advise the defendant personally that the court is not required to follow the plea agreement and give the defendant an opportunity to withdraw the plea; and

(C) advise the defendant personally that if the plea is not withdrawn, the court may dispose of the case less favorably toward the defendant than the plea agreement contemplated.

(d) Withdrawing a Guilty or Nolo Contendere Plea. A defendant may withdraw a plea of guilty or nolo contendere:

(1) before the court accepts the plea, for any reason or no reason; or

(2) after the court accepts the plea but before it imposes sentence if:

(A) the court rejects a plea agreement under Rule 11(c)(5); or

(B) the defendant can show a fair and just reason for requesting the withdrawal.

(e) Finality of a Guilty or Nolo Contendere Plea. After the court imposes sentence, the defendant may not withdraw a plea of guilty or nolo contendere, and the plea may be set aside only on direct appeal or collateral attack.

(f) Admissibility or Inadmissibility of a Plea, Plea Discussions, and Related Statements. The admissibility or inadmissibility of a plea, a plea discussion, and any related statement is governed by Federal Rule of Evidence 410.

(g) Recording the Proceedings. The proceedings during which the defendant enters a plea must be recorded by a court reporter or by a suitable recording device. If there is a guilty plea or a nolo contendere plea, the record must include the inquiries and advice to the defendant required under Rule 11(b) and (c).

(h) Harmless Error. A variance from the requirements of this rule is harmless error if it does not affect substantial rights.

Rule 14. Relief from Prejudicial Joinder

(a) Relief. If the joinder of offenses or defendants in an indictment, an information, or a consolidation for trial appears to prejudice a defendant or the government, the court may order separate trials of counts, sever the defendants' trials, or provide any other relief that justice requires.

(b) Defendant's Statements. Before ruling on a defendant's motion to sever, the court may order an attorney for the government to deliver to the court for in camera inspection any defendant's statement that the government intends to use as evidence.

Rule 16. Discovery and Inspection

(a) Government's Disclosure.

(1) Information Subject to Disclosure.

(A) Defendant's Oral Statement. Upon a defendant's request, the government must disclose to the defendant the substance of any relevant oral statement made by the defendant, before or after arrest, in response to interrogation by a person the defendant knew was a government agent if the government intends to use the statement at trial.

(B) Defendant's Written or Recorded Statement. Upon a defendant's request, the government must disclose to the defendant, and make available for inspection, copying, or photographing, all of the following:

(i) any relevant written or recorded statement by the defendant if:

- the statement is within the government's possession, custody, or control; and
- the attorney for the government knows—or through due diligence could know—that the statement exists;

(ii) the portion of any written record containing the substance of any relevant oral statement made before or after arrest if the defendant made the statement in response to interrogation by a person the defendant knew was a government agent; and

(iii) the defendant's recorded testimony before a grand jury relating to the charged offense.

(C) Organizational Defendant. Upon a defendant's request, if the defendant is an organization, the government must disclose to the defendant any statement described in Rule 16(a)(l)(A) and (B) if the government contends that the person making the statement:

(i) was legally able to bind the defendant regarding the subject of the statement because of that person's position as the defendant's director, officer, employee, or agent; or

(ii) was personally involved in the alleged conduct constituting the offense and was legally able to bind the defendant regarding that conduct because of that person's position as the defendant's director, officer, employee, or agent.

(D) Defendant's Prior Record. Upon a defendant's request, the government must furnish the defendant with a copy of the defendant's prior criminal record that is within the government's possession, custody, or control if the attorney for the government knows—or through due diligence could know—that the record exists.

(E) Documents and Objects. Upon a defendant's request, the government must permit the defendant to inspect and to copy or photograph books, papers, documents, data, photographs, tangible objects, buildings or places, or copies or portions of any of these items, if the item is within the government's possession, custody, or control and:

(i) the item is material to preparing the defense;

(ii) the government intends to use the item in its case-in-chief at trial; or

(iii) the item was obtained from or belongs to the defendant.

(F) Reports of Examinations and Tests. Upon a defendant's request, the government must permit a defendant to inspect and to copy or photograph the results or reports of any physical or mental examination and of any scientific test or experiment if:

(i) the item is within the government's possession, custody, or control;

(ii) the attorney for the government knows—or through due diligence could know—that the item exists; and

(iii) the item is material to preparing the defense or the government intends to use the item in its case-in-chief at trial.

(G) Expert Witnesses. At the defendant's request, the government must give to the defendant a written summary of any testimony that the government intends to use under Rules 702, 703, or 705 of the Federal Rules of Evidence during its case-in-chief at trial. If the government requests discovery under subdivision (b)(1)(C)(ii) and the defendant complies, the government must, at the defendant's request, give to the defendant a written summary of testimony that the government intends to use under Rules 702, 703, or 705 of the Federal Rules of Evidence as evidence at trial on the issue of the defendant's mental condition. The summary provided under this subparagraph must describe the witness's opinions, the bases and reasons for those opinions, and the witness's qualifications.

(2) Information Not Subject to Disclosure. Except as Rule 16 (a)(1) provides otherwise, this rule does not authorize the discovery or inspection of reports, memoranda, or other internal government documents made by an attorney for the government or other government agent in connection with investigating or prosecuting the case. Nor does this rule authorize the discovery or inspection of statements made by prospective government witnesses except as provided in 18 U.S.C. §3500.[2]

(3) Grand Jury Transcripts. This rule does not apply to the discovery or inspection of a grand jury's recorded proceedings, except as provided in Rules 6, 12(h), 16(a)(l), and 26.2.

(b) Defendant's Disclosure.

(1) Information Subject to Disclosure.

(A) Documents and Objects. If a defendant requests disclosure under Rule 16(a)(1)(E) and the government complies, then the defendant must permit the government, upon request, to inspect and to copy or photograph books, papers, documents, data, photographs, tangible objects, buildings or places, or copies or portions of any of these items if:

(i) the item is within the defendant's possession, custody, or control; and

2. For a description of § 3500, see Note 2 at page 1136 in the casebook.—Eds.

(ii) the defendant intends to use the item in the defendant's case-in-chief at trial.

(B) Reports of Examinations and Tests. If a defendant requests disclosure under Rule 16(a)(1)(F) and the government complies, the defendant must permit the government, upon request, to inspect and to copy or photograph the results or reports of any physical or mental examination and of any scientific test or experiment if:

(i) the item is within the defendant's possession, custody, or control; and

(ii) the defendant intends to use the item in the defendant's case-in-chief at trial, or intends to call the witness who prepared the report and the report relates to the witness's testimony.

(C) Expert Witnesses. The defendant must, at the government's request, give to the government a written summary of any testimony that the defendant intends to use under Rules 702, 703, or 705 of the Federal Rules of Evidence as evidence at trial, if —

(i) the defendant requests disclosure under subdivision (a)(1)(G) and the government complies; or

(ii) the defendant has given notice under Rule 12.2(b) of an intent to present expert testimony on the defendant's mental condition.

This summary must describe the witness's opinions, the bases and reasons for those opinions, and the witness's qualifications[.]

(2) Information Not Subject to Disclosure. Except for scientific or medical reports, Rule 16(b)(1) does not authorize discovery or inspection of:

(A) reports, memoranda, or other documents made by the defendant, or the defendant's attorney or agent, during the case's investigation or defense; or

(B) a statement made to the defendant, or the defendant's attorney or agent, by:

(i) the defendant;

(ii) a government or defense witness; or

(iii) a prospective government or defense witness.

(c) Continuing Duty to Disclose. A party who discovers additional evidence or material before or during trial must promptly disclose its existence to the other party or the court if:

(1) the evidence or material is subject to discovery or inspection under this rule; and

(2) the other party previously requested, or the court ordered, its production.

(d) Regulating Discovery.

(1) Protective and Modifying Orders. At any time the court may, for good cause, deny, restrict, or defer discovery or inspection, or grant other appropriate relief. The court may permit a party to show good cause by a written statement that the court will inspect ex parte. If relief is granted, the court must preserve the entire text of the party's statement under seal.

(2) Failure to Comply. If a party fails to comply with this rule, the court may:

(A) order that party to permit the discovery or inspection; specify its time, place, and manner; and prescribe other just terms and conditions;

(B) grant a continuance;

(C) prohibit that party from introducing the undisclosed evidence; or

(D) enter any other order that is just under the circumstances.

Rule 26.2. Producing a Witness's Statement

(a) Motion to Produce. After a witness other than the defendant has testified on direct examination, the court, on motion of a party who did not call the witness, must order an attorney for the government or the defendant and the defendant's attorney to produce, for the examination and use of the moving party, any statement of the witness that is in their possession and that relates to the subject matter of the witness's testimony.

(b) Producing the Entire Statement. If the entire statement relates to the subject matter of the witness's testimony, the court must order that the statement be delivered to the moving party.

(c) Producing a Redacted Statement. If the party who called the witness claims that the statement contains information that is privileged or does not relate to the subject matter of the witness's testimony, the court must inspect the statement in camera. After excising any privileged or unrelated portions, the court must order delivery of the redacted statement to the moving party. If the defendant objects to an excision, the court must preserve the entire statement with the excised portion indicated, under seal, as part of the record.

(d) Recess to Examine a Statement. The court may recess the proceedings to allow time for a party to examine the statement and prepare for its use.

(e) Sanction for Failure to Produce or Deliver a Statement. If the party who called the witness disobeys an order to produce or deliver a statement, the court must strike the witness's testimony from the record. If an attorney for the government disobeys the order, the court must declare a mistrial if justice so requires.

(f) "Statement" Defined. As used in this rule, a witness's "statement" means:

(1) a written statement that the witness makes and signs, or otherwise adopts or approves;

(2) a substantially verbatim, contemporaneously recorded recital of the witness's oral statement that is contained in any recording or any transcription of a recording; or

(3) the witness's statement to a grand jury, however taken or recorded, or a transcription of such a statement.

(g) Scope. This rule applies at trial, at a suppression hearing under Rule 12, and to the extent specified in the following rules:

(1) Rule 5.1(h) (preliminary hearing);

(2) Rule 32(i)(2) (sentencing);

(3) Rule 32.1(e) (hearing to revoke or modify probation or supervised release);

(4) Rule 46(j) (detention hearing); and

(5) Rule 8 of the Rules Governing Proceedings under 28 U.S.C. §2255.

Rule 41. Search and Seizure

(a) Scope and Definitions.

(1) Scope. This rule does not modify any statute regulating search or seizure or the issuance and execution of a search warrant in special circumstances.

(2) Definitions. The following definitions apply under this rule:

(A) "Property" includes documents, books, papers, any other tangible objects, and information.

(B) "Daytime" means the hours between 6:00 A.M. and 10:00 P.M. according to local time.

(C) "Federal law enforcement officer" means a government agent (other than an attorney for the government) who is engaged in enforcing the criminal laws and is within any category of officers authorized by the Attorney General to request a search warrant.

(b) Authority to Issue a Warrant. At the request of a federal law enforcement officer or an attorney for the government:

(1) a magistrate judge with authority in the district—or if none is reasonably available, a judge of a state court of record in the district—has authority to issue a warrant to search for and seize a person or property located within the district;

(2) a magistrate judge with authority in the district has authority to issue a warrant for a person or property outside the district if the person or property is located within the district when the warrant is issued but might move or be moved outside the district before the warrant is executed; and

(3) a magistrate judge—in an investigation of domestic terrorism or international terrorism (as defined in 18 U.S.C. §2331)—having authority in any district in which activities related to the terrorism may have occurred, may issue a warrant for a person or property within or outside that district

(c) Persons or Property Subject to Search or Seizure. A warrant may be issued for any of the following:

(1) evidence of a crime;

(2) contraband, fruits of crime, or other items illegally possessed;

(3) property designed for use, intended for use, or used in committing a crime; or

(4) a person to be arrested or a person who is unlawfully restrained.

(d) Obtaining a Warrant.

(1) Probable Cause. After receiving an affidavit or other information, a magistrate judge or a judge of a state court of record must issue the warrant if there is probable cause to search for and seize a person or property under Rule 41(c).

(2) Requesting a Warrant in the Presence of a Judge.

(A) Warrant on an Affidavit. When a federal law enforcement officer or an attorney for the government presents an affidavit in support of a warrant, the judge may require the affiant to appear personally and may examine under oath the affiant and any witness the affiant produces.

(B) Warrant on Sworn Testimony. The judge may wholly or partially dispense with a written affidavit and base a warrant on sworn testimony if doing so is reasonable under the circumstances.

(C) Recording Testimony. Testimony taken in support of a warrant must be recorded by a court reporter or by a suitable recording device, and the judge must file the transcript or recording with the clerk, along with any affidavit.

(3) Requesting a Warrant by Telephonic or Other Means.

(A) In General. A magistrate judge may issue a warrant based on information communicated by telephone or other appropriate means, including facsimile transmission.

(B) Recording Testimony. Upon learning that an applicant is requesting a warrant, a magistrate judge must:

(i) place under oath the applicant and any person on whose testimony the application is based; and

(ii) make a verbatim record of the conversation with a suitable recording device, if available, or by a court reporter, or in writing.

(C) Certifying Testimony. The magistrate judge must have any recording or court reporter's notes transcribed, certify the transcription's accuracy, and file a copy of the record and the transcription with the clerk. Any written verbatim record must be signed by the magistrate judge and filed with the clerk.

(D) Suppression Limited. Absent a finding of bad faith, evidence obtained from a warrant issued under Rule 41(d)(3)(A) is not subject to suppression on the ground that issuing the warrant in that manner was unreasonable under the circumstances.

(e) Issuing the Warrant.

(1) In General. The magistrate judge or a judge of a state court of record must issue the warrant to an officer authorized to execute it.

(2) Contents of the Warrant. The warrant must identify the person or property to be searched, identify any person or property to be seized, and designate the magistrate judge to whom it must be returned. The warrant must command the officer to:

(A) execute the warrant within a specified time no longer than 10 days;

(B) execute the warrant during the daytime, unless the judge for good cause expressly authorizes execution at another time; and

(C) return the warrant to the magistrate judge designated in the warrant.

(3) Warrant by Telephonic or Other Means. If a magistrate judge decides to proceed under Rule 41(d)(3)(A), the following additional procedures apply:

(A) Preparing a Proposed Duplicate Original Warrant. The applicant must prepare a "proposed duplicate original warrant" and must read or otherwise transmit the contents of that document verbatim to the magistrate judge.

(B) Preparing an Original Warrant. The magistrate judge must enter the contents of the proposed duplicate original warrant into an original warrant.

(C) Modifications. The magistrate judge may direct the applicant to modify the proposed duplicate original warrant. In that case, the judge must also modify the original warrant.

(D) Signing the Original Warrant and the Duplicate Original Warrant. Upon determining to issue the warrant, the magistrate judge must immediately sign the original warrant, enter on its face the exact time it is issued, and direct the applicant to sign the judge's name on the duplicate original warrant.

(f) Executing and Returning the Warrant.

(1) Noting the Time. The officer executing the warrant must enter on its face the exact date and time it is executed.

(2) Inventory. An officer present during the execution of the warrant must prepare and verify an inventory of any property seized. The officer must do so in the presence of another officer and the person from whom, or from whose premises, the property was taken. If either one is not present, the officer must prepare and verify the inventory in the presence of at least one other credible person.

(3) Receipt. The officer executing the warrant must:

(A) give a copy of the warrant and a receipt for the property taken to the person from whom, or from whose premises, the property was taken; or

(B) leave a copy of the warrant and receipt at the place where the officer took the property.

(4) Return. The officer executing the warrant must promptly return it—together with a copy of the inventory—to the magistrate judge designated on the warrant. The judge must, on request, give a copy of the inventory to the person from whom, or from whose

premises, the property was taken and to the applicant for the warrant.

(g) Motion to Return Property. A person aggrieved by an unlawful search and seizure of property or by the deprivation of property may move for the property's return. The motion must be filed in the district where the property was seized. The court must receive evidence on any factual issue necessary to decide the motion. If it grants the motion, the court must return the property to the movant, but may impose reasonable conditions to protect access to the property and its use in later proceedings.

(h) Motion to Suppress. A defendant may move to suppress evidence in the court where the trial will occur, as Rule 12 provides.

(i) Forwarding Papers to the Clerk. The magistrate judge to whom the warrant is returned must attach to the warrant a copy of the return, of the inventory, and of all other related papers and must deliver them to the clerk in the district where the property was seized.

Rule 44. Right to and Appointment of Counsel

(a) Right to Appointed Counsel. A defendant who is unable to obtain counsel is entitled to have counsel appointed to represent the defendant at every stage of the proceeding from initial appearance through appeal, unless the defendant waives this right.

(b) Appointment Procedure. Federal law and local court rules govern the procedure for implementing the right to counsel.

(c) Inquiry into Joint Representation.

(1) Joint Representation. Joint representation occurs when:

(A) two or more defendants have been charged jointly under Rule 8(b) or have been joined for trial under Rule 13; and

(B) the defendants are represented by the same counsel or counsel who are associated in law practice.

(2) Court's Responsibilities in Cases of Joint Representation. The court must promptly inquire about the propriety of joint representation and must personally advise each defendant of the right to the effective assistance of counsel, including separate representation. Unless there is good cause to believe that no conflict of interest is likely to arise, the court must take appropriate measures to protect each defendant's right to counsel.

Rule 52. Harmless and Plain Error

(a) Harmless Error. Any error, defect, irregularity, or variance that does not affect substantial rights must be disregarded.

(b) Plain Error. A plain error that affects substantial rights may be considered even though it was not brought to the court's attention.

Bail Reform Act of 1984 (as amended)

18 U.S.C. §3141. Release and Detention Authority Generally

(a) Pending trial. A judicial officer authorized to order the arrest of a person under section 3041 of this title before whom an arrested person is brought shall order that such person be released or detained, pending judicial proceedings, under this chapter [18 U.S.C. §§ 3141 et seq.].

(b) Pending sentence or appeal. A judicial officer of a court of original jurisdiction over an offense, or a judicial officer of a Federal appellate court, shall order that, pending imposition or execution of sentence, or pending appeal of conviction or sentence, a person be released or detained under this chapter [18 U.S.C. §§3141 et seq.].

18 U.S.C. §3142. Release or Detention of a Defendant Pending Trial

(a) In general. Upon the appearance before a judicial officer of a person charged with an offense, the judicial officer shall issue an order that, pending trial, the person be —

(1) Released on personal recognizance or upon execution of an unsecured appearance bond, under subsection (b) of this section;

(2) released on a condition or combination of conditions under subsection (c) of this section;

(3) temporarily detained to permit revocation of conditional release, deportation, or exclusion under subsection (d) of this section; or

(4) detained under subsection (e) of this section.

(b) Release on personal recognizance or unsecured appearance bond. The judicial officer shall order the pretrial release of the person on personal recognizance, or upon execution of an unsecured appearance bond in an amount specified by the court, subject to the condition that the person not commit a Federal, State, or local crime during the period of release, unless the judicial officer determines that such release will not reasonably assure the appearance of the person as required or will endanger the safety of any other person or the community.

(c) Release on conditions.

(1) If the judicial officer determines that the release described in subsection (b) of this section will not reasonably assure the appearance of the person as required or will endanger the safety of any other person or the community, such judicial officer shall order the pretrial release of the person —

(A) subject to the condition that the person not commit a Federal, State, or local crime during the period of release; and

(B) subject to the least restrictive further condition, or combination of conditions, that such judicial officer determines will reasonably assure the appearance of the person as required and the safety of any other person and the community, which may include the condition that the person —

(i) remain in the custody of a designated person, who agrees to assume supervision and to report any violation of a release condition to the court, if the designated person is able reasonably to assure the judicial officer that the person will appear as required and will not pose a danger to the safety of any other person or the community;

(ii) maintain employment, or, if unemployed, actively seek employment;

(iii) maintain or commence an educational program;

(iv) abide by specified restrictions on personal associations, place of abode, or travel;

(v) avoid all contact with an alleged victim of the crime and with a potential witness who may testify concerning the offense;

(vi) report on a regular basis to a designated law enforcement agency, pretrial services agency, or other agency;

(vii) comply with a specified curfew;

(viii) refrain from possessing a firearm, destructive device, or other dangerous weapon;

(ix) refrain from excessive use of alcohol, or any use of a narcotic drug or other controlled substance, as defined in section 102 of the Controlled Substances Act (21 U.S.C. § 802), without a prescription by a licensed medical practitioner;

(x) undergo available medical, psychological, or psychiatric treatment, including treatment for drug or alcohol dependency, and remain in a specified institution if required for that purpose;

(xi) execute an agreement to forfeit, upon failing to appear as required, property of a sufficient unencumbered value, including money, as is reasonably necessary to assure the appearance of the person as required, and shall provide the court with proof of ownership and the value of the property along with information regarding existing encumbrances as the judicial office may require;

(xii) execute a bail bond with solvent sureties; who will execute an agreement to forfeit in such amount as is reasonably necessary to assure appearance of the person as required and shall provide the court with information regarding the value of the assets and liabilities of the surety if other than an approved surety and the nature and extent of encumbrances against the surety's property; such surety shall have a net worth which shall have sufficient unencumbered value to pay the amount of the bail bond;

(xiii) return to custody for specified hours following release for employment, schooling, or other limited purposes; and

(xiv) satisfy any other condition that is reasonably necessary to assure the appearance of the person as required and to assure the safety of any other person and the community.

(2) The judicial officer may not impose a financial condition that results in the pretrial detention of the person.

(3) The judicial officer may at any time amend the order to impose additional or different conditions of release.

(d) Temporary detention to permit revocation of conditional release, deportation, or exclusion. If the judicial officer determines that —

(1) such person —

(A) is, and was at the time the offense was committed, on —

(i) release pending trial for a felony under Federal, State, or local law;

(ii) release pending imposition or execution of sentence, appeal of sentence or conviction, or completion of sentence, for any offense under Federal, State, or local law; or

(iii) probation or parole for any offense under Federal, State, or local law; or

(B) is not a citizen of the United States or lawfully admitted for permanent residence, as defined in section 101(a)(20) of the Immigration and Nationality Act (8 U.S.C. § 1101(a)(20)); and

(2) the person may flee or pose a danger to any other person or the community; such judicial officer shall order the detention of the person, for a period of not more than ten days, excluding Saturdays, Sundays, and holidays, and direct the attorney for the Government to notify the appropriate court, probation or parole official, or State or local law enforcement official, or the appropriate official of the Immigration and Naturalization Service. If the official fails or declines to take the person into custody during that period, the person shall be treated in accordance with the other provisions of this section, notwithstanding the applicability of other provisions of law governing release pending trial or deportation or exclusion proceedings. If temporary detention is sought under paragraph (1)(B) of this subsection, the person has the burden of proving to the court such person's United States citizenship or lawful admission for permanent residence.

(e) Detention.

(1) If, after a hearing pursuant to the provisions of subsection (f) of this section, the judicial officer finds that no condition or combination of conditions will reasonably assure the appearance of the person as required and the safety of any other person and the community, such judicial officer shall order the detention of the person before trial.

(2) In a case described in subsection (f)(l) of this section, a rebuttable presumption arises that no condition or combination of conditions will reasonably assure the safety of any other person and the community if such judicial officer finds that—

(A) the person has been convicted of a Federal offense that is described in subsection (f)(l) of this section, or of a State or local offense that would have been an offense described in subsection (f)(l) of this section if a circumstance giving rise to Federal jurisdiction had existed;

(B) the offense described in paragraph (A) of this subsection was committed while the person was on release pending trial for a Federal, State, or local offense; and

(C) a period of not more than five years has elapsed since the date of conviction, or the release of the person from imprisonment, for the offense described in paragraph (A) of this subsection, whichever is later.

(3) Subject to rebuttal by the person, it shall be presumed that no condition or combination of conditions will reasonably assure the appearance of the person as required and the safety of the community if the judicial officer finds that there is probable cause to believe that the person committed—

(A) an offense for which a maximum term of imprisonment of ten years or more is prescribed in the Controlled Substances Act (21 U.S.C. 801 et seq.), the Controlled Substances Import and Export Act (21 U.S.C. 951 et seq.), or chapter 705 of title 46;

(B) an offense under section 924(c), 956(a), or 2332b of this title;

(C) an offense listed in section 2332b(g)(5)(B) of title 18, United States Code, for which a maximum term of imprisonment of 10 years or more is prescribed;

(D) an offense under chapter 77 of this title for which a maximum term of imprisonment of 20 years or more is prescribed; or

(E) an offense involving a minor victim under section 1201, 1591, 2241, 2242, 2244(a)(1), 2245, 2251, 2251A, 2252(a)(1), 2252(a)(2), 2252(a)(3), 2252A(a)(1), 2252A(a)(2), 2252A(a)(3), 2252A(a)(4), 2260, 2421, 2422, 2423, or 2425 of this title.

(f) Detention hearing. The judicial officer shall hold a hearing to determine whether any condition or combination of conditions set forth in subsection (c) of this section will reasonably assure the appearance of the person as required and the safety of any other person and the community —

(1) upon motion of the attorney for the Government, in a case that involves —

(A) a crime of violence;

(B) an offense for which the maximum sentence is life imprisonment or death;

(C) an offense for which a maximum term of imprisonment often years or more is prescribed in the Controlled Substances Act (21 U.S.C. §§ 801 et seq.), the Controlled Substances Import and Export Act (21 U.S.C. §§951 et seq.), or the Maritime Drug Law Enforcement Act (46 U.S.C. App. §§1901 et seq.); or

(D) any felony if the person has been convicted of two or more offenses described in subparagraphs (A) through (C) of this paragraph, or two or more State or local offenses that would have been offenses described in subparagraphs (A) through (C) of this paragraph if a circumstance giving rise to Federal jurisdiction had existed, or a combination of such offenses; or

(2) upon motion of the attorney for the Government or upon the judicial officer's own motion, in a case that involves —

(A) a serious risk that such person will flee; or

(B) a serious risk that the person will obstruct or attempt to obstruct justice, or threaten, injure, or intimidate, or attempt to threaten, injure, or intimidate, a prospective witness or juror.

The hearing shall be held immediately upon the person's first appearance before the judicial officer unless that person, or the attorney for the Government, seeks a continuance. Except for good cause, a continuance on motion of the person may not exceed five days (not including any intermediate Saturday, Sunday, or legal holiday), and a continuance on motion of the attorney for the Government may not exceed three days (not including any intermediate Saturday, Sunday, or legal holiday). During a continuance, the person shall be detained and the judicial officer, on motion of the attorney for the Government or sua sponte, may order that, while in custody, a person who appears to be a narcotics addict receive a medical examination to determine whether such person is an addict. At the hearing, the person has the right to be represented by counsel and, if financially unable to obtain adequate representation, to have counsel appointed. The person shall be afforded an opportunity to testify, to present witnesses, to cross-examine witnesses who appear at the hearing, and to present information by proffer or otherwise. The rules concerning admissibility of evidence in criminal trials do not apply to the presentation and consideration of information at the hearing. The facts the judicial officer uses to support a finding pursuant to subsection (e) that no condition or combination of conditions will reasonably assure the safety of any other person and the community shall be supported by clear and convincing evidence. The person may be detained pending completion of the hearing. The hearing may be reopened, before or after a determination by the judicial officer, at any time before trial if the judicial officer finds that information exists that was not known to the movant at the time of the hearing and that has a material bearing on the issue whether there are conditions of release that will reasonably assure the appearance of the person as required and the safety of any other person and the community.

(g) Factors to be considered. The judicial officer shall, in determining whether there are conditions of release that will reasonably assure the appearance of the person as required and the safety of any other person and the community, take into account the available information concerning —

(1) the nature and circumstances of the offense charged, including whether the offense is a crime of violence or involves a narcotic drug;

(2) the weight of the evidence against the person;

(3) the history and characteristics of the person, including —

(A) the person's character, physical and mental condition, family ties, employment, financial resources, length of residence in the community, community ties, past conduct, history relating to drug or alcohol abuse, criminal history, and record concerning appearance at court proceedings; and

(B) whether, at the time of the current offense or arrest, the person was on probation, on parole, or on other release pending trial, sentencing, appeal, or completion of sentence for an offense under Federal, State, or local law; and

(4) the nature and seriousness of the danger to any person or the community that would be posed by the person's release. In considering the conditions of release described in subsection (c)(1)(B)(xi) or (c)(1)(B)(xii) of this section, the judicial officer may, upon his own motion, or shall, upon the motion of the Government, conduct an inquiry into the source of the property to be designated for potential forfeiture or offered as collateral to secure a bond, and shall decline to accept the designation, or the use as collateral, of property that, because of its source, will not reasonably assure the appearance of the person as required.

(h) Contents of release order. In a release order issued under subsection (b) or (c) of this section, the judicial officer shall —

(1) include a written statement that sets forth all the conditions to which the release is subject, in a manner sufficiently clear and specific to serve as a guide for the person's conduct; and

(2) advise the person of —

(A) the penalties for violating a condition of release, including the penalties for committing an offense while on pretrial release;

(B) the consequences of violating a condition of release, including the immediate issuance of a warrant for the person's arrest; and

(C) sections 1503 of this title (relating to intimidation of witnesses, jurors, and officers of the court), 1510 (relating to obstruction of criminal investigations), 1512 (tampering with a witness, victim, or an informant), and 1513 (retaliating against a witness, victim, or an informant).

(i) Contents of detention order. In a detention order issued under subsection (e) of this section, the judicial officer shall —

(1) include written findings of fact and a written statement of the reasons for the detention;

(2) direct that the person be committed to the custody of the Attorney General for confinement in a corrections facility separate, to the extent practicable, from persons awaiting or serving sentences or being held in custody pending appeal;

(3) direct that the person be afforded reasonable opportunity for private consultation with counsel; and

(4) direct that, on order of a court of the United States or on request of an attorney for the Government, the person in charge of the corrections facility in which the person is confined deliver the person to a United States marshal for the purpose of an appearance in connection with a court proceeding.

The judicial officer may, by subsequent order, permit the temporary release of the person, in the custody of a United States marshal or another appropriate person, to the extent that the judicial officer determines such release to be necessary for preparation of the person's defense or for another compelling reason.

(j) Presumption of innocence. Nothing in this section shall be construed as modifying or limiting the presumption of innocence.

18 U.S.C. §3143. Release or Detention of a Defendant Pending Sentence or Appeal

(a) Release or detention pending sentence.

(1) Except as provided in paragraph (2), the judicial officer shall order that a person who has been found guilty of an offense and who is awaiting imposition or execution of sentence, other than a person for whom the applicable guideline promulgated pursuant to 28 U.S.C. §994 does not recommend a term of imprisonment, be

detained, unless the judicial officer finds by clear and convincing evidence that the person is not likely to flee or pose a danger to the safety of any other person or the community if released under section 3142(b) or (c). If the judicial officer makes such a finding, such judicial officer shall order the release of the person in accordance with section 3142(b) or (c).

(2) The judicial officer shall order that a person who has been found guilty of an offense in a case described in subparagraph (A), (B), or (C) of subsection (f)(l) of section 3142 and is awaiting imposition or execution of sentence be detained unless —

(A) (i) the judicial officer finds there is a substantial likelihood that a motion for acquittal or new trial will be granted; or

(ii) an attorney for the Government has recommended that no sentence of imprisonment be imposed on the person; and

(B) the judicial officer finds by clear and convincing evidence that the person is not likely to flee or pose a danger to any other person or the community.

(b) Release or detention pending appeal by the defendant.

(1) Except as provided in paragraph (2), the judicial officer shall order that a person who has been found guilty of an offense and sentenced to a term of imprisonment, and who has filed an appeal or a petition for a writ of certiorari, be detained, unless the judicial officer finds —

(A) by clear and convincing evidence that the person is not likely to flee or pose a danger to the safety of any other person or the community if released under section 3142(b) or (c) of this title; and

(B) that the appeal is not for the purpose of delay and raises a substantial question of law or fact likely to result in —

(i) reversal

(ii) an order for a new trial,

(iii) a sentence that does not include a term of imprisonment, or

(iv) a reduced sentence to a term of imprisonment less than the total of the time already served plus the expected duration of the appeal process.

If the judicial officer makes such findings, such judicial officer shall order the release of the person in accordance with section 3142

(b) or (c) of this title, except that in the circumstance described in subparagraph (B)(iv) of this paragraph, the judicial officer shall order the detention terminated at the expiration of the likely reduced sentence.

(2) The judicial officer shall order that a person who has been found guilty of an offense in a case described in subparagraph (A), (B), or (C) of subsection (f)(1) of section 3142 and sentenced to a term of imprisonment, and who has filed an appeal or a petition for a writ of certiorari, be detained.

(c) Release or detention pending appeal by the government. The judicial officer shall treat a defendant in a case in which an appeal has been taken by the United States under section 3731 of this title, in accordance with section 3142 of this title, unless the defendant is otherwise subject to a release or detention order. Except as provided in subsection (b) of this section, the judicial officer, in a case in which an appeal has been taken by the United States under section 3742, shall —

(1) if the person has been sentenced to a term of imprisonment, order that person detained; and

(2) in any other circumstance, release or detain the person under section 3142.

18 U.S.C. §3144. Release or Detention of a Material Witness

If it appears from an affidavit filed by a party that the testimony of a person is material in a criminal proceeding, and if it is shown that it may become impracticable to secure the presence of the person by subpoena, a judicial officer may order the arrest of the person and treat the person in accordance with the provisions of section 3142 of this title. No material witness may be detained because of inability to comply with any condition of release if the testimony of such witness can adequately be secured by deposition, and if further detention is not necessary to prevent a failure of justice. Release of a material witness may be delayed for a reasonable period of time until the deposition of the witness can be taken pursuant to the Federal Rules of Criminal Procedure.

18 U.S.C. §3145. Review and Appeal of a Release or Detention Order

(a) Review of a release order. If a person is ordered released by a magistrate [United States magistrate judge], or by a person other than a judge of a court having original jurisdiction over the offense and other than a Federal appellate court —

(1) the attorney for the Government may file, with the court having original jurisdiction over the offense, a motion for revocation of the order or amendment of the conditions of release; and

(2) the person may file, with the court having original jurisdiction over the offense, a motion for amendment of the conditions of release. The motion shall be determined promptly.

(b) Review of a detention order. If a person is ordered detained by a magistrate [United States magistrate judge], or by a person other than a judge of a court having original jurisdiction over the offense and other than a Federal appellate court, the person may file, with the court having original jurisdiction over the offense, a motion for revocation or amendment of the order. The motion shall be determined promptly.

(c) Appeal from a release or detention order. An appeal from a release or detention order, or from a decision denying revocation or amendment of such an order, is governed by the provisions of section 1291 of title 28 and section 3731 of this title. The appeal shall be determined promptly. A person subject to detention pursuant to section 3143(a)(2) or (b)(2), and who meets the conditions of release set forth in section 3143(a)(l) or (b)(l), may be ordered released, under appropriate conditions, by the judicial officer if it is clearly shown that there are exceptional reasons why such person's detention would not be appropriate.

18 U.S.C. §3146. Penalty for Failure to Appear

(a) Offense. Whoever, having been released under this chapter [18 U.S.C. §§ 3141 et seq.] knowingly —

(1) fails to appear before a court as required by the conditions of release; or

(2) fails to surrender for service of sentence pursuant to a court order;

shall be punished as provided in subsection (b) of this section.

(b) Punishment.

(1) The punishment for an offense under this section is —

(A) if the person was released in connection with a charge of, or while awaiting sentence, surrender for service of sentence, or appeal or certiorari after conviction for —

(i) an offense punishable by death, life imprisonment, or imprisonment for a term of 15 years or more, a fine under this title or imprisonment for not more than ten years, or both;

(ii) an offense punishable by imprisonment for a term of five years or more, a fine under this title or imprisonment for not more than five years, or both;

(iii) any other felony, a fine under this title or imprisonment for not more than two years, or both; or

(iv) a misdemeanor, a fine under this title or imprisonment for not more than one year, or both; and

(B) if the person was released for appearance as a material witness, a fine under this chapter [18 U.S.C. §§3141 et seq.] or imprisonment for not more than one year, or both.

(2) A term of imprisonment imposed under this section shall be consecutive to the sentence of imprisonment for any other offense.

(c) Affirmative defense. It is an affirmative defense to a prosecution under this section that uncontrollable circumstances prevented the person from appearing or surrendering, and that the person did not contribute to the creation of such circumstances in reckless disregard of the requirement to appear or surrender, and that the person appeared or surrendered as soon as such circumstances ceased to exist.

(d) Declaration of forfeiture. If a person fails to appear before a court as required, and the person executed an appearance bond pursuant to section 3142(b) of this title or is subject to the release condition set forth in clause (xi) or (xii) of section 3142(c)(l)(B) of this title, the judicial officer may, regardless of whether the person has been charged with an offense under this section, declare any property designated pursuant to that section to be forfeited to the United States.

18 U.S.C. §3147. Penalty for an Offense Committed While on Release

A person convicted of an offense committed while released under this chapter [18 U.S.C. §§3141 et seq.] shall be sentenced, in addition to the sentence prescribed for the offense, to —

(1) a term of imprisonment of not more than ten years if the offense is a felony; or

(2) a term of imprisonment of not more than one year if the offense is a misdemeanor.

A term of imprisonment imposed under this section shall be consecutive to any other sentence of imprisonment.

18 U.S.C. §3148. Sanctions for Violation of a Release Condition

(a) Available sanctions. A person who has been released pursuant to the provisions of section 3142 of this title, and who has violated a condition of his release, is subject to a revocation of release, an order of detention, and a prosecution for contempt of court.

(b) Revocation of release. The attorney for the Government may initiate a proceeding for revocation of an order of release by filing a motion with the district court. A judicial officer may issue a warrant for the arrest of a person charged with violating a condition of release, and the person shall be brought before a judicial officer in the district in which such person's arrest was ordered for a proceeding in accordance with this section. To the extent practicable, a person charged with violating the condition of release that such person not commit a Federal, State, or local crime during the period of release, shall be brought before the judicial officer who ordered the release and whose order is alleged to have been violated. The judicial officer shall enter an order of revocation and detention if, after a hearing, the judicial officer —

(1) finds that there is —

(A) probable cause to believe that the person has committed a Federal, State, or local crime while on release; or

(B) clear and convincing evidence that the person has violated any other condition of release; and

(2) finds that —

(A) based on the factors set forth in section 3142(g) of this title, there is no condition or combination of conditions of release that will assure that the person will not flee or pose a danger to the safety of any other person or the community; or

(B) the person is unlikely to abide by any condition or combination of conditions of release.

If there is probable cause to believe that, while on release, the person committed a Federal, State, or local felony, a rebuttable presumption arises that no condition or combination of conditions will assure that the person will not pose a danger to the safety of any other person or the community. If the judicial officer finds that there are conditions of release that will assure that the person will not flee or pose a danger to the safety of any other person or the community, and that the person will abide by such conditions, the judicial officer shall treat the person in accordance with the provisions of section 3142 of this title and may amend the conditions of release accordingly.

(c) Prosecution for contempt. The judicial officer may commence a prosecution for contempt, under section 401 of this title, if the person has violated a condition of release.

18 U.S.C. §3149. Surrender of an Offender by a Surety

A person charged with an offense, who is released upon the execution of an appearance bond with a surety, may be arrested by the surety, and if so arrested, shall be delivered promptly to a United States marshal and brought before a judicial officer. The judicial officer shall determine in accordance with the provisions of section 3148(b) whether to revoke the release of the person, and may absolve the surety of responsibility to pay all or part of the bond in accordance with the provisions of Rule 46 of the Federal Rules of Criminal Procedure. The person so committed shall be held in official detention until released pursuant to this chapter [18 U.S.C. §§3141 et seq.] or another provision of law.

18 U.S.C. §3150. Applicability to a Case Removed from a State Court

The provisions of this chapter [18 U.S.C. §§3141 et seq.] apply to a criminal case removed to a Federal court from a State court.

Speedy Trial Act of 1974 (as amended)

18 U.S.C. §3161. Time Limits and Exclusions

(a) In any case involving a defendant charged with an offense, the appropriate judicial officer, at the earliest practicable time, shall, after consultation with the counsel for the defendant and the attorney for the Government, set the case for trial on a day certain, or list it for trial on a weekly or other short-term trial calendar at a place within the judicial district, so as to assure a speedy trial.

(b) Any information or indictment charging an individual with the commission of an offense shall be filed within thirty days from the date on which such individual was arrested or served with a summons in connection with such charges. If an individual has been charged with a felony in a district in which no grand jury has been in session during such thirty-day period, the period of time for filing of the indictment shall be extended an additional thirty days.

(c) (1) In any case in which a plea of not guilty is entered, the trial of a defendant charged in an information or indictment with the commission of an offense shall commence within seventy days from the filing date (and making public) of the information or indictment, or from the date the defendant has appeared before a judicial officer of the court in which such charge is pending, whichever date last occurs. If a defendant consents in writing to be tried before a magistrate [United States magistrate judge] on a complaint, the trial shall commence within seventy days from the date of such consent.

(2) Unless the defendant consents in writing to the contrary, the trial shall not commence less than thirty days from the date on which the defendant first appears through counsel or expressly waives counsel and elects to proceed pro se.

(d) (1) If any indictment or information is dismissed upon motion of the defendant, or any charge contained in a complaint filed against an individual is dismissed or otherwise dropped, and thereafter a complaint is filed against such defendant or individual charging him with the same offense or an offense based on the same conduct or arising from the same criminal episode, or an information or indictment is filed charging such defendant with the same offense or an offense based on the same conduct or arising from the same criminal episode, the provisions of subsections (b) and (c) of this section shall be applicable with respect to such subsequent complaint, indictment, or information, as the case may be.

(2) If the defendant is to be tried upon an indictment or information dismissed by a trial court and reinstated following an appeal, the trial shall commence within seventy days from the date the action occasioning the trial becomes final, except that the court retrying the case may extend the period for trial not to exceed one hundred and eighty days from the date the action occasioning the trial becomes final if the unavailability of witnesses or other factors resulting from

the passage of time shall make trial within seventy days impractical. The periods of delay enumerated in section 3161(h) are excluded in computing the time limitations specified in this section. The sanctions of section 3162 apply to this subsection.

(e) If the defendant is to be tried again following a declaration by the trial judge of a mistrial or following an order of such judge for a new trial, the trial shall commence within seventy days from the date the action occasioning the retrial becomes final. If the defendant is to be tried again following an appeal or a collateral attack, the trial shall commence within seventy days from the date the action occasioning the retrial becomes final, except that the court retrying the case may extend the period for retrial not to exceed one hundred and eighty days from the date the action occasioning the retrial becomes final if unavailability of witnesses or other factors resulting from passage of time shall make trial within seventy days impractical. The periods of delay enumerated in section 3161(h) are excluded in computing the time limitations specified in this section. The sanctions of section 3162 apply to this subsection.

(f) Notwithstanding the provisions of subsection (b) of this section, for the first twelve-calendar-month period following the effective date of this section as set forth in section 3163(a) of this chapter[,] the time limit imposed with respect to the period between arrest and indictment by subsection (b) of this section shall be sixty days, for the second such twelve-month period such time limit shall be forty-five days and for the third such period such time limit shall be thirty-five days.

(g) Notwithstanding the provisions of subsection (c) of this section, for the first twelve-calendar-month period following the effective date of this section as set forth in section 3163(b) of this chapter, the time limit with respect to the period between arraignment and trial imposed by subsection (c) of this section shall be one hundred and eighty days, for the second such twelve-month period such time limit shall be one hundred and twenty days, and for the third such period such time limit with respect to the period between arraignment and trial shall be eighty days.

(h) The following periods of delay shall be excluded in computing the time within which an information or an indictment must be filed, or in computing the time within which the trial of any such offense must commence:

(1) Any period of delay resulting from other proceedings concerning the defendant, including but not limited to —

(A) delay resulting from any proceeding, including any examinations, to determine the mental competency or physical capacity of the defendant;

(B) delay resulting from trial with respect to other charges against the defendant;

(C) delay resulting from any interlocutory appeal;

(D) delay resulting from any pretrial motion, from the filing of the motion through the conclusion of the hearing on, or other prompt disposition of, such motion;

(E) delay resulting from any proceeding relating to the transfer of a case or the removal of any defendant from another district under the Federal Rules of Criminal Procedure;

(F) delay resulting from transportation of any defendant from another district, or to and from places of examination or hospitalization, except that any time consumed in excess of ten days from the date an order of removal or an order directing such transportation, and the defendant's arrival at the destination shall be presumed to be unreasonable;

(G) delay resulting from consideration by the court of a proposed plea agreement to be entered into by the defendant and the attorney for the Government; and

(H) delay reasonably attributable to any period, not to exceed thirty days, during which any proceeding concerning the defendant is actually under advisement by the court.

(2) Any period of delay during which prosecution is deferred by the attorney for the Government pursuant to written agreement with the defendant, with the approval of the court, for the purpose of allowing the defendant to demonstrate his good conduct.

(3) (A) Any period of delay resulting from the absence or unavailability of the defendant or an essential witness.

(B) For purposes of subparagraph (A) of this paragraph, a defendant or an essential witness shall be considered absent when his whereabouts are unknown and, in addition, he is attempting to avoid apprehension or prosecution or his whereabouts cannot be determined by due diligence. For purposes of such subparagraph, a defendant or an essential witness shall be considered unavailable whenever his whereabouts are known but his presence for trial cannot be obtained by due diligence or he resists appearing at or being returned for trial.

(4) Any period of delay resulting from the fact that the defendant is mentally incompetent or physically unable to stand trial.

(5) If the information or indictment is dismissed upon motion of the attorney for the Government and thereafter a charge is filed against the defendant for the same offense, or any offense required to be joined with that offense, any period of delay from the date the charge was dismissed to the date the time limitation would commence to run as to the subsequent charge had there been no previous charge.

(6) A reasonable period of delay when the defendant is joined for trial with a codefendant as to whom the time for trial has not run and no motion for severance has been granted.

(7) (A) Any period of delay resulting from a continuance granted by any judge on his own motion or at the request of the defendant or his counsel or at the request of the attorney for the Government, if the judge granted such continuance on the basis of his findings that the ends of justice served by taking such action outweigh the best interest of the public and the defendant in a speedy trial. No such period of delay resulting from a continuance granted by the court in accordance with this paragraph shall be excludable under this subsection unless the court sets forth, in the record of the case, either orally or in writing, its reasons for finding that the ends of justice served by the granting of such continuance outweigh the best interests of the public and the defendant in a speedy trial.

(B) The factors, among others, which a judge shall consider in determining whether to grant a continuance under subparagraph (A) of this paragraph in any case are as follows:

(i) Whether the failure to grant such a continuance in the proceeding would be likely to make a continuation of such proceeding impossible, or result in a miscarriage of justice.

(ii) Whether the case is so unusual or so complex, due to the number of defendants, the nature of the prosecution, or the existence of novel questions of fact or law, that it is unreasonable to expect adequate preparation for pretrial proceedings or for the trial itself within the time limits established by this section.

(iii) Whether, in a case in which arrest precedes indictment, delay in the filing of the indictment is caused because the arrest occurs at a time such that it is unreasonable to expect return and filing of the indictment within the period specified in section 3161 (b) or because the facts upon which the grand jury must base its determination are unusual or complex.

(iv) Whether the failure to grant such a continuance in a case that, taken as a whole, is not so unusual or so complex as to fall within clause (ii), would deny the defendant reasonable time to obtain counsel, would unreasonably deny the defendant or the Government continuity of counsel, or would deny counsel for the defendant or the attorney for the Government the reasonable time necessary for effective preparation, taking into account the exercise of due diligence.

(C) No continuance under subparagraph (A) of this paragraph shall be granted because of general congestion of the court's calendar, or lack of diligent preparation or failure to obtain available witnesses on the part of the attorney for the Government.

(8) Any period of delay, not to exceed one year, ordered by a district court upon an application of a party and a finding by a preponderance of the evidence that an official request, as defined in section 3292 of this title, has been made for evidence of any such offense and that it reasonably appears, or reasonably appeared at the time the request was made, that such evidence is, or was, in such foreign country.

(i) If trial did not commence within the time limitation specified in section 3161 because the defendant had entered a plea of guilty or nolo contendere subsequently withdrawn to any or all charges in an indictment or information, the defendant shall be deemed indicted with respect to all charges therein contained within the meaning of section 3161 on the day the order permitting withdrawal of the plea becomes final.

(j) (1) If the attorney for the Government knows that a person charged with an offense is serving a term of imprisonment in any penal institution, he shall promptly —

(A) undertake to obtain the presence of the prisoner for trial; or

(B) cause a detainer to be filed with the person having custody of the prisoner and request him to so advise the prisoner and to advise the prisoner of his right to demand trial.

(2) If the person having custody of such prisoner receives a detainer, he shall promptly advise the prisoner of the charge and of the prisoner's right to demand trial. If at any time thereafter the prisoner informs the person having custody that he does demand trial, such person shall cause notice to that effect to be sent promptly to the attorney for the Government who caused the detainer to be filed.

(3) Upon receipt of such notice, the attorney for the Government shall promptly seek to obtain the presence of the prisoner for trial.

(4) When the person having custody of the prisoner receives from the attorney for the Government a properly supported request for temporary custody of such prisoner for trial, the prisoner shall be made available to that attorney for the Government (subject, in cases of interjurisdictional transfer, to any right of the prisoner to contest the legality of his delivery).

(k) (1) If the defendant is absent (as defined by subsection (h)(3)) on the day set for trial, and the defendant's subsequent appearance before the court on a bench warrant or other process or surrender to the court occurs more than twenty-one days after the day set for trial, the defendant shall be deemed to have first appeared before a judicial officer of the court in which the information or indictment is pending within the meaning of subsection (c) on the date of the defendant's subsequent appearance before the court.

(2) If the defendant is absent (as defined by subsection (h)(3)) on the day set for trial, and the defendant's subsequent appearance before the court on a bench warrant or other process or surrender to the court occurs not more than twenty-one days after the day set for trial, the time limit required by subsection (c), as extended by subsection (h), shall be further extended by twenty-one days.

18 U.S.C. §3162. Sanctions

(a) (1) If, in the case of any individual against whom a complaint is filed charging such individual with an offense, no indictment or information is filed within the time limit required by section 3161(b) as extended by section 3161(h) of this chapter, such charge against that individual contained in such complaint shall be dismissed or otherwise dropped. In determining whether to dismiss the case with or without prejudice, the court shall consider, among others, each of the following factors: the seriousness of the offense; the facts and circumstances of the case which led to the dismissal; and the impact of a reprosecution on the administration of this chapter [18 U.S.C. §§ 3161 et seq.] and on the administration of justice.

(2) If a defendant is not brought to trial within the time limit required by section 3161(c) as extended by section 3161(h), the information or indictment shall be dismissed on motion of the defendant. The defendant shall have the burden of proof of supporting such motion but the Government shall have the burden of going

forward with the evidence in connection with any exclusion of time under subparagraph 3161(h)(3).

In determining whether to dismiss the case with or without prejudice, the court shall consider, among others, each of the following factors: the seriousness of the offense; the facts and circumstances of the case which led to the dismissal; and the impact of a reprosecution on the administration of this chapter [18 U.S.C. §§3161 et seq.] and on the administration of justice. Failure of the defendant to move for dismissal prior to trial or entry of a plea of guilty or nolo contendere shall constitute a waiver of the right to dismissal under this section.

(b) In any case in which counsel for the defendant or the attorney for the Government

(1) knowingly allows the case to be set for trial without disclosing the fact that a necessary witness would be unavailable for trial;

(2) files a motion solely for the purpose of delay, which he knows is totally frivolous and without merit;

(3) makes a statement for the purpose of obtaining a continuance that he knows to be false and that is material to the granting of a continuance; or

(4) otherwise willfully fails to proceed to trial without justification consistent with section 3161 of this chapter, the court may punish any such counsel or attorney, as follows:

(A) in the case of an appointed defense counsel, by reducing the amount of compensation that otherwise would have been paid to such counsel pursuant to section 3006A of this title in an amount not to exceed 25 per centum thereof;

(B) in the case of a counsel retained in connection with the defense of a defendant, by imposing on such counsel a fine of not to exceed 25 per centum of the compensation to which he is entitled in connection with his defense of such defendant;

(C) by imposing on any attorney for the Government a fine of not to exceed $250;

(D) by denying any such counsel or attorney for the Government the right to practice before the court considering such case for a period of not to exceed 90 days; or

(E) by filing a report with an appropriate disciplinary committee.

The authority to punish provided for by this subsection shall be in addition to any other authority or power available to such court.

(c) The court shall follow procedures established in the Federal Rules of Criminal Procedure in punishing any counsel or attorney for the Government pursuant to this section.

18 U.S.C. §3164. Persons Detained or Designated As Being of High Risk

(a) The trial or other disposition of cases involving —

(1) a detained person who is being held in detention solely because he is awaiting trial, and

(2) a released person who is awaiting trial and has been designated by the attorney for the Government as being of high risk, shall be accorded priority.

(b) The trial of any person described in subsection (a)(l) or (a)(2) of this section shall commence not later than ninety days following the beginning of such continuous detention or designation of high risk by the attorney for the Government. The periods of delay enumerated in section 3161(h) are excluded in computing the time limitation specified in this section.

(c) Failure to commence trial of a detainee as specified in subsection (b), through no fault of the accused or his counsel, or failure to commence trial of a designated releasee as specified in subsection (b), through no fault of the attorney for the Government, shall result in the automatic review by the court of the conditions of release. No detainee, as defined in subsection (a), shall be held in custody pending trial after the expiration of such ninety-day period required for the commencement of his trial. A designated releasee, as defined in subsection (a), who is found by the court to have intentionally delayed the trial of his case shall be subject to an order of the court modifying his nonfinancial conditions of release under this title to insure that he shall appear at trial as required.

18 U.S.C. §3173. Sixth Amendment Rights

No provision of this chapter [18 U.S.C. §§3161 et seq.] shall be interpreted as a bar to any claim of denial of speedy trial as required by amendment VI of the Constitution.

Criminal Appeals Act of 1970 (as amended)

18 U.S.C. §3731. Appeal by United States

In a criminal case an appeal by the United States shall lie to a court of appeals from a decision, judgment, or order of a district court dismissing an indictment or information or granting a new trial after verdict or judgment, as to any one or more counts, or any part thereof, except that no appeal shall lie where the double jeopardy clause of the United States Constitution prohibits further prosecution.

An appeal by the United States shall lie to a court of appeals from a decision or order of a district court suppressing or excluding evidence or requiring the return of seized property in a criminal proceeding, not made after the defendant has been put in jeopardy and before the verdict or finding on an indictment or information, if the United States attorney certifies to the district court that the appeal is not taken for purpose of delay and that the evidence is a substantial proof of a fact material in the proceeding.

An appeal by the United States shall lie to a court of appeals from a decision or order, entered by a district court of the United States, granting the release of a person charged with or convicted of an offense, or denying a motion for revocation of, or modification of the conditions of, a decision or order granting release.

The appeal in all such cases shall be taken within thirty days after the decision, judgment, or order has been rendered and shall be diligently prosecuted.

The provisions of this section shall be liberally construed to effectuate its purposes.

Habeas Corpus Act of 1867 (as amended by Antiterrorism and Effective Death Penalty Act of 1996)

28 U.S.C. §2241. Power to Grant Writ

(a) Writs of habeas corpus may be granted by the Supreme Court, any justice thereof, the district courts, and any circuit judge within their respective jurisdictions. The order of a circuit judge shall be entered in the records of the district court of the district wherein the restraint complained of is had.

(b) The Supreme Court, any justice thereof, and any circuit judge may decline to entertain an application for a writ of habeas corpus and may transfer the application for hearing and determination to the district court having jurisdiction to entertain it.

(c) The writ of habeas corpus shall not extend to a prisoner unless —

(1) He is in custody under or by color of the authority of the United States or is committed for trial before some court thereof; or

(2) He is in custody for an act done or omitted in pursuance of an Act of Congress, or an order, process, judgment or decree of a court or judge of the United States; or

(3) He is in custody in violation of the Constitution or laws or treaties of the United States; or

(4) He, being a citizen of a foreign state and domiciled therein, is in custody for an act done or omitted under any alleged right, title, authority, privilege, protection, or exemption claimed under the commission, order or sanction of any foreign state, or under color thereof, the validity and effect of which depend upon the law of nations; or

(5) It is necessary to bring him into court to testify or for trial.

(d) Where an application for a writ of habeas corpus is made by a person in custody under the judgment and sentence of a State court of a State which contains two or more Federal judicial districts, the application may be filed in the district court for the district wherein such person is in custody or in the district court for the district within which the State court was held which convicted and sentenced him and each of such district courts shall have concurrent jurisdiction to entertain the application. The district court for the district wherein such an application is filed in the exercise of its discretion and in furtherance of justice may transfer the application to the other district court for hearing and determination.

28 U.S.C. §2242. Application

Application for a writ of habeas corpus shall be in writing signed and verified by the person for whose relief it is intended or by someone acting in his behalf.

It shall allege the facts concerning the applicant's commitment or detention, the name of the person who has custody over him and by virtue of what claim or authority, if known.

It may be amended or supplemented as provided in the rules of procedure applicable to civil actions.

If addressed to the Supreme Court, a justice thereof, or a circuit judge, it shall state the reasons for not making application to the district court of the district in which the applicant is held.

28 U.S.C. §2243. Issuance of Writ; Return; Hearing; Decision

A court, justice, or judge entertaining an application for a writ of habeas corpus shall forthwith award the writ or issue an order directing the respondent to show cause why the writ should not be granted, unless it appears from the application that the applicant or person detained is not entitled thereto.

The writ, or order to show cause, shall be directed to the person having custody of the person detained. It shall be returned within three days unless for good cause additional time, not exceeding twenty days, is allowed.

The person to whom the writ or order is directed shall make a return certifying the true cause of the detention.

When the writ or order is returned a day shall be set for hearing, not more than five days after the return unless for good cause additional time is allowed.

Unless the application for the writ and the return present only issues of law, the person to whom the writ is directed shall be required to produce at the hearing the body of the person detained.

The applicant or the person detained may, under oath, deny any of the facts set forth in the return or allege any other material facts.

The return and all suggestions made against it may be amended, by leave of court, before or after being filed.

The court shall summarily hear and determine the facts and dispose of the matter as law and justice require.

28 U.S.C. §2244. Finality of Determination

(a) No circuit or district judge shall be required to entertain an application for a writ of habeas corpus to inquire into the detention of a person pursuant to a judgment of a court of the United States if it appears that the legality of such detention has been determined by a judge or court of the United States on a prior application for a writ of habeas corpus, except as provided in section 2255.

(b) (1) A claim presented in a second or successive habeas corpus application under section 2254 that was presented in a prior application shall be dismissed.

(2) A claim presented in a second or successive habeas corpus application under section 2254 that was not presented in a prior application shall be dismissed unless —

(A) the applicant shows that the claim relies on a new rule of constitutional law, made retroactive to cases on collateral review by the Supreme Court, that was previously unavailable; or

(B) (i) the factual predicate for the claim could not have been discovered previously through the exercise of due diligence; and

(ii) the facts underlying the claim, if proven and viewed in light of the evidence as a whole, would be sufficient to establish by clear and convincing evidence that, but for constitutional error, no reasonable factfinder would have found the applicant guilty of the underlying offense.

(3) (A) Before a second or successive application permitted by this section is filed in the district court, the applicant shall move in the appropriate court of appeals for an order authorizing the district court to consider the application.

(B) A motion in the court of appeals for an order authorizing the district court to consider a second or successive application shall be determined by a three-judge panel of the court of appeals.

(C) The court of appeals may authorize the filing of a second or successive application only if it determines that the application makes a prima facie showing that the application satisfies the requirements of this subsection.

(D) The court of appeals shall grant or deny the authorization to file a second or successive application not later than 30 days after the filing of the motion.

(E) The grant or denial of an authorization by a court of appeals to file a second or successive application shall not be appealable and shall not be the subject of a petition for rehearing or for a writ of certiorari.

(4) A district court shall dismiss any claim presented in a second or successive application that the court of appeals has authorized to be filed unless the applicant shows that the claim satisfies the requirements of this section.

(c) In a habeas corpus proceeding brought in behalf of a person in custody pursuant to the judgment of a State court, a prior judgment of the Supreme Court of the United States on an appeal or review by a writ of certiorari at the instance of the prisoner of the decision of such State court, shall be conclusive as to all issues of fact or law with respect to an asserted denial of a Federal right which constitutes ground for discharge in a habeas corpus proceeding, actually adjudicated by the Supreme Court therein, unless the applicant for the writ of habeas corpus shall plead and the court shall find the existence of a material and controlling fact which did not appear in the record of the proceeding in the Supreme Court and the court shall further find that the applicant for the writ of habeas corpus could not have caused such fact to appear in such record by the exercise of reasonable diligence.

(d) (1) A one-year period of limitation shall apply to an application for a writ of habeas corpus by a person in custody pursuant to the judgment of a State court. The limitation period shall run from the latest of —

(A) the date on which the judgment became final by the conclusion of direct review or the expiration of the time for seeking such review;

(B) the date on which the impediment to filing an application created by State action in violation of the Constitution or laws of the United States is removed, if the applicant was prevented from filing by such State action;

(C) the date on which the constitutional right asserted was initially recognized by the Supreme Court, if the right has been newly recognized by the Supreme Court and made retroactively applicable to cases on collateral review; or

(D) the date on which the factual predicate of the claim or claims presented could have been discovered through the exercise of due diligence.

(2) The time during which a properly filed application for State post-conviction or other collateral review with respect to the pertinent judgment or claim is pending shall not be counted toward any period of limitation under this subsection.

28 U.S.C. §2253. Appeal

(a) In a habeas corpus proceeding or a proceeding under section 2255 before a district judge, the final order shall be subject to review, on appeal, by the court of appeals for the circuit in which the proceeding is held.

(b) There shall be no right of appeal from a final order in a proceeding to test the validity of a warrant to remove to another district or place for commitment or trial a person charged with a criminal offense against the United States, or to test the validity of such person's detention pending removal proceedings.

(c) (1) Unless a circuit justice or judge issues a certificate of appealability, an appeal may not be taken to the court of appeals from —

(A) the final order in a habeas corpus proceeding in which the detention complained of arises out of process issued by a State court; or

(B) the final order in a proceeding under section 2255.

(2) A certificate of appealability may issue under paragraph (1) only if the applicant has made a substantial showing of the denial of a constitutional right.

(3) The certificate of appealability under paragraph (1) shall indicate which specific issue or issues satisfy the showing required by paragraph (2).

28 U.S.C. §2254. State Custody; Remedies in Federal Courts

(a) The Supreme Court, a Justice thereof, a circuit judge, or a district court shall entertain an application for a writ of habeas corpus in behalf of a person in custody pursuant to the judgment of a State court only on the ground that he is in custody in violation of the Constitution or laws or treaties of the United States.

(b) (1) An application for a writ of habeas corpus on behalf of a person in custody pursuant to the judgment of a State court shall not be granted unless it appears that —

(A) the applicant has exhausted the remedies available in the courts of the State; or

(B) (i) there is an absence of available State corrective process; or

(ii) circumstances exist that render such process ineffective to protect the rights of the applicant.

(2) An application for a writ of habeas corpus may be denied on the merits, notwithstanding the failure of the applicant to exhaust the remedies available in the courts of the State.

(3) A State shall not be deemed to have waived the exhaustion requirement or be estopped from reliance upon the requirement unless the State, through counsel, expressly waives the requirement.

(c) An applicant shall not be deemed to have exhausted the remedies available in the courts of the State, within the meaning of this section, if he has the right under the law of the State to raise, by any available procedure, the question presented.

(d) An application for a writ of habeas corpus on behalf of a person in custody pursuant to the judgment of a State court shall not be granted with respect to any claim that was adjudicated on the merits in State court proceedings unless the adjudication of the claim —

(1) resulted in a decision that was contrary to, or involved an unreasonable application of, clearly established Federal law, as determined by the Supreme Court of the United States; or

(2) resulted in a decision that was based on an unreasonable determination of the facts in light of the evidence presented in the State court proceeding.

(e) (1) In a proceeding instituted by an application for a writ of habeas corpus by a person in custody pursuant to the judgment of a State court, a determination of a factual issue made by a State court shall be presumed to be correct. The applicant shall have the burden of rebutting the presumption of correctness by clear and convincing evidence.

(2) If the applicant has failed to develop the factual basis of a claim in State court proceedings, the court shall not hold an evidentiary hearing on the claim unless the applicant shows that —

(A) the claim relies on —

(i) a new rule of constitutional law, made retroactive to cases on collateral review by the Supreme Court, that was previously unavailable; or

(ii) a factual predicate that could not have been previously discovered through the exercise of due diligence; and

(B) the facts underlying the claim would be sufficient to establish by clear and convincing evidence that but for constitutional error, no reasonable factfinder would have found the applicant guilty of the underlying offense.

(f) If the applicant challenges the sufficiency of the evidence adduced in such State court proceeding to support the State court's determination of a factual issue made therein, the applicant, if able, shall produce that part of the record pertinent to a determination of the sufficiency of the evidence to support such determination. If the applicant, because of indigency or other reason is unable to produce such part of the record, then the State shall produce such part of the record and the Federal court shall direct the State to do so by order directed to an appropriate State official. If the State cannot provide such pertinent part of the record, then the court shall determine under the existing facts and circumstances what weight shall be given to the State court's factual determination.

(g) A copy of the official records of the State court, duly certified by the clerk of such court to be a true and correct copy of a finding, judicial opinion, or other reliable written indicia showing such a factual determination by the State court shall be admissible in the Federal court proceeding.

(h) Except as provided in section 408 of the Controlled Substance Acts [21 U.S.C. § 848], in all proceedings brought under this section, and any subsequent proceedings on review, the court may appoint counsel for an applicant who is or becomes financially unable to afford counsel, except as provided by a rule promulgated by the Supreme Court pursuant to statutory authority. Appointment of counsel under this section shall be governed by section 3006A of title 18.

(i) The ineffectiveness or incompetence of counsel during Federal or State collateral post-conviction proceedings shall not be a ground for relief in a proceeding arising under section 2254.

Collateral Review for Federal Prisoners

28 U.S.C. §2255. Federal Custody; Remedies on Motion Attacking Sentence

A prisoner in custody under sentence of a court established by Act of Congress claiming the right to be released upon the ground that the sentence was imposed in violation of the Constitution or laws of the United States, or that the court was without jurisdiction to impose such sentence, or that the sentence was in excess of the maximum authorized by law, or is otherwise subject to collateral attack, may move the court which imposed the sentence to vacate, set aside or correct the sentence.

Unless the motion and the files and records of the case conclusively show that the prisoner is entitled to no relief, the court shall cause notice thereof to be served upon the United States attorney, grant a prompt hearing thereon, determine the issues and make findings of fact and conclusions of law with respect thereto. If the court finds that the judgment was rendered without jurisdiction, or that the sentence imposed was not authorized by law or otherwise open to collateral attack, or that there has been such a denial or infringement of the constitutional rights of the prisoner as to render the judgment vulnerable to collateral attack, the court shall vacate and set the judgment aside and shall discharge the prisoner or resentence him or grant a new trial or correct the sentence as may appear appropriate.

A court may entertain and determine such motion without requiring the production of the prisoner at the hearing.

An appeal may be taken to the court of appeals from the order entered on the motion as from the final judgment on application for a writ of habeas corpus.

An application for a writ of habeas corpus in behalf of a prisoner who is authorized to apply for relief by motion pursuant to this section, shall not be entertained if it appears that the applicant has failed to apply for relief, by motion, to the court which sentenced him, or that such court has denied him relief, unless it also appears that the remedy by motion is inadequate or ineffective to test the legality of his detention.

A one-year period of limitation shall apply to a motion under this section. The limitation period shall run from the latest of —

(1) the date on which the judgment of conviction becomes final;

(2) the date on which the impediment to making a motion created by governmental action in violation of the Constitution or laws of the United States is removed, if the movant was prevented from making a motion by such governmental action;

(3) the date on which the right asserted was initially recognized by the Supreme Court, if that right has been newly recognized by the Supreme Court and made retroactively applicable to cases on collateral review; or

(4) the date on which the facts supporting the claim or claims presented could have been discovered through the exercise of due diligence.

Except as provided in section 408 of the Controlled Substances Act [21 U.S.C. § 848], in all proceedings brought under this section, and any subsequent proceedings on review, the court may appoint counsel, except as provided by a rule promulgated by the Supreme Court pursuant to statutory authority. Appointment of counsel under this section shall be governed by section 3006A of title 18.

A second or successive motion must be certified as provided in section 2244 by a panel of the appropriate court of appeals to contain —

(1) newly discovered evidence that, if proven and viewed in light of the evidence as a whole, would be sufficient to establish by clear and convincing evidence that no reasonable factfinder would have found the movant guilty of the offense; or

(2) a new rule of constitutional law, made retroactive to cases on collateral review by the Supreme Court, that was previously unavailable.